WITHDRAWN
FROM
UNIVERSITY OF PLYMOUTH

Principles of Business Taxation

Principles of Business Taxation

JOHN POINTON and DEREK SPRATLEY

CLARENDON PRESS · OXFORD
1988

Oxford University Press, Walton Street, Oxford OX2 6DP

Oxford New York Toronto
Delhi Bombay Calcutta Madras Karachi
Petaling Jaya Singapore Hong Kong Tokyo
Nairobi Dar es Salaam Cape Town
Melbourne Auckland

and associated companies in
Beirut Berlin Ibadan Nicosia

Oxford is a trade mark of Oxford University Press

Published in the United States
by Oxford University Press, New York

British Library Cataloguing in Publication Data
Pointon, John
Principles of business taxation.
1. Business enterprises—taxation
—Great Britain
I. Title II. Spratley, Derek
336.2'07'0941 HD2753.G7

ISBN 0–19–877257–2
ISBN 0–19–877258–0 Pbk

Library of Congress Cataloging-in-Publication Data
Pointon, John, 1951–
Principles of business taxation.
Bibliography: p. Includes index.
1. Taxation—Great Britain. 2. Business enterprises—Taxation—Great Britain. 3. Business enterprises—Taxation. I. Spratley, Derek, 1937– . II. Title.
HJ2621.P65 1988 336.24'3'0941 87–28129

ISBN 0–19–877257–2
ISBN 0–19–877258–0 (pbk.)

Typeset by Macmillan India Ltd., Bangalore 560 025
Printed and bound in
Great Britain by Biddles Ltd,
Guildford and Kings Lynn

Preface

Principles of Business Taxation is intended to provide a rigorous analysis of the theory and practice of both the present UK and alternative systems of taxation as they affect the commercial activities of businesses. It is mainly designed to meet the needs of undergraduate and postgraduate (MBA) students in accountancy and business studies, although Parts Two and Three should be highly relevant to the BTEC HND Business and Finance student. We also expect the book to be of general interest to professionally qualified executives, although not as a comprehensive reference text on tax practice. We assume in our presentation that readers have already been exposed to some formal tuition in basic financial accounting, economics, statistics, and discounted cash flow analysis.

The book begins with a discussion of the theoretical choice of alternative tax bases, including income and consumption taxes. An in-depth study is made of alternative systems of business taxation, including different inflation-adjusted tax systems. There follows a critical appraisal of the main UK taxes and a rigorous study of the effects of taxation on various business decisions. Special attention is devoted to sole traders, partnerships, corporate status, financial policy, project appraisal, leasing, and fiscal implications of overseas operations.

Although tax practice is susceptible to frequent change in its detail, we have attempted to concentrate on those significant broad principles of business taxation, which should be of more lasting relevance. Throughout the course of the book we have provided detailed numerical examples to help the reader to become familiar with these broad principles. Guidance is given on further reading material to follow-up specific points in more detail, of which the reader is advised to refer to up-to-date editions. Since we do not hold limited liability status, we disclaim responsibility for consequential loss or damage, financial or otherwise, although we have sincerely made every effort to ensure accuracy and a high standard of presentation.

We are indebted to Carol York and Gill Payne for their careful typing and processing of our original manuscript. Finally, we hope that you will enjoy reading the book and not find it too taxing!

J.P.
D.S.

January 1987

Contents

1
Introduction

This book is primarily concerned with the impact of the present UK and alternative systems of taxation on business policy and decision-making. Thus we do not confine ourselves to a description of the complex tax rules operative in the UK, although there is a strong UK bias. Instead, we provide first, a conceptual framework for the evaluation of alternative systems of business taxation; second, an analysis of the broad principles of the UK tax system; and third, an appraisal of the impact of the UK tax system on selected business decisions.

We begin with an interest in a number of fundamental questions. What is required from a tax system? How can a tax system be designed so as not to interfere with business decision-making? Is value added tax an efficient system? Is there a case for a separate system of corporation tax? In what ways do tax systems discriminate for or against dividend policy or borrowing? What is meant by classical and imputation systems? Should business taxes be raised on profits or cash flows? How might adjustments be made for the impact of inflation?

With regard to the UK tax system, we will focus upon the administration and practice of income tax, capital gains tax, corporation tax, value added tax, and other taxes or similar instruments such as national insurance contributions, customs and excise duties, local authority rates, and North Sea oil taxation. Emphasis is placed upon significant broad principles of business taxation, which should be of lasting relevance, rather than a comprehensive coverage of tax rules in minute detail. Nevertheless, we shall provide numerous practical examples to help the reader become familiar with the broad principles, and guidance on further reading. Such examples include important topics such as bases of assessment, computation of profits or gains, exemptions and reliefs, allowances for capital expenditure, the treatment of tax losses, and the commencement and cessation of a trade.

Having described the broad principles of the main taxes in the UK relevant to businesses and developed a conceptual basis for the evaluation of alternative tax systems, we shall examine the particular characteristics of selected business decisions. The areas which we consider to be important are: the choice of business medium, a sole proprietorship, partnership, or a limited company; tax-efficient borrowing, leasing, and dividend policies; capital investment decisions; and the fiscal implications of overseas operations.

The book is organized into three parts plus an introduction and conclusion. Part One—Tax Theory and Alternative Tax Systems, Part Two—Taxes in the UK, and Part Three—Tax Implications of Selected Business Decisions. We begin in the next chapter with an examination of some important concepts in tax design.

PART ONE
Tax Theory and Alternative Tax Systems

In this part we attempt to lay the theoretical foundations for our subsequent analysis. We begin in Chapter 2 with a discussion of the theoretical choice of alternative tax systems, including income and consumption taxes. Chapter 3 focuses primarily upon the design of a cash-flow tax system and its non-distortionary effect on investment decisions. Alternative types of corporation tax systems are analysed in Chapter 4 with particular emphasis upon implications for dividend policy and borrowing. Chapter 5 looks at inefficiencies under an historic profits tax system, which has special relevance when we later examine selected business decisions in Part Three. Finally we examine in Chapter 6 the implications of alternative inflation-adjusted tax systems for investment and financing decisions.

2
Alternative Bases for Taxation

Introduction

The intention in this chapter is to introduce some basic concepts in public finance theory, to set out the overall requirements of a tax system, and to examine alternative bases of taxation. Our focus of attention will mainly be directed at income and consumption taxes, although in our analysis we shall make some references to capital gains tax, wealth tax, and a poll tax. Since our ultimate concern is to analyse the effects of different taxes on business decisions, we shall pay some attention to the micro-economic effects of different tax systems, and in particular we shall evaluate the implications of alternative taxes for capital investment decision-making.

Requirements of a tax system

In Part Two we shall provide an exposition of the main taxes in the UK which affect business activity, but first we need to address ourselves to the question of whether there is an ideal form of taxation, first, from the viewpoint of central government and second, from the position of a business enterprise. A sceptic may feel that as far as firms are concerned, an optimal tax is one that can be completely avoided and does not interfere with the decision-making processes within the firm, whether routine, operational, or strategic. To some extent there is some merit in this view although, in order to make progress in our analysis, we need to determine a more comprehensive set of criteria against which we can judge alternative tax bases.

One starting point is a consideration of the need for taxes; why should they be raised? What purposes do they serve? An extreme position is that the provision of all goods and services should be determined in a free market where those who benefit pay the competitively determined market price. In this way, in the long run, over- or under-production should be avoided, and the consumer has free choice over his or her spending decisions. Business firms whose operations are efficient should provide goods and services until the marginal revenue is equal to the marginal cost. Such goods are referred to as private goods if ownership and usage are passed on to a private individual. By contrast, public goods are those whose benefits are enjoyed by the general public who do not have a private claim. A special characteristic of a public good is that once available, it can generally be enjoyed at zero marginal cost to the consumer. An isolated example to demonstrate the point is the case of the provision of policing activities to uphold law and order within a given community. Once the service is financed it is enjoyed by all within the locality, except perhaps the criminal fraternity, at zero marginal cost. In the absence of a tax system, there is no automatic mechanism to raise the necessary initial finance in an equitable way. Nor is there an incentive to make a financial contribution to the provision of the public service.

In a democratic society the political voting process is used as a vehicle for representation of the public on specified issues to ensure that the welfare needs of society are met. Public goods and services are financed through the application of tax revenues, borrowing, or self-funding, if practicable. If the central government borrows to finance public goods and services, then the methods by which the interest on debt and capital repayments are met need to be determined. Future taxes can be raised to finance the interest or capital repayment, or the debt can be rolled over by the issue of new debt. In a limited way public goods and services can be self-financed; for example, fines can be imposed on individuals for civil or criminal offences and applied to policing activities. Similarly, revenues from vehicle licences or VAT on petrol may be used to help finance motorway repairs. How the revenues are applied is a political decision and the same is true of the basis on which a tax is raised.

Following our example of financing motorway costs, one basis of revenue-raising is to follow the benefit principle, which states that those who benefit from a public good or service share the cost according to the extent of their usage. An alternative position is based on the taxpayer's ability to pay. For a business enterprise, does this refer to its operating cash flow? Should taxable capacity be increased in line with a firm's unused borrowing capacity? Taking an opposite view, should there be allowances for commitments to pay interest? Thus, are profits after interest the appropriate criterion of a firm's ability to pay? On the other hand, should capital expenditure commitments reduce a firm's ability to pay? Then there is the question of the impact of inflation. Should inflationary adjustments be made at the firm level, or does this lock inflation into the system to such an extent that it would run counter to a policy of reducing the general rate of inflation in the economy?

We have established that certain goods and services should be financed centrally because the free market mechanism is not always appropriate. If we apply the free market approach to the provision of labour and the determination of wage levels, to be efficient in production, one view is that a person should be paid, at the margin, according to the value of the marginal product or service derived from his or her efforts. In this way there is an efficient allocation of the labour resources, and skills are developed and rewarded according to demand. In a caring society, however, there must be some limit on this otherwise those who are socially or physically disadvantaged suffer. Accordingly, one would wish that their rewards, whether in terms of money or social benefits, were in excess of the value of their marginal product. The extent of social provisions and the redistribution of income and wealth is, in a democratic society, largely determined through the political system by the revenue-raising capacity of the tax system as a whole. For the same marginal tax rate, a tax system with a broad base can generally raise more revenue than one with a narrower base. Furthermore, high marginal tax rates may create distortions in business decision-making. On the other hand, a narrower base, if appropriately designed, may be superior in terms of minimization of distortions in economic choices. Thus, in tax design we have to consider the welfare needs of the community, the extent to which those needs are financed by taxation, and the effects of alternative taxes on the decision-making processes of firms and individuals.

Once the nature of a tax base is determined, it is important for it to be equitable both horizontally and vertically. By horizontal equity, taxpayers with equal taxable capacity should bear the same tax, whereas vertical equity suggests that those whose need is greater suffer less tax. To some extent those tax structures which are equitable by nature of their breadth of coverage and circumstances are not necessarily economically efficient.

An important aspect of tax design is the extent to which taxes do not distort economic choices. As far as a capital investment is concerned, this may relate to whether the internal rate of return on a project is different when expressed on a post-tax basis or whether the overall cost of financing a project is distorted. Tax neutrality exists when a given tax system does not discriminate in economic choices. Under a VAT system, tax neutrality in the product market implies that all goods and services are taxed at the same rate so that, although goods and services are priced differently according to quality and other factors, the marginal rate of substitution of one product for another is the same whether taxation is imposed or not. For example, if products A and B are initially free from VAT and priced at £1 and £2, respectively, then at the margin consumers may substitute two items of A to buy one item of product B, costing, £2. Now suppose VAT is introduced such that the price of A increases to £1.15 and B, which is twice as expensive, increase to £2.30. Although there is an income effect of the tax in that consumers suffer a loss of purchasing power in real terms, since they can buy fewer items with their money, the rate of substitution of product A for B remains the same, since the consumer can sacrifice two items of A, saving £2.30, in order to buy one item of B. However, if VAT had been raised on item A only then there would be an economic inefficiency through the distortion in economic choices. A substitution effect would be evident, since now 40 items of A can be sacrificed at a cost of £46, in order to buy 23 items of B, at a cost of 23 × £2 = £46, whereas previously only 20 items of B could have been acquired in place of 40 items of A. The substitution effect is no longer neutral or nil, since product B is relatively more attractive than before. Although there is an income effect, which represents the loss of spending power in real terms, this is theoretically offset by the benefits gained from the provision of public goods and services financed by the taxes raised. In theory, at the margin these should cancel so that the social disutility of the loss of income is equal to the social utility from the additional public goods and services. However, the burden of taxation is not confined to the value of the tax raised, but also includes the social loss resulting from the distortion in economic choice. This additional burden is known as the excess burden of taxation.

A transposition of this principle to the capital investment decision can be seen in terms of a project whose net present value ignoring tax effects is £50,000, yet when expressed on an after-tax basis its net present value is negative. If the firm does not proceed with the investment, there is a substitution effect. It may have substituted an inferior project which may not have been financed due to an insufficiency of funds available, perhaps due to a market imperfection or a constraint imposed by the internal administration of the firm. Alternatively, the firm may distribute a dividend rather than finance a project by way of retained funds. The economy suffers in a number of ways. Firstly, there is an estimated loss of wealth to the shareholders of £50,000 before any personal taxes. Secondly, there may be repercussions for the local community to the extent that the project requires labour in addition to that provided in the absence of the project. Thirdly, the central government has not directly raised any taxes on the venture, although there may be some taxes, indirectly raised, through the substitution effects, on dividend distributions or taxes on the inferior project.

From the standpoint of central government, rather than impose taxes which have neutral effects on economic choices, there may be deliberate attempts through fiscal policy to promote spending instead of investment, or consumption of certain types of product rather than another. An important aspect of fiscal policy relates to its role in the management of aggregate demand. To minimize the cyclical fluctuations in aggregate demand, taxes may be reduced to stimulate demand during a downturn in economic activity and increased at times of an upward trend in the rate of economic growth. Such types of neo-classical Keynesian remedies are of course more complex in character than this would suggest and tend to be used in conjunction with monetary policies, which attempt to influence demand by controlling the volume of money available. As far as the individual firm is concerned the main point here is that over time there are likely to be some dramatic changes in government fiscal policies which can affect business decisions covering a number of areas, including business forecasting, financial planning, the choice of business medium, capital investment appraisal, the choice of location, working capital management, financial policy, lease or buy decisions, and the management of overseas operations. Furthermore, there may be fundamental differences between the impact on business decisions associated with changes in tax structure and changes in the rates of taxation even within a stable structure. For example, a tax system which taxes true economic profit at an increasing rate each year may not be as harmful as one which taxes cash flows at increasing rates over time, since the latter may very well form the basis of a capital investment appraisal proposal, which may incorporate predictions of a small tax benefit on cash outflows when expenditures are made in early years, and large tax payments based on future inflows. The measurement of true economic profit in a period of inflation and the evaluation of the impact on decision-making of cash-flow-based or other tax systems will be the subject of our scrutiny in due course.

Some consideration also needs to be given to the economic impact of the taxation of foreign-controlled enterprises in the UK as well as foreign taxes on UK operations overseas. To a large extent this may be reflected in tax treaties between countries. Clearly, the central government cannot maintain absolute stability in tax design and operation if it is to respond to domestic and international economic events. For the individual firm, as an aid to commercial decision-making, absolute stability is sought in both the design of the tax base and, normally, the tax rates applied. Furthermore, there needs to be certainty regarding how tax laws are to be applied and simplicity in the derivation of estimated tax liabilities and savings; otherwise the opportunity cost of the expense in obtaining first-rate tax advice and legal representation on points of dispute with the Inland Revenue and Customs and Excise may be substantially uneconomic.

The costs imposed on the taxpayer in complying with a given tax are known as compliance costs and represent a burden of taxation which also arises to a significant degree in cases where the firm operates as a tax collector on behalf of the central government, as evidenced by PAYE collections and value added tax, whose formal statutory incidence is on employees and customers, respectively. These costs arise in addition to the administrative costs of government bodies directly associated with tax collection.

Before we turn to an overview of alternative tax bases let us briefly summarize the requirements of a tax system. The tax bases need to take account of (i) their revenue-raising capacity in relation to the size of the provision of public goods and services to be funded by taxes, (ii) the intended redistribution of income and wealth, (iii) their role in aggregate demand management in the economy, (iv) horizontal and vertical equity, (v) economic efficiency, (vi) international implications, and (vii) administrative and compliance costs. As far as corporate financial management is concerned, once a tax is imposed, the compliance costs are largely unavoidable, and thus in later chapters our main concern will be distortions in economic efficiency in commercial decision-making. But before we proceed to such issues we need to have a clear picture of the merits of alternative tax bases in relation to the overall requirements of a tax system.

A true economic income tax

In Chapter 7 we describe the essential features of the UK income tax system. Account is taken of personal circumstances by way of personal allowances and the progressive nature of the tax rates which increase in line with a person's taxable income. The concept of horizontal and vertical equity can be seen to be applied in practice. Those with more taxable capacity not only pay more tax, but at an increasing rate. To some extent this reflects a utilitarian view that the disutility of a £1 tax payment is greater for a poor man or woman than for a rich person, who can afford to sacrifice more. For a sole trader or partnership, i.e. an unincorporated business, the appropriate share of the income of the firm is treated as income of the individual who is assessed to tax accordingly. If the system is truly equitable, however, adjustments need to be made for the impact of inflation, not only on personal allowances through adjustments linked to the retail price index, but also on business income. For if the capital base of the firm is eroded by inflation, that part of income necessary to maintain capital should be exempt from tax, otherwise true income is not being measured correctly. But should the capital base be expressed in financial terms or on the basis of physical operating capability? Should appropriate adjustments be made for the general rate of inflation or only the specific rates of inflation which impinge upon the firm's expenses, including payroll costs, material costs, and overheads? Financing costs can reasonably be expected to rise in line with inflation since an investor needs an appropriate adjustment to be made so that the required rate of return is maintained in real terms. But should adjustments be made for the effects of inflation on financing costs? An insight into these problems in intended to be gained after reading the next few chapters. At this stage we can appreciate that if the income tax base is to be sufficiently comprehensive there may indeed be complex adjustments for inflationary effects. Although developments in standard accounting practice may pave the way for business profits to reflect, to some degree, the impact of inflation, the income and corporation tax systems are primarily based on historic cost profits as far as businesses are concerned. Special problems arise, in attempting to make an income tax base more comprehensive, when fixed assets are included in the analysis. The asset value at the beginning of a period can be regarded as the capitalized value of the income stream, generated from asset use.

We shall now demonstrate that if an income-based tax system allows true economic depreciation, as a tax deduction, in addition to interest costs on project finance, then there should be a neutral effect on the investment decision. Thus, in example A, suppose a capital asset costs £90,000 and generates pre-tax net operating cash inflows of £44,000, £36,300, and £26,620 at the end of each of the next three years, respectively, at the end of which there is no scrap value on the asset. The project earns its required economic rate of return which we assume to be merely 10 per cent per annum, for the sake of simplicity. This may be verified by discounting the relevant cash flows:

$$£44{,}000/(1.10) + £36{,}300/(1.10)^2 + £26{,}620/(1.10)^3 = £90{,}000.$$

But by discounting the future cash flows we can also determine the economic value of the asset at the end of the first and second years, respectively. Thus, the economic value at the end of the first year is:

$$£36{,}300/(1.10)+£26{,}620/(1.10)^2=£55{,}000,$$

and the value at the end of the second year is simply derived by discounting the final cash flow for one year:

$$£26{,}620/(1.10)=£24{,}200.$$

In this way the asset depreciates by £35,000 during the first year, from £90,000 to £55,000, by £30,800 during the second year, from £55,000 to £24,200, and by £24,200 in the final year, thus fully depreciating the asset. In Table 2.1 we deduct this true economic depreciation from the net operating cash flows to derive true economic income each year. The question which now presents itself is how much interest is payable each year on the project finance. We assume that the asset is funded entirely by borrowing and that the pre-tax net operating cash flows from the project are used to pay the interest and debt capital. The debt repayment schedule, which can now be derived, is illustrated in Table 2.2. But we observe that the annual interest payments on debt, which we assume to be 10 per cent per annum, are exactly the same as the annual true economic incomes before interest, given in Table 2.1. We may hasten to add that this conclusion is not just specific to this numerical example, but is a general result. Hence, where a project earns its required rate of return, and the income tax system allows both true economic depreciation and interest deductibility, net taxable income is nil. Clearly, since there is a nil tax liability, such a tax system should not distort the investment decision.

We have assumed that the only source of finance is debt, and so, by implication, to maintain tax neutrality we need to allow full corporate tax deductibility for dividends or retentions in the case of an equity financed

TABLE 2.1. *True economic income: example A* (£)

Item	End of year t			
	$t=0$	$t=1$	$t=2$	$t=3$
Capitalized value of future inflows (V_t)	90,000	55,000	24,200	nil
Pre-tax net operating cash flow (F_t)	—	44,000	36,300	26,620
True economic depreciation ($D_t=V_{t-1}-V_t$)	—	35,000	30,800	24,200
True economic income before interest (F_t-D_t)	—	9,000	5,500	2,420
Less: interest on debt	—	(9,000)	(5,500)	(2,420)
Net taxable income	—	nil	nil	nil

TABLE 2.2. *Debt repayment schedule: example A* (£)

Item	Year		
	1	2	3
Debt capital outstanding at the beginning of the year	90,000	55,000	24,200
Add: interest on debt	9,000	5,500	2,420
	99,000	60,500	26,620
Less: repayment	(44,000)	(36,300)	(26,620)
Debt capital outstanding at the end of the year	55,000	24,200	nil

project. However, this is a contradiction in the meaning of true economic income since an appropriation of income, by way of dividends, cannot be regarded as an expense in the derivation of that income.

For the moment we shall assume that all finance is raised by borrowing. To gain a deeper understanding of the tax concept of economic income we shall introduce some variations into the analysis. In example B the firm borrows £90,000 at a fixed rate of interest of 10 per cent per annum as before, but immediately afterwards there is a change in the general rate of inflation in the economy such that the required rate of return increases to 11 per cent per annum. Happily, the project is inflation-proof such that its pre-tax net operating cash flows, which are shown in Table 2.3, rise accordingly. Thus the project earns an 11 per cent rate of return per annum before tax:

$$£44{,}400/(1.11)+£36{,}963/(1.11)^2+£27{,}353/(1.11)^3=£90{,}000.$$

The capitalized value of the future inflows is determined by the same process as before but results in different figures for the true economic depreciation. During the first year the interest on debt is £9,000, assuming a 10 per cent annual cost of debt before tax, so the first year's net taxable income from the project, which is derived in Table 2.3 is £900. To demonstrate an extreme situation we shall evaluate the consequences of a 100 per cent tax rate, such that each annual tax due is equal to the net taxable income. We find that the net operating cash flow after tax is £43,500 for the first year, which is used to make repayments towards debt capital and interest, as shown in Table 2.4. It follows that the interest for the next year is £5,550, which for tax purposes is offset against true economic income before interest. Once again the figure for the derived post-tax net operating cash flow from Table 2.3 forms the basis of the debt repayment, which in turn, following Table 2.4, determines the interest for the final year. We find that the post-tax net operating cash flows for the final year exactly match the debt repayment needed to completely eliminate

TABLE 2.3. *True economic income: example B* (£)

	End of year t			
	$t=0$	$t=1$	$t=2$	$t=3$
Capitalized value of future inflows (V_t)	90,000	55,500	24,642	—
Pre-tax net operating cash flow (F_t)	—	44,400	36,963	27,353
True economic depreciation ($D_t = V_{t-1} - V_t$)	—	34,500	30,858	24,642
True economic income before interest ($F_t - D_t$)	—	9,900	6,105	2,711
Less: interest on debt	—	(9,000)	(5,550)	(2,465)
Net taxable income	—	900	555	246
Taxes raised at 100% (T_t)	—	900	555	246
Post-tax net operating cash flow ($F_t - T_t$)	—	43,500	36,408	27,107

TABLE 2.4. *Debt repayment schedule: example B* (£)

Item	Year		
	1	2	3
Debt capital outstanding at the beginning of the year	90,000	55,500	24,642
Add: interest on debt	9,000	5,550	2,465
	99,000	61,050	27,107
Less: repayment	(43,500)	(36,408)	(27,107)
Debt capital outstanding at the end of the year	55,500	24,642	nil

the liability. Thus, when the pre-tax rate of return on an asset exceeds the pre-tax cost of borrowing, there will be tax liabilities under this economic income tax system, unlike the case of example A where there were no taxes due. With a tax rate of 100 per cent of net taxable economic income after interest, the project is still economic, since the post-tax returns can finance the capital required for the project, as demonstrated in example B. There is no distortion in economic efficiency since the project is financially attractive even though there are no longer excess returns after tax. With a tax rate at less than 100 per cent, an acceleration in the debt repayment schedule would be facilitated, and hence there would be surplus funds available from the project after all liabilities for taxes, interest, and debt capital were settled. However, the same non-distortionary feature is displayed in that this tax system has a neutral effect on the investment decision. Whether the project is acceptable, should not be affected when account is taken of the fiscal ramifications. Another feature of this tax system, which we have demonstrated, is that where the actual rate of return exceeds the minimum required rate of return, that is, where returns exceed pure profits, then tax revenues are raised. This is an important issue especially when we shall later make a comparison with an expenditure, or cash-flow, tax system. A third feature is that the tax rate can vary between zero and 100 per cent each year and still maintain neutrality. For instance, if we amend example B and raise taxes at 100 per cent for two years and 50 per cent for the final year, we can see that half the final year's original tax liability is eliminated so that £123 of surplus funds remain after the debt has been repaid. Although the post-tax value of the investment is now different, there is no tax distortion in the decision to proceed with the investment on economic grounds.

In the previous example, a perfect capital market was assumed even though there was a change in expectations. However, let us now suppose that in example C the firm perceives an opportunity to make excess profits, before evaluating the tax implications. The future net operating cash flows before tax are given in the original analysis of example A, but on this occasion the cost of the asset is only £80,000. The future cash flows are discounted at 10 per cent per annum as before, which is equivalent to the cost of borrowing, when expressed on a pre-tax basis. Hence, before tax, the project is worth £90,000 as originally envisaged, and thus there is a £10,000 net present value before tax. However, at the end of year zero there is a negative figure for true economic depreciation, which represents the instantaneous capital appreciation of £10,000, from the cost of £80,000 to the economic value of £90,000. Under a true economic income tax system this would be taxable. One extreme situation is that taxes may be raised at 100 per cent in which case the firm needs to raise a further £10,000, perhaps by borrowing, in which instance the firm borrows a total of £90,000 as originally planned in example A. The total debt repayment schedule is the same as that depicted in Table 2.2 and the derivation of net taxable income for the following three years is exactly the same as that shown in Table 2.1. The project is still marginal on a post-tax basis since it earns the required rate of return and has a zero net present value after deducting the initial tax liability. For tax rates between zero and 100 per cent there is no disincentive to invest. Hence the tax system is economically efficient in the maintenance of tax neutrality even when there was a market imperfection.

In example C we included a capital gain as part of true economic income. Over long time horizons, the distinctions between income and capital gains become blurred. The capital appreciation from a venture which lasts ten years, for instance, should be reconcilable with the total of ten annual profits or losses. Capital gains taxes and income taxes fit together quite logically. The question of an additional tax on wealth though, is not entirely consistent with income and capital gains taxes, since income generated from wealth is taxed under an income tax, and thus to tax wealth as well, whether through the taxation of the stock of wealth by an annual wealth tax or through the taxation of transfers of wealth, is really a form of double taxation. Nevertheless, to move towards a socially desirable distribution of income and wealth, there are strong grounds for additional taxes on wealth because of the benefits that such privilege brings. Income, capital gains, and wealth taxes together provide a broad basis for taxation. Since the flow of income can be used on either consumption or savings, consumption provides a narrower base than income. Marginal tax rates may therefore be much lower under an income tax than those under an expenditure or consumption tax system, if the same amount of revenue is required to be raised.

Unfortunately the design of the income tax system is such that income is not measured in its true economic sense. It is impracticable to measure wealth accurately by discounting future cash flows since there is no certainty in the figures, either with regards to the discount rate, the size, or time pattern of the cash flows. To some extent asset valuations based on inflation-adjusted figures may be a move in the right direction, but essentially income tax is based on the concept of a transactions flow and not measured by changes in capital stock, despite academic devices that can be used to reconcile these concepts.

A further problem is that under the income tax system, which taxes profits of unincorporated businesses, the tax rates are progressive in nature and so businesses whose profits fluctuate more violently may be penalized. An example of this is provided in Table 2.5, where each £10,000 slice of profits is taxed at 30, 40, and 50 per cent, respectively, up to £30,000. Firm X pays a total of £7,000 per annum in tax comprised of £3,000 tax on its first £10,000 slice of profits and £4,000 on its next tranche. Profits remain constant at £20,000 per annum, and so the total tax bill for three years is £21,000. On the other hand, firm Y suffers on account of its fluctuations in profits since it finds that its total tax liability exceeds that of firm X despite the same total taxable profits.

Finally, an income tax discriminates against work rather than leisure especially where the marginal tax rates are high, and so under a personal tax system with progressive tax rates there are potential disincentives to

TABLE 2.5. *Progressive tax rates and equity considerations* (£)

	Item	Year			Total
		1	2	3	
Firm X	Profits	20,000	20,000	20,000	60,000
	Taxes	7,000	7,000	7,000	21,000
Firm Y	Profits	10,000	30,000	20,000	60,000
	Taxes	3,000	12,000	7,000	22,000

entrepreneurship and work effort. To redistribute income within an economy, however, progressive tax rates are a useful part of tax design.

In the next section we turn our attention to a tax on corporate income independent of the income tax system.

A separate corporation tax

Just as income tax is raised on unincorporated businesses, we shall describe in Chapter 10 how similar principles are applied to the assessment of taxes on companies. But why should there be a separate tax on companies? One view is that corporate status conveys the privilege of limited liability and should therefore be subject to tax on the benefit. An opposing view is that those who provide debt finance or trade credit are aware of the limited liability and are likely to charge appropriate interest and credit costs according to their perceptions of the financial risk of not receiving full repayment of the firm's liabilities to them.

Although companies have legal personalities in their own right, their financial success or failure primarily accrues to those who have a financial stake in the business. If a company pays out a dividend, then, under income tax rules, this investment forms part of the taxable capacity of the shareholder. Alternatively, to the extent that profits are retained within the business, in a perfect market, the share price should rise accordingly. Under a true economic income tax system, the change in wealth, through the capitalization of the retention, would form part of income, so in theory an income tax system should effectively tax the capital gain and a separate corporation tax is unnecessary. In practice, the derivation of true economic income is not possible due to the uncertainties in the figures upon which the calculations would be based. In practice, a separate capital gains tax already attempts to deal with changes in wealth, yet its application is based on the taxation of only realized gains. As such, capital gains tax is avoidable, at least in the short run. A capital gains tax system could in theory include unrealized share price appreciation as part of taxable capacity, and shareholders with insufficient funds to pay the tax liabilities could dispose of some shares to raise the necessary personal finance. Alternatively, the income tax system could include retained profits per share as part of an individual's net taxable income and collect tax at the basic rate, through a corporate withholding tax, and additional personal income tax liabilities direct from higher rate taxpayers. If this approach were adopted, tax credits could be given against capital gains tax to avoid double taxation on retentions.

In our analysis we have assumed that the statutory incidence of a corporation tax is the same as its economic incidence, that is to say, that the economic effects of the tax fall on the owners of a company, its shareholders. In a perfect market, one would expect this to be the case. However, in practice, this depends upon the elasticity of supply and demand in the product and labour markets. Some tax-shifting may occur by a firm increasing the price of goods and services to attempt to recoup the corporation tax and thereby loading the tax burden onto consumers. Another option is to resist wage demands by squeezing pay increases so that employees effectively bear some of the corporate tax, and a further alternative is to take excess credit and penalize suppliers. Interest groups may, of course, resist such moves and pass the burden back onto the firm, perhaps by consumers buying fewer products; by employees reducing productivity, changing employment, or taking industrial action; or by suppliers tightening terms of credit or refusing to trade. However, the very nature of imperfections in economic markets means that corporate taxes can be used to become effectively, to some extent, taxes on jobs, goods, and services. Additionally, a corporate tax system can be used as an instrument to influence capital investment, either favourably or not, depending upon central government objectives. But if such devices are to be achieved through an indirect route when other alternatives exist, perhaps through income and value added taxes or government grants, there still remains a question mark over the rationale for a separate corporate tax system.

In a perfect market, apart from tax distortions, not only do shareholders suffer taxes at the corporate level, but also personal taxes penalize both dividends, by way of higher rate taxes, and capital gains on the disposal of shares, the values of which may have appreciated through corporate growth induced by retained profits. Although under the UK imputation tax system some of the underlying corporation tax is effectively treated as a tax credit at the personal level, there may still be a net mainstream corporation tax liability for the company, and so a double taxation exists. The design of alternative corporate tax systems is an interesting issue on which we shall elaborate further in the remaining chapters of this part.

Since unincorporated businesses are not subjected to this double taxation, effectively, on the introduction of a corporate tax system, capital is likely to be transferred from the corporate sector to the unincorporated sector. In the short run this reduces the rate of return on investment until the after-tax rate of return for both sectors is equalized after adjusting for risk. Thus the tax burden shifts in the short run to the unincorporated sector, assuming a perfect capital market which allows free flow of capital at zero transaction costs. But although the average rate of return on investment in the unincorporated sector falls, as the incremental capital earns at the margin a lower marginal rate of return than previously, the marginal rate of return on investments previously undertaken in the unincorporated sector does not fall, and so the entrepreneurs who financed only the original capital base in the unincorporated sector have not borne additional taxes. As output falls in the corporate sector and rises in the unincorporated sector, prices of goods and services from the former may rise and those from the latter fall, with the result that some consumers gain whilst others lose according to their demand for goods and services from each sector (Musgrave and Musgrave 1980).

Most of the discussion so far of the rationale for a corporation tax has been fairly negative, so we now briefly turn our attention to its support. First, if the tax were abolished there would be windfall gains to those who bought shares at prices which reflected the view that the tax would continue to exist. Second, it is an efficient tax in that it is administratively convenient to collect. Third, it raises finance from foreign-controlled companies that may otherwise escape the tax net.

Consumption taxes

An obvious alternative to the taxation of true economic income, or its practical substitute in the form of a set of taxes based on a combination of income, capital gains, and wealth, is the taxation of consumer spending. A consumption tax may take several forms, one of which is a general sales tax covering a wide range of goods. But where there is no tax credit for sales taxes paid by a firm on its purchases, a discriminatory form of double taxation may result. In Table 2.6 we illustrate this by considering firm A, whose inputs of items X, Y, and Z cost £3m in total, whose profit is £300,000, and whose tax collection under a general sales tax is 15 per cent on a tax exclusive basis, or 15/115 on a tax inclusive basis. Thus, from Table 2.6 the general sales tax is 15 per cent of £3.3m, or £495,000, which is 15/115 of £3,795,000. Now, firm C competes in the same product market, but buys an intermediate product, derived from inputs X and Y only, from firm B. The two operations of firms B and C considered together are just as efficient as A, earning profits of £150,000 each. The sales tax collected by firm B is 15 per cent of £2,150,000, or £322,500, as shown in the table. Therefore, the value of the intermediate product sold to

TABLE 2.6. *Operating a general sales tax* (£)

Item	Firm		
	A	B	C
Inputs:			
X	1,000,000	1,000,000	—
Y	1,000,000	1,000,000	—
X & Y	—	—	2,472,500
Z	1,000,000	—	1,000,000
	3,000,000	2,000,000	3,472,500
Add: profit	300,000	150,000	150,000
	3,300,000	2,150,000	3,622,500
Add: sales tax	495,000	322,500	543,375
Output	3,795,000	2,472,500	4,165,875

C is £2,472,500. Firm C's production process also requires the addition of input Z making it comparable with firm A. However, when the sales tax is raised at 15 per cent, we find that the value of the final product exceeds that of A's product by £370,875. This is represented by the extent to which the total tax bill for B and C exceeds the tax collected by firm A, as we show in Table 2.7. Therefore the consumers of firm A's product pay substantially less than those who consume firm C's product due to the tax discrimination. Clearly, this represents a disequilibrium position, and market forces may subsequently drive down the price of C's product, squeezing profit margins such that firm C is only willing to buy the intermediate product from B at a lower price, which in turn squeezes firm B's profit margin. In the long run, under a general sales tax, multi-stage production would be abandoned so that all firms in the market would be engaged in the whole production process and not manufacture intermediate products.

As an alternative, a VAT system at 15 per cent would tax outputs at 15/115 but allow tax credits for VAT on eligible inputs. In this case firms B and C can maintain their profit margins, and C can sell the final product at the same price as firm A as shown in Table 2.8. The VAT on firm C's output is 15/115 × £3,795,000, or £495,000, but offset against this is a tax credit of £322,500 for the VAT on the inputs. With a reduced tax liability firm C can compete with firm A in the market-place.

It is not necessary however for consumption taxes to be indirect taxes collected by firms yet intended as taxes on consumer products. Instead there may be direct taxes raised on individuals on the basis of their consumption. Since it is impracticable to itemize individual amounts of spending on a tax return, a personal expenditure tax system could assess consumption merely by excluding investment from taxable expenditure. More specifically it could measure cash receipts, whether from capital, income, or gifts received, but allow as tax-deductible items, cash payments for registered assets and gifts

TABLE 2.7. *Discrimination by a general sales tax* (£)

Output:	
Firm C	4,165,875
Firm A	3,795,000
Difference	370,875
Sales tax:	
Firm B	322,500
Firm C	543,375
Subtotal	865,875
Less: Firm A's sales tax	(495,000)
	370,875

TABLE 2.8. *Value added tax (£)*

Item	Firm		
	A	B	C
Output	3,795,000	2,472,500	3,795,000
VAT on output at 15/115	495,000	322,500	495,000
Less: VAT on input	—	—	(322,500)
Net VAT	495,000	322,500	172,500
Inputs, including VAT	3,000,000	2,000,000	3,472,500
Add: profit	300,000	150,000	150,000
Subtotal	3,300,000	2,150,000	3,622,500
Add: VAT	495,000	322,500	172,500
Output	3,795,000	2,472,500	3,795,000

made. Furthermore, in order to redistribute income and wealth in the economy, consumption taxes could be raised at progressive rates.

An important feature of an expenditure tax, which maintains a constant marginal tax rate, is that it does not distort the yield on a capital investment. This result contrasts sharply with that of an income tax system, which is illustrated in Table 2.9. The potential investor is faced with a choice of using income for immediate consumption or fully investing the income for one year and spending all the accumulated wealth at the end of the year.

Under example 1 of Table 2.9 the investor can enjoy immediate consumption of £700 after paying income tax of £300 on gross income of £1,000. Alternatively, the £700 can be reinvested to generate income at a rate we assume to be 10 per cent before tax, which accumulates of £749 after income tax. By deferring consumption for a year, the investor sacrifices consumption of £700, and thus the yield on the investment is 49/700, or 7 per cent per annum. On account of the taxes on income at 30 per cent, the rate of return has declined by 30 per cent of 10 per cent, that is a reduction of 3 percentage points. With a 40 per cent income tax rate the yield reduces from 10 per cent to 6 per cent, as shown in example 2. We are not suggesting that to replace a 30 per cent income tax by a 30 per cent consumption tax, the revenue raised would be the same, especially since present taxes can be avoided by entering the process of investment and wealth accumulation. However, the principle we wish to stress here is that the pre-tax yield of an investment, which we assume to be 10 per cent in these few examples, is the same as the post-tax yield, assuming a constant rate of consumption tax. In example 3 of Table 2.9 a consumption tax is raised at 30 per cent thus reducing present consumption from £1,000 before tax to £700, assuming no investment takes place. However, if consumption is delayed for one year, the £1,000 initial income escapes the consumption tax net

TABLE 2.9. *Income versus consumption taxes: constant tax rates* (£)

	Income tax		Consumption tax	
	Example 1	Example 2	Example 3	Example 4
(i) *Immediate consumption*				
Income	1,000	1,000	1,000	1,000
Less: income tax	(300)	(400)	—	—
	700	600	1,000	1,000
Less: consumption tax	—	—	(300)	(400)
Present consumption (i)	*700*	*600*	*700*	*600*
(ii) *Deferred consumption*				
Income	1,000	1,000	1,000	1,000
Less: income tax	(300)	(400)	—	—
	700	600	1,000	1,000
Less: investment	(700)	(600)	(1,000)	(1,000)
Present consumption	nil	nil	nil	nil
Income at end of year	70	60	100	100
Less: income tax	(21)	(24)	—	—
Net income	49	36	100	100
Add: original capital	700	600	1,000	1,000
Accumulated wealth	749	636	1,100	1,100
Less: consumption tax	—	—	(330)	(440)
Consumption at end of year (ii)	*749*	*636*	*770*	*660*
Additional consumption (iii) = (ii) − (i)	*49*	*36*	*70*	*60*
Yield (iv) = (iii)/(i)	7%	6%	10%	10%

and grows to £1,100 before tax by the end of the year. A 30 per cent consumption tax raises £330 revenue, leaving £770 for consumption at the end of the year. But the investor has only sacrificed £700 of present consumption, so the £70 cash return on the investment results in an after-tax yield of 70/700, or 10 per cent per annum, which is exactly, the yield before tax. Example 4 of Table 2.9 utilizes a 40 per cent consumption tax rate, yet the same conclusion remains, which is that the yield on the investment is not distorted by a constant rate of consumption tax, unlike the case of an investment undertaken within an income tax system.

A problem arises, however, if the tax rate changes. In Table 2.10, we have reworked the examples on the assumption that if the tax rate is 30 per cent in the first year, then it will be 40 per cent in the second year, and vice versa for a 40 per cent tax rate in the first year. Under an income tax system the post-tax

TABLE 2.10. *Income versus consumption taxes: fluctuating tax rates* (£)

	Income tax		Consumption tax	
	Example 5	Example 6	Example 7	Example 8
(i) *Immediate consumption*				
Income	1,000	1,000	1,000	1,000
Less: income tax	(300)	(400)	—	—
	700	600	1,000	1,000
Less: consumption tax	—	—	(300)	(400)
Present consumption (i)	*700*	*600*	*700*	*600*
(ii) *Deferred consumption*				
Income	1,000	1,000	1,000	1,000
Less: income tax	(300)	(400)	—	—
	700	600	1,000	1,000
Less: investment	(700)	(600)	(1,000)	(1,000)
Present consumption	nil	nil	nil	nil
Income at end of year	70	60	100	100
Less: income tax	(28)	(18)	—	—
Net income	42	42	100	100
Add: original capital	700	600	1,000	1,000
Accumulated wealth	742	642	1,100	1,100
Less: consumption tax	—	—	(440)	(330)
Consumption at end of year (ii)	*742*	*642*	*660*	*770*
Additional consumption (iii) = (ii) − (i)	*42*	*42*	*−40*	*170*
Yield (iv) = (iii)/(i)	6%	7%	−5.7%	28.3%

yield is unaffected by the income tax rate in the first year, since yield is merely a relative measure, although accumulated wealth at the end of the first year is dependent upon the rate at which taxation is imposed on the original income stream which is used to finance the investment. Thus, we see that the rate of return on the investment is effectively reduced from 10 per cent to 6 per cent, under a 40 per cent tax rate during the second year, and to 7 per cent, under a 30 per cent tax rate on the investment income. A 10 percentage point change in the income tax rate has made little impact on the effective yield.

Such is not the case when we focus our analysis on a consumption tax. When the tax rate increases from 30 to 40 per cent, the yield on the investment declines dramatically to minus 5.7 per cent, as derived in example 7 of Table 2.10. Alternatively, when the rate of taxation falls from 40 per cent to 30 per cent, under example 8, there is a dramatic improvement in the rate of return from 10 per cent before tax to 28.3 per cent on a post-tax basis. The reason for the sensitivity of the yield to changes in consumption tax rates is that the accumulated wealth on the investment is not dependent upon the tax rate operative at the beginning of the period since investment financed from income is, by definition, excluded from the measurement of consumption. However, the denominator in the yield calculation is distorted by the rate of consumption tax applied to the alternative choice of full consumption at the beginning of the period. In this way there is a gearing effect which increases the yield when initial consumption taxes are at a high rate, but subsequently fall, but decreases the yield when taxes increase, since in the latter instance there is a higher figure for the present immediate consumption employed in the denominator of the yield calculation.

However, we argued that if income tax is applied to true economic income after interest, then an investment financed by debt is non-distortionary. In our above example, if the investment of £1,000 is financed entirely by debt at a cost of 10 per cent per annum, then the £100 interest on debt is offset against the £100 gross income on the investment so the true economic income is zero and there is no tax to pay. But for investments financed out of income, there is a distortionary effect.

But with constant tax rates, although consumption taxes are non-distortionary with regards to investment decisions, there are instances of excess burden whenever consumption taxes are raised on some goods and not on others, or whenever there are different tax rates applied to different goods and services. This arises because the rate of substitution of one good for another changes when a selective consumption tax is imposed. The burden of the tax initially falls on consumers of the selectively-taxed product if the demand is inelastic, or on producers if supply is inelastic. Otherwise, the burden is shared according to the elasticity of supply and demand. In general equilibrium, there is likely to be a shift in the production of goods which are untaxed so that, if they are produced under conditions of increasing cost, the price of the untaxed product rises, and consumers of the untaxed product effectively bear some of the tax. As far as the taxed product is concerned a reduction in production levels may result in cost savings at the margin such that the price of the product rises by an amount less than the tax. However, if there are no additional cost savings because both the taxed and the untaxed products are manufactured at constant cost, the burden remains with the consumers of the taxed product. But where there are changes in production levels of different products, secondary effects may result such that employees in the untaxed industry may find that their earnings increase. The pattern of their increased spending may create further ripple effects in the economy.

In practice the VAT system in the UK is selective in that certain items of goods and services bear no tax because they are classified as exempt or zero-rated. However, these items could largely be regarded as necessaries and therefore would not generally be subject to increased demand because of the favourable tax treatment. For those on low incomes this type of tax system is reasonably equitable and should enable prices of necessaries to be lower than they would otherwise be. As we move up the income scale we note that the system is initially progressive since individuals who have a little more to spend feel the burden of tax on a few luxury goods. However, higher up the consumption scale the system is very regressive in that the loss in utility on each luxury product, through payments of VAT, is lower for individuals with large consumption potential, if a flat tax rate is applied to all luxury goods, than the loss of the utility to those who can afford fewer luxury products. To redistribute income and wealth within the economy, a VAT system which applies the same flat rate to most products is ineffective.

As far as administrative and compliance costs are concerned, a VAT system is perhaps an inefficient tax especially when account is taken of the costs connected with numerous collection points. By comparison a retail sales tax on the final product may be cheaper to collect.

Even if consumption taxes are not selective, there is still an excess burden since the marginal rate of substitution of leisure for work expressed on a pre-tax basis differs from that post-tax. Either people work harder to generate even more income to maintain purchasing power, or they enjoy more leisure which is not taxed. A theoretical alternative tax base is a poll tax, or head tax, the execution of which (sorry for the pun) does not result in an excess burden. Clearly, some work may be needed to generate income to pay for such a tax, but at the margin, whether a person substitutes work for leisure, or vice versa, is not distorted by a head tax, since there is no extra tax to pay on the generation of more income or consumption of more goods and services. Although such a tax base is efficient, it is clearly inequitable since income and wealth generating potential differs substantially between individuals.

Conclusion

In this chapter we introduced a number of concepts in public finance theory, including the meaning and significance of public and private goods, taxable capacity, income and substitution effects, and excess burden of taxation. We stated that the tax base needs to take account of its revenue-raising capacity, the intended redistribution of income and wealth, its role in aggregate demand management, horizontal and vertical equity, economic efficiency, international implications, and administrative and compliance costs.

We examined the operation of a true economic income tax system and its neutral effect on an investment decision for projects funded entirely by debt finance. Where such an investment earns its required rate of return, and the income tax system allows both true economic depreciation and interest deductibility, net taxable income is nil. However, tax liabilities arise if the pre-tax rate of return exceeds the pre-tax cost of borrowing, although the investment decision should not be distorted by the imposition of tax under this style of tax system. In practice, a true economic income tax system is impractical to design, although separate systems of income, capital gains, and wealth taxes operating together do provide a fair basis of taxation in their breadth of coverage. Special problems arise with progressive income tax rates both on grounds of equity and economic efficiency with regard to work effort and entrepreneurship.

The case for a separate corporation tax was considered and felt to be rather weak on theoretical grounds, although in practice it is a convenient device for the collection of revenue and the taxation of foreign-controlled operations. There followed discussions of alternative ways of taxing profits attributable to shareholders and tax-shifting in product, labour, and capital markets.

General sales taxes were compared with a system of VAT with respect to the economic effects on multi-stage production. With constant tax rates, a consumption tax was shown to have a neutral effect on capital investment decisions unlike that of an income tax system, except for projects financed by debt under a system based on true economic income. However, we explained that distortions may arise when marginal tax rates change. Tax-shifting between producers, consumers, and employees was considered under selective consumption taxes, and equity considerations and administrative and compliance costs were discussed under a VAT system. Finally, we stated the theoretical justification for a poll tax and its economic superiority over both consumption and income taxes in the work versus leisure decision.

Recommendations for further reading

Further discussion of the economic incidence of taxes can be found in Musgrave and Musgrave (1980), which also provides an excellent introduction to both the theory of public finance and practical applications in the United States. For a more advanced economic treatment, Atkinson and Stiglitz (1980) is recommended. The notion of a true economic income tax system with interest deductibility can be traced back to a seminal paper by Samuelson (1964). The Meade report, which is a major study of the structure and reform of direct taxation in the UK by a committee set up by the Institute for Fiscal Studies and chaired by James Meade (1978), contains a thorough discussion of the required characteristics of a good tax system, alternative tax bases, and the case for a separate corporation tax. Finally, for a lively introduction to the economics of the British tax system, Kay and King (1986) may usefully be consulted.

References

Atkinson, A. B., and Stiglitz, J. E. (1980), *Lectures on Public Economics* (New York: McGraw-Hill).

Kay, J. A., and King, M. A. (1986), *The British Tax System* (Oxford: Oxford University Press).

Meade, J. E. (1978), *The Structure and Reform of Direct Taxation* (London: Institute for Fiscal Studies).

Musgrave, R. A., and Musgrave, P. B. (1980), *Public Finance in Theory and Practice* (New York: McGraw-Hill).

Samuelson, P. A. (1964), 'Tax Deductibility of Economic Depreciation to Insure Invariant Valuations', *Journal of Political Economy*, 72: 604–6.

3
A Cash-Flow Tax System

Introduction

In Chapter 2 we discussed the properties of a consumption-based tax system, including the neutral effect on the investment decision, given certain assumptions. We now explain how a corporate consumption tax can be considered as a cash-flow tax system and discuss alternative variations. The assumptions required for tax neutrality will be examined, and later relaxed, in order to evaluate the implications for investment incentives with reference to a project's net present value and internal rate of return. Finally, we shall briefly consider under what circumstances a cash-flow tax system can raise revenue for the central government.

Tax neutrality

We shall introduce three different ways of designing a cash-flow tax system. For the moment, we shall concentrate solely on model I, which is based on the difference between the firm's cash receipts and cash payments. Transactions relating to long-term finance, however, are excluded, such as issues of debt or shares, debt capital repayments, interest paid, and dividend distributions. If the taxable capacity is negative because allowable cash payments exceed taxable cash receipts then we assume that a tax rebate is given, such an arrangement being referred to as a perfect loss offset, since the tax loss is treated in a perfect reciprocal way to a net taxable receipt. The central government is thus effectively providing a negative tax through the subsidization of the firm's tax losses. The elapsed time between the occurrence of a taxable cash flow, positive or negative, and the related payment of tax or rebate, we shall refer to as a tax lag. Initially, we also assume constancy of tax lags and tax rates, which enables us to demonstrate the principle of tax neutrality. Thus, at this stage we are considering a cash-flow tax system with no interest deductibility, no imputed tax credits on dividends, certainty of both constant tax rates and tax time lags, and perfect loss offsets. To appreciate the rationale behind these requirements we shall first of all demonstrate that a cash-flow tax system which adopts these rules results in a neutral effect on the capital investment decision.

We shall consider three capital projects, an analysis of which is summarized in Table 3.1. Project X costs £10,000 and generates a net cash flow of £12,100

TABLE 3.1. *Tax neutrality for capital projects under a cash-flow tax system*

	Project		
	X	Y	Z
Before tax:			
net present value (i)	0	+£182.64	−£180.99
internal rate of return (ii)	10%	11%	9%
After tax (zero lag):			
net present value (70% of (i))	0	+£127.85	−£126.69
internal rate of return (= (ii))	10%	11%	9%
After tax (one-year lag):			
net present value (72.727% of (i))	0	+£132.83	−£131.63
internal rate of return (= (ii))	10%	11%	9%

two years later, and so, assuming a cost of capital of only 10 per cent per annum, its net present value is zero:

$$-£10{,}000+£12{,}100/(1.10)^2=0.$$

Since the net present value is zero, the internal rate of return on the project is 10 per cent per annum. The tax implications of the project have so far been completely ignored in both the cash flows and the discount rate.

But given our tax parameters, the discount rate is unaffected by tax, since there is no interest deductibility for tax purposes and no imputed tax credits on dividends. If we assume a 30 per cent tax rate, then the cash payment of £10,000 gives rise to a tax rebate of £3,000, and the £12,100 cash receipt provides the basis for a £3,630 tax payment. With no tax lag, we find that the net present value of the project after tax, discounting at the 10 per cent after-tax cost of capital is:

$$-£10{,}000+£3{,}000+£12{,}100/(1.10)^2-£3{,}630/(1.10)^2=0.$$

The project is equally attractive whether expressed on a before-tax or after-tax basis since its net present value is zero and its internal rate of return is still 10 per cent per annum.

With a tax lag of one year the tax rebate occurs in one year's time, and the tax payment is made in three years' time, one year after the taxable inflow. The after-tax net present value is now:

$$-£10{,}000+£3{,}000/(1.10)+£12{,}100(1.10)^2-£3{,}630(1.10)^3=0.$$

The net present value is still zero after tax, and thus the internal rate of return after tax remains at 10 per cent per annum. Hence, there is no distortion in the investment decision as a result of the constant tax lag.

We now introduce a small complication by the evaluation of a project which offers a superior return, the results of which are summarized in Table 3.1.

Project Y also costs £10,000 but generates a cash return of £12,321 in two years' time. Its before-tax internal rate of return of 11 per cent can be verified by discounting at 11 per cent, the rate at which the sum of the discounted cash flows is zero:

$$-£10{,}000 + £12{,}321/(1.11)^2 = 0.$$

When we incorporate tax into the analysis, given our parameters, including a zero tax time lag, we find that there is an immediate tax rebate of £3,000 and a tax payment two years later of 30 per cent of £12,321 or £3,696.30. However, the internal rate of return is still 11 per cent per annum after tax, since a zero value is given to the sum of the after-tax discounted cash flows when the discount rate is 11 per cent per annum:

$$-£10{,}000 + £3{,}000 + £12{,}321/(1.11)^2 - £3{,}696.30/(1.11)^2 = 0.$$

Under a cash-flow tax system, with a proportional tax rate and a constant tax time lag, the internal rate of return before tax is the same as the internal rate of return after tax.

In order to appreciate the underlying process, let us examine the effects of this tax system on project Y's net present value. If the cost of capital is 10 per cent per annum as before, then project Y's net present value before tax is:

$$-£10{,}000 + £12{,}321/(1.10)^2 = £182.64.$$

With a zero tax time lag the net present value after tax is reduced to:

$$-£10{,}000 + £3{,}000 + £12{,}321/(1.10)^2 - £3{,}696.30/(1.10)^2 = £127.85.$$

The net present value is still positive and so it is financially attractive after tax. However, the tax rate at 30 per cent has reduced the net present value to 70 per cent of its former value:

$$£182.64 \times 0.70 = £127.85.$$

The reduction in net present value of £54.79 represents the net present value for the central government, assuming a governmental cost of capital of 10 per cent per annum. The government has effectively become a business partner in the venture with a 30 per cent initial stake of £3,000, represented by the tax rebate, with expectations of tax revenue returns to the government of £3,696.30, two years later. The government's net present value from the project is:

$$-£3{,}000 + £3{,}696.30/(1.10)^2 = £54.79, \text{ as expected.}$$

The cost of the investment to the firm is only 70 per cent of the outlay, after deducting the tax rebate, and the firm receives only 70 per cent of the future returns after tax. However, we showed that the internal rate of return for the firm is still 11 per cent despite the tax implications. For, although the yield is the same, it is earned on a smaller outlay, being 70 per cent of its pre-tax cost.

Likewise, the yield for the central government is 11 per cent per annum on its 30 per cent stake, as demonstrated by discounting its cash flows at 11 per cent per annum:

$$-£3{,}000+£3{,}696.30/(1.11)^2=0.$$

With a slight relaxation in our initial assumptions, we can recompute our results for a one year tax time lag. The tax rebate now occurs in one year's time and the tax payment falls due in three years' time, yet the internal rate of return after tax remains at 11 per cent:

$$-£10{,}000+£3{,}000/(1.11)+£12{,}321(1.11)^2-£3{,}696.30/(1.11)^3=0.$$

The implications for the net present value, however, are more interesting and demonstrate an increase in value after tax from £127.85 to:

$$-£10{,}000+£3{,}000/(1.10)+£12{,}321(1.10)^2-£3{,}696.30/(1.10)^3=£132.83.$$

Because of the time delay the effective tax rate is reduced from 30 per cent to $0.30/(1.10)=27.273$ per cent. Thus, the net present value after tax is given by the net present value before tax of £182.64, reduced by 27.273 per cent to:

$$£182.64-(0.27273\times £182.64)=£132.83,$$

being 72.727 per cent of its pre-tax value, as itemized in Table 3.1.

We now turn our attention to project Z which is financially unattractive, since it costs £10,000 but generates a pre-tax return of only £11,881 in two years' time. Its net present value and internal rate of return are provided in Table 3.1 under similar assumptions to those previously given. The internal rate of return is 9 per cent per annum before tax, since this is the discount rate at which the sum of the discounted cash flows is zero:

$$-£10{,}000+£11{,}881/(1.09)^2=0.$$

It is also found to be 9 per cent per annum after tax, as expected. At a cost of capital of 10 per cent per annum, the net present value before tax is:

$$-£10{,}000+£11{,}881/(1.10)^2=-£180.99.$$

With a zero tax time lag, the after-tax net present value is:

$$-£10{,}000+£3{,}000+£11{,}881/(1.10)^2-£11{,}881(0.30)/(1.10)^2=-£126.69,$$

which is 70 per cent of the before-tax net present value. Finally, if the tax time lag is one year, the after-tax net present value is:

$$-£10{,}000+£3{,}000/(1.10)+£11{,}881/(1.10)^2$$
$$-£11{,}881(0.30)/(1.10)^3=-£131.63,$$

representing a 27.273 per cent change in value compared with the net present value before tax:

$$-£180.99(1-0.27273)=-£131.63.$$

The general results are the same as the case found in the example of project Y, except that since the net present value of project Z is negative, the effect of the central government's participation in the investment, in the provision of the tax rebate in return for a share of future returns, is to reduce the loss in wealth for the firm. Ignoring the tax time lag, the central government bears 30 per cent of the negative net present value before tax, leaving the firm with the remaining 70 per cent loss in value. If taxes were instantaneously raised at 50 per cent, then clearly the negative net present value before tax would be split in such a way that both the firm and the central government would bear an equal loss in wealth. An extreme theoretical case of taxes raised at 100 per cent would effectively make the firm an agent for the central government who would take all the risks and bear all the loss.

In general, for a discount rate of k, and a constant tax time lag of y years, the net present value, after taxes at the rate T on cash flows, is represented by:

$$\{1-(T/(1+k)^y)\} \times \text{net present value before tax.} \tag{3.1}$$

Provided the tax rate is set between zero and 100 per cent, the sign, positive or negative, of the net present value after tax will be the same as the net present value before tax. In the example of project Y we saw that, for a positive net present value, both the firm and the central government share in the investment and increase wealth according to the size of the discounted tax rate. Alternatively, if the net present value is zero before tax, it will also be zero after tax, as shown in the case of project X. When there is a negative net present value of an investment, as illustrated by the example of project Z, the net present values of both the firm's and the central government's stakes in the project are also negative after tax, and its acceptance by the firm would decrease wealth for the two parties. The operation of such a tax system is very efficient since it does not distort the yield on an investment and ensures that pursuance of projects on economic grounds should not result in a loss of wealth for the central government. Provided the firm can find projects with positive net present values, the financial objectives of the firm should be congruent with the revenue-raising aims of the central government. However, there are problems regarding the revenue-raising capacity of a cash-flow tax system which we shall briefly re-examine later in the chapter.

An interesting point is whether tax neutrality holds if risk is taken into account. Suppose, for example, that ignoring tax, project W costs £10,000 and provides a mean return of £11,600 at the end of the year with a £2,000 standard deviation. If we assume that the risk-adjusted discount rate is 15 per cent per annum, then by discounting the mean return and deducting the cost of the project we find that its net present value before tax is:

$$-£10{,}000+£11{,}600/(1.15)=£86.96,$$

and the internal rate of return before tax is 16 per cent per annum, since this is the discount rate at which the sum of the discounted cash flows is zero:

$$-£10{,}000 + £11{,}600/(1.16) = 0.$$

The project is therefore financially attractive. Now suppose there is a zero tax time lag, and taxes are raised on cash flows at 30 per cent. The net cost of the investment after deducting the tax rebate is now:

$$£10{,}000 - £3{,}000 = £7{,}000.$$

However, the mean return on the investment after deducting tax is:

$$£11{,}600 - 0.30 \times £11{,}600 = £8{,}120.$$

Thus, the after-tax mean rate of return on the investment is:

$$(8{,}120 - 7{,}000)/7{,}000 = 16\%,$$

which is the same as that before tax. But what happens to these rates of return which differ from the mean? If the before-tax return at the end of the year is £13,600, for example, that is one standard deviation above its mean value, then the rate of return before tax will be:

$$(13{,}600 - 10{,}000)/10{,}000 = 36\%.$$

After taxes raised at 30 per cent, the superior cash return is reduced by 30 per cent from £13,600 to £9,520, but the net cost of the outlay is reduced also by the same proportion from £10,000 to £7,000, because of the tax rebate on the investment. Hence the superior rate of return after-tax is:

$$(9{,}520 - 7{,}000)/7{,}000 = 36\%,$$

which is identical to the rate of return before tax. Just as the yield on a riskless investment is the same whether expressed on a before-tax or after-tax basis, similarly for a risky investment the after-tax yield, for every possible outcome, is the same as that before tax. We must remember, of course, that we assume a cash-flow tax system with perfect loss offset, proportional tax rates, and constant tax lags.

Marginal tax rates

We demonstrated in Chapter 2 that to maintain tax neutrality in investment decisions, a consumption tax needs to apply a constant tax rate over time. By the same token, project X which was marginal, with taxes raised at 30 per cent each year, would be financially attractive if the tax rate initially was set at 30 per cent, but the rate of tax applied only to the inflows dropped to, say 25 per cent, since the net present value after taxes, settled one year in arrears, would be:

$$-£10{,}000 + £3{,}000/(1.10) + £12{,}100/(1.10)^2$$
$$-£12{,}100(0.25)/(1.10)^3 = £454.55,$$

which is, of course, positive. Alternatively, if taxes on the inflows were raised at 35 per cent, whilst the tax rebate on the outlay remained at 30 per cent, the after-tax net present value would be negative:

$$-£10{,}000+£3{,}000/(1.10)+£12{,}100/(1.10)^2$$
$$-£12{,}100(0.35)/(1.10)^3=-£454.55,$$

and therefore financially unattractive. Generally, under a cash-flow tax system, when tax rates are increasing, there is a disincentive to invest in capital projects which are marginal before tax, whereas when they are falling, there is an incentive to proceed with such projects. But, for a capital investment with a positive net present value before tax, there may still be an incentive to invest, as evidenced by a positive net present value after tax, even if tax rates are increasing, provided the before-tax net present value is sufficiently large. However, if the tax rate applied to the initial outlay is 30 per cent and the rate of tax on the future inflow is 32 per cent, project Y's net present value changes from positive to negative, assuming a one year tax time lag:

$$-£10{,}000+£3{,}000(1.10)+£12{,}321(1.10)^2$$
$$-£12{,}321(0.32)/(1.10)^3=-£52.31.$$

Alternatively, a project which has a negative net present value before tax may benefit from falling tax rates to such an extent that its after-tax net present value is positive.

Tax time lags

In our analysis so far we have assumed constant tax time lags. The delay between expenditure on a capital asset and receipt of a tax rebate was regarded as the same length of time as that between receipt of a future cash flow and the resultant tax payment. Given that cash and bank transactions of a firm occur on most working days of the year it is impracticable to raise taxes and receive tax rebates following every single taxable or tax-deductible transaction. If the tax base is determined on an annual basis, then if all transactions theoretically occurred midway during the year, the tax time lag would comprise the six-month period until the end of the year plus the delay from the end of the year until the tax date. If we assume that taxes are settled one year after the end of an assessable period, taxes are raised, on average, 18 months in arrears. However, for taxable cash flows occurring at the beginning of an assessable period, the tax lag is two years, whereas those cash flows arising at the end of the period result in future taxes only one year later.

If we reconsider project X which, you may recall, was marginal before tax, we find that even with a constant tax rate of 30 per cent, if the outlay occurs at the beginning of the first accounting period and the pre-tax inflow arises at the end of the second accounting period, that is two years later, there is a disincentive to invest since its net present value is negative:

$$-\pounds10{,}000+\pounds3{,}000/(1.10)^2+\pounds12{,}100/(1.10)^2$$
$$-\pounds3{,}630/(1.10)^3=-\pounds247.94.$$

The tax time lag for the rebate is two years, whereas the tax time lag for the tax liability is only one year, resulting in a recommendation to reject the project. Conversely, if the outlay occurs at the end of period one and the inflow arises at the beginning of period four, again only two years (and one day) later, then the value of the cash flows discounted to the time of the initial expenditure is positive:

$$-\pounds10{,}000+\pounds3{,}000/(1.10)+\pounds12{,}100/(1.10)^2-\pounds3{,}630/(1.10)^4=\pounds247.94.$$

The tax time lags of one and two years are reversed, and since the timing of the rebate is accelerated compared with the delay in settling tax liabilities on future inflows, an investment incentive is created.

Tax losses

Although we have assumed that there are perfect loss offsets, it is useful to consider distortionary effects which may arise if tax rebates are not given for losses. Outlays on capital expenditure which are not covered by taxable receipts in the same period of assessment would result in a tax loss. Provided the loss can be carried forward and inflated at the firm's reinvestment rate there is no distortion.

If we assume a constant tax lag of one year, then if the firm had no cash flows other than those relating to project X, the £10,000 outlay would be carried forward but inflated at 10 per cent per annum to $\pounds10{,}000(1.10)^2=\pounds12{,}100$ in two years' time and exactly offset against the future inflow, wiping out the taxable capacity completely. Since there would be no taxes raised, the net present value and internal rate of return would not be distorted by taxation. If the firm undertook only project Y, then project Y's tax loss would be inflated, but now at the 11 per cent reinvestment rate, and so taxes due in three years' time would be equal to 30 per cent of the difference between the inflow of £12,321 and the inflated loss of $\pounds10{,}000(1.11)^2=\pounds12{,}321$. Once again this would wipe out the firm's taxable capacity and so no taxes would be raised.

However, if tax losses are carried forward and inflated at a rate less than the firm's reinvestment rate, there would be potential disincentives to invest.

Alternative bases

The intention in this section is to extend the analysis to two further alternative bases for a cash-flow tax system. The design of the tax base used so far in this chapter has ignored cash inflows and outflows between the firm and those who supply long-term capital. This type of cash-flow tax system we should label model I. It is slightly different from a real base, as described in the Meade report (1978), since although it reflects real goods and services, we assume that a net taxable inflow is a cash transaction and not, typically, sales less purchases of revenue or capital items. For example, if goods are sold on credit to a customer then, in model I, the taxable inflow is not strictly the sale but the cash receipt which may occur in a different time period. Conversely, the purchase of goods is not a tax-deductible expense, since they may have been acquired on credit. In this case, the allowable outflow relates to the cash payment to the supplier. This distinction is important and will be re-examined in Chapter 5, when we discuss an historic profits tax system.

Under model II there are taxable inflows and tax-deductible outflows, additional to those under model I, to take account of cash transactions between the firm and suppliers of borrowed funds. Typically, interest costs and capital repayments are tax-deductible, but debt capital receipts are taxable. Conversely, money lent by the firm is tax-deductible, whereas interest and capital received are taxable.

Model III is based solely on transactions between the shareholders, and the firm; taxes are raised on distributions, but tax relief is provided on issues of shares. The efficiency of models II and III will be demonstrated by way of an extension of the example of project X, which costs £10,000 and generates, two years later, net cash inflows of £12,100, thus earning a 10 per cent rate of return per annum.

Suppose the project is financed by debt costing 10 per cent annum, the required cost of capital. If there is a 'balloon' repayment of interest and capital two years later, then we find that the immediate net taxable inflow is given by the £10,000 issue of debt less the £10,000 capital outlay on the project, and the net taxable inflow two years later is represented by the £12,100 net cash inflow from the project less the sum of the £10,000 debt capital repayment and the £2,100 accumulated interest for two years. Consequently, the taxable capacity is completely wiped out, and there is no tax to pay.

But the reader may now enquire as to what happens if there is no 'balloon' repayment and interest costs are paid annually. In Table 3.2 we derive the after-tax cash flows relating to the debt finance, assuming a tax time lag of one year and a 30 per cent tax rate. The debt capital received by the firm forms the basis of a £3,000 tax payment one year later, whereas the interest and capital costs give rise to tax rebates, also lagged for a year. If we discount the after-tax cash flows for debt finance at 10 per cent per annum, we discover that the sum of the discounted net cash flows is:

$$£10{,}000 - £4{,}000/(1.10) - £10{,}700/(1.10)^2 + £3{,}300/(1.10)^3 = 0.$$

This signifies that the after-tax cost of debt is 10 per cent per annum, exactly the same as the before-tax cost of debt. Thus, under model II there is no tax

TABLE 3.2. *After-tax cash flows for debt finance under Model II*

	End of year			
	0	1	2	3
Issue	10,000	—	—	—
Less: interest	—	(1,000)	(1,000)	—
Less: repayment	—	—	(10,000)	—
Subtotal	10,000	(1,000)	(11,000)	—
Less: tax payment	—	(3,000)	—	—
Add: tax rebate	—	—	300	3,300
After-tax cash flows	10,000	(4,000)	(10,700)	3,300

incentive to issue debt finance. But share issues are not taxable and dividend distributions do not give rise to tax payments, since equity finance is exempt from the tax base, both from the standpoint of taxable items and tax reliefs. Hence, both equity and debt finance are effectively treated equally for different reasons, first, because of the tax neutralizing effect on debt and second, on account of the exclusion of equity finance for tax purposes. Thus, the after-tax cost of finance is the same as the before-tax cost, and the net present value of a project is not distorted by financing arrangements. This applies in all cases, no matter whether the net present value before tax is positive, negative, or zero.

Let us now turn our focus of attention to model III. Ignoring share and dividend transcactions between companies, the only tax-deductible items under model III are issues of shares, and tax payments are based solely on dividend distributions.[1] But how much equity finance is required to fund an investment, such as project X? What dividend distributions can be made out of the project's inflows in two years' time? Since dividends give rise to tax payments under model III, it is convenient first of all to convert a 30 per cent rate on a tax-inclusive basis to 3/7 on a tax-exclusive basis, when expressed in proportionate form. Thus, assuming a zero tax time lag, we show in Table 3.3 that a £7,000 new issue is sufficient to fund the project and that the dividend distribution in two years' time is £8,470. The tax rebate of £3,000, being 3/7 of the issue, allows the firm to finance the £10,000 cost of the project. The dividend distribution is equal to 70 per cent of the project's inflows, with a provision of sufficient funds to pay taxes at a rate of 3/7 on the dividends. If we discount the shareholder cash flows at 10 per cent per annum we find that the sum of the discounted cash flows is:

$$-£7{,}000+£8{,}470/(1.10)^2=0.$$

[1] At first, this may seem the wrong way round, until we view dividends as spending or shareholder consumption!

TABLE 3.3. *Tax rebate and payment under Model III* (£)

End of year 0	
New issue (i)	7,000
Add: tax rebate (= 3/7 × (i))	3,000
Subtotal	10,000
Less: project outlay	(10,000)
	nil
End of year 2	
Inflow from project (ii)	12,100
Less: dividend ((iii) = 70% × (ii))	(8,470)
Less: tax on dividend (= 3/7 × (iii))	(3,630)
	nil

Hence, the after-tax cost of equity capital is the same as the before-tax cost under model III. However, since debt capital raised is not taxable under model III, and interest and capital costs are not allowable for tax purposes, on this occasion equity capital is tax neutral and debt capital is exempt, which is effectively just as efficient.

Now suppose instead that the project were financed by a reduction in dividends. The intended dividend distribution could be reduced by £7,000, saving £3,000 tax, to enable the firm to fund the £10,000 required outlay on the project, again on the basis of a zero tax time lag, in order to simplify the anlaysis. So, the dividend distribution two years later would be the same as that shown in Table 3.3. Pursuance of this strategy results in a £7,000 sacrifice in present consumption in return for shareholder dividends of £8,470 in two years' time, with a resultant 10 per cent rate of return per annum maintained.

The three models are indeed variants of a shareholder consumption tax. Finance by new issues or retentions are both tax neutral with respect to investment decisions following a model III cash-flow tax system with proportional tax rates.

Revenue-raising

We have demonstrated that the three alternative models of a cash-flow tax system should result in neutral effects in investment decision-making. The sceptic may, however, query whether a cash-flow tax system would raise any revenue. For, if we use the example of the model I tax system, for ease of illustration, then provided the firm continually reinvests net operating cash inflows, the taxable capacity is nil and thus, taxes can be avoided completely.

However, if the firm's total net present value is positive, some taxes are expected to be paid on final liquidation, should the company voluntarily liquidate. This can be seen by reference to project Y which earned a positive net present value both for the firm and the central government. For project Y there is a tax rebate of £3,000, and tax revenues of £3,696.30 two years later. Thus, if the government borrowed at 10 per cent per annum in order to fund the rebate to the firm and repaid its loan with interest two years later, the government would use the tax revenues to repay its debts which, with interest accumulated over two years, would compound to $£3{,}000(1.10)^2 = £3{,}630$, and hence the government would have surplus net tax revenues of $£3{,}696.30 - £3{,}630 = £66.30$.

However, if a firm always exactly earns its required rate of return, there would be no net revenues raised for the government since the initial tax rebate would be equal to the sum of the discounted values of future taxes, provided the government's cost of capital were the same as that of the firm. For example, project X generates a tax rebate of £3,000 but suffers taxes of £3,630 two years later. The central government's accumulated debts on the £3,000 additional governmental borrowing to fund the rebate would be exactly equal to the tax revenues raised two years later, and so, net of governmental financing costs, there would be no revenue raised.

The revenue-raising capacity of a cash-flow tax system thus depends on the extent to which firms can generate wealth. However, such a system seems fair to those who query why a firm should pay tax if it cannot increase wealth.

Conclusion

We discussed three alternative designs of a corporate cash-flow tax system. Under model I tax payments less rebates are based on the firm's cash receipts less cash payments, ignoring transactions which relate to long-term finance. Interest and debt capital repayments are tax-deductible under model II, but debt capital receipts are taxable. Model III is based solely on share transactions of the firm, and under this model taxes are raised on distributions, although tax relief on issues of shares is provided. The three models were shown to be equally efficient in both capital investment and financing decisions.

In each case a project's internal rate of return is the same both before and after tax, assuming perfect loss offsets, proportional tax rates, and a constant tax time lag. Since rates of return are not distorted if the above conditions hold, the inclusion of taxation in the analysis does not alter the riskiness of alternative rates of return under different economic outcomes. Under model I the sign of the net present value of a project, whether positive, negative, or zero, is unchanged based on these parameters. However, for projects with positive net present values before tax, the net present value after tax will be smaller than the before-tax value, because of the central government's effective equity stake in the project. If projects with negative net present values were undertaken, then both the firm and the government would share in the loss in wealth.

With a relaxation in assumptions, incentives and disincentives can be created. High marginal tax rates applied in the determination of tax rebates, together with low marginal tax rates on taxable inflows may create incentives to invest. Dependent upon the timing of cash flows in relation to an assessable period for taxation, some further distortions may also arise. It is generally beneficial to the firm, and detrimental to the central government, if expenditure is incurred towards the end of an assessable period and taxable inflows at the beginning of assessable periods, so that the tax time lags applied to rebates are reduced and those applied to tax payments are extended. Even when tax rates and tax times lags are non-distortionary, there may be potential disincentives to invest where there is imperfect tax relief for losses, such that immediate rebates are not given, but instead tax losses are carried forward and inflated at a rate less than the firm's reinvestment rate.

Finally, we demonstrated that a cash-flow tax system is generally ineffective in raising revenue for the central government, where firms can invest only in projects which do not earn returns in excess of the cost of capital.

Recommendations for further reading

The implications of a cash-flow tax system for project appraisal are discussed in Brown (1948). In this chapter we have ignored cases of multiple internal rates of return that may arise especially when tax time lags occur. Readers unfamiliar with this problem may like to refer to chapter 3 of Davis and Pointon (1984). Further detailed discussion of different bases of a cash-flow tax system can be found in chapter 12 of the Meade Report (1978). The classic article by Domar and Musgrave (1944), which attacks the problem of imperfect relief for losses in a risk context, is reviewed in the books by Musgrave and Musgrave (1980) and Atkinson and Stiglitz (1980). The effects of taxation on project risk in a portfolio context is analysed by Pointon (1980). MacDonald (1980) raises the issue as to whether a cash-flow corporate tax system can raise revenue. Other objections to such a system are given in a Green Paper (HMSO 1982), although refuted by Edwards (1982).

References

Atkinson, A. B., and Stiglitz, J. E. (1980), *Lectures on Public Economics* (New York: McGraw-Hill).

Brown, E. C. (1948), 'Business Income Taxation and Investment Incentives', in *Income, Employment and Public Policy: Essays in Honor of Alvin Hansen* (New York: Norton).

Davis, E. W., and Pointon, J. (1984), *Finance and the Firm* (Oxford: Oxford University Press).

Domar, E. D., and Musgrave, R. A. (1944), 'Proportional Income Taxation and Risk-Taking', *Quarterly Journal of Economics*, 58: 388–422.

Edwards, J. S. S. (1982) 'On the Case for a Flow-of-Funds Corporation Tax', IFS Working Paper No. 35 (August).

HMSO (1982), *Corporation Tax*, Cmnd. 8456 (London: HMSO).

Macdonald, G. (1980), 'Can a Corporation Tax Under an Expenditure Tax Regime be Non-Distortionary?', *Accounting and Business Research*, (Winter): 66–70.

Meade, J. E. (1978), *The Structure and Reform of Direct Taxation* (London: Institute for Fiscal Studies).

Musgrave, R. A., and Musgrave, P. B. (1980), *Public Finance in Theory and Practice* (New York: McGraw-Hill).

Pointon, J. (1980), 'Investment and Risk: The Effect of Capital Allowances', *Accounting and Business Research*, (Autumn): 432–9.

4
Classical and Imputation Systems

Introduction

The intention in this chapter is to provide a review of alternative systems of corporation tax, classified according to the degree of imputation and according to whether there is a lower tax rate applied to distributed profits. Under a partial imputation system, which is the UK corporation tax system which we shall describe more fully in Chapter 10, credit is given, in personal tax computations, for part of the underlying corporation tax on profits paid out as dividends. By contrast, under a pure classical tax system, a flat tax rate is applied to profits, whether distributed or not, and so dividends effectively suffer double taxation, once at the corporate level and then again at the personal level. Full credit is given under a full imputation system for all the corporation tax on the underlying profits distributed, and so this provides a way of eliminating double taxation. An alternative way of fully relieving double taxation is under a dual rate imputation system, which taxes distributed profits at a lower rate than the rate at which undistributed profits are taxed, yet provides relief against personal taxes on dividends, in personal tax computations, for all the underlying corporation tax. Under some tax systems, the company deducts withholding taxes from gross dividends. These taxes are not regarded as part of the corporation tax, but merely represent a device for the collection of personal tax revenues on behalf of shareholders. Finally, we shall briefly mention alternative tax systems which are operated in different countries.

A partial imputation system

Under a partial imputation system there is a tax credit, in the determination of personal income taxes on dividends, that relates to part of the underlying corporation tax. In Table 4.1 the effects of a partial imputation tax system on a full dividend distribution is illustrated. We assume that there is a 35 per cent corporate tax rate and no special rate for companies with small profits, that imputed taxes on dividends are at 30 per cent of the gross dividend, and that shareholders each pay personal income taxes at a marginal rate of 44 per cent. Profits of £70,000 bear corporation tax of £24,500, leaving a balance of £45,500, which is paid out as a net dividend. There is an imputed tax credit of £19,500, which represents 3/7 of the net dividend, or 30 per cent of the gross

TABLE 4.1 *Full distributions under a partial imputation tax system*

Profits before tax	70,000
Less: corporation tax (at 35%)	(24,500)
Profits after tax	45,500
Less: net dividend	(45,500)
Cash retained	nil
Net dividend	45,500
Add: imputed tax	19,500
Taxable income	65,000
Income tax (at 44%)	28,600
Less: tax credits	(19,500)
Income tax payable	9,100
Net gain (net dividend – income tax payable)	36,400
Effective tax (profits before tax – net gain)	33,600
Effective tax rate (effective tax/profits before tax)	48%

dividend of £65,000. Based on taxable income of £65,000, total personal income tax at 44 per cent is £28,600, but since there is a tax credit for the imputed tax, the net amount of tax payable at the personal level is £9,100. If the representative shareholder suffers income tax at a flat rate of 30 per cent, then clearly there would be no further taxes to pay. However, shareholders receive net dividends of £45,500, but have to pay £9,100 in personal taxes, since their marginal tax rates exceed the basic rate of income tax. The underlying profits of £70,000 result in a net gain to shareholders of only £36,400. Thus, the effective tax is £70,000 – £36,400 = £33,600, and the effective tax rate is 48 per cent as shown in Table 4.1. The effective tax rate exceeds the marginal tax rate suffered by shareholders because under a partial imputation system there is still some remaining corporation tax not imputed to shareholders.

The reader may ask whether the firm would be better advised to retain profits instead. So let us analyse the tax implications of a policy of full retentions. Provided retentions are used to finance projects which earns the required rate of return, the value of the firm should increase by £45,500, compared with a nil increase in value when the firm makes a full distribution. We assume that each shareholder suffers capital gains taxes at an effective rate of 20 per cent on any increase in wealth, although typically, under the UK system, this occurs on realization of the shares. From Table 4.2 we see that the effective tax rate is 48 per cent as before. Consequently, under a partial imputation tax system, with tax credits of 30 per cent of gross dividends, there is a financial equivalence between dividends suffering personal taxes at 44 per cent and retentions subject to a 20 per cent capital gains tax rate. But what is

TABLE 4.2. *Full retentions under an imputation tax system*

Profits before tax	70,000
Less: corporation tax (at 35%)	(24,500)
Cash retained	45,500
Capital gain	45,500
Less: capital gains tax (at 20%)	(9,100)
Net gain	36,400
Effective tax (profits before tax – net gain)	33,600
Effective tax rate (effective tax/profits before tax)	48%

the underlying relationship when tax rates are imposed at rates different from these in our example.

In the next section we shall determine a mathematical relationship to show that under specified rigid conditions, including the absence of imperfections other than taxes, dividends and retentions are fiscally equivalent under an imputation system if:

$$(1-m)=(1-b)(1-g) \tag{4.1}$$

where m = the marginal rate of income tax on gross dividend income,
b = the rate of imputed tax credit on gross dividends, and
g = the rate of capital gains tax.

In our numerical example, with personal income taxes raised at 44 per cent, the above equality holds since:

$$(1-m)=(1-0.44)=0.56, \text{ and}$$

$$(1-b)(1-g)=(1-0.30)(1-0.20)=0.56$$

which demonstrates that, for the given tax rates, dividends and retentions are fiscally equivalent under a partial imputation tax system. For a different rate of capital gains tax an alternative critical marginal tax rate on investment income can be computed. For example, if the capital gains tax rate is 30 per cent and raised on the retention, rather than on the strict realization of the gain, the critical marginal tax rate on gross dividend income is:

$$1-(1-b)(1-g)=1-(1-0.30)(1-0.30)=51\%.$$

Dividends are preferred to retentions if the marginal rate of tax on investment income is less than 51 per cent; retentions are preferred if the marginal income tax rate exceeds 51 per cent.

Dividends or retentions: an algebraic analysis

In this short section we set out a proof of this simple mathematical relationship for dividend policy. There is no loss of continuity, however, by moving on to the next section headed 'Debt finance', which may be of partial relief!

We assume that tax rates and cash flows are known with certainty, although the broad relationsips are similar when risk is introduced. We recall that b denotes the rate of imputed tax credit on the gross dividend and that $b/(1-b)$ represents the tax rate on the net dividend. For example, when $b=0.30$, $b/(1-b)$ is 3/7.

A net dividend of £1 has a related tax credit of £$b/(1-b)$, so that the gross equivalent is worth:

$$\begin{aligned} 1+b/(1-b) &= (1-b)/(1-b)+b/(1-b) \\ &= (1-b+b)/(1-b) \\ &= 1/(1-b). \end{aligned}$$

At a marginal tax rate of m, personal tax of $m/(1-b)$ is borne, which can be decomposed into the tax credit of $b/(1-b)$ and the remaining tax payable after the credit of $(m-b)/(1-b)$. After all taxes, the dividend is worth the £1 net dividend received less the additional tax payable of £$(m-b)/(1-b)$:

$$\begin{aligned} 1-(m-b)/(1-b) &= (1-b)/(1-b)-(m-b)/(1-b) \\ &= (1-b-m+b)/(1-b) \\ &= £(1-m)/(1-b) \end{aligned}$$

Now let us switch our focus onto retained funds. A retention of £1, earning the required rate of return, is worth £1 before personal tax and suffers capital gains tax of £g and thus its value is £$(1-g)$ after capital gains tax. Hence, the retention and distribution are equivalent if:

$$(1-m)/(1-b)=(1-g), \text{ or}$$

$$(1-m)=(1-b)(1-g) \tag{4.2}$$

which we previously labelled equation (4.1), without proof. But this simple relationship provides a valuable guide to the tax implications of dividend policy.

Debt finance

We now evaluate the tax implications of debt finance with reference to the previous numerical example. With deductibility of debenture interest, corporation tax could be avoided by the payment of £70,000 in interest, which would completely eliminate taxable profits, of which the implications are shown in

Table 4.3. We assume that the firm deducts a withholding tax of 30 per cent of the gross interest and pays this to the central government on behalf of debenture-holders who may treat the £21,000 deduction as a personal tax credit. On this occassion we assume that debenture holders bear income taxes on the gross equivalent of interest received at a marginal income tax rate of 48 per cent, which we deliberately choose to be higher than that suffered by shareholders. Income tax payable is thus £12,600, which leaves cash of £36,400 after the settlement of tax liabilities. The important point we wish to stress is that the effective tax rate, derived in Table 4.3, is 48 per cent, exactly the same as that in the first example in which equity finance was raised instead. Hence with the chosen tax rates, debt and equity finance are fiscally equivalent.

We shall now refer to some further simple algebraic relationships for debt finance, the derivations of which are given in the next section.

Debt finance or retentions are fiscally equivalent if:

$$(1-t)=(1-T)(1-g) \tag{4.3}$$

where $t=$ the marginal income tax rate on gross interest received,
$T=$ the marginal corporate tax rate, and
$g=$ the rate of capital gains tax.

From equation (4.3) we can derive the critical marginal tax rate on gross interest received, when the effective rate of capital gains tax is 20 per cent and the marginal corporate tax rate is 35 per cent:

$$\begin{aligned} t &= 1-(1-T)(1-g) \\ &= 1-(1-0.35)(1-0.20) \\ &= 0.48. \end{aligned}$$

TABLE 4.3. *Debt finance and interest deductibility*

Profits before tax	70,000
Less: interest	(70,000)
Taxable profits	nil
Net interest	49,000
Add: withholding tax	21,000
Taxable income	70,000
Income tax (at 48%)	33,600
Less: tax credit	(21,000)
Income tax payable	12,600
Net gain (net interest − income tax payable)	36,400
Effective tax (profits before tax − net gain)	33,600
Effective tax rate (effective tax/profits before tax)	48%

This is the reason why 48 per cent was chosen in the numerical example. If the personal income tax rate on interest had been less than 48 per cent, perhaps the 44 per cent rate which was the critical rate used in the dividend versus retention decision, then debt finance would be fiscally preferable to retentions. However, if the marginal rate of income tax on gross interest received exceeded 48 per cent, then, to the company, retentions taxed at 20 per cent at the personal level would be preferable to debt finance.

In the next section we compare interest payments with dividends to show that they are fiscally equivalent if:

$$(1-m)/(1-b)=(1-t)/(1-T). \tag{4.4}$$

For example, we can verify that this is so when (i) the marginal rate of income tax on gross dividend income is 44 per cent ($m=0.44$), (ii) the rate of imputed tax credit on gross dividends is 30 per cent ($b=0.30$), (iii) the marginal income tax rate on gross interest received is 48 per cent ($t=0.48$), and (iv) the marginal corporate tax rate is 35 per cent:

$$(1-m)/(1-b)=(1-0.44)/(1-0.30)=0.80, \text{ and}$$

$$(1-t)/(1-T)=(1-0.48)/(1-0.35)=0.80.$$

However, when both shareholders and debenture holders pay income tax on investment income at the same marginal tax rate, then, under an imputation system, dividends and interest payments are fiscally equivalent if:

$$b=T \tag{4.5}$$

Thus, for a company which pays corporate taxes at a marginal rate of 30 per cent, then the equivalence holds when the full imputation rate is 30 per cent of the gross dividends. But when the marginal corporate tax rate exceeds this imputed rate, for example, if the marginal corporate tax rate is 35 per cent, then debt finance is preferred to raising new issues of equity and paying dividends.

Debt or equity finance: an algebraic analysis

As promised, we now explain the derivations of equations (4.3), (4.4), and (4.5). A deeper understanding of the underlying processes may be gained by following the algebra, although there is some comfort, to those who move on directly to the next section, that there is no loss in continuity.

We begin by a comparison of retentions with debt finance. A retention of £1 which earns the required rate of return after tax can be financed by profit before tax of £$1/(1-T)$. The reason for this is that the corporate tax on the profit is T times £$1/(1-T)$ and so the profit after tax is (in £'s):

$$1/(1-T)-T/(1-T)=(1-T)/(1-T)=1,$$

as required. Now, debenture interest of £$1/(1-T)$ wipes out the taxable profits and bears total personal tax of £$t/(1-T)$, where t is the marginal income tax rate on gross interest received. The withholding tax at the rate w on gross interest is given by £$w/(1-T)$, and thus the net tax payable is £$(t-w)/(1-T)$. The gross interest is reduced by the withholding tax to provide a net interest of:

$$1/(1-T)-w/(1-T)=(1-w)/(1-T).$$

Thus, the net interest after deduction for the net tax payable is:

$$(1-w)/(1-T)-(t-w)/(1-T)=(1-w-t+w)/(1-T)=(1-t)/(1-T).$$

Hence, debt finance and retentions are equivalent if:

$$(1-t)/(1-T)=(1-g), \text{ or}$$

$$(1-t)=(1-T)(1-g), \tag{4.6}$$

which we previously labelled as equation (4.3).

The fiscal equivalence of dividends and debenture interest can be seen by the elimination of the capital gains tax rate from equation (4.1) and (4.3) to give:

$$(1-m)/(1-b)=(1-g), \text{ and}$$

$$(1-t)/(1-T)=(1-g), \text{ so}$$

$$(1-m)/(1-b)=(1-t)/(1-T), \tag{4.7}$$

of which the latter relationship has previously been labelled equation (4.4).

If the marginal income tax rates for shareholders and debenture holders are the same ($m=t$), interest and dividends are fiscally equivalent only if:

$$(1-t)/(1-b)=(1-t)/(1-T), \text{ or}$$

$$b=T, \tag{4.8}$$

as already stated in equation (4.5). This represents a full imputation system. Under a full imputation system we shall find that the imputed credit is given by the full corporate tax rate, and so we expect no tax bias between interest paid and dividend distributions.

A full imputation system

Under a full imputation system, the tax credit attached to dividends, in the personal tax computation, relates to all the underlying corporation tax. This is demonstrated in Table 4.4, in which the full corporate tax liability is treated as an imputed tax credit to determine total personal taxable income of £70,000. Table 4.2 showed that when the capital gains tax rate is 20 per cent, the effective tax rate on the retention is 48 per cent. This applies to a full retention under both a partial and full imputation tax system. When no dividends are paid, there is no complication arising over the imputed tax credits. We can

TABLE 4.4. *Full distributions under a full imputation tax system*

Profits before tax	70,000
Less: corporation tax (at 35%)	(24,500)
Profits after tax	45,500
Less: net dividend	(45,500)
Cash retained	nil
Net dividend	45,500
Add: imputed tax	24,500
Taxable income	70,000
Income tax (at 48%)	33,600
Less: tax credits	(24,500)
Income tax payable	9,100
Net gain (net dividend – income tax payable)	36,400
Effective tax (profits before tax – net gain)	33,600
Effective tax rate (effective tax/profits before tax)	48%

apply equation (4.1) and show that for an imputed tax credit of 35 per cent of gross dividends, and an effective capital gains tax rate of 20 per cent, then

$$m = 1-(1-b)(1-g)$$
$$= 1-(1-0.35)(1-0.20) = 0.48.$$

This result signifies that if the marginal income tax rate on gross dividends is 48 per cent, then dividends are fiscally equivalent to a retention, assuming no potential imperfections other than tax. To verify this we find from Table 4.4 that the net gain to shareholders is given by the net dividend of £45,500 less the tax payable, which is represented by 48 per cent of the £70,000 gross dividend, less the £24,500 tax credit:

$$\pounds 45{,}000-(0.48\times \pounds 70{,}000-\pounds 24{,}500) = \pounds 36{,}400,$$

which is exactly the amount of the net gain under the retention alternative as shown in Table 4.2.

For dividends and retentions, the effective tax rate on the underlying profits is 48 per cent. But 48 per cent represents the personal tax rate on investment income. Thus, under a full imputation system, the corporate tax liability is effectively eliminated and distributed profits are subjected to taxation only once. The elimination of double taxation, at the corporate and personal level, is the key feature of a full imputation tax system. Notice, however, that the critical marginal income tax rate on investment income, at which dividends and retentions are equivalent, is different from that experienced under the partial imputation system.

We know from equation (4.5) that when both shareholders and debenture holders pay income tax on investment income at the same marginal tax rate, then dividends and interest payments are fiscally equivalent if b, which denotes the rate of imputed tax credit on the gross dividend, equals T, the marginal corporate tax rate. But under a full imputation system, this relationship always holds. If a company never raises equity finance by retentions, but always by way of new issues of shares instead, then debt and equity finance are fiscally equivalent, ignoring issue costs. In Table 4.3 we showed that when debenture holders pay income tax at a marginal rate of 48 per cent on investment income, then the effective tax rate on profits, which financed the interest, is 48 per cent, which is equivalent to the effective tax rate for shareholders, when full distributions are made, as shown in Table 4.4. Debt interest is tax-deductible at the corporate level, whereas dividends under a full imputation system effectively wipe out the corporate tax liability through granting a full tax credit at the personal level. Thus, for different reasons debt and equity finance, ignoring retentions, are equivalent under this type of tax system.

A pure classical system

A classical tax system is a corporate tax system which operates separately from the personal tax system with no imputed tax credits given for any underlying corporation tax. A pure classical system is one which does not use discriminatory tax rates on profits retained or distributed. The implication is that there is a double taxation of profits distributed, first at the corporate level and subsequently at the personal level. However, it must be remembered that capital gains taxes may be applied on disposal of shares, which should appreciate in line with retained profits. Hence, there is still a potential double taxation of undistributed profits. Since there is no imputed tax credit ($b = 0$), equation (4.1) condenses to:

$$m = g, \tag{4.9}$$

which signifies that dividends and retentions are fiscally equivalent, under a classical tax system, when the marginal rate of income tax on gross dividend income is equal to the rate of capital gains tax.

Table 4.5 sets out the effective tax rate on underlying profits when there is a full distribution, initially assuming a 35 per cent corporate tax rate and then on the basis of a $7\frac{1}{7}$ per cent corporate tax rate. The implications of a full retention policy is provided in Table 4.6. In each instance, the capital gains tax rate and the marginal rate of income tax on gross dividend income are both set at 20 per cent, although we assume a withholding tax on gross dividends of 30 per cent.

Assuming a 35 per cent rate of corporation tax, a net dividend of £31,850 can be paid, which forms part of the £45,500 personal taxable income. Since the withholding tax exceeds the income tax at only 20 per cent of the gross dividend, there is a tax repayment of £4,550 due to the shareholders, However,

TABLE 4.5. *Full distributions under a pure classical tax system*

	35% rate of corporation tax	7 1/7% rate of corporation tax
	(i)	(ii)
Profits before tax	70,000	70,000
Less: corporation tax	(24,500)	(5,000)
Profits after tax	45,500	65,000
Less: net dividend	(31,850)	(45,500)
Less: withholding tax (30% of gross dividend)	(13,650)	(19,500)
Cash retained	nil	nil
Net dividend	31,850	45,500
Add: withholding tax	13,650	19,500
Taxable income	45,500	65,000
Income tax (at 20%)	9,100	13,000
Less: tax credit	(13,650)	(19,500)
Income tax payable (repayable)	(4,550)	(6,500)
Net gain (net dividend + income tax repayable)	36,400	52,000
Effective tax (profits before tax − net gain)	33,600	18,000
Effective tax rate (effective tax/ profits before tax)	48%	25.7%

TABLE 4.6. *Full retentions under a classical tax system*

	35% rate of corporation tax	7 1/7% rate of corporation tax
	(i)	(ii)
Profits before tax	70,000	70,000
Less: corporation tax	(24,500)	(5,000)
Cash retained	45,500	65,000
Capital gain	45,500	65,000
Less: capital gains tax (at 20%)	(9,100)	(13,000)
Net gain	36,400	52,000
Effective tax (profit before tax − net gain)	33,600	18,000
Effective tax rate (efficive tax/ profits before tax)	48%	25.7%

the net gain to shareholders of £36,400, which is represented by the net dividend plus the income tax rebate, is the same as the net gain to shareholders when a full retention policy is adopted instead. With a lower corporate tax rate of $7\frac{1}{7}$ per cent, the net gains under the two financial policies are both equal to £52,000. Because there is some double taxation of dividends, the effective tax rates as shown in Table 4.5 exceed the 20 per cent marginal rate of income tax on gross dividend income.

We know that when the income tax rate on investment income exceeds the capital gains tax rate, retentions are preferred to dividends under a classical tax system. But what is the position regarding debt finance? Is debt finance more attractive under a classical system? Where there is no imputation ($b = 0$), we can amend equation (4.4) to show that interest payments and dividends are fiscally equivalent if:

$$(1-m) = (1-t)/(1-T). \tag{4.10}$$

For example, if the marginal rate of income tax on gross dividend income is only 20 per cent and the corporate tax rate is 35 per cent, then the critical marginal income tax rate on gross interest received is found by:

$$t = 1-(1-m)(1-T) = 1-(1-0.20)(1-0.35) = 48\%.$$

This is consistent with Table 4.5, which shows that a full distribution from £70,000 profits before tax is worth £36,400 after tax to shareholders, and Table 4.3, which demonstrates that the use of £70,000 to finance debenture interest is worth, to debenture holders, also £36,400 after tax, assuming that the latter pay income taxes at 48 per cent. Note, however, that we assume presently that debenture holders pay income taxes at a higher rate than the rate at which shareholders pay income taxes on their investment income.

Under a pure classical tax system, there is a fundamental distortion when shareholders and debenture holders pay income taxes on investment income at the same marginal tax rate. From equation (4.10), interest is fiscally superior to dividends if the corporate tax rate is positive.[1] Under a classical tax system dividends are taxed twice, whereas profits applied towards the payment of debenture interest escape from the corporate tax net. Hence, interest is preferred unless debenture holders suffer a marginal tax rate on interest income which is sufficiently higher than the marginal tax rate on gross dividends received by shareholders. Clearly, when an investor holds both

[1] Resetting equation (4.10) as an inequality, interest is preferred to dividends if: $(1-t)/(1-T) > (1-m)$.

Multiplying by $(1-T)$: $(1-t) > (1-m)(1-T)$.

Setting $t = m$: $(1-m) > (1-m)(1-T)$.

Dividing by $(1-m)$: $1 > 1-T$.

Hence: $T > 0$.

stocks and shares in the same firm, interest income should be preferred to dividends under a classical tax system.

Before moving on to consider an alternative classical tax system, it is interesting to compare the pure classical tax system, which applies a $7\frac{1}{7}$ per cent tax rate, with a partial imputation tax system, which imposes a 35 per cent corporate tax rate and allows imputed tax credits at 30 per cent of gross dividends (please refer back to Tables 4.1 and 4.5). As far as full distributions are concerned, these two tax systems are effectively identical, since personal taxable income is £65,000 in each example. But if we assume a marginal income tax rate on gross dividends of 44 per cent instead of a 20 per cent rate, then the net gain would have been the same as that under the partial imputation system.

A major problem, however, is that the two systems are not equivalent, when a full retention policy is chosen, on the assumption that the previous tax rates still hold. Table 4.2 and the second column of Table 4.6 explain the derivation of the net gain to shareholders when the corporate tax rates are 35 per cent under the imputation system and $7\frac{1}{7}$ per cent under the classical system. With a lower corporate tax rate, retentions are more favourably treated under the classical system. Alternatively, we could apply a 35 per cent corporate tax rate to each system and demonstrate that retentions are equivalent under both systems. This can be seen from a comparison of Table 4.2 with the first column of Table 4.6, where we show that the effective tax rate is 48 per cent in each case. However, for a full distribution, the marginal tax rate on gross dividends needs to be 20 per cent for a classical tax system (see Table 4.5, column (i), whereas under a partial imputation system, the marginal tax rate needs to be 44 per cent (see Table 4.1), in order to derive an effective tax rate of 48 per cent in each example. Thus, it is not possible to design a classical tax system which is equivalent to a partial imputation system in its treatment of both retentions and dividends, unless the dividend payout rate is fixed.

A dual rate classical system

We now discuss a tax system which applies different tax rates to distributed and undistributed profits. But because there are no imputed tax credits, we categorize it as a classical system rather than an imputation system. Such a system is called a dual rate classical system. In our numerical example, we assume a 5 per cent corporate tax rate on gross dividends of £65,000 and a 35 per cent corporate tax rate on the remaining £5,000 profits before tax, of which the total is £70,000, as before. The ramifications of this are set out in Table 4.7. The total corporate tax liability is shown to be £5,000, which is exactly the amount under a pure classical tax system with a corporate tax rate of $7\frac{1}{7}$ per cent. However, such is not the case when we consider the alternative option of a full retention since under the dual rate classical tax system the retained profits are taxed at 35 per cent. In Table 4.7, a 44 per cent income tax rate results in a 48 per cent effective tax rate on profits and is equivalent to the application of a 20 per cent rate of capital gains tax, as shown in column (i) of Table 4.6. Hence, a dual rate classical system is not a perfect substitute for a pure classical system.

An interesting feature of the dual rate classical system is appreciated in the determination of a maximum gross dividend, such that there is no cash retained. Profits before tax are used to finance the net dividend, the withholding tax, and also the corporation tax on the gross dividend and the corporation tax on the remainder. It sounds paradoxical that there should be any remaining profits after a full distribution is made, but an inspection of the numerical example in Table 4.7 shows that the gross dividends do not fully wipe out the profits of £70,000. For a nil retention, the gross dividends will be less than the profits before tax. We can determine the amount of the maximum gross dividends from the following formula:[1]

$$P(1-u)/(1+d-u)$$

where P = profits before tax,
u = corporate tax rate on undistributed income,
d = corporate tax rate on gross distributed income.

In our arithmetical example, P = £70,000, $u = 0.35$, $d = 0.05$. and so the maximum gross dividend is:

$$£70{,}000\ (1-0.35)/(1+0.05-0.35) = £65{,}000,\text{ as expected.}$$

Under the policy of full distribution, the total tax liability is:[2]

$$dP/(1+d-u),$$

and so we can calculate the overall corporate tax liability as a percentage.

[1] The corporation tax on the maximum distribution is:

$$dP(1-u)/(1+d-u),$$

and the corporation tax on the undistributed profits is:

$$u(P-P(1-u)/(1+d-u)).$$

The total corporate tax liability is thus:

$$\begin{aligned}&dP(1-u)/(1+d-u)+uP(1-(1-u)/(1+d-u))\\&=(P/(1+d-u))(d(1-u)+u(1+d-u)-u(1-u))\\&=(P/(1+d-u))(d-du+u+ud-u^2-u+u^2)\\&=dP/(1+d-u).\end{aligned}$$

Hence, profit after tax is:

$$\begin{aligned}&P-dP/(1+d-u)=(P(1+d-u)-dP)/(1+d-u)\\&=P(1-u)/(1+d-u).\end{aligned}$$

Since this represents the gross dividend, then there is no cash to retain. Hence the final expression represents the maximum gross dividend.

[2] See above.

TABLE 4.7. *Full distributions under a dual rate classical tax system*

Profits before tax		70,000
Corporation tax on gross dividends (65,000 at 5%) (i)	3,250	
Corporation tax on remainder (5,000 at 35%) (ii)	1,750	
Less: total corporation tax ((i) + (ii))		(5,000)
Profits after tax		65,000
Less: net dividend		(45,500)
Less: withholding tax (30% of gross dividend)		(19,500)
Cash retained		nil
Net dividend		45,500
Add: withholding tax		19,500
Taxable income		65,000
Income tax (at 44%)		28,600
Less: tax credit		(19,500)
Income tax payable		9,100
Net gain (net dividend − income tax payable)		36,400
Effective tax (profits before tax − net gain)		33,600
Effective tax rate (effective tax/profits before tax)		48%

Using the same parameters we find that the overall effective corporate tax rate is 7 1/7 per cent:

$$dP/(1+d-u) = P(0.05)/(1+0.05-0.35)$$

$$= P \times 7\,1/7\%$$

Clearly, for a full retention the tax rate is merely the tax rate on undistributed profits.

A further useful result is that the dual rate classical system is equivalent to a partial imputation system when:

$$d = u - b \tag{4.11}$$

that is, when the rate of corporation tax on gross dividends is equal to the difference between the tax on undistributed profits and the rate of imputation on gross dividends.[1] Consequently, given a corporate tax rate of 35 per cent on retentions ($u = 0.35$), and an imputation tax rate of 30 per cent on gross dividends ($b = 0.30$), then the rate of tax on gross dividends under the dual rate

[1] Under a dual rate classical tax system, a full distribution is worth, after income tax:

$$(1-m)P(1-u)/(1+d-u),$$

and a retention, after capital gains tax, is worth:

$$(1-g)P(1-u).$$

classical tax system was deliberately chosen to be equal to the difference of 5 per cent ($d = 0.05$).

We can see that a dual rate classical tax system can be equivalent to a partial imputation system by an examination of Tables 4.1, 4.2, and 4.7. Under a dual rate classical tax system, with a 5 per cent corporate tax rate on gross dividends and a 35 per cent corporate tax rate on the remaining profits, the effective tax rate on the profits from which a full distribution is made is 48 per cent, as shown in Table 4.7, which is identical to the effective tax rate on the profits from which a full distribution is made under a partial imputation system, as revealed in Table 4.1. Although in each case the marginal tax rate of the shareholder was assumed to be 44 per cent, the two systems, imposing corporate tax rates as already described, would also provide the same effective tax rate on the underlying profits, since in each case the taxable income of the shareholders is the same. But are there any distortions if a full retention is made? Clearly, if there are no distributions, then the lower of the two corporate tax rates under the dual rate classical system is inoperative, and so a flat 35 per cent corporate tax rate would apply to both the dual rate classical tax system and the partial imputation system, as in Table 4.2. Hence, a dual rate classical tax system can be designed so as to be equivalent to an imputation system.

A dual rate imputation system

The final corporate tax system we shall consider is a dual rate imputation tax system. Under this version we assume that there is full imputation of any corporation tax on profits, from which dividends are paid, and that, in addition, there is a withholding tax equal to 30 per cent of the gross dividend. Unlike the dual rate classical tax system we assume that a 5 per cent tax rate is applied to profits distributed, not to gross dividends, and that the remaining profits are taxed at 35 per cent. Table 4.8 shows that from profits of £70,000 before tax, a net dividend of £46,550 can be paid. Personal taxable income takes account of both the full imputed corporation tax as well as the withholding tax although, in the settlement of the final personal tax liability, full credit is given for the withholding tax as well as the imputed tax. We see from Table 4.8 that the effective tax rate on the underlying profits is 48 per cent,

Hence, the two are equivalent if:

$$(1-m)P(1-u)/(1+d-u) = (1-g)P(1-u), \text{ or}$$

$$(1-m) = (1+d-u)(1-g).$$

However, dividends and retentions are equivalent under a partial imputation system if:

$$(1-m) = (1-b)(1-g).$$

Thus, the two tax systems are equivalent if:

$$1+d-u = 1-b, \text{ or}$$

$$d = u-b.$$

TABLE 4.8. *Full distributions under a dual rate imputation system*

	Dual rate imputation tax system (5% on distributed profits)	Pure classical tax system (zero tax rate)
Profits before tax	70,000	70,000
Less: corporation tax	(3,500)	nil
Profits after tax	66,500	70,000
Less: net dividend	(46,550)	(49,000)
Less: withholding tax	(19,950)	(21,000)
Cash retained	nil	nil
Net dividend	46,550	49,000
Add: withholding tax	19,950	21,000
Add: imputed tax	3,500	—
Taxable income	70,000	70,000
Income tax (at 48%)	33,600	33,600
Less: imputed tax credit	(3,500)	—
Less: withholding tax credit	(19,950)	(21,000)
Income tax payable	10,150	12,600
Net gain (net dividend – income tax payable)	36,400	36,400
Effective tax (profits before tax – net gain)	33,600	33,600
Effective tax rate (effective tax/ profits before tax)	48%	48%

which equals the marginal income tax rate on gross dividends received, and this is shown to be equivalent to a pure classical tax system with a zero tax rate! Thus, the dual rate imputation system, as described, completely eliminates the double taxation of distributions, since full credit is given for all the underlying corporation tax when a full distribution is made.

If cash profits are retained in the business, share values are expected to increase, hence potential personal capital gains taxes are raised in addition to corporate taxes on the underlying corporate profits. But in this instance, corporation tax is raised at 35 per cent, and there is no imputed tax credit against the capital gains tax liability, as shown in Table 4.9. Thus, double taxation is not eliminated and hence the dual rate imputation system is not always equivalent to a pure classical tax system with a zero corporation tax rate. However, in our numerical illustration it can be equivalent to a full

TABLE 4.9. *Full retentions under a dual rate imputation system*

	Dual rate imputation tax system (35% on retained profits)	Pure classical tax system (zero tax rate)
	(i)	(ii)
Profits before tax	70,000	70,000
Less: corporation tax	(24,500)	nil
Cash retained	45,500	70,000
Capital gain	45,500	70,000
Less: capital gains tax (at 20%)	(9,100)	(14,000)
Net gain	36,400	56,000
Effective tax (profits before tax – net gain)	33,600	14,000
Effective tax rate (effective tax/ profits before tax)	48%	20%

imputation tax system, with a 35 per cent corporate tax rate, for which the effective tax rate was also 48 per cent. This has previously been demonstrated in Table 4.4 for a full distribution, and, as far as a full retention is concerned, the calculation under a full imputation system is the same as that shown in column (i) of Table 4.9.

A dual rate imputation system, as described, is fiscally neutral with respect to interest and dividends, unless shareholders and debenture holders pay income taxes at different marginal rates. The underlying corporation tax on profits paid as dividends is wiped out in the personal tax computation. Alternatively, when profits are used to pay interest, no corporation tax is paid, assuming interest deductibility. Hence, from an economic standpoint, the result is the same for interest and dividends, although technically their tax treatments are different.

International comparisons

Tax systems in different countries are liable to change and so the use of practical examples needs to be treated with caution. The examples of different tax systems, as shown in Table 4.10, can thus be regarded as those presently adopted or having been adopted in different countries. Most countries have experienced other tax systems. In the UK, for example, a classical tax system was in operation from 1966 to 1973. It also needs to be stated that the tax rates used in the examples within this chapter do not necessarily coincide with those

TABLE 4.10. *Corporate tax systems operated in different countries*

Partial imputation system	*Dual rate imputation system*
Belgium	Japan
Canada	West Germany
France	
Italy	*Classical system*
Republic of Ireland	Netherlands
United Kingdom	USA

in a specific country, since we are more concerned with broad principles. Furthermore, in practice there are numerous small variations from the main systems which we have described. For example, in the USA the corporate tax system has retained an element of tax progressivity with lower rates applied to small profits. Also in some countries there are local taxes as well as national taxes.

In France the tax credit, known as *avoir fiscal*, is based on a fraction of the corporation tax. For example, with profits of 12,000 fr., a 50 per cent corporate tax rate leaves 6,000 fr. available for net dividends. But the *avoir fiscal* of 50 per cent of the tax, is equal to 3,000 fr which is $33\frac{1}{3}$ per cent of the gross dividend:

$$\tfrac{1}{3} \times (6{,}000 + 3{,}000) \text{ fr.} = 3{,}000 \text{ fr.}$$

In our examples, we have expressed the rate of imputed tax on the gross dividend, although it is simple to convert the rate to an imputed tax on either the net dividend or the underlying corporation tax. In Table 4.1, if we were describing the French system, the rate of *avoir fiscal* would be:

$$19{,}500 \text{ (imputed tax)}/24{,}500 \text{ (corporate tax)} = 80\%.$$

The tax rates for 1986/87 in the UK are slightly different from those used in Table 4.1. The full rate of corporation tax is 35 per cent, whereas the rate of imputed tax is 29 per cent of the gross dividend and not 30 per cent. On this basis the rate of *avoir fiscal* would be:

$$29/71 \times 45{,}500/24{,}500 = 76\% \text{ approximately.}$$

But this does not meet the proposals of the EEC Commission's draft directive on tax harmonization, which proposes that the rate of *avoir fiscal* should be between 45 and 55 per cent of the corporation tax on the relevant profits. Furthermore, the draft directive also proposes that the corporate tax rate should be between 45 and 55 per cent, which is higher than the full rate of corporation tax in the UK.

The intention of the change in the UK corporation tax system, in 1973, from a classical tax system to an imputation tax system was not only to reduce the element of double taxation of dividends, for this could have been partly achieved by a lowering of the corporate tax rate, but also to move towards European harmonization of tax systems. Although, most European countries adopt the imputation system, there are still significant variations in the tax rates. Furthermore, in West Germany a dual rate imputation system is operated, and so, as far as dividend distributions are concerned, double taxation is completely eliminated unlike in other European countries.

Problems can arise when dividends are paid to companies in overseas countries who operate different tax systems. When a dual rate classical system is adopted, then dividends paid to foreign shareholders may effectively bear lower corporate tax rates, resulting in a loss of revenue to the government of the dividend-paying company. Dividends received from companies in countries, which suffer high corporate tax rates, may be penalized by companies in countries which operate a dual rate classical system. However, double taxation agreements frequently exist which can eliminate major distortions. Also, imputed tax credits may not be given to foreign shareholders, and rates of withholding taxes can be varied for foreign shareholders.

Conclusion

In this chapter we introduced alternative systems of corporation tax, which were variants of either classical or imputation systems, of which the latter allowed partial or full credit in personal tax computations for the underlying corporation tax on a distribution.

When a full distribution is made, under a partial imputation system, the effective tax rate on the underlying profits exceeds the marginal tax rate suffered by shareholders. We derived several simple models to determine critical marginal tax rates at which dividends and retentions are fiscally equivalent. By varying the rate of imputed credit from zero to the full corporate tax rate, alternative tax systems can be analysed. With interest deductibility, debt finance is generally treated more favourably than dividends unless there is provision for full imputation. However, where debenture holders pay income taxes on interest received at marginal tax rates sufficiently higher than those at which gross dividends are taxed in the hands of shareholders, then distortions at the personal level may eliminate financing preferences at the corporate level, induced by corporate tax design.

Under a full imputation system, the effective tax rate on underlying profits fully distributed is equal to the marginal income tax rate on gross dividends received, thus eliminating double taxation. With a pure classical tax system, double taxation of distributed profits occurs. A pure classical tax system is not equivalent to an imputation system, unless the dividend payout rate is fixed and the tax rates are adjusted accordingly.

Under a dual rate classical system different tax rates are applied to distributed and undistributed profits. The intention of such a system is to reduce the double taxation of distributed profits. It can be equivalent to an imputation system when (i) the tax rate on distributed profits is set to equal the difference between the corporate tax rate on undistributed profits less the imputed tax rate and (ii) the corporate tax rate on undistributed profits equals the corporate tax rate under the imputation system. In our examples, we assumed that the tax rate applied to distributions is based on the gross dividends and that a higher rate is applied to profits before tax, less gross dividends. We produced a number of formulae to derive the maximum gross dividends and to determine the overall tax rate which makes this system equivalent, in terms of revenue-raising, to a pure classical tax system, when a full distribution is made.

Under the dual rate imputation system we assumed that the intention in tax design is to eliminate double taxation, and so, although a lower rate of tax is applied to distributed profits, full imputation is given in personal tax computations for the full imputed corporation tax as well as any withholding taxes. Consequently, the effective tax rate on underlying profits equals the marginal income tax rate on gross dividends received. This is equivalent to a pure classical tax system with a zero tax rate! It completely eliminates the double taxation of distributions. However, where some profits are retained there may remain some double taxation since there is no imputation on retentions and retained funds may lead to capital gains taxes on the realization of shares, which have appreciated through the retention of profits. Since interest is treated as tax-deductible, and profits used to pay dividends effectively escape double taxation, a dual rate imputation system is fiscally neutral with respect to interest and dividends, assuming that shareholders and debenture holders suffer income taxes on investment income at the same marginal rate.

Finally, we categorized corporate tax systems of different countries and noted a few minor variations from the basic systems described earlier.

Recommendations for further reading

Nobes (1980) provides a clear discussion of imputation systems of corporation tax within the EEC and some of the problems of tax harmonization. An article by Chown (1971), which focuses on alternative tax systems, is worth noting especially since it was written in the context of the political and economic environment just before the UK government changed the corporation tax system from a classical to an imputation system. Chapter 12 of the Meade report (1978), including one of the appendices to that chapter, also provides a brief discussion of classical and imputation systems. In addition, there is some discussion of alternative systems of corporation tax in HMSO (1982) which includes an appendix of some international comparisons. An integration of personal and corporate tax arrangements, for dividend and debt policy, with the tax treatment of capital expenditure, can be found in Macdonald (1981). For a financial policy perspective, readers may refer to the book by King (1977). A risk-adjusted model for dividend policy and debt finance within the UK framework is provided by Pointon (1981), whereas Stapleton and Burke (1978) include international comparisons as well.

References

Chown, J. (1971), 'The Reform of Corporation Tax', *Accounting and Business Research*, (Spring): 93–117.

HMSO (1982), *Corporation Tax*, Cmnd. 8456 (London: HMSO).

King, M. A. (1977), *Public Policy and the Corporation* (London: Chapman and Hall).

Macdonald, G. (1981), 'Taxation and Corporate Finance and Investment', *Accounting and Business Research*, (Winter): 41–54.

Meade, J. E. (1978), *The Structure and Reform of Direct Taxation* (London: Institute for Fiscal Studies).

Nobes, C. W. (1980), 'Imputation Systems of Corporation Tax within the EEC', *Accounting and Business Research*, (Spring): 221–31.

Pointon, J. (1981), 'Optimal Capital Structure Under the Imputation System', *Accounting and Business Research*, (Summer): 217–26.

Stapleton, R. C., and Burke, C. M. (1978), *Tax Systems and Corporate Financing Policy*, Monograph Series in Finance and Economics (New York: New York University).

5
An Historic Profits Tax System

Introduction

In this chapter we examine the implications of an historic profits tax system[1] from the standpoint of the firm and make appropriate comparisons with both a cash-flow tax system and a true economic income tax system. We begin with a comparison of cash flow and profit and explain the fundamental differences. The question of interest deductibility is our focus of attention, with regard to its effects upon a project's valuation. Complications are introduced to deal with the impact of inflation on firms whose profits are assessed to tax on historic profits, with particular emphasis on working capital. Alternative depreciation methods are discussed, with a view to the determination of an optimal method under an historic profits tax system. Finally, we evaluate the general effects of historic depreciation charges on risk and return.

Cash flow versus profit

It does not take great imagination to infer that an historic profits tax system is a tax system based on historic profits! But since capital projects should be assessed on the basis of discounted cash flows rather than profit, if they are to reflect the time value of money, then it is instructive to begin with a comparison of the tax implications of productive investment under an historic profits tax system with those under a cash-flow tax system.

Profits differ from cash flows primarily on account of the accruals concept in accounting. Sales are included in profit determination when they are made even if customers have not yet settled their accounts at the end of the financial period. Such revenues are matched with associated costs, and so the cost of unsold stocks are not matched against revenues of the period in which the stocks were paid for, but carried forward against the future sale of such stocks. Furthermore, the cost of a fixed asset is normally allocated to accounting periods in such a way that a fair proportion is expensed to each period in order to reflect the useful life of the asset. These policies are based on standard accounting practice following historic cost accounting principles.

To illustrate, we shall examine the implications of an historic profits tax system for project HP, which requires a capital investment outlay of £123,000,

[1] We are not discussing here the detailed mechanics of a profits tax system which was operative in the UK before the introduction of corporation tax!

for which there is no scrap value at the end of its useful life three years later. Details of sales, purchases, and stock movements are provided in Table 5.1, which sets out the tax implications of the project, when taxes are raised at a flat 35 per cent, and depreciation is calculated on a straight-line basis at £41,000 per annum. Clearly, in practice there are other expenses to be charged against profit but, for simplicity, these are ignored. It is assumed that there is a tax rebate following the tax loss incurred in the third year.

The net operating cash flow is determined in Table 5.2 by an adjustment for opening and closing debtors, to derive the amount of cash to be received from

TABLE 5.1. *Taxes based on historic profits* (£)

	Year		
	1	2	3
Sales (i)	*154,000*	*258,000*	*216,000*
Opening stocks	nil	25,000	48,000
Add: purchases	112,000	194,000	138,000
Subtotal	112,000	219,000	186,000
Less: closing stocks	(25,000)	(48,000)	nil
Cost of goods sold (ii)	*87,000*	*171,000*	*186,000*
Profit before depreciation ((i) – (ii))	67,000	87,000	30,000
Less: depreciation	(41,000)	(41,000)	(41,000)
Profit or (loss) before tax	26,000	46,000	(11,000)
Tax or (rebate) at 35%	9,100	16,100	(3,850)

TABLE 5.2. *Net operating cash flow before tax* (£)

	Year			
	1	2	3	3+
Sales	154,000	258,000	216,000	—
Opening debtors	—	15,400	25,800	21,600
Less: closing debtors	(15,400)	(25,800)	(21,600)	—
Cash received from customers (i)	*138,600*	*247,600*	*220,200*	*21,600*
Purchases	112,000	194,000	138,000	—
Opening creditors	—	11,200	19,400	13,800
Less: closing creditors	(11,200)	(19,400)	(13,800)	—
Cash paid to suppliers (ii)	*100,800*	*185,800*	*143,600*	*13,800*
Net operating cash flow ((i) – (ii)) before tax	37,800	61,800	76,600	7,800

customers, and then by an adjustment to the purchases figures for movements in creditor balances, to calculate cash payments to suppliers. In Table 5.3 the profit before tax is reconciled with the net operating cash flow before tax. The principles employed follow those used in an accounting statement of source and application of funds. First, depreciation is not a cash flow and thus should not be treated as a deduction, so it is added back to the profit figure. Second, there are working capital adjustments. We recall that net working capital is comprised of stocks and debtors less creditors. The stock movements included in profit determination are not cash flows and are therefore reversed. Purchases and sales are not the same as cash payments to suppliers and cash received from customers, respectively, because of movements in the balances for debtors and creditors. Thus, the second adjustment is to calculate the increase in net working capital over the period and deduct this from profit before depreciation.

In order to enable us to appraise the project on an after-tax basis, let us make a few assumptions:

1. The net operating cash flows arise midway through each year, and thus the cash flows for the first three years will be discounted for 0.5, 1.5, and 2.5 years.

TABLE 5.3. *A reconciliation of profit and cash flow* (£)

	Year			
	1	2	3	3+
Profit or (loss) after depreciation, before tax	26,000	46,000	(11,000)	—
Add back: depreciation	41,000	41,000	41,000	—
Subtotal (i)	*67,000*	*87,000*	*30,000*	—
Working capital movements:				
Closing stocks	25,000	48,000	—	—
Add: closing debtors	15,400	25,800	21,600	—
Less: closing creditors	(11,200)	(19,400)	(13,800)	—
Subtotal (ii)	*29,200*	*54,400*	*7,800*	—
Opening stocks	—	25,000	48,000	—
Add: opening debtors	—	15,400	25,800	21,600
Less: opening creditors	—	(11,200)	(19,400)	(13,800)
Subtotal (iii)	—	*29,200*	*54,400*	*7,800*
Periodic investment in net working capital (iv) = (ii) − (iii)	29,200	25,200	(46,600)	(7,800)
Net operating cash flow before tax ((i) − (iv))	37,800	61,800	76,600	7,800

2. Amounts owing to suppliers and owed by customers at the end of the third year are all settled on the same day, which arises one-tenth of the way through the next year, and so these cash flows are discounted for 3.1 years.
3. The capital expenditure is fully paid in one instalment at the beginning of the first year and is therefore not discounted.
4. Taxes are paid on profits, and rebate given on losses, one year after each year-end.
5. The discount rate is 20 per cent per annum.

We know that project HP costs £123,000 and thus, from the net operating cash flows provided in Table 5.2, we can calculate the net present value of the project before tax, using the 20 per cent discount rate:

$$-123{,}000 + 37{,}800/(1.20)^{0.5} + 61{,}800/(1.20)^{1.5} + 76{,}600/(1.20)^{2.5} + 7{,}800/(1.20)^{3.1} = £11{,}511.$$

The tax effects of the project are given in Table 5.1 and so, remembering to apply a one year tax lag, we can calculate the discounted cost of the tax effects, net of the tax rebate on the third year's tax loss:

$$9{,}100/(1.20)^2 + 16{,}100/(1.20)^3 - 3{,}850/(1.20)^4 = £13{,}780.$$

Thus, the after-tax net present value of the project is:

$$11{,}511 - 13{,}780 = £-2{,}269,$$

which is negative, indicating a recommendation to reject the project. In the project evaluation, it is worth noting that although an historic profits tax system is not based on cash flows it was necessary to calculate the project's pre-tax cash flows as well as to determine the historic profits for the tax caculations.

But we know from the reconciliation of profit and cash flow that the profit after depreciation is equal to the net operating cash flow plus the periodic investment in net working capital minus depreciation. To see the factors underlying an historic profits tax system, we can isolate the tax effects into three components. First, we can calculate the present value of the taxes on the net operating cash flows; second, we can determine the present value of the effective tax on working capital investment; and third, we can calculate the present value of the tax savings through depreciation deductions, which we shall call the depreciation tax shield. In order to maintain a constant tax time lag, we assume that taxes on cash flows occur 1.5 years later. With a tax rate of 35 per cent and a discount rate of 20 per cent per annum, the present value of the depreciation tax shield is:

$$41{,}000(0.35)/(1.20)^2 + 41{,}000(0.35)/(1.20)^3 + 41{,}000(0.35)/(1.20)^4 = £25{,}190.$$

The discounted cost of taxes on cash flows is:

$$37{,}800(0.35)/(1.20)^2 + 61{,}800(0.35)/(1.20)^3 + 76{,}600(0.35)/(1.20)^4 + 7{,}800(0.35)/(1.20)^{4.6} = £35{,}814.$$

Finally, the discounted cost of the effective tax on working capital is:

$$29{,}200(0.35)/(1.20)^2 + 25{,}200(0.35)/(1.20)^3 - 46{,}600(0.35)/(1.20)^4 - 7{,}800(0.35)/(1.20)^{4.6} = £3{,}156.$$

Consequently, the net present value of the tax effects is:

$$25{,}190 - 35{,}814 - 3{,}156 = £-13{,}780.$$

As expected, the net tax effects are the same as we previously evaluated when we applied the tax rates to the historic profits. However, it is instructive to examine, under an historic profits tax system, the isolated effects on cash flow, working capital, and the depreciation shield, because it provides an insight into the underlying factors at work.

We know from Chapter 2 that a perfect cash-flow tax system, with a proportional tax rate and constant tax time lags, should have a non-distortionary effect on capital investment decisions. But the tax depreciation shield under an historic profits tax system is inferior to instant relief under a cash-flow tax system because of the discounting effect. With a 35 per cent tax rate, the depreciation tax shield, under a cash-flow tax system, is worth:

$$123{,}000(0.35)/(1.20)^{1.5} = £32{,}749,$$

which is substantially in excess of the historic cost depreciation tax shield of £25,190.

We have assumed that the tax payments are made one year in arrears of the financial year-end, but that the net operating cash flows arise mid-year. Hence, the tax time lag is 1.5 years from the time that the cash flows arise to the relevant tax payment date. Thus, in our comparison of an historic profits tax system with a cash-flow tax system, it is convenient to assume a tax time lag of 1.5 years between cash flows and tax payments or rebates. Furthermore, the effective tax on working capital, which has a discounted cost of £3,156 is not a feature of the cash-flow tax system and provides a further potential disincentive to invest. Hence, the project is taxed more heavily under an historic profits tax system than under a cash-flow tax system when the same tax rate is applied to each system. Under the cash-flow tax system, the net present value after tax is £8,446, which is determined by taking the before-tax value of £11,511 less the discounted cost of the taxes on operating cash flows of £35,814, plus the depreciation tax shield of £32,749.

A positive net present value after tax is expected, since the net present value before tax is positive, and the cash-flow tax system under consideration has a proportional tax rate less than 100 per cent, a constant tax time lag, and it offers perfect relief for losses. Under this neutral tax system, the sign of the net present value after tax is the same as the sign of the net present value before tax. There is no distortionary effect on the investment decision. If the project is financially attractive before tax, then it should also be financially attractive after tax, otherwise there is a distortion in economic efficiency.

However, we find that under an historic profits tax system, this condition does not hold. Ignoring tax, the project generates wealth of £11,511, yet the tax effects reduce wealth by £13,780, which leads to a negative net present value after tax of minus £2,269. Effectively, to proceed with the project would result in fiscal costs in excess of the pre-tax value of the project. The reader may query whether it is proper for a tax system to extract wealth, through tax payments less rebates, to a greater extent than the pre-tax wealth that can be generated.

It is interesting to examine at what rate a cash-flow tax system would raise the same net taxes as those under an historic profits tax system, which applies a 35 per cent tax rate. In the above example, for the discounted cost of the tax effects, under the cash-flow tax system, to be the same as that which results from an historic profits tax system, the tax rate under the cash-flow tax system is equal to:[1]

$$(\text{discounted cost of tax effects}) \times (\text{one} + \text{annual discount rate})^{1.5}/(\text{net present value before tax}) = 13{,}780\ (1.20)^{1.5}/11{,}511 = 157.37\,\%!$$

By taking into account the cash flows given in Table 5.2, the discounted cost of the tax effects under the cash-flow tax system with a tax rate of 157.37 per cent is:

$$-123{,}000(1.5737)/(1.20)^{1.5} + 37{,}800(1.5737)/(1.20)^2 + 61{,}800(1.5737)/(1.20)^3 + 76{,}600(1.5737)/(1.20)^4 + 7{,}800(1.5737)/(1.20)^{4.6} = £13{,}780,$$

as required. The overall tax burden is now the same as that under the historic profits tax system, even though the tax rate has increased from 35 per cent to over 150 per cent. For a neutral effect on the investment decision, the effective marginal tax rate should be between zero and 100 per cent. However, under an historic profits tax system the actual tax rate may seem misleadingly low yet result in potential disincentives to invest due to (i) the inadequacy of depreciation provisions and (ii) the lack of relief for working capital

[1] Let: B = net present value before tax
A = net present value after tax
E = discounted cost of tax effects
T = tax rate, and
k = discount rate.

Thus, for a tax lag of 1.5 years:

$$A = B - BT/(1+k)^{1.5}$$

But, $A = B - E$,

So, $BT/(1+k)^{1.5} = E$

and, $T = E(1+k)^{1.5}/B$.

investment. But before we dismiss the historic profits tax system, we shall introduce a further factor into the analysis. This relates to the question of interest deductibility.

Interest deductibility: historic profits and true economic income

The analysis so far has assumed that the project was funded by a firm financed entirely by equity capital. There is also an implicit assumption that a classical tax system is in operation. In order to make the example more intriguing we shall assume that the firm is approximately 100 per cent debt-financed. Although this is unrealistic in practice, it serves as a useful device to illustrate a simple but important principle, which is that under an historic profits tax system, interest payments on debt are tax-deductible, since they are deducted in profit determination under historic cost principles. We shall discover that this may have a dramatic effect on the net present value of the project. We are not suggesting that a project should necessarily be evaluated at the after-tax cost of debt, for the increased financial risk, through interest commitments against profit, may very well result in increases in returns required by shareholders. Instead, the emphasis here is on tax design. However, if the project is of very low risk, then the after-tax cost of debt may be a useful surrogate for the correct discount rate.

If interest rates are 20 per cent and if taxes, settled 1.5 years in arrears, are raised at 35 per cent, then the after-tax cost of the interest is less than 20 per cent. But how do we determine the cost? If we assume that interest payments are made annually and debt is raised and repaid at discrete annual intervals, then, for every £1,000 of debt raised, there is a payment of £1,200 one year later, of which the interest of £200 results in a tax saving of 0.35 times £200, eighteen months after the interest is paid. By choosing a discount rate at which the net present value of the relevant cash flows is zero, we can find the after-tax cost of the debt. We discover that the after-tax cost of debt is 14.27 per cent per annum:[1]

$$1{,}000 - 1{,}200/(1.1427) + 200(0.35)/(1.1427)^{2.5} = 0.$$

[1] Another method to derive the after-tax cost of debt proceeds as follows. First, let b = the before-tax cost per annum, and a = the after-tax cost per annum. With a time lag of 1.5 years and a tax rate equal to T:

$$b(1 - T/(1+a)^{1.5}) = a.$$

Let e = an estimate for the after-tax cost, such that the first estimate:

$$e_1 = b(1 - T) = 0.20(1 - 0.35) = 0.13.$$

Hence, a revised estimate for a is e_2 such that:

$$\begin{aligned} e_2 &= b/(1 - T/(1+e_1)^{1.5}) \\ &= 0.20(1 - 0.35/(1+0.13)^{1.5}) \\ &= 0.1417. \end{aligned}$$

On the basis of the capital cost of £123,000, we now find that the net present value of project HP is positive when discounted at the after-tax cost of debt as shown in Table 5.4.

Hence, although an historic profits tax system appears deficient in design due to the inadequacy of depreciation provisions and the effective tax on working capital, we must remember that our conclusion was based on a comparison with a cash-flow tax system. Such a conclusion was initially valid when the firm was funded by retentions. However, when the principal source of finance is debt, then under the historic profits tax system interest is tax-deductible, whereas under a cash-flow tax system interest should not be tax-deductible, a principle we established in Chapter 3. Therefore, it is more valid to compare an historic profits tax system with a true economic income tax system, which allows for interest deductibility (see Chapter 2).

We have already established that profit differs from operating cash flow primarily because of the treatment of depreciation and working capital. Under an historic profits tax system the tax base, ignoring interest deductibility, is equivalent to net operating cash flow less depreciation plus the periodic investment in net working capital. By comparison, again ignoring interest deductibility, the true economic income tax system is based upon net

TABLE 5.4. *Discounting at the after-tax cost of debt*

Item	Cash flow (£)	Discount factor	Present value (£)
Outlay	(123,000)	1	(123,000)
First net operating cash flow	37,800	$1/(1.1427)^{0.5}$	35,361
Second net operating cash flow	61,800	$1/(1.1427)^{1.5}$	50,593
Tax on first year's profit	(9,100)	$1/(1.1427)^{2}$	(6,969)
Third net operating cash flow	76,600	$1/(1.1427)^{2.5}$	54,878
Tax on second year's profit	(16,100)	$1/(1.1427)^{3}$	(10,790)
Final net operating cash flow	7,800	$1/(1.1427)^{3.1}$	5,158
Tax rebate on third year's loss	3,850	$1/(1.1427)^{4}$	2,258
Net present value after tax			7,489

Using this revised estimate, e_2, in the formula we derive a third estimate e_3:

$$e_3 = b/(1 - T/(1 + e_2)^{1.5})$$
$$= 0.20(1 - 0.35/(1 + 0.1417)^{1.5}) = 0.1426,$$

A similar process determines e_4 as 0.1427,

which satisfies the original expression:

$$a = b(1 - T/(1 + a)^{1.5})$$
$$= 0.20(1 - 0.35/(1 + 0.1427)^{1.5}) = 0.1427.$$

Hence, by iteration we have found the after-tax cost.

operating cash flow less true economic depreciation. Hence, the issue is now whether the historic cost depreciation figures less the periodic investments in net working capital in each period are equivalent to true economic depreciation.

In Table 5.5 we evaluate the same project under a true economic income tax system. It is assumed that the tax rate is 35 per cent and that interest deductibility is reflected in the discount rate of 14.27 per cent per annum after tax relief. The capitalized values of future inflows, shown in Table 5.5, are derived by discounting the pre-tax net operating cash flows of future periods, given in the first row of Table 5.5. For example at time $t = 2.5$, the £7,200 capitalized value of the future inflow is found by discounting £7,800 for $3.1 - 2.5 = 0.6$ years, at 14.27 per cent per annum:

$$7{,}800/(1.1427)^{0.6} = £7{,}200.$$

Correspondingly, the capitalized value of future inflows, at time $t = 1.5$, is found by discounting £76,600 and £7,200 for $2.5 - 1.5 = 1$ year:

$$76{,}600/(1.1427) + 7{,}200/(1.1427) = £73{,}335.$$

Initially there is no true economic depreciation, since the project costs £123,000 but generates discounted inflows worth £145,990. Hence, there is a true economic appreciation of £22,990, which is taxable. At time $t = 0.5$, the project suffers economic depreciation of £145,990 − £118,259 = £27,731, as shown in Table 5.5. Thus, true economic income, set out in Table 5.5, is £37,800 − £27,731 = £10,069. We calculate the discounted cost of the tax payments by the application of a 35 per cent tax rate and the inclusion of a tax lag of 1.5 years:

$$22{,}990(0.35)/(1.1427)^{1.5} + 10{,}069(0.35)/(1.1427)^{2} + 16{,}876(0.35)/(1.1427)^{3} + 10{,}465(0.35)/(1.1427)^{4} + 600(0.35)/(1.1427)^{4.6} = £15{,}507.$$

TABLE 5.5. *A true economic income tax*

	Waiting period in years (t)				
	$t=0$	$t=0.5$	$t=1.5$	$t=2.5$	$t=3.1$
Pre-tax net operating cash flow	—	37,800	61,800	76,600	7,800
Capitalized value of future inflows	145,990	118,259	73,335	7,200	—
Outlay	(123,000)	—	—	—	—
True economic depreciation (appreciation)	(22,990)	27,731	44,924	66,135	7,200
True economic income	22,990	10,069	16,876	10,465	600

We know that the capitalized value of the inflows is £145,990, when discounted at the after-tax cost of debt, so the net present value after tax is equal to:

$$145{,}990 - 123{,}000 - 15{,}507 = £7{,}483.$$

The final after-tax net present value can be compared with that under the historic profits tax system of £7,489, as shown in Table 5.4. Thus, an historic profits tax system is virtually equivalent to a true economic income tax system for this particular project.

Inflation, taxes, and cash flows

The effects of inflation on tax arrangements cannot be ignored since there are potential economic inefficiencies that may arise. Inflation is likely to impact upon sales, purchases, fixed assets, as well as financing costs, at differential rates depending upon expectations in different real and financial markets. Under an historic profits tax system actual money interest costs are deductible in profit determination, whereas depreciation expenses are based on historic asset costs. In project evaluation, the actual pre-tax money cash flows should be discounted at the actual money rate of interest, according to the risk category of the investment, and then a deduction should be made for the discounted cost of the incremental tax payments less tax savings based on historic profits attributable to the project.

Initially, let us assume that there is uniform inflation at the rate of 5 per cent per annum so that sales, purchases, stocks, debtors, and creditors are all inflated at this rate. For the sake of computational convenience, working capital balances are inflated to the end of the appropriate year, whereas sales and purchases are based on mid-year figures. Finally, the net operating cash flow for each year is deemed to arise at mid-year. In Table 5.6 the tax payments and rebate are recalculated for project HP, which was previously evaluated ignoring these inflationary effects. The revised net operating cash flows are given in Table 5.7.

Previously the after-tax cost of debt was used, for which the before-tax cost was 20 per cent per annum, which we now assume was on the basis of a nil general rate of inflation. However, debenture holders should now demand 26 per cent per annum, if the general rate is expected to be 5 per cent per annum. There is a 5 percentage point increase plus a further increase for inflation on interest of 20 per cent of 5 percentage points, which is 1 percentage point. Arithmetically, we can check that one plus the revised rate demanded by debenture holders is equal to:

$$(1.20)(1.05) = 1.26,$$

providing a 26 per cent annual discount rate before tax. But for every £1,000 of one year debt raised now, £260 is paid one year later as interest on which 35 per cent times £260 is saved in taxes in 2.5 years' time, given an 18-month tax time

TABLE 5.6. *Uniform inflationary effects of taxes on historic profits* (£)

	Year		
	1	2	3
Sales (i)	*154,000 $(1.05)^{0.5}$*	*258,000 $(1.05)^{1.5}$*	*216,000 $(1.05)^{2.5}$*
Opening stocks	nil	25,000 (1.05)	48,000 $(1.05)^2$
Purchases	112,000 $(1.05)^{0.5}$	194,000 $(1.05)^{1.5}$	138,000 $(1.05)^{2.5}$
Subtotal	114,766	234,980	208,822
Less: closing stocks	(25,000) (1.05)	(48,000) $(1.05)^2$	nil
Cost of goods sold (ii)	*88,516*	*182,060*	*208,822*
Profit before depreciation ((i) – (ii))	69,287	95,530	35,199
Less: depreciation	(41,000)	(41,000)	(41,000)
Profit or (loss) before tax	28,287	54,530	(5,801)
Tax or (rebate) at 35%	9,900	19,086	(2,030)

lag as before. By trial and error we can find the after-tax cost of debt, which is denoted by a in the following equation, which discounts the relevant cash flows:

$$+1{,}000-1{,}000/(1+a)-260/(1+a)+0.35(260)/(1+a)^{2.5}=0.$$

A discount rate of 19 per cent per annum satisfies this equation and therefore represents the after-tax cost of debt.[1]

We now know the pre-tax cash flows, the tax payments or rebate, and the after-tax discount rate, so we are well-equipped to calculate the after-tax net present value. The derivation, set out in Table 5.8, reveals that the final

[1] An alternative derivation is through iteration. Let e = an estimate for the after-tax cost, such that the first estimate, which ignores the tax lag on the interest deductibility, is:

$$e_1 = b(1-T) = 0.26(1-0.35) = 0.169.$$

Hence a second estimate for a is e_2, such that:

$$e_2 = b(1-T/(1+e_1)^{1.5})$$
$$= 0.26(1-0.35/(1.169)^{1.5}) = 0.188.$$

A third estimate is:

$$e_3 = b(1-T/(1+e_2)^{1.5})$$
$$= 0.26(1-0.35/(1.188)^{1.5}) = 0.190,$$

which satisfies:

$$a = b(1-T/(1+a)^{1.5})$$
$$= 0.26(1-0.35/(1.190)^{1.5}) = 0.190,$$

and so the after-tax cost is 19 per cent per annum.

TABLE 5.7. *Uniform inflationary effects on cash flow* (£)

	Year			
	1	2	3	3+
Profit before depreciation and tax (i)	*69,287*	*95,530*	*35,199*	—
Working capital movements:				
Closing stocks	25,000(1.05)	48,000$(1.05)^2$	—	—
Add: closing debtors	15,400(1.05)	25,800$(1.05)^2$	21,600$(1.05)^3$	—
Less: closing creditors	(11,200)(1.05)	(19,400)$(1.05)^2$	(13,800)$(1.05)^3$	—
Subtotal (ii)	*30,660*	*59,976*	*9,029*	—
Opening stocks	—	25,000(1.05)	48,000$(1.05)^2$	—
Add: opening debtors	—	15,400(1.05)	25,800$(1.05)^2$	21,600$(1.05)^3$
Less: opening creditors	—	(11,200)(1.05)	(19,400)$(1.05)^2$	(13,800)$(1.05)^3$
Subtotal (iii)	—	*30,660*	*59,976*	*9,029*
Periodic investment in net working capital (iv) = (ii) − (iii)	30,660	29,316	(50,947)	(9,029)
Net operating cash flow ((i) − (iv))	38,627	66,214	86,146	9,029

valuation is approximately the same as before. For, although inflation has generally increased the operating cash flows, the net result is roughly neutralized because of the increase in the discount rate. It must be stressed, however, that inflation rates were deemed to be uniform across all real and financial markets.

However, if the firm could not increase its prices as fast as the rate of its product cost inflation, then there would be lower profits and a reduction in net present value. The impact upon profits and taxes is shown in Table 5.9, and the cash flow repercussions are set out in Table 5.10, assuming a 5 per cent inflation rate on purchases, stocks, and creditors, and a 2 per cent inflation rate applied to sales and debtors. The after-tax net present value is derived in Table 5.11 and shows that the project is now financially unattractive. On account of the specific inflation rates being discriminatory against the firm the cash inflows are lower than those under conditions of uniform inflation, as summarized in Table 5.12. Furthermore, the cash flows under uniform

TABLE 5.8. *Net present value after tax, given uniform inflation*

Item	Cash flow (£)	Discount factor	Present value (£)
Outlay	(123,000)	1	(123,000)
First net operating cash flow	38,627	$1/(1.19)^{0.5}$	35,409
Second net operating cash flow	66,214	$1/(1.19)^{1.5}$	51,007
Tax on first year's profit	(9,900)	$1/(1.19)^{2}$	(6,991)
Third net operating cash flow	86,146	$1/(1.19)^{2.5}$	55,766
Tax on second year's profit	(19,086)	$1/(1.19)^{3}$	(11,326)
Final net operating cash flow	9,029	$1/(1.19)^{3.1}$	5,266
Tax rebate on third year's loss	2,030	$1/(1.19)^{4}$	1,012
Net present value after tax			7,143

TABLE 5.9. *Specific inflationary effects of taxes on historic profits* (£)

	Year		
	1	2	3
Sales	154,000 $(1.02)^{0.5}$	258,000 $(1.02)^{1.5}$	216,000 $(1.02)^{2.5}$
Less: cost of goods sold	(88,516)	(182,060)	(208,822)
Profit before depreciation	67,016	83,719	18,141
Less: depreciation	(41,000)	(41,000)	(41,000)
Profit or (loss) before tax	26,016	42,719	(22,859)
Tax or (rebate) at 35%	9,106	14,952	(8,001)

inflation exceed those generated by the project when there is no inflation. Such is little comfort to the firm, however, since there is an offsetting effect through the discounting process, due to the rise in the discount rate to reflect the anticipated general rate of inflation.

A particularly interesting feature of Table 5.12 is the discrepancy, in each case, between profit and cash flow. For each pair of rows, the total profit over the life of the project is equal to the total cash flow. However, initially there is no loss recorded despite the large cash outflow, whereas towards the end of the project life, cash flows exceed profits. But is this merely a question of financial swings and roundabouts? The answer must be in the negative from a valuation standpoint, since the time value of money stresses greater importance to sums of money in earlier years. Hence a tax system based on profits discriminates against projects generally, since they typically have outflows in earlier years in

TABLE 5.10. *Specific inflationary effects on cash flow* (£)

	Year 1	2	3	3+
Profit before depreciation and tax (i)	*67,016*	*83,719*	*18,141*	—
Working capital movements:				
Closing stocks	25,000 (1.05)	48,000 $(1.05)^2$	—	—
Add: closing debtors	15,400 (1.02)	25,800 $(1.02)^2$	21,600 $(1.02)^3$	—
Less: closing creditors	(11,200) (1.05)	(19,400) $(1.05)^2$	(13,800) $(1.05)^3$	—
Subtotal (ii)	*30,198*	*58,374*	*6,947*	—
Opening net working capital (iii)	—	*30,198*	*58,374*	*6,947*
Periodic investment in net working capital (iv) = (ii) − (iii)	30,198	28,176	(51,427)	(6,947)
Net operating cash flow ((i) − (iv))	36,818	55,543	69,568	6,947

TABLE 5.11. *Specific inflationary effects upon the net present value after tax*

Item	Cash flow (£)	Discount factor	Present value (£)
Outlay	(123,000)	1	(123,000)
First net operating cash flow	36,818	$1/(1.19)^{0.5}$	33,751
Second net operating cash flow	55,543	$1/(1.19)^{1.5}$	42,787
Tax on first year's profit	(9,106)	$1/(1.19)^2$	(6,430)
Third net operating cash flow	69,568	$1/(1.19)^{2.5}$	45,034
Tax on second year's profit	(14,952)	$1/(1.19)^3$	(8,873)
Final net operating cash flow	6,947	$1/(1.19)^{3.1}$	4,051
Tax rebate on third year's loss	8,001	$1/(1.19)^4$	3,990
Net present value after tax			(8,690)

anticipation of future inflows, whereas levels of profits less losses are likely to be smoother. Primarily, the smoothing process is a reflection of the impact of depreciation provisions. But it may be of little consolation that tax depreciation rules allow a full write-off spread over the useful life of the asset, if the asset is paid for in one lump sum. The spreading of allowances does not provide full compensation because of the discounting effect. Furthermore, when the general rate of inflation is anticipated and reflected in an increased

TABLE 5.12. *Profits and cash flow under varying levels of inflation* (£)

	Year				
	0	1	2	3	3+
With specific inflation					
Profit or (loss) before tax	—	26,016	42,719	(22,859)	—
Cash inflow or (outflow)	(123,000)	36,818	55,543	69,568	6,947
With uniform inflation					
Profit or (loss) before tax	—	28,287	54,530	(5,801)	—
Cash inflow or (outflow)	(123,000)	38,627	66,214	86,146	9,029
Without inflation					
Profit or (loss) before tax	—	26,000	46,000	(11,000)	—
Cash inflow or (outflow)	(123,000)	37,800	61,800	76,600	7,800

market rate of interest, the discounted value of the depreciation tax shield is further reduced.

The working capital projections under alternative inflationary conditions are shown in Table 5.13. Even ignoring inflation, we can see the building up of working capital in the early years, followed by a release of working capital, which is a reflection of the normal working capital cycle. But under a profits tax system there is an effective tax on working capital invested but an effective tax relief on disinvestment, although this is not by tax design! If interest rates were zero there would be no distortionary effects on investment incentives as far as the working capital dimension of project evaluation is concerned. However, in reality not only are interest rates positive, but with inflation the working capital investment and disinvestment may be more pronounced, as illustrated in Table 5.13. Furthermore, inflationary-induced increases in interest rates may reduce the compensations for higher levels of disinvestment, on account of the discounting process.

TABLE 5.13. *Working capital projections under varying levels of inflation* (£)

	Year			
	1	2	3	3+
With specific inflation (from Table 5.10)	30,198	28,176	(51,427)	(6,947)
With uniform inflation (from Table 5.7)	30,660	29,316	(50,947)	(9,029)
Without inflation (from Table 5.3)	29,200	25,200	(46,600)	(7,800)

Depreciation methods

An historic profits tax system allows for the tax deductibility of depreciation based on historic cost accounting principles.[1] Thus, the tax depreciation expense is typically based on original cost. Depreciation charges reduce profits and therefore result in lower tax liabilities. But although alternative methods of depreciation may allocate the same total depreciation charge over an asset's useful life, it is normally preferable to receive the tax benefits in earlier years, on account of the time value of money, and thus any choice of depreciation method may be financially significant.

The straight-line method allocates equal annual amounts over the life of the asset, whereas the reducing or declining balance method applies a fixed percentage to the written-down value of the asset. The double-declining balance method is an example of the declining balance method where the depreciation rate is twice that under the straight-line method for an asset of equal life. Another approach is the sum-of-the-years'-digits method, under which depreciation is charged on the basis of the proportion of the number of remaining years of useful life to the sum of all the years from one onwards to the estimated total life in years. There are, of course, other depreciation methods, which we shall presently ignore, such as the depletion method, more suitable for mining and oil wells, and the revaluation method, which is used for livestock. The tax implications of different methods can best be illustrated by example.

Table 5.14 sets out the depreciation charges under alternative methods, for an asset which costs £1,000 and has an expected life of seven years, at the end of which the estimated scrap value is £133. Under the straight-line method, the cost less scrap value, of £1,000 – £133 = £867, is written off in equal instalments of one-seventh of £867, which is rounded up to £124 per annum for six years and rounded down to £123 in the seventh year merely to balance the arithmetic. The depreciation rate under the reducing balance method is set at 25 per cent per annum. At this rate, in this example, the asset can be written down to its scrap value in seven years' time. In the first year, 25 per cent of the cost is written off, which leaves a written-down value of £750. Thus in the second year the depreciation expense is reduced to 25 per cent of £750, which equals £188. In the third column of Table 5.14, we set out the depreciation charges under the double-declining balance method. We recall that the straight-line depreciation was at the rate of one-seventh per annum, thus the double-declining rate will be set at double this rate, or two-sevenths per annum. In the first year the depreciation charge is two-sevenths of £1,000, which equals £286, leaving a written-down value of £714. However, the method follows the reducing balance procedure, and correspondingly the charge in the second year is two-sevenths of the £714, or £204. By year six the

[1] We assume here a theoretical tax system, not the actual one used in the UK.

TABLE 5.14. *Alternative depreciation methods* (£)

	Straight-line	Reducing balance	Double-declining	Sum-of-the-years' digits
Cost	1,000	1,000	1,000	1,000
Less: depreciation (yr. 1)	(124)	1000/4 = (250)	1,000 × 2/7 = (286)	867 × 7/28 = (216)
Written-down value	876	750	714	784
Less: depreciation (yr. 2)	(124)	750/4 = (188)	714 × 2/7 = (204)	867 × 6/28 = (186)
Written-down value	752	562	510	598
Less: depreciation (yr. 3)	(124)	562/4 = (141)	510 × 2/7 = (146)	867 × 5/28 = (155)
Written-down value	628	421	364	443
Less:depreciation (yr. 4)	(124)	421/4 = (105)	364 × 2/7 = (104)	867 × 4/28 = (124)
Written-down value	504	316	260	319
Less: depreciation (yr. 5)	(124)	316/4 = (79)	260 × 2/7 = (74)	867 × 3/28 = (93)
Written-down value	380	237	186	226
Less: depreciation (yr. 6)	(124)	237/4 = (59)	186 × 2/7 = (53)	867 × 2/28 = (62)
Written-down value	256	178	133	164
Less: depreciation (yr. 7)	(123)	178/4 = (45)	nil	867 × 1/28 = (31)
Written-down value	133	133	133	133
Less: scrap proceeds	(133)	(133)	(133)	(133)
Balance	nil	nil	nil	nil
Present value of tax savings:				
(case 1)	157	181	188	178
(case 2)	258	248	246	258

asset is already written down to its estimated scrap value, and so there is no depreciation charge in year seven. Because the written-down value declines year by year, the reducing balance method, of which the double-declining balance method is one example, results in heavier depreciation charges in earlier years. It is thus sometimes referred to as a form of accelerated depreciation. This type of depreciation profile is also illustrated in the final column of Table 5.14, where the choice of depreciation is focused upon the sum-of-the-years'-digits method. The asset life is seven years and so the sum of the digits is $1+2+3+4+5+6+7=28$. The total depreciation charge over the asset's life is given by the original cost of £1,000 less the net scrap proceeds of £133, which equals £867. Thus in the first year, the depreciation charge is 7/28 of £867, or £216; in the second year the charge is 6/28 of the £867, or £186 and so on, until the asset is written down to its expected scrap value, as shown in Table 5.14.

The value of the tax savings resulting from allowances for depreciation depends upon the marginal tax rate in each year, the tax time lag, and the discount rate. In Table 5.14 it is assumed in the penultimate row that the tax rate is fixed at 35 per cent, that the tax lag is one year from the end of each respective year, and that the discount rate is 15 per cent per annum. Under the reducing balance method the present value of tax savings from depreciation deductions is:

$$250(0.35)/(1.15)^2+188(0.35)/(1.15)^3+141(0.35)/(1.15)^4+105(0.35)/(1.15)^5 \\ +79(0.35)/(1.15)^6+59(0.35)/(1.15)^7+45(0.35)/(1.15)^8=£181.$$

The other present value calculations for alternative depreciation methods, shown in Table 5.14, follow the same principles.[1]

The preference for earlier tax write-offs implicitly assumes that tax rates are constant or decreasing. However, in Table 5.14 in the final row, we have calculated the present value of the tax savings under the four methods on the basis of a 10 per cent marginal tax rate in the first year, followed by a 70 per cent marginal tax rate in subsequent years. We now discover that the double-declining balance method is least attractive and that the straight-line method, which previously ranked fourth, now lies equal first with the sum-of-the-

[1] It is interesting to note that in the United States the tax depreciation system, known as the Accelerated Cost Recovery System, set out in the 1981 Economic Recovery Act, is based upon a hybrid of all four of these methods. Assets are classified according to type, such as buildings, cars, and plant and machinery, other than for research, which determines the maximum tax life of the asset. The depreciation method, adopted in 1986, is initially the double-declining balance method, although the legislation assumes that in the first year the asset is acquired midway throughout the year, except for buildings, and so only half the annual depreciation charge is allowed initially. However, the depreciation system assumes that the depreciation method changes to either the straight-line method or the sum-of-the-years'-digits method in that year which will accelerate the remaining depreciation expenses. The final result is a depreciation system which moves slightly away from normal historic cost accounting principles, in that asset costs are normally fully written off before the end of their useful lives.

years'-digits method. Thus, with changes in marginal tax rates it is not always immediately obvious which depreciation method is superior, although it is reasonable to expect that the greater the degree of acceleration in a depreciation method, the more likely it is to be adopted unless there are expectations of significantly large increases in the marginal tax rate over time.

Depreciation and risk

We have established that the spreading of capital allowances into future tax periods reduces the present value of tax savings from allowable depreciation expenses when tax rates are constant. The rate of return on a project falls as the depreciation tax shield declines in value. An interesting feature, however, is that there is also a reduction in risk. But why does this occur? And does the reduction in risk compensate for the rate of return now at a lower level?

In order to provide an insight into this phenomenon we shall consider a hypothetical project. We shall base our analysis on the Capital Asset Pricing Model, for which references for further reading are provided at the end of the chapter. Basically, this model states that the minimum required rate of return is calculated by the sum of two components: a risk-free rate and a premium, of which the latter varies proportionately according to the beta risk of the investment. In turn, beta risk is measured by (i) the covariance of the rate of return on the investment with the rate of return on the efficient market portfolio, divided by (ii) the variance of the rate of return on the market portfolio. Presently, we are primarily concerned with the covariance calculation which is a relative measure of risk. As we proceed with a numerical example, the tax effects on risk should soon become apparent.

The hypothetical project costs £1m, for which there are three possible outcomes A, B, and C, under which the project earns 18, 19, and 20 per cent per annum, respectively, at the end of the first year and continues to earn the same return in subsequent years into perpetuity. We further assume that there is a 60 per cent probability that the rate of return will be 19 per cent per annum and that the other two possible outcomes are equally likely, each with a 20 per cent probability. The mean rate of return is thus a weighted average:

$$(0.20 \times 18\%) + (0.60 \times 19\%) + (0.20 \times 20\%) = 19\%.$$

In Tables 5.15 and 5.16 we examine the covariance of the project with that of the market as a whole, assuming that there are only three outcomes A, B, and C. If the project earns 18 per cent before tax, this rate of return is 1 per cent less than the weighted average. Hence the deviation of the project's rate of return before tax is given in Table 5.15 as -0.01 under outcome A, zero under outcome B since the outcome does not deviate from the expectation, and $+0.01$ under outcome C, under which the performance is better than the average. In our illustration, we assume that different deviations have already been computed for the efficient market portfolio as a whole, on an after-tax

TABLE 5.15. *Initial covariance of the rate of return on a project before tax with that of the market after tax*

	Possible outcomes		
	A	B	C
Project return per annum before tax (£'000) (i)	180	190	200
Project rate of return on outlay of £1m (ii)	0.18	0.19	0.20
Deviation of project rate of return before tax, for a given outcome, from the average for all outcomes (ii) − 0.19 = (iii)	−0.01	0	+0.01
Deviation of after-tax yield on efficient market, for a given outcome from the average for all outcomes (iv)	−0.02	−0.01	+0.05
Probability of occurrence (v)	0.20	0.60	0.20
Calculation towards deriving covariance of rate of return on project before tax with that of the market after tax (vi) = (iii) × (iv) × (v)	0.00004	0	0.00010
Initial covariance (vii) = (0.00004 + 0 + 0.00010)	0.00014	0.00014	0.00014

basis, as shown in row (iv) of Table 5.15. The covariance of the rate of return on the project before tax, with that of the market after tax is determined in two stages. First, in row (vi) we multiply the project's deviation in yield by the market yield deviation and by the probability of occurrence. Second, the covariance is found by adding together the results from the first operation. Thus, the initial covariance is 0.00014. We assume that the variance of the market yield is 0.00064, and so the project's initial beta coefficient is 14/64 or 0.21875, and as such it is a low risk project. By initial beta, we imply that tax has been taken into account as far as the market yield is concerned but excluded from the project's financial specifications.

In Table 5.16 we reiterate the calculations, on this occasion by the incorporation of the tax effects of the project. The marginal tax rate is T, expressed in proportionate rather than percentage form, for each outcome. Thus the cash returns per annum are reduced to $(1-T)$ times their former values. For convenience we shall ignore the small tax lag between earning the cash returns and paying taxes on them. We assume that £1m times a represents the discounted depreciation. Hence a represents the present value of tax depreciation as a proportion of cost. But the depreciation expenses save taxes at the rate T, and so the present value of the tax shield is given by aT expressed in £ms. The cost of the investment after tax relief is:

$$£1\text{m} - £1\text{m}(aT) = £1\text{m}(1-aT),$$

TABLE 5.16. *Final covariance after tax*

	Possible outcomes		
	A	B	C
Project return per annum after tax (£'000) (i)	$180(1-T)$	$190(1-T)$	$200(1-T)$
Project rate of return on net investment of £1m$(1-aT)$ (ii)	$0.18(1-T)/(1-aT)$	$0.19(1-T)/(1-aT)$	$0.20(1-T)/(1-aT)$
Deviation of project rate of return after tax, for a given outcome, from the average for all outcomes (iii) = (ii) $-0.19(1-T)/(1-aT)$	$-0.01(1-T)/(1-aT)$	0	$+0.01(1-T)/(1-aT)$
Deviation of after-tax yield on efficient market, for a given outcome, from average for all outcomes (iv)	-0.02	-0.01	$+0.05$
Probability of occurrence (v)	0.20	0.60	0.20
Calculation towards deriving covariance of rate of return on project after tax with that of the market after tax (vi) = (iii) × (iv) × (v)	$0.00004(1-T)/(1-aT)$	0	$0.00010(1-T)/(1-aT)$
Final covariance (vii) = $0.00004(1-T)/(1-aT)+0+0.00010(1-T)/(1-aT)$	$0.00014(1-T)/(1-aT)$	$0.00014(1-T)/(1-aT)$	$0.00014(1-T)/(1-aT)$

and the project rate of return on the net investment is derived accordingly in row (ii) of Table 5.16. The deviation from the average outcome is given in row (iii) following the same principles as before, and the covariance term is calculated in the normal way. We multiply the probability of occurrence by the deviation on the project's yield and by the deviation of the market yield and sum of the component factors. The final covariance after tax is given by $(1-T)/(1-aT)$ times the initial covariance of 0.00014. Hence, given a market variance of 0.00064, the after-tax beta coefficient is:

$$(0.00014/0.00064)(1-T)/(1-aT)=0.21875(1-T)/(1-aT).$$

But what does this signify? The important point is that the level of beta risk after tax is $(1-T)/(1-aT)$ times the initial beta, when tax considerations were excluded from the project's financial profile, although included in the market parameters. But the reason why this is significant is that the project's mean rate of return has also changed by the same factor from 19 per cent before tax to $(1-T)/(1-aT)$ times 19 per cent after tax. We shall refer to this factor as the tax reduction factor.

Now, if the present value of tax depreciation as a proportion of cost is 0.60, that is $a=0.60$, and the marginal tax rate is 35 per cent, then the tax reduction factor is:

$$(1-T)/(1-aT)=(1-0.35)/(1-0.60(0.35))=0.82,$$

and the after-tax project yield is:

$$0.82\times 19\%=15.6\%.$$

But, although the rate of return on the project is 82 per cent of its former value because of the discounting effect on the tax depreciation shield, the beta risk is also 82 per cent of its former value.

In Fig. 5.1 the market line depicts the cut-off threshold, or minimum required mean rate of return, for varying levels of beta risk. Point B represents the before-tax position of a project's beta risk and mean rate of return. After-tax the risk is reduced to 82 per cent of its former value, but the mean rate of return is also reduced by the same amount. The after-tax position is labelled A in Fig. 5.1, which demonstrates that the mean yield for A lies above the market line, which represents the minimum required mean rate of return. Thus, the project is still financially attractive after tax. In Fig. 5.2 the project is deemed only marginal after tax, despite the fact that, in this instance, the before-tax position appears financially attractive, since the yield for position B, the before-tax position, lies above the minimum required yield, in accordance with the market line. An example of a project, which is financially attractive excluding tax, but is unacceptable after tax, is depicted in Fig. 5.3. The after-tax position, at point A, represents a beta risk of 82 per cent of the beta before the project's tax adjustment and an after-tax yield of only 82 per cent of its pre-tax value. This is clearly an example of an excess burden of taxation, since the

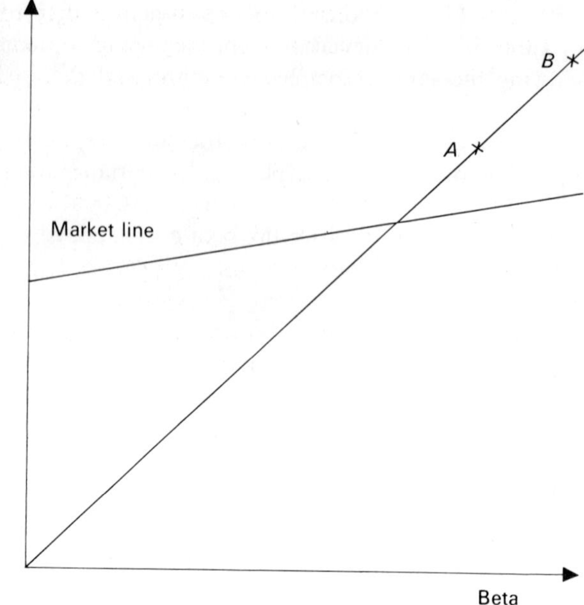

Fig. 5.1 Acceptable project after tax

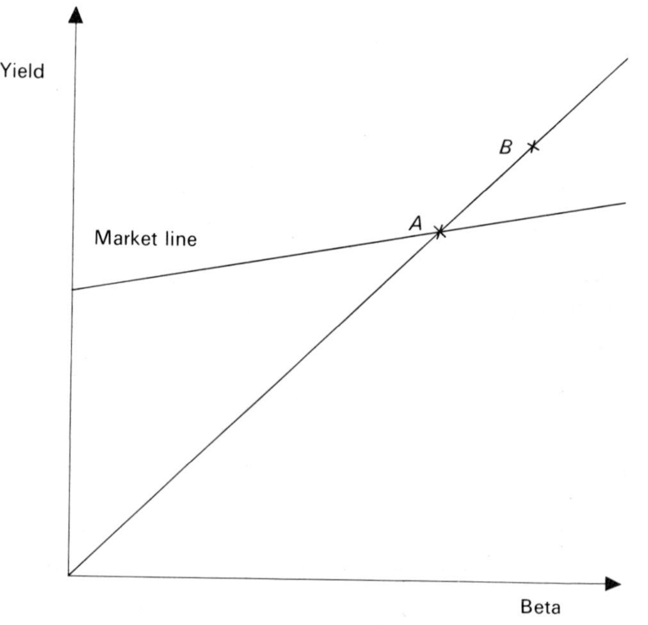

Fig. 5.2 Marginal project after tax

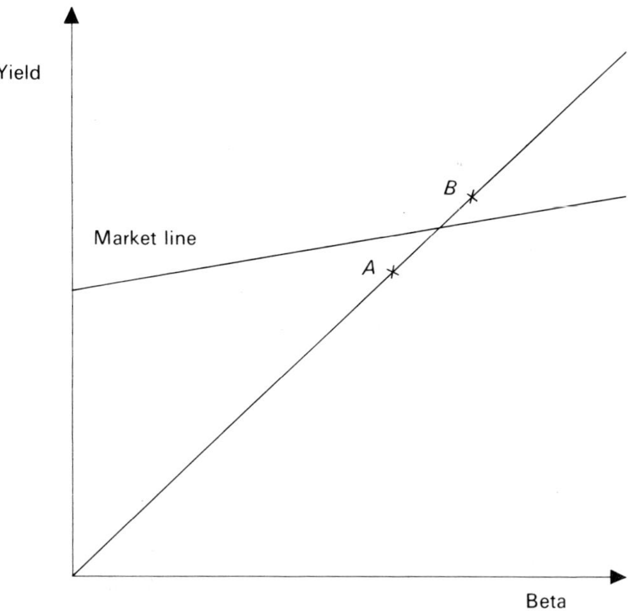

Fig. 5.3 Attractive project without tax, unacceptable after tax

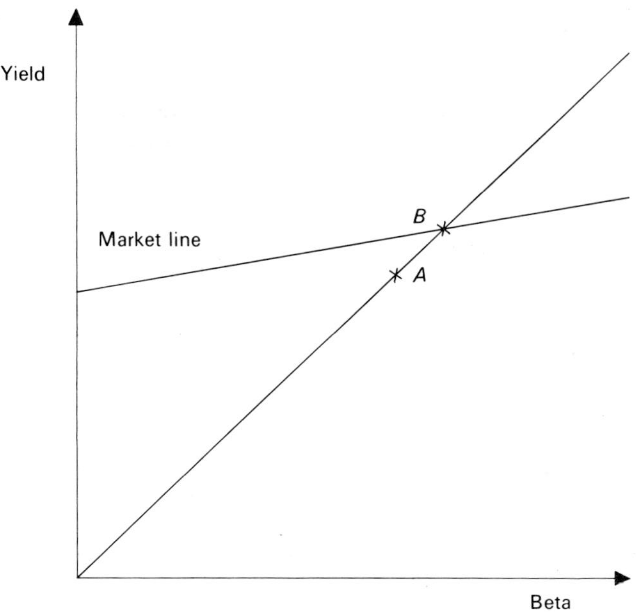

Fig. 5.4 Marginal project before tax, unattractive after tax

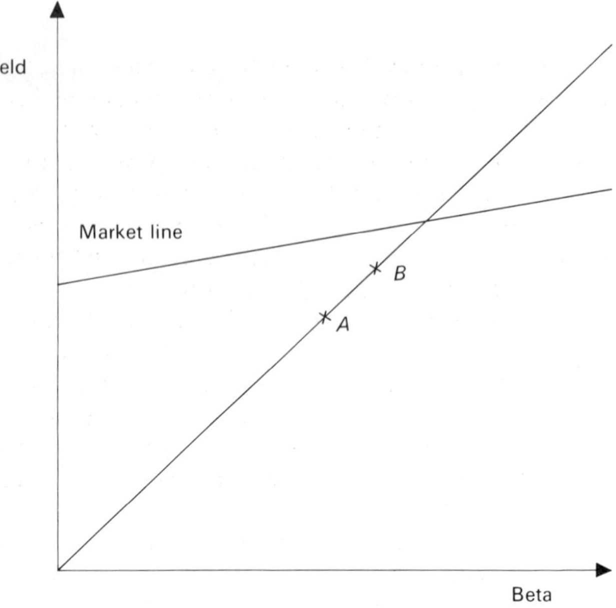

Fig. 5.5 Unattractive project with or without tax

design of the tax system leads to a recommendation to reject a project, which would be wealth-creating under a neutral tax system. When the present value of capital allowances as a proportion of cost is less than 100 per cent, that is when $a < 1$, a project which is marginal before tax becomes financially unattractive after tax, as depicted in Fig. 5.4. We assume, as before, a constant marginal tax rate in this figure and also in Fig. 5.5, where a project is unattractive with or without tax considerations. In the latter instance, despite the risk reduction induced by depreciation expenses for tax purposes, the reduction in the mean rate of return is too excessive to make the project worthwhile, even for a lower beta risk.

Thus, the depreciation tax shield rducés the rate of return on the investment, but also reduces the beta risk. For a lower level of risk, a revised minimum mean rate of return is required and set at a lower level than that for the initial beta risk. However, the decline in the expected rate of return is sharper than the decline in the required rate of return, as depicted in Figs 5.1 to 5.5, in which the line *AB* is steeper than the slope of the market, or cut-off, line. Whether the project is still acceptable on an after-tax basis, depends on the individual financial characteristics of the project. With heavy investments in working capital, a profits tax system would tend to exaggerate the features presented here of risk-reduction and declining yields. However, with an increasing marginal tax rate over time and any possible tax reliefs on financing costs, the final picture is less clear.

Conclusion

Although projects should be evaluated on the basis of discounted cash flows in order to incorporate the effects of the time value of money, an historic profits tax system is based, quite naturally, upon profits and not cash flows. But profits before depreciation generally exceed cash flows due to the periodic investment in net working capital. Thus, under an historic profits tax system, taxes are raised on profits which, ignoring depreciation, generally exceed, during the early years of a project, operating cash flows and hence the returns are penalized. Furthermore, although the cash outlay on the investment normally occurs at or near the start of a capital project, the tax savings from allowable depreciation expenses are spread into the future. With inflation, the picture can be distorted further, since the present value of the tax shield is reduced when the discount rate reflects inflationary expectations. Also, the working capital cycle can be more pronounced under inflationary conditions.

A separate analysis evaluated the effects of allowable depreciation on the beta risk of an investment. It was demonstrated that, with a constant marginal tax rate, there may be a dramatic reduction in beta risk, according to the size of the depreciation tax shield. However, the corresponding decline in the mean rate of return on a project may be excessive despite the risk reduction.

The general bleak picture of an historic profits tax system is not, however, painted when account is taken of interest deductibility for tax purposes. For, in profit determination, interest is deductible. From a legal standpoint, the interest costs reduce the chargeable profits, and result in lower tax liabilities. From a financial appraisal perspective, it may be more enlightening to accommodate the fiscal savings into the discount rate, rather than to adjust the cash flows, although mathematically, they have the equivalent overall impact. In the final analysis, the interest deductibility issue may weigh in favour of an historic profits tax system, from the standpoint of the taxpaying firm, which is contemplating capital investment. With interest deductibility, the historic profits tax system is more appropriately compared with a true economic income tax system and can in certain circumstances be virtually equivalent, dependent upon the particular depreciation pattern and the working capital requirements of a project.

Recommendations for further reading

The distribution of the tax burden on industrial sectors, under an historic profits tax system, may be found in HMSO (1982). There is a worthwhile discussion of the difference between profit and cash flow in Lawson and Stark (1975), whose focus of attention is, in fact, directed towards the UK liquidity crisis in the first half of the 1970s. The lessons learnt from a fundamental understanding of the financial effects of a tax system, which does not allow for working capital adjustments, let alone inflationary effects on working capital, are still relevant today. An early piece of analysis on the effects of taxation on risk-taking can be found in Domar and Musgrave (1944), which has particular emphasis on the treatment of tax losses. More recent theoretical and empirical work is reviewed in Atkinson and Stiglitz (1980). A portfolio treatment of risk under the Capital Asset Pricing Model was developed by Sharpe (1964) and others, on which discussions can be found in business finance texts, such as Davis and Pointon (1984). Extensions to deal with the effects of capital allowances on beta risk and rates of return are given by Pointon (1980).

References

Atkinson, A., and Stiglitz, J. (1980), *Lectures on Public Economics* (New York: McGraw-Hill).

Davis, E. W., and Pointon, J. (1984), *Finance and the Firm* (Oxford: Oxford University Press).

Domar, E. D., and Musgrave, R. A. (1944), 'Proportional Income Taxation and Risk-Taking', *Quarterly Economic Journal*, (May): 388–422.

HMSO (1982). *Corporation Tax*, Cmnd. 8456 (London: HMSO).

Lawson, G. H., and Stark, A. W. (1975), 'The Concept of Profit for Fund Raising', *Accounting and Business Research*, (Winter): 21–41.

Pointon, J. (1980), 'Investment and Risk: The Effect of Capital Allowances', *Accounting and Business Research*, (Autumn): 432–9.

Sharpe, W. F. (1964), 'Capital Asset Prices: A Theory of Market Equilibrium under Conditions of Risk', *Journal of Finance*, 19, no. 3 (September): 425–42.

6
Inflation-Adjusted Tax Systems

Introduction

In the previous chapter we explained some of the deficiencies of an historic profits tax system under inflationary conditions. A natural extension is to look at various ways in which profit calculations can be indexed to take account of specific and general inflationary effects. We begin with a brief discussion of the need for inflationary adjustments to tax brackets for consumption, income, and capital taxes. We explain the superiority of consumption-based tax systems, provided that they are based on values and not physical measurements, in that inflationary adjustments to capital or income are not necessary. Calculations for capital or income adjustments are explained, and we investigate how to take account of the interest factor when capital gains taxes would otherwise be based on realizations rather than reflect benefits of ownership before disposal.

Potential distortions are highlighted under both current purchasing power and current cost tax systems. An indepth study is made of the treatment of depreciation and stocks under these two tax systems. In passing, we also note several methods to adjust trading stocks for inflation, which are not related to these two tax systems. Our overall analysis is extended to adjustments to other working capital items, and we address the issues of gearing adjustments under a current cost tax system and inflationary gains on debt under a current purchasing power tax system. Finally, we discuss inefficiencies even when tax losses are indexed.

Inflationary distortions

Where a tax structure has levels of taxable capacity, between which different tax rates apply, then it is necessary to index the tax brackets for inflation; otherwise taxpayers may find themselves dragged into a different tax bracket solely due to the effects of inflation. The problem is known as fiscal drag. Exemption levels under income tax and capital gains tax are examples of the need for bracket indexation. Furthermore, with progressive tax structures, all tax brackets need to be index-linked in order to avoid higher marginal tax rates being applied, even though there may be no increase in real taxable capacity. Clearly, the pattern of personal expenditures will vary for different individuals, and so there will be some anomalies since the same index is likely to be used for all taxpayers, for administrative convenience.

A more difficult problem is to make allowance, in a tax system, for the inflationary erosion of capital and income. For example, holders of debt during a period of inflation suffer a loss of purchasing power when the debt is repaid. Hence, either taxes on income need to be based upon real returns rather than actual money returns, or capital taxes need to make allowances for the decline in the real capital value.

However, the effects of inflation on different taxes varies considerably. Consumption taxes need to allow for bracket indexation in exemption levels or in higher tax brackets, if different marginal tax rates apply. But where such consumption or expenditure taxes are *ad valorem* taxes, i.e. where they are based on values and not physical units, there is no need for a capital-income adjustment. For example, let us consider the simple case of £150 VAT raised at 15 per cent on a taxable flow of £1,000 net. If, through inflation at, say, 10 per cent, the taxable flow increases to, say, £1,100, the VAT now increases to 15 per cent of £1,100 or £165. But if the specific inflation rate on the taxable flow is the same as the general, broadly representative rate of inflation in the economy, then for every £1 before inflation, £1.10 is now needed for the maintenance of purchasing power. The purchasing power of the £165 tax at the end of the period is equal to £165/1.10 = £150 in terms of the purchasing power at the beginning of the period. Hence, the tax raised is maintained in real terms. Furthermore, the after-tax real value at the end of the period, of £1,100, is also maintained for it has a value of £1,100/1.10 = £1,000, in terms of the purchasing power at the beginning of the period. For *ad valorem* expenditure taxes, capital-income adjustments are not required, since current taxes are raised on current expenditure at current prices.

However, where taxes are based on physical units, tax rates need to be increased. Assume that tax is raised at 15p per litre on a commodity. Then, for an inflationary price increase of 10 per cent, from £1 per litre to £1.10 per litre, the tax rate would need to be increased by 10 per cent to 16.5p per litre. For 1,000 litres the initial tax would have been £0.15 per litre, or £150 for 1,000 litres, whereas the final tax would be £0.165 per litre, or £165 for 1,000 litres. But in real terms the tax raised is maintained, since the purchasing power of £165 at the end of the period is equal to £165/1.10 or £150, which is the same as the purchasing power of the tax at the beginning of the period. Thus, there is a need for indexation of tax rates, for expenditure taxes based on physical units, but not for *ad valorem* expenditure taxes.

For taxes based on capital or income, inflation-induced adjustments are needed, in order to avoid inequities. But how should appropriate adjustments be made? Should changes be made to the measurement of income and not capital, or vice versa? In the next section we consider the measurement problem.

Capital–income adjustments

For investments which span a number of periods, there is a potential measurement problem of both income and capital during the intervening periods. In the long run, as assets are disposed of, capital gains and income are essentially the same. Income flows can be converted into new capital stock and capital stock can be realized to simulate income. If income is taxed but capital gains are not, then there is an incentive to trade some assets so as to generate capital inflows, rather than to retain assets in order to receive income flows from productive investment. Thus, there is a good case for an income tax system to coexist with a system of capital gains tax. Theoretically, income and capital gains should be taxed at the same rate. However, capital gains are likely to arise at irregular intervals over time and, under a progressive tax system, may be unduly penalized. Thus, there are sound reasons for the application of rules for spreading the gains over several years and treating them as income, with a resultant re-computation of tax borne. Alternatively, capital gains may be subject to a separate tax rate, for administrative convenience. For the moment, it is instructive to consider income and capital gains under one tax system.

First of all, let us dwell upon the income adjustment for inflation, by use of an example, in which a year ago an asset was acquired at a cost of £100,000. It earned a nominal return of 10 per cent for the year and maintained its value in nominal terms. The general rate of inflation for the year was 7 per cent. The question now is how we measure the real income for the period. We can view the problem from a number of perspectives. The accumulated wealth in terms of purchasing power is £110,000, composed of the asset's stock of wealth of £100,000 and a stock of cash of £10,000 which was derived from the 10 per cent income flow. But the original capital of £100,000 has a current purchasing power of £107,000, since the general rate of inflation was 7 per cent for the year. In terms of current purchasing power, wealth has increased from £107,000 to £110,000. Hence the real rate of growth was:

$$(110{,}000 - 107{,}000)/107{,}000 = 2.80373\%.$$

Real income is measured by the real growth on the current purchasing power of the original investment:

$$2.80373\% \times £107{,}000 = £3{,}000.$$

Thus, under an inflation-adjusted income tax system, taxable capacity is given by the £3,000 real income and not the £10,000 nominal income.

An alternative procedure is to adjust the capital, so that real income is comprised of the nominal income flow less the capital erosion by inflation. With an inflation rate of 7 per cent per annum, the loss in the purchasing power of capital is 7 per cent of £100,000, or £7,000. Hence, given a downward capital adjustment of £7,000, the real income is reduced from £10,000 to £3,000. The two approaches yield the same conclusion.

A more interesting case is to consider capital gains over several periods, during which general price levels are changing. Where assets can be traded in competitive markets, in which prices are quoted at the end of each interim period, it is possible to measure real income for each period. However, administratively it is simpler to assess capital gains when they are realized and to assume for tax purposes that the inflation rate was at a constant compound rate per annum. Indexation of capital is relatively straightforward under these conditions. For example, consider an asset which costs £10,000 and is realized for £14,181 three years later. There is no cash income during the intervening period. Further assume that the annual compound rate of inflation for the period was 7 per cent as before. The assessable real gain is therefore £1,931, which is given by the final cash inflow realized less the inflated cost indexed for inflation, as shown in Table 6.1. Fortunately, for the taxpayer, such a system by itself fails to allow for all the benefits derived from asset ownership during earlier years. If taxes had been raised annually then the resultant intermediate taxes could have earned interest for the central government. Annual valuation procedures can be expensive to administer, yet it is possible to estimate the real gains and effectively assess them retrospectively. Such a system is known as tax deferral.

Tax deferral

To accommodate interest lost by the central government, under a system of capital gains taxation which is based on realizations rather than accruals, it is necessary to allow for tax deferral as well as indexation. We can appreciate the factors at work by use of the previous example in which an asset costing £10,000 is held for three years, during which the annual compound rate of inflation is 7 per cent, and at the end of which, the asset is realized for £14,181. Let us further assume that the interest rate under the tax deferral procedure is 9 per cent per annum and tax exempt. But how do we evaluate the real rate of capital growth? What is the gain for each year? And how do we take into account the interest factor?

TABLE 6.1. *Indexation of cost at 7 per cent per annum* (£)

Realized value	14,181
Less: indexed cost (£10,000 $(1.07)^3$)	(12,250)
Real gain	1,931

First of all, let us calculate the actual or nominal compound rate of capital growth per annum, which we shall denote by a. Since the investment is for three years:

$$£10{,}000\ (1+a)^3 = £14{,}181$$

$$(1+a)^3 = 1.4181.$$

Thus for every £1 of original investment, the accumulated wealth is £1.4181. Depressing the cubed root function on a calculator, gives $1+a = 1.1235$. Hence the actual growth rate is 12.35 per cent per annum.

Second, we need to estimate the intermediate asset values. The overall actual growth rate was 12.35 per cent per annum, and so the estimated values at the end of each year are:

$$£10{,}000\ (1.1235) = £11{,}235 \text{ for the first year, and}$$

$$£11{,}235\ (1.1235) = £12{,}623 \text{ for the second year.}$$

The closing values at the end of each year, comprising intermediate values and the final realized figure, are shown in row (i) of Table 6.2. The opening values are index-linked by the rate of inflation, and thus the revised indexed values are derived, by adding to each respective opening value, the inflation rate times the opening value, and are shown in row (ii) of the Table. The real gain is given by the closing value less the indexed opening value, as tabulated in row (iii). However, to the gain for the first year is added an interest factor at 9 per cent

TABLE 6.2. *Indexation at 7 per cent and deferral adjustments* (£)

	End of year		
	1	2	3
Closing value (i)	*11,235*	*12,623*	*14,181*
Opening value	10,000	11,235	12,623
Indexation adjustments:			
$10{,}000 \times 0.07$ (yr. 1)	700	—	—
$11{,}235 \times 0.07$ (yr. 2)	—	786	—
$12{,}623 \times 0.07$ (yr. 3)	—	—	884
Indexed opening value (ii)	*10,700*	*12,021*	*13,507*
Real gain (iii) = (i) − (ii)	535	602	674
Tax deferral adjustment:			
$535(1.09)^2 - 535$ (yr. 1)	101	—	—
$602(1.09) - 602$ (yr. 2)	—	54	—
0 (yr. 3)	—	—	nil
Real gain + tax deferral adjustment	636	656	674

for the two years' delay until the realization date, and a one year adjustment factor is added to the gain for the second year, to account for the one year delay until the final year. The tax deferral adjustments are merely interest factors and thus apply compound interest to the real gains. The real gains and the tax deferral adjustments are added together for each year, as shown in the final row of Table 6.2. Hence, the taxable gain is equal to the sum of the three gains:

$$£636 + £656 + £674 = £1{,}966.$$

The taxable gain, with deferral adjustments, of £1,966 exceeds the previously calculated taxable gain without the tax deferral adjustment of £1,931, which we derived in Table 6.1. But is the reason for the discrepancy solely because there is a positive interest rate applied to the real gain, or is it because the interest rate exceeds the inflation rate? In Table 6.3, we derive the taxable gains attributable to each year, when the deferral adjustment is included, on the basis of an inflation rate of 9 per cent per annum, which is equal to the interest rate. Following the same principles as before we discover, from the final row of Table 6.3, that the total taxable gain is:

$$£398 + £411 + £422 = £1{,}231.$$

But this gain is exactly the same as the taxable gain under indexation, when the inflation rate is 9 per cent per annum, as shown in Table 6.4. Thus, when the inflation rate is equal to the interest rate for deferral calculations, the assessment of real gains per annum for tax deferral is unnecessary. Under these

TABLE 6.3. *Indexation at 9 per cent and deferral adjustments* (£)

	End of year		
	1	2	3
Closing (i)	*11,235*	*12,623*	*14,181*
Opening value	10,000	11,235	12,623
Indexation adjustment:			
10,000 × 0.09 (yr. 1)	900	—	—
11,235 × 0.09 (yr. 2)	—	1,011	—
12,623 × 0.09 (yr. 3)	—	—	1,136
Indexed opening value (ii)	*10,900*	*12,246*	*13,759*
Real gain (iii) = (i) − (ii)	335	377	422
Tax deferral adjustment:			
$335(1.09)^2 - 335$ (yr. 1)	63	—	—
$377(1.09) - 377$ (yr. 2)	—	34	—
0 (yr. 3)	—	—	nil
Real gain + tax deferral adjustment	398	411	422

TABLE 6.4. *Indexation of cost at 9 per cent per annum* (£)

Realized value	14,181
Less: indexed cost (£10,000 $(1.09)^3$)	(12,950)
Real gain	1,231

conditions, the two methods are equivalent. However, indexation without deferral will produce a smaller gain when the inflation rate is less than the deferral interest rate, and a larger gain when the interest rate exceeds the deferral interest rate.

Depreciation

We established in Chapter 5 that, under a corporation tax system with no interest deductibility, the present value of depreciation expenses based on historic cost accounting principles is worth less than 100 per cent depreciation in the first year and therefore is a potential disincentive to invest. Alternatively, where interest deductibility is allowed, depreciation expenses need to be compared with true economic depreciation. The reason for these two results is that we have expounded two tax systems which have neutral effects on economic efficiency, of which the first is a cash-flow tax system, and the second is a true economic income tax system with interest deductibility. Our purpose here is to reconsider the implications for economic efficiency when indexation is applied in the calculation of depreciation expenses. In our analysis we shall consider two forms of indexation, based on current purchasing power and current costs, respectively.

Under a current purchasing power tax system, the original cost of a fixed asset is inflated by a general price index to reflect the general rate of inflation in the economy. In Table 6.5 depreciation expenses are calculated under the straight-line method, for an asset which costs £100,000 and has a three year life. For convenience, depreciation is based on the current purchasing power of the asset at the end of the year, rather than at mid-year. The anticipated general rate of inflation is assumed to be 10 per cent per annum. Asset costs are

TABLE 6.5. *Depreciation under a current purchasing power tax system* (£)

Year	Current purchasing power of asset cost (at end of year) before depreciation	Depreciation for year
1	100,000 (1.10) = 110,000	110,000/3 = 36,667
2	110,000 (1.10) = 121,000	121,000/3 = 40,333
3	121,000 (1.10) = 133,100	133,100/3 = 44,367

indexed at 10 per cent per annum, and the depreciation expense is simply one-third of the indexed cost. But does this represent an incentive to invest? In order to answer this, let us defer the question of interest deductibility until later in the chapter and compare the present value of tax savings from depreciation expenses under a current purchasing power tax system with the present value of tax savings from a cash-flow tax system, which allows a 100 per cent write-off in the first year. We shall consider three discount rates: 8, 10, and 12 per cent per annum. Also, we shall assume that the asset is acquired on the last day of year zero and that there is a one year tax time lag from the end of each accounting period. On the basis of a 35 per cent marginal tax rate, the present value of tax savings from depreciation under a current purchasing power tax system is shown in Table 6.6. The present value of tax savings from the first depreciation expense is given by discounting for two years, because of the tax time lag, and similarly in calculating the tax savings for the second year, we discount for three years, and so on. When the general rate of inflation exceeds the discount rate, for example, when the discount rate is 8 per cent per annum, as shown in Table 6.6, the present value of each annual tax saving from depreciation increases over time, because the tax rules allow for indexation in excess of that required for the time value of money. When the two rates are the same, the present value of each annual tax saving is constant over time, as illustrated in Table 6.6 when the discount rate is 10 per cent per annum. However, when the inflation rate is less than the discount rate, the present value of each annual tax saving decreases over time, for example when the discount rate is 12 per cent per annum.

By contrast, the present values of tax savings (£s) under a cash-flow tax system, maintaining the one year tax time lag are:

(0.35)100,000/(1.08) = 32,407 (at an 8% discount rate),

(0.35)100,000/(1.10) = 31,818 (at 10%), and

(0.35)100,000/(1.12) = 31,250 (at 12%).

TABLE 6.6. *Present value of tax savings from depreciation expenses under a current purchasing power tax system* (£)

Year of depreciation expense	Tax saving @ 35% tax rate	Present value of tax saving @ different discount rates		
		8%	10%	12%
1	36,667 × 0.35 = 12,833	11,002	10,606	10,230
2	40,333 × 0.35 = 14,117	11,207	10,606	10,048
3	44,367 × 0.35 = 15,528	11,414	10,606	9,868
		33,623	31,818	30,146

In Table 6.7 these results are compared with those under a current purchasing power tax system. But, a cash-flow tax system has a neutral effect on the capital investment decision, provided that the marginal tax rate is constant, that there is perfect loss offset, and that the tax time lag is constant. Thus from Table 6.7 we see that, under a current purchasing power tax system, there is an incentive to invest when the discount rate is less than the general rate of inflation, because the tax savings exceed those under a cash-flow tax system; there is a neutral effect on the investment decision when the discount rate equals the general rate of inflation; and there is a disincentive to invest when the discount rate exceeds the general rate of inflation.

But normally, market rates of interest should exceed the general rate of inflation in the economy, otherwise investors receive a negative real rate of return. Thus, in general, a disincentive to invest is expected under a current purchasing power tax system with no interest deductibility. However, we shall return to the thorny question of interest deductibility later on in the chapter.

An alternative tax system is one based on current cost accounting principles. Assets are recorded at their value to the business, normally the replacement cost, net of depreciation, of an identical asset of the same age. For the moment we shall ignore any adjustments for gearing, or borrowing, levels. Inflationary adjustments to asset values thus reflect specific price changes relating to each particular asset category rather than general price level changes in the economy. But, if the rate of price inflation on a specific asset is 10 per cent, then for a three year asset costing £100,000, the annual depreciation charges under a current cost tax system are exactly the same as those under a current purchasing power tax system, with a 10 per cent general rate of inflation in the economy. Under asset category A, the depreciation each year, under the straight-line method is the same as that given under Table 6.5 for a current purchasing power tax system. However, for asset category B, the asset inflation rate is equal to 12 per cent per annum and thus the current cost of the asset at the end of the first year is £112,000. By the end of the second year, the current cost of the asset for category B grows by a further 12 per cent to £112,000 (1.12) = £125,440. The annual depreciation expenses are therefore more than those

TABLE 6.7 *Tax savings under current purchasing power and cash-flow tax systems* (£)

Basis for tax system	Total present value of tax savings at different annual discount rates, assuming a 10% general rate of inflation per annum		
	8%	10%	12%
Current purchasing power	33,623	31,818	30,146
Cash-flow	32,407	31,818	31,250

under category A, because the specific inflation rate under category B is higher. Finally, under category C, the asset inflation rate is assumed to be 14 per cent per annum.

The tax savings are set out in Table 6.9 for each asset category. The depreciation expenses from Table 6.8 are multiplied by 35 per cent, to determine the tax savings. The discount rate is assumed to be 12 per cent per annum, and there is an implied tax time lag of one year from the end of each accounting period. Under category A, the present value of tax savings is thus £12,833.3/(1.12)^2 = £10,230.6 for the first year as shown in Table 6.9. The current cost of a new but otherwise identical asset increases year by year under category A, and thus the depreciation expense increases, and the annual tax savings increase also. However, because the discount rate of 12 per cent exceeds the asset inflation rate of only 10 per cent, the present value of the annual tax savings declines year by year.

Under category B, the asset price inflation rate is the same as the discount rate, and so, although the annual tax savings increase in line with the rate of asset price inflation, the present value of the annual tax savings remains the same each year. The compounding effect on the depreciation expenses is exactly cancelled by the discounting effect, which allows for the time value of money. Both rates are assumed to be equal at 12 per cent per annum. The total present value of tax savings is given by £31,250 in Table 6.9. Finally, for category C, the asset price inflation rate exceeds the discount rate, and so the present value of the annual tax savings increases year by year.

The yardstick for economic efficiency, however, is a total present value of £31,250, which is set out in Table 6.7 and represents the total present value of tax savings under a cash-flow tax system, for a discount rate of 12 per cent per

TABLE 6.8. *Depreciation under a current cost tax system* (£)

Asset category	Asset inflation rate per annum (%)	Year	Current cost of asset (at end of year) before depreciation	Depreciation for year
A	10	1	110,000.0	110,000/3 = 36,667.7
	10	2	121,000.0	121,000/3 = 40,333.3
	10	3	133,100.0	133,100/3 = 44,366.7
B	12	1	112,000.0	112,000/3 = 37,333.3
	12	2	125,440.0	125,440/3 = 41,813.3
	12	3	140,492.8	140,492.8/3 = 46,830.9
C	14	1	114,000.0	114,000/3 = 38,000.0
	14	2	129,960.0	129,960/3 = 43,320.0
	14	3	148,154.4	148,154.4/3 = 49,384.8

TABLE 6.9. *Present value of tax savings from depreciation expenses under a current cost tax system* (£)

Asset category	Year of depreciation expense	Tax saving @ 35% tax rate	Present value of tax savings at 12% annual discount rate
A	1	12,833.3	10,230.6
	2	14,116.7	10,048.0
	3	15,528.3	9,868.5
Total			30,147.1
B	1	13,066.7	10,416.7
	2	14,634.7	10,416.7
	3	16,390.8	10,416.6
Total			31,250.0
C	1	13,300.0	10,602.7
	2	15,162.0	10,792.0
	3	17,284.7	10,984.7
Total			32,379.4

annum. We know that for a cash-flow tax system with a constant tax time lag, a constant marginal tax rate, and full immediate offsets for losses, there is a neutral effect on the investment decision. Thus, from Table 6.9, there is a neutral effect for category B under a current cost tax system, since the total present value of tax savings is equal to the required amount of £31,250, under a cash-flow tax system. The reason for this result is that for category B, the specific asset price inflation rate is the same as the discount rate. By contrast, for category A the asset inflation rate is insufficient, whereas for category C, the depreciation expense under a current cost tax system should lead to a fiscal incentive to invest.[1] However, we are ignoring the question of interest deductibility, which we shall examine later in the chapter.

Stocks

We shall shortly turn our focus of attention to the issue of the extent to which the valuation of trading stocks and the calculation of the cost of goods sold can be adjusted to reflect the impact of inflation under alternative tax systems. But temporarily, we shall indirectly avoid an examination of inflation-adjusted costs, until we look at a more conventional flow of costs for trading stocks.

[1] Although market rates of interest should exceed asset cost inflation rates in general, for specific assets the discrepancies can be wildly different, hence the importance of categories A and C.

Since it is often impracticable to identify each item of sale with its actual cost, the accounting system may be based on a broad assumption of a particular flow of costs. One assumption is that the oldest goods are treated as those first expensed against revenues. This system is known as FIFO, or first-in-first-out. An alternative system, not generally recommended in the UK, is LIFO, or last-in-first-out, under which those items most recently acquired are deemed to be those first expensed against revenues.

The profit implications under these two systems are illustrated in Table 6.10. We assume that, in period 1, 100 units are acquired at £10 and then a further 100 units at £11 each, totalling 200 units; and at the end of the period there are 100 units remaining. Under FIFO, the oldest goods are deemed sold first, and so the 100 units sold are costed at the old price of £10 each. Hence the profit for the first period is £1,000, as shown in Table 6.10. The stocks are costed at the

TABLE 6.10. *Taxable profits under FIFO and LIFO* (£)

	FIFO	LIFO
Period 1		
Opening stocks (nil)	—	—
Add: purchases (a) 100 units at £10	1,000	1,000
(b) then a further 100 units at £11	1,100	1,100
Subtotal (200 units)	2,100	2,100
Less: closing stocks (100 units)	(1,100)	(1,000)
Cost of goods sold (100 units)	1,000	1,100
Profit (sales – cost of goods sold)	*1,000*	*900*
Sales (100 units at £20)	2,000	2,000
Period 2		
Opening stocks (100 units)	1,100	1,000
Add: purchases (50 units at £12)	600	600
Subtotal (150 units)	1,700	1,600
Less: closing stocks (25 units)	(300)	(250)
Cost of goods sold (125 units)	1,400	1,350
Profit (sales – cost of goods sold) (ii)	*1,100*	*1,150*
Sales (125 units at £20)	2,500	2,500
Period 3		
Opening stocks (25 units)	300	250
Add: purchases (nil)	—	—
Less: closing stocks (nil)	—	—
Cost of goods sold (25 units)	300	250
Profit (sales – cost of goods sold) (iii)	*200*	*250*
Sales (25 units at £20)	500	500
Total profits ((i) + (ii) + (iii))	2,300	2,300

new price of £11, and so at the beginning of period 2 the opening stocks are valued at £1,100. During this period 50 items are acquired at £12 each, and so there are 150 items of stock available for sale, at a total cost of £1,700. There are 25 units remaining in stock at the end of the second period, which are valued at the new price under FIFO, since the oldest ones are deemed already sold first. Hence the 25 items in stock are valued at £12, giving a valuation of £300. With a selling price of £20 each, the profit in the second period is £1,100 as shown in Table 6.10. Finally in period 3, 25 units are sold and no further items are acquired.

Under LIFO, the same total profit is determined over the three periods although the profit pattern is now different. In the first period, the goods sold are costed at the more recent price of £11, leaving a profit of £900. However, this valuation approach results in an opening stock of only £1,000 in period two, which is based on the old price. But in period two, only 50 items are purchased compared with 125 items sold, and so there is a reduction in stock levels. Given the LIFO flow of costs, although the next 50 items sold are costed at the new price of £12, the remaining 75 units sold have to be based on the very old price of £10. The cost of goods sold under LIFO in the second period is less than that under FIFO because stock levels have fallen. Consequently, the profit recorded under LIFO exceeds that under FIFO, in both the second and final periods. Hence, although generally one would expect LIFO to determine a lower profit figure, and hence a lower tax bill, if LIFO is an allowable method for tax purposes and chosen in preference to a FIFO system, it should be implicitly assumed that unit costs are rising and that stock levels in volume terms do not fall. When unit costs or stock levels are falling, then a switch to a FIFO system may record lower profit figures, and hence may result in greater tax savings instead.

Now that we have highlighted some of the problems of a LIFO flow of costs for tax purposes, let us redirect our attention to a FIFO system, but use alternative methods of indexation, based on current costs and current purchasing power. Under an historic profits tax system, the cost of goods sold is determined by (i) the cost of the stock available for sale, calculated by the addition of the opening stock to the cost of production during the period, less (ii) the cost of the closing stock. For a tax system based on current costs, the cost of production during the period is likely to be at current costs, so it does not normally require adjustment. However, the opening stock less the closing stock needs to be matched against the sales of the period at the current costs of the stocks at the time of the sales. Specific stock indices are given in Table 6.11. It is assumed that, in our illustration, three months' stock is held so that the stock at the beginning of 1988 was acquired during October, November, and December of 1987, and that on average, the cost index of the opening stock was approximately 100, the mid-November figure. General price changes in the economy may not necessarily move in the same way as those for the specific trading stock category of the firm. They may rise at a lower rate, under trend A of Table 6.11, at the same rate as indicated by trend B, or at a higher rate as illustrated by the general price index under trend C.

In order to derive the current cost of sales, under a current cost tax system, the opening and closing stocks are revalued at mid-year current costs. Thus, the historic cost of the opening stock is multiplied by the specific stock index at mid-year and divided by the specific stock index for mid-November 1987; whereas the historic cost of the closing stock is multiplied by the specific stock index at mid-year and divided by the mid-November 1988 specific stock index. Sales and costs of production are assumed to flow evenly throughout the year and thus should not require any adjustment for current costs. It is assumed that actual cash sales are equal to 150 per cent of the historic cost of goods sold. From Table 6.12, we see that the taxable profit under a current cost tax system is reduced from £49,000 to £47,000.

Table 6.12 also restates the profit under a current purchasing power tax system, on the assumption that the general rate of inflation may follow three different patterns under trends A, B and C, respectively. The opening stock, cost of production, closing stock, and sales figures are multiplied by the general price index at the end of the year and divided by the general price index with reference to the appropriate category, as shown in Table 6.11. For example, the cost of production is deemed to arise mid-year, and so in order to restate production costs at their end of year purchasing power equivalents under trend A, we multiply the actual cost by 112, the end of year general price index, and divide by 105, the mid-year price index. Under a current cost tax system, specific stock indices at mid-year are used in the numerators of the indexation adjustments, whereas under a current purchasing power tax system, general price indices at the end of the year are used.

We assume in our example that there are no credit sales and purchases, and so the operating cash flow is £47,000, given by cash sales of £147,000 less production costs of £100,000. This coincides with the profit figure under a

TABLE 6.11. *Changes in a general price index and a specific stock index*

Date	Reference	General price index			Specific stock index
		Trend A	Trend B	Trend C	
Mid-November 1987	Opening stock	100	100	100	100
End-June 1988	Sales or cost of production	105	110	112	110
Mid-November 1988	Closing stock	110	120	128	120
End-December 1988	Year-end	112	123	135	123

Table 6.12. *Indexation of trading stocks: constant volume*

	Historic profits tax system (£)	Current cost tax system		Current purchasing power tax system					
				Trend A		Trend B		Trend C	
		Adj.	(£)	Adj	(£)	Adj	(£)	Adj.	(£)
Opening stock	10,000	$\frac{110}{100}$	11,000	$\frac{112}{100}$	11,200	$\frac{123}{100}$	12,300	$\frac{135}{100}$	13,500
Add: cost of production	100,000		100,000	$\frac{112}{105}$	106,667	$\frac{123}{110}$	111,818	$\frac{135}{112}$	120,536
	110,000		111,000		117,867		124,118		134,036
Less: closing stock	(12,000)	$\frac{110}{120}$	(11,000)	$\frac{112}{110}$	(12,218)	$\frac{123}{120}$	(12,300)	$\frac{135}{128}$	(12,656)
Cost of goods sold	98,000		100,000		105,649		111,818		121,380
Profit (balance)	49,000		47,000		51,151		52,555		55,808
Sales	147,000		147,000	$\frac{112}{105}$	156,800	$\frac{123}{110}$	164,373	$\frac{135}{112}$	177,188

current cost tax system. The reason for this result is that there is a costant stock volume. We can observe this from two points of view. First, the current mid-year costs of the opening and closing stocks are both £11,000, thus the volume of stock has not changed. Second, the specific stock index has increased from 100 to 120, as shown in Table 6.11, a reflection of a 20 per cent annual rate of cost inflation, which coincides with the rate at which the actual cost of end of year stocks has increased, also by 20 per cent, from £10,000 to £12,000. We know that a cash-flow tax system can have a neutral effect on the investment decision, and so, as far as trading stocks are concerned, with a constant stock volume a current cost tax system can also be neutral to the investment decision. If we assume that the operating cash flow of £47,000 arises mid-year, then we can restate this in terms of its purchasing power equivalent at the end of the year. If general prices increase according to those shown under trend B of Table 6.11, then we can divide the cash flow by 110 and multiply by 123 to give an end-of-year purchasing power equivalent of:

$$£47{,}000 \times 123/110 = £52{,}555.$$

But this is exactly the same as the taxable profit under a current purchasing power tax system for trend B. Thus, with constant volume and a general rate of inflation equal to the rate of inflation on the unit costs of trading stocks, a current purchasing power tax system is equivalent to a current cost tax system, as far as stocks are concerned, except that the former, effectively, partially allows for tax deferral, in that general inflationary effects on cash flows from mid-year to the end of the year are taken into account.

In Table 6.13 we consider a different pattern of trading and stockholding. Opening stocks and production costs are the same as before, but closing stocks are higher in volume terms. The nature of the indexation adjustments follow the same principles as those discussed previously. The operating cash flow is given by the cash sales of £93,000 less the cash production costs of £100,000, which equals minus £7,000. However, from Table 6.13 we see that the three tax systems, based on historic profits, current costs, and current purchasing power, respectively, all reveal profits rather than losses. This demonstrates inefficiencies in tax design of these three tax systems. Both the current cost and the current purchasing power tax systems allow for specific and general price changes, respectively, and hence deal with price changes, but neither addresses the question of adjustments for volume changes. Furthermore, the historic profits tax system accomodates neither volume nor price changes in stocks.

In Table 6.14, we again assume the same opening stocks and costs of production, but this time we show a decline in the volume of the closing stocks. The operating cash flow is equal to cash sales of £156,000 less cash production costs of £100,000, which nets out to £56,000. This exceeds the taxable profits based under the historic profits tax system and the current cost tax system. Hence, there are potential incentives to decrease stock volume under these two tax systems. Whether the taxable profit exceeds the operating cash flow under

TABLE 6.13. *Indexation of trading stocks: increase in volume*

	Historic profits tax system (£)	Current cost tax system		Current purchasing power tax system					
				Trend A		Trend B		Trend C	
		Adj	(£)	Adj.	(£)	Adj	(£)	Adj	(£)
Opening stock	10,000	$\frac{110}{100}$	11,000	$\frac{112}{100}$	11,200	$\frac{123}{100}$	12,300	$\frac{135}{100}$	13,500
Add: cost of production	100,000		100,000	$\frac{112}{105}$	106,667	$\frac{123}{110}$	111,818	$\frac{135}{112}$	120,536
	110,000		111,000		117,867		124,118		134,036
Less: closing stock	(48,000)	$\frac{110}{120}$	(44,000)	$\frac{112}{110}$	(48,873)	$\frac{123}{120}$	(49,200)	$\frac{135}{128}$	(50,625)
Cost of goods sold	62,000		67,000		68,994		74,918		83,411
Profit (balance)	31,000		26,000		30,206		29,073		28,687
Sales	93,000		93,000	$\frac{112}{105}$	99,200	$\frac{123}{110}$	103,991	$\frac{135}{112}$	112,098

TABLE 6.14. *Indexation of trading stocks: fall in volume*

	Historic profits tax system (£)	Current cost tax system		Current purchasing power tax system					
				Trend A		Trend B		Trend C	
		Adj	(£)	Adj	(£)	Adj	(£)	Adj	(£)
Opening stock	10,000	$\frac{110}{100}$	11,000	$\frac{112}{100}$	11,200	$\frac{123}{100}$	12,300	$\frac{135}{100}$	13,500
Add: cost of production	100,000		100,000	$\frac{112}{105}$	106,667	$\frac{123}{110}$	111,818	$\frac{135}{112}$	120,536
	110,000		111,000		117,867		124,118		134,036
Less: closing stock	(6,000)	$\frac{110}{120}$	(5,500)	$\frac{112}{110}$	(6,109)	$\frac{123}{120}$	(6,150)	$\frac{135}{128}$	(6,328)
Cost of goods sold	104,000		105,500		111,758		117,968		127,708
Profit (balance)	52,000		50,500		54,642		56,468		60,328
Sales	156,000		156,000	$\frac{112}{105}$	166,400	$\frac{123}{110}$	174,436	$\frac{135}{112}$	188,036

a current purchasing power tax system depends upon the trend of the general price index.

As far as the working capital cycle is concerned, trading stocks are likely to rise at the beginning and fall near the end of the life of a particular project. Thus, in present value terms, the potential disincentive to increase stock volume at the start of a project, under both current cost and current purchasing power tax systems, is likely to outweigh any potential tax incentive to reduce stocks in the future. However, if trading stock prices are rising faster than the discount rate, there may be a tax incentive to increase stocks. But we can observe from Table 6.13 that, under a current cost tax system, trading stocks at mid-year prices increase by £33,000, from £11,000 to £44,000. This represents the difference between current cost profit (+£26,000) and cash flow (−£7,000). An alternative way to derive the current cost profit is thus to add to the cash flow the volume increase in stocks times the mid-year cost per item, for each stock category. Taking a different example, let us assume that the annual net operating cash flow is £500 and that a firm increases stocks by 100 units over the year, but decreases stocks by the same volume during the following year. The current cost of stocks at mid-year is £1.10 per item for the first year and £2.20 per item for the second year. Taxes are paid on current costs at 35 per cent, one year in arrears after the end of each year. Finally, the discount rate is 20 per cent per annum. In Table 6.15 we provide detailed calculations to show that an additional tax payment of £27, in present value terms, results from the stock increase, and there is a consequential discounted tax saving of £45 from the decline in stocks at a later date, with a net saving of

TABLE 6.15. *Current cost tax incentives to manipulate stocks*

	Year	
	1	2
Net operating cash flow	£500	£500
Volume change in stocks	+100 units	−100 units
Mid-year cost of stocks per item	£1.10	£2.20
Periodic investment in stocks	100 × £1.10 = +£110	−100 × £2.20 = −£220
Current cost profit	£500 + £110 = £610	£500 − £220 = £280
Tax @ 35% before investment, or disinvestment, in stocks	£500 × 0.35 = £175	£500 × 0.35 = £175
Tax on current cost profit	£610 × 0.35 = £214	£280 × 0.35 = £98
Incremental tax effect	£175 − £214 = −£39	£175 − £98 = +£77
Discounted incremental tax effect	$-£39/(1.20)^2 = -£27$	$+£77/(1.20)^3 = +£45$

£18. Thus, because stock prices are increasing at a rate in excess of the discount rate, there is a tax incentive to invest in stocks. Similarly, under a current purchasing power tax system, when the general price index is rising faster than the discount rate, there is a potential tax incentive to increase stocks.

Before leaving the discussion on stock valuation, it is interesting to examine various other methods of tax relief on trading stocks which were used in the UK from April 1973 to March 1984.[1] Under the first variation, which we shall call method A, and which was adopted from 1973 to 1975, relief was given on the increase in the valuation of stock over the period, less a deduction of 10 per cent of trading profits *before* capital allowances. The second variation, which we call method B and was effective from April 1975 until November 1980, requires that the relief is calculated on the increase in valuation of trading stocks less 15 per cent of trading profits *after* capital allowances. Finally, under method C the relief is determined by multiplying (i) the excess of the opening stock valuation over £2,000 by (ii) the rate of inflation on an index of all stocks published by the Department of Industry. Method C was operative from November 1980 until March 1984. Under each method the tax relief was temporary in that if stocks substantially fell, then relief given during the preceding six years would be withdrawn and become taxable under provisions known as claw-back.

In Table 6.16 we set out examples of each method under five alternative financial situations, as listed in the table. Under example I, each method gives the same stock relief figure of £5,000, which is tax-deductible and reduces profits after capital allowances to £295,000. Example II differs in that there is an extra £10,000 of capital allowances. This alters the deduction under method B and so the stock relief for method B increases to £6,500. On account of the extra £10,000 capital allowances the tax bill has been reduced by £5,750, from £147,500 to £141,750. Hence, the marginal tax rate, on the £10,000, changes from 50 to 57.5 per cent. Thus, under method B, given that a firm is likely to claim stock relief, the marginal tax rate at which relief is given on capital expenditure increases. However, we discover under example III, specified in Table 6.16, that when profits increase by £10,000, the tax liability increases by £5,500 (£153,000 – £147,500) under method A, and by £5,750 (£153,250 – £147,500) under method B. Thus, when stock relief is claimed under these two methods the marginal tax rate on profits increases from 50 to 55 and 57.5 per cent, respectively. Under example IV, also specified in Table 6.16, there is no increase in stocks and so there is no stock relief under methods A and B. However, method C generously allows relief since it is based upon the opening stocks. Finally, under example V, stocks in excess of £2,000 increase by 5 per cent, which may be due to volume or cost increases. We discover from Table 6.16 that under methods A and B there is no stock relief in this case because of the 10 and 15 per cent restrictions. However, the stock relief under method C

[1] We have excluded a discussion of stock relief in Part Two since it was abandoned in 1984.

TABLE 6.16. *Some other alternative methods of stock relief* (£)

	Financial situation: examples				
	I	II	III	IV	V
Opening stocks	102,000	102,000	102,000	102,000	102,000
Closing stocks	152,000	152,000	152,000	102,000	107,000
Trading profits before capital allowances (i)	*450,000*	*450,000*	*460,000*	*450,000*	*450,000*
Capital allowances (ii)	*150,000*	*160,000*	*150,000*	*150,000*	*150,000*
Inflation rate on all stocks index	5%	5%	5%	5%	5%
Marginal tax rate	50%	50%	50%	50%	50%
Method A					
Closing stocks	152,000	Calculation as in I	152,000	102,000	107,000
Less: opening stocks	(102,000)	—	(102,000)	(102,000)	(102,000)
	50,000	—	50,000	nil	5,000
Less: 10% of trading profits before capital allowances	(45,000)	—	(46,000)	N/A	Restricted to (5,000)
Stock relief (iii)	*5,000*	*5,000*	*4,000*	*nil*	*nil*
Taxable profit ((i) – (ii) – (iii))	295,000	285,000	306,000	300,000	300,000
Tax @ 50%	147,500	142,500	153,000	150,000	150,000
Method B					
Closing stocks	152,000	152,000	152,000	102,000	107,000
Less: opening stocks	(102,000)	(102,000)	(102,000)	(102,000)	(102,000)
	50,000	50,000	50,000	nil	5,000
Less: 15% of trading profits after capital allowances	(45,000)	(43,500)	(46,500)	N/A	Restricted to (5,000)
Stock relief (iv)	*5,000*	*6,500*	*3,500*	*nil*	*nil*
Taxable profit ((i) – (ii) – (iv))	295,000	283,500	306,500	300,000	300,000
Tax @ 50%	147,500	141,750	153,250	150,000	150,000
Method C					
Opening stocks	102,000	Calculation as in I	Calculation as in I	Calculation as in I	Calculation as in I
Less: standard deduction	*(2,000)*	—	—	—	—
	100,000	—	—	—	—
Multiply: inflation rate on all stocks	× 0.05	—	—	—	—
Stock relief (v)	*5,000*	*5,000*	*5,000*	*5,000*	*5,000*
Taxable profit ((i) – (ii) – (v))	295,000	285,000	305,000	295,000	295,000
Tax @ 50%	147,500	142,500	152,500	147,500	147,500

exactly matches the additional working capital investment of £5,000, from £102,000 to £107,000. However in general, although method C does not alter the marginal tax rate on profits or capital allowances, the method fails to take account of volume increases and broadly allows only for actual cost inflation, if the actual inflation rate on the particular stocks of the firm is the same as the inflation rate on an all stocks index, which is calculated from the cost inflation on stocks on all firms on which the index is based. On the other hand, methods A and B allow for both volume and price changes, apart from the effects of the 10 and 15 per cent restrictions.

Net monetary working capital

Earlier we demonstrated how adjustments to the cost of sales might be made for inflationary losses. This was achieved through the indexation of stocks. But there are other components of working capital on which gains can be made instead. For example, trade creditor balances result in a loss of purchasing power to the creditor and a gain to the debtor firm. Thus, gains on creditor balances, caused by inflation, should be taxable under an inflation-adjusted tax system. On the other hand, there is a strong argument too for tax relief on inflationary losses on debtor balances. Hence, the opening and closing balances of monetary assets, such as cash and debtors, and also monetary liabilities, such as creditors and overdrafts, need to be indexed in order to calculate changes in taxable capacity induced by inflation.

Technically, for current cost calculations, the index used for each component of net monetary working capital needs to reflect the specific inflation rate on each input price. Also, account should be taken of the point in time in which the asset or liability arose. However, for convenience we shall assume that both a current cost tax system and a current purchasing power tax system use the same general price index at the beginning, middle, and end of the year in our calculations. The only difference we shall assume is that the relief under a current cost tax system is based on the mid-year reading of the index, whereas the final relief under a current purchasing power tax system reflects the end of year value of the index. In our example, the general price index at the beginning, middle and end of the year is 100,108, and 115, respectively. Accordingly, we calculate in Table 6.17 the current cost of the periodic investment in net monetary working capital during the year and compare this with the historic cost of the periodic investment. The historic cost of the net monetary working capital has increased by £9,500 compared with a current cost of only £8,640. Since the periodic investment is lower by £9,500 – £8,640 = £860, this represents a tax-deductible item. Finally, we see from Table 6.17 that, under a current purchasing power tax system, the tax relief is converted from a mid-year indexed figure to an end-of-year purchasing power equivalent and is slightly higher at £916. Alternatively, where monetary liabilities exceed

TABLE 6.17. *Tax relief on inflationary losses in holding net monetary working capital* (£)

Historic costs	
Closing balance of net monetary working capital	11,500
Less: opening balance	(2,000)
Periodic investment in net monetary working capital	*9,500*
Current costs	
Closing balance (11,500 × 108/115)	10,800
Less: opening balance (2,000 × 108/100)	(2,160)
Periodic investment in net monetary working capital	*8,640*
Tax relief	
(i) under a current cost tax system (9,500 – 8,640)	860
(ii) under a current purchasing power tax system (860 × 115/108)	916

monetary assets, there may be a resultant increase in taxable profits through the inflationary gain.

Long-term debt

Our analysis of a current cost tax system was compared with a cash-flow tax system so that we could determine potential incentives and disincentives. However, we know that for neutrality under a cash-flow tax system, with respect to investment decisions, there should not be any deductibility for interest payments. The issues which now arise are (i) whether interest on debt is eliminated by any tax adjustments relating to inflationary effects on debt finance, and thus (ii) to what extent interest deductibility can be ignored. A current cost tax system may indeed include a taxable gearing adjustment, the details of which we shall demonstrate by way of example.

In Table 6.18 we evaluate the extent to which additional tax liabilities arise for a firm which can be financed by varying levels of debt. Annual market interest rates on debt are assumed to be either 8, 10, or 12 per cent. The level of debt as a proportion of the current cost of net operating assets is either 10, 25, or 40 per cent. The current cost operating adjustments for the year are £400,000. These represent the total expenses charged to the profit and loss account before interest, gearing adjustments, and tax under a current cost tax system less the total expenses under an historic profits tax system. When the gearing ratio is 10 per cent, then an extra £40,000 is taxable as a gearing adjustment (see line (v) of Table 6.18). Correspondingly, the gearing adjustment increases to £100,000 and to £160,000 as the gearing ratio is raised to 25 and then to 40 per cent, respectively. However, interest on debt is considered to be tax-deductible and is thus deducted from the gearing adjustment to

TABLE 6.18. *Tax liabilities from gearing adjustments net of interest deductions*

Annual interest rate	8%			10%			12%		
Gearing	Low	Medium	High	Low	Medium	High	Low	Medium	High
Debt capital (£000) (i)	400	1,000	1,600	400	1,000	1,600	400	1,000	1,600
Current cost of net operating assets (£000) (ii)	4,000	4,000	4,000	4,000	4,000	4,000	4,000	4,000	4,000
Gearing ratio (iii) = (i)/(ii)	0.10	0.25	0.40	0.10	0.25	0.40	0.10	0.25	0.40
Current cost of operating adjustments (£000) (iv)	400	400	400	400	400	400	400	400	400
Gearing adjustment (£000) (v) = (iii) × (iv)	40	100	160	40	100	160	40	100	160
Interest on debt (£000) (vi) = (i) × rate	32	80	128	40	100	160	48	120	192
Additional taxable capacity (£000) (vii) = (v) − (vi)	8	20	32	nil	nil	nil	(8)	(20)	(32)
Additional tax Liability or (saving) (£000) (viii) = 0.35 × (vii)	2.8	7.0	11.2	nil	nil	nil	(2.8)	(7.0)	(11.2)

determine the additional net taxable capacity, as shown in line (vii) of Table 6.18. The marginal tax rate is assumed to be 35 per cent.

We see from Table 6.18 that when the interest rate on debt is 10 per cent per annum, the additional taxable capacity is zero. This occurs no matter whether the gearing ratio is low, medium, or high. The critical factor which determines this is that the total current cost operating adjustments as a proportion of the current cost of the net operating assets (£400,000/£4,000,000) is equal to the annual market rate of interest on debt. When the interest rate is only 8 per cent, there is an additional tax liability which increases from £2,800 to £11,200 as gearing grows from 10 to 40 per cent, respectively. Finally, when the annual interest rate on debt is 12 per cent, there is a tax saving, which also increases in line with increases in the gearing ratio.

Under a current purchasing power tax system, the inflationary gain from holding debt may be taxable. This may more than offset the benefits derived from tax deductibility of interest. As an example, we shall consider the tax implications of holding £1m of debt for one year on which interest is payable at 10 per cent per annum at the end of the year in one instalment. In a period of inflation, there is a gain in purchasing power from holding the debt, since its value declines in real terms. From Table 6.19 we see that the gains on this monetary liability increases in line with inflation. When the general rate of inflation is less than the interest rate on debt, there is a net tax saving since the tax benefit from interest deductibility outweighs the tax liability on the inflationary gain. If the general rate of inflation is the same as the interest rate on debt, then clearly there is a nil tax liability. Finally, when the general rate of inflation exceeds the interest rate on debt, there is an increase in taxable capacity, which results in a tax liability.

TABLE 6.19. *Tax liabilities from gains on monetary liabilities net of interest deductions*

	General rate of inflation per annum		
	5%	10%	15%
Gain on monetary liability (inflation rate × £1m)	50,000	100,000	150,000
Less: interest on debt (10% × £1m)	(100,000)	(100,000)	(100,000)
Net taxable capacity	(50,000)	Nil	50,000
Tax liability or (saving) (35% × net taxable capacity)	(17,500)	Nil	17,500

Tax losses

In our analysis we have generally assumed that relief for tax purposes can be offset against taxable profits. But if there are inadequate profits then tax losses arise. Losses that cannot immediately be offset against recent taxable profits may need to be carried forward and offset against future profits. Under an inflation-adjusted tax system, it would seem appropriate to index the losses. However, the rate of inflation on the index, used for tax purposes, might be lower than the relevant market rate of interest, which reflects how the company should discount the future tax saving from the loss relief claim. In this instance, the present value of the tax loss would be reduced. By contrast if the inflation rate on the index exceeds the discount rate, then there is a tax inefficiency, but on this occasion in favour of the company.

Conclusion

Inflation distorts the measurement of income and capital and may create the need for appropriate tax adjustments. However, *ad valorem* consumption taxes do not need capital-income adjustments because they are designed on a different basis, although bracket indexation is still necessary. Under an interlocking tax system based on capital and income, either real income should be measured or the inflationary erosion of capital should be tax-deductible, whilst nominal income remains subject to tax. Under a capital gains tax on realized gains, a further issue relates to tax deferral, which is necessary to take account of benefits from not paying taxes during earlier years of asset ownership, before the time of disposal. This problem can be solved by a retrospective calculation of real gains during earlier years and by an adjustment for the interest factor. If the inflation rate exceeds the deferral interest rate, then a capital gains tax which operates without a deferral adjustment is excessive. However, when the inflation rate is less than the deferral interest rate, there is an under assessment of tax. Finally, a deferral adjustment is unnecessary if the inflation rate equals the interest rate.

Our focus of attention turned towards the measurement of depreciation under current cost and current purchasing power tax systems. Under a current purchasing power tax system there is an incentive to invest if the discount rate is less than the general rate of inflation, a neutral effect if the two rates are the same, and a disincentive to invest when the discount rate exceeds the general rate of inflation. Similarly, under a current cost tax system there is a neutral effect if the specific asset price inflation rate is the same as the discount rate, a disincentive if the asset inflation rate is less than the discount rate, and an incentive to invest if the asset inflation rate exceeds the discount rate.

Our discussion of trading stocks began with a review of the FIFO and LIFO flow of costs for stock valuation purposes. We found that if unit costs of stocks are rising and stock levels in volume terms do not fall, then under a LIFO system there is a lower taxable profit figure than under a FIFO system. However, when unit costs or stock levels are falling, FIFO may result in greater tax savings.

We then turned our discussion towards indexation in relation to trading stocks. If there is a constant stock volume, then as far as stocks are concerned, a current cost tax system is non-distortionary. The same result may occur if there is a current purchasing power tax system provided that there is a constant stock volume, except that the current purchasing power tax system allows for tax deferral unlike the current cost tax system. A critical assumption, however, is that the general rate of inflation is equal to the rate of inflation on unit costs of trading stocks. When specific stock prices and general prices are rising, both tax systems imply excessive taxable profits when there are volume increases in stocks. Although the current cost and current purchasing power tax systems allow for specific and general price changes, respectively, neither is designed to address itself to the question of volume increases because it does not directly relate to profit measurement. Conversely, there are potential incentives to decrease stocks when unit costs are rising under a current cost tax system. Incentives under a current purchasing power tax system depend upon the general rate of inflation. We noted that the working capital cycle is such that stock levels associated with particular projects are likely to rise initially and then fall. Thus, if trading stock prices are rising faster than the discount rate, there may be a tax incentive to increase stocks under a current cost tax system, and similarly under a current purchasing power tax system if general prices are rising faster than the discount rate.

We also examined three methods of stock relief used in the UK from 1973 to 1984 and discussed potential distortionary effects. In addition, we extended our review to possible net monetary working capital adjustments under current cost and current purchasing power tax systems.

In our attempt to analyse the implications of long-term debt under a current cost tax system, we calculted the ratio of the total current cost operating adjustments to the current cost of the net operating assets. This proportion, which is not the gearing ratio, is a critical ratio that affects potential tax distortions. When the interest rate on debt is less than this critical ratio, there is an excessive tax burden which increases in line with the degree of gearing. If the interest rate on debt is the same as the critical ratio, then there is a nil tax liability associated with debt financing. But if the interest rate exceeds the critical ratio, there is a tax saving which increases with the degree of gearing.

Under a current purchasing power tax system, we explained how to assess inflationary gains on holding debt, which would not outweigh tax savings through interest deductibility, unless the general rate of inflation exceeded the interest rate.

Finally, we mentioned that tax losses should be indexed under inflation-adjusted tax systems, although there are potential inefficiencies in favour of the taxpayer during periods in which the inflation rate on the appropriate index exceeds the relevant market discount rate.

Recommendations for further reading

For readers who wish to become more acquainted with the inflation accounting debate, references to Kirkman (1978), Whittington (1983) and Kay and Mayer (1984) are well worth noting. In the Meade report (1978, chapters 6 and 7) there is an illuminating discussion of indexation. A book by Morley (1974) addresses itself to the question of a current purchasing power tax system. The implications of a current cost tax system are discussed in the Government Green Paper (1982) and an article by Pointon (1986), which concentrates on investment appraisal and capital structure.

References

HMSO (1982), *Corporation Tax*, Cmnd. 8456 (London: HMSO).

Kay, J., and Mayer, C. P. (1984), *Inflation Accounting*, IFS Report Series No 10 (May).

Kirkman, P. R. A. (1978), *Accounting Under Inflationary Conditions*, Second Edn. (London: George Allen and Unwin).

Meade, J. E. (1978), *The Structure and Reform of Direct Taxation* (London: Institute for Fiscal Studies).

Morley, M. F. (1974), *The Fiscal Implications of Inflation Accounting* (London: Institute for Fiscal Studies and the Trustees of the Chartered Accountants Trust for Education and Research).

Pointon, J. (1986), 'Investment Appraisal and Financial Policy Under a Current Cost Tax System', *British Accounting Review*, 18, no. 3 (Autumn): 61–89.

Whittington, G. (1983), *Inflation Accounting: An Introduction to the Debate* (Cambridge: Cambridge University Press).

PART TWO

Taxes in the United Kingdom

Having examined some important concepts of tax theory and the design of alternative tax systems, we now turn towards a critical appraisal of the main taxes operative in the UK. We attempt to concentrate on those significant broad principles of business taxation which should be of more lasting relevance. Typical of the rest of the book, we have provided detailed numerical examples to help the reader to become familiar with these broad principles. Chapter 7 introduces the complex system of income tax and is followed in Chapter 8 by its application to unincorporated businesses, either sole traders or partnerships. An introduction to capital gains tax is presented in Chapter 9. Similarities to income tax and important differences, are given in Chapter 10, when we appraise the UK system of corporation tax. In Chapter 11 we discuss value added tax and finally in Chapter 12 introduce some other taxes and similar instruments, such as national insurance contributions, customs and excise duties, local authority rates, and North Sea oil taxation.

7
Introduction to Income Tax

Introduction

This chapter will commence with a brief review of the development of the UK income tax system and will then explain how that system is governed by statute law and the way in which it is administered. It will then concentrate on aspects of the law and practice which we consider necessary for a fuller understanding of business taxation.

Historic development

Over the centuries taxation has been accredited with changing the course of history—often violent change and even war. Conversely, to finance wars governments have often found it necessary to impose additional taxation to meet the costs of conflict.

Income tax in the UK was imposed initially by Pitt in January 1799 as a method of financing the Napoleonic Wars. Unfortunately, the actual collection of income tax fell short of the estimated revenue expected by the Government of the time, and this resulted in corrective measures being introduced by Addington in his 1803 Finance Act. These measures tackled specifically the dual problem of persons not making tax returns or, where assessments were made, payments to the Government were extremely slow in forthcoming. The first part of the problem was solved by allocating various types of income to distinct schedules, labelled A to E, and then requiring that separate tax returns for each category of income be submitted to different assessors. This concept overcame the natural reluctance of potential taxpayers to disclose their income levels. The fact that five tax assessors knew part of their income rather than one assessor knowing the whole was more acceptable. The second part of the problem was tackled by the introduction of the concept of taxing certain classes of income at source. The consequence of this legislation was twofold—taxpayers effectively paid their tax in advance to the Government, which speeded up its tax revenue cash flows and left far smaller sums outstanding at any one time where assessments were still necessary.

It is interesting to note that these two concepts are still part of the income tax legislation at the current time, although it should be stressed that taxpayers now submit only one return, covering all income under the various schedules, to the Inland Revenue. The maintenance of confidentiality by the Inland Revenue appears to be widely accepted by the taxpayer.

At the cessation of the Napoleonic hostilities in 1815 an event occurred the like of which is not likely to be repeated—income tax was abolished including the destruction of all records. For the next twenty-six years the UK citizen was free of income tax, but in 1842 Sir Robert Peel found it necessary to reintroduce it as a temporary tax. Although a temporary tax, it has remained with us ever since, but nevertheless it is by law only an annual tax which has to be revived in each Finance Act. From these somewhat simple beginnings the UK direct tax system has evolved into a multi-tax system as shown in Table 7.1. However, despite the number of additional direct taxes introduced since 1894, income tax has always remained the most important tax in terms of revenue raised.

Legal machinery for imposition

At the outset it must be stressed that the sole source of tax law in the UK is that created by statute law and no other method. The courts, as will be discussed in the next section, merely play an interpretative role. The courts are not lawmakers.

TABLE 7.1 *Development of UK direct taxation system*

1799	Introduction of income tax
1803	Revision of income tax
1816–42	No income tax
1842	Reimposition of income tax on three-yearly basis
1860	Reimposition of income tax on indefinite basis
1894	Estate duty introduced
1909	Super tax imposed
1918	First Consolidation Act
1927	Super tax renamed surtax
1944	Introduction of PAYE system
1945	Introduction of capital allowances
1946	First double tax agreement
1952	Second Consolidation Act
1965	Introduction of capital gains tax
1965	Introduction of corporation tax
1970	Third Consolidation Act
1975	Capital transfer tax replaced estate duty
1976	Development land tax introduced
1979	Capital Gains Tax Acts consolidated
1984	Capital Transfer Tax Acts consolidated
1985	Abolition of development land tax
1986	Inheritance tax replaced capital transfer tax

The statute law is contained in a series of annual Finance Acts which, of course, over the years amount to a large volume of tax legislation. After a period of time it becomes cumbersome to trace, through numerous Finance Acts, the current law on a given situation, and for this reason, at intervals, all parts of the Finance Acts which are still in force are codified into a single Consolidating Act. By reference to Table 7.1 it will be seen that the last Consolidating Act relative to income tax and corporation tax was in 1970. It is referred to as the Income and Corporation Taxes Act 1970 (TA 1970). The capital taxes have or had their own Consolidating Acts.

The process by which the annual Finance Act is created is shown in Fig. 7.1. The start of the chain of events which culminates in the birth of a Finance Act is that well-known British institution, the Budget speech. This speech, delivered by the Chancellor of the Exchequer, puts forward to Parliament, among other matters, proposed changes in taxation for the coming fiscal year, i.e. commencing 6 April to the following 5 April. The Chancellor's speech is normally in March or very early April, but in recent years has been in the third week of March. After the Budget speech the proposals are debated in the House of Commons, and Budget Resolutions are passed, which are published a few weeks after the Budget in the Finance Bill. The annual Finance Bill sets out, clause by clause, the Chancellor's new tax proposals in detail, and for the first time, by reading the small print, the business community may appreciate the full impact of those proposals. However, the reader should appreciate at this stage that the proposals are in no way legally enforceable and may be subject to considerable amendment in the ensuing Parliamentary Debate. In

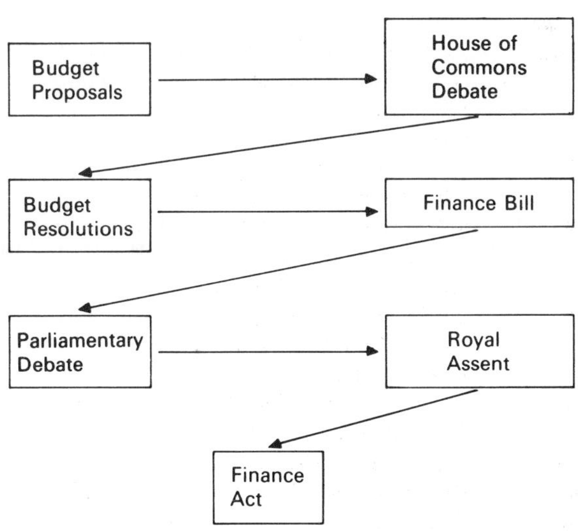

Fig. 7.1 Creation of a Finance Act

1982 the Finance Bill grew substantially in the course of its passage through the House of Commons, from its original 189 pages to a final length of 256 pages. The 1983 Finance Bill was severely truncated as a direct result of severe time pressures imposed by the dissolution of Parliament prior to the general election. Finally, the amended Finance Bill receives the Royal Assent about the end of July at which point its contents assume legal status.

It will be recalled that income tax is merely an annual tax which is revived each year in the Finance Act and one might pose this question. Why do I or others pay income tax between April and the end July when it ceases to be a legal tax on 6 April and is not reintroduced onto the statutes until three months later? The answer to this question lies in a rather obscure, but nonetheless important, piece of legislation, namely the Provisional Collection of Taxes Act 1968 (PCTA 1968). This act authorizes the Government to collect taxes, including income tax, at the rates proposed in the Budget speech until 5 August; by which time the Finance Act will be in force.

Administration and practice

The UK direct tax system, of which income tax is a part, is administered under various statutory provisions contained in the Taxes Management Act 1970 (TMA 1970). This act provides that the care and management of income tax shall be vested in the Board of Inland Revenue. It also specifies how this is to be done. Fig. 7.2 shows the important functionaries in the administration of income tax within the UK. Taxpayers or their advisors would normally only have dealings with the bottom row administrators, but before considering these officials in more detail, a brief description of the upper levels is given for the interested reader.

The Board of Inland Revenue sometimes referred to as the Commissioners of Inland Revenue (not to be confused with Special and General Commissioners) is a body of permanent civil servants under control of the Treasury. The Board is charged with advising the Treasury and Chancellor of Exchequer on proposals for new or amended legislation in addition to its duties contained in the TMA 1970. To ease the process of administration the UK is divided into fifteen regions including Wales, Scotland and Northern Ireland with controllers in charge of each region. Each region is further divided into tax districts and collection offices. A regional controller is in overall charge of both inspectors and collectors who operate within his or her region. Throughout the UK there are some 600 tax districts and about 135 local collectors' offices.

Both collectors and inspectors are permanent civil servants. However, their roles within the administrative system are quite different and also separate, although they are part of a single staff group. The Collector of Taxes is responsible for the collection of tax as assessed by the Inspector and is not empowered by the legislation to issue demand notes for tax for which a corresponding assessment is not already in existence. Where income tax

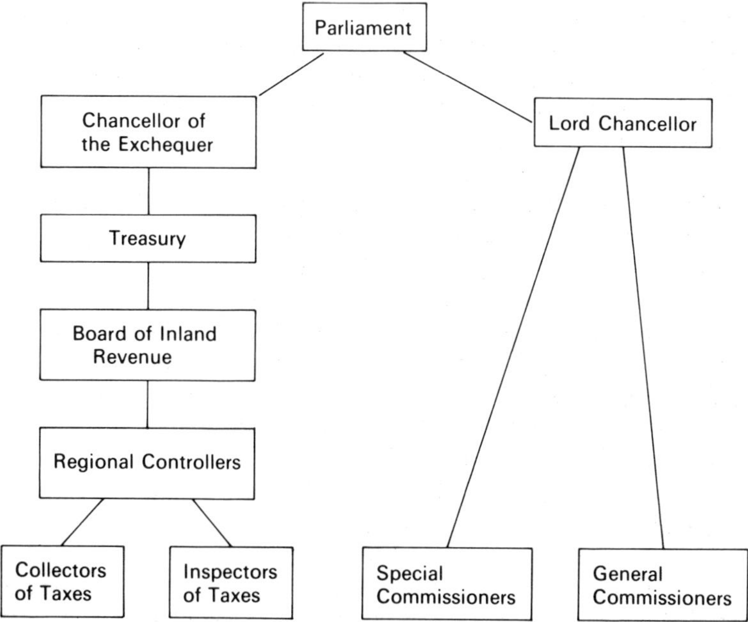

Fig. 7.2 UK Income Tax Administration

remains unpaid after the due payment date the collector is authorized by the TMA 1970 to obtain payment, if necessary, by distraining upon the taxpayer's goods and chattels. However, this approach is not attractive to the Inland Revenue, and so the collector will normally attempt to collect the outstanding tax by seeking a judgment in the courts.

In their day to day tax affairs taxpayers or their advisors will normally have most dealings with HM Inspector of Taxes. Table 7.2 may perhaps give some

TABLE 7.2. *Some duties of HM Inspector of Taxes*

(i)	The issue of tax returns
(ii)	The examination of completed returns.
(iii)	Preparation and issue of assessments based on completed returns
(iv)	Issue of estimated assessments where no return is received or he disagrees with the information contained therein
(v)	Where the taxpayer appeals against the estimated assessment, the Inspector attempts to settle the appeal informally by agreement.
(vi)	If this is not possible the Inspector lists the appeal for hearing by the Commissioners and appears before them to put the Inland Revenue's case.

indication of why this is. Although reference is made to HM Inspector of Taxes it should, of course, be realized that in each tax district there is a team carrying out this wide range of duties. The taxpayer may be dealing with the district inspector (difficult cases or large taxpayers), more junior assistant inspectors, or clerical staff who are often involved in handling low-level, straightforward cases under Schedule E.

HM Inspector of Taxes is charged under the TMA 1970 with the duty of issuing tax returns and, after completion and signature by the taxpayer, examining the details provided of the taxpayer's income, charges on income, and claim to personal reliefs. Not all taxpayers are issued with a tax return each year; particularly employees with no income other than that from their employment. However, it is important to note that in circumstances where a taxpayer has not received a tax return but income arises upon which a tax liability accrues, then there is a legal obligation for that taxpayer to inform HM Inspector of Taxes.

There are a wide range of different tax returns, each designed to highlight the type of taxpayer from whom information is required. nevertheless the information requested is, as already indicated, fairly standard. The majority of tax returns are issued either just before or immediately after the commencement of the tax year. In law, these returns must be completed and returned to HM Inspector of Taxes within a specified time limit and where a taxpayer is a married man must contain details of his wife's income, if any.

The tax return is clearly an extremely important document to the inspector, and providing he or she is satisfied with the information contained therein, will issue an assessment showing the income assessable and the income tax payable. Apart from the situation where higher rate tax applies to the taxpayer's taxable income, the inspector will only raise assessments on income which has not already suffered tax at source. This method of assessment and tax collection is known as direct assessment. If the taxpayer does not submit his or her return or the inspector suspects the information shown is incomplete or incorrect, then the inspector has a powerful weapon at his disposal to force the issue. He is legally empowered to raise an assessment showing an estimate, usually excessive, of the income assessable. The UK tax law does, however, provide that taxpayers may appeal against any assessment they receive, including estimates, providing some basic rules are followed. These are that the time limit of 30 days from issue of the assessment, not date of receipt, is strictly observed, and that the appeal is made in writing and addressed and delivered to HM Inspector of Taxes who raised the assessment. The taxpayer may also apply to have any disputed tax liability deferred until the appeal, has been resolved, although care should be exercised in view of the interest on overdue tax provisions. It is recommended that taxpayers use the standard Inland Revenue forms obtainable from any local tax district or perhaps, even better, seek the assistance of a professional advisor.

On the assumption that a valid appeal is made, then HM Inspector of Taxes will attempt to settle the matter informally either directly with the taxpayer or his professional advisor. Whatever method of informality is adopted, if agreement is achieved, an exchange of letters is required by law to ratify what has been agreed. If agreement cannot be reached in this way a formal meeting before the General or Special Commissioners will be instigated by the inspector at which he will appear as the Inland Revenue's representative.

The function of the General and Special Commissioners is identical in that each is an independent body which hears disputes between the taxpayer and the Inland Revenue and gives a decision which binds both parties. Although both bodies are now appointed by the Lord Chancellor, their qualifications are somewhat different. The General Commissioners are normally business and professional persons local to the division which is to hear the appeals. Their appointment is unpaid and part-time, and they are not experts in tax law—their main asset being a good knowledge of local business, trade, and other relevant conditions. The General Commissioners have their own clerk, usually a solicitor, who may advise them upon legal matters. By contrast the Special Commissioners are tax experts who are appointed on a full-time, paid basis. They are based in London but throughout the tax year travel on circuit to the provinces. At either type of Commissioners' meeting the taxpayer has the right to appear in person, but it is advisable that a suitably qualified advisor appears for the taxpayer and it is considered essential before the Special Commissioners. Indeed, in many cases specially briefed tax counsel are vital. The taxpayer may elect as to which body of Commissioners he appears before, but the Inland Revenue will not allow an appeal before the Special Commissioners where it is felt that the reasons are to gain time, waste time, or indeed merely frivolous. Nevertheless, despite this proviso in making his decision the taxpayer or his advisor may do well to heed the words of Hepker: 'an appeal to the heart would do better before the General Commissioners, an appeal to the head before the Special Commissioners' (Hepker 1975, p. 37).

Despite both taxpayer and HM Inspector of Taxes being bound by the decision of the Commissioners, one side will be dissatisfied with it. The legislation lays down that where the decision is erroneous on a point of law, providing certain formalities are conducted at the meeting and within specified time limits thereafter, appeal may be made to the High Court Chancery Division. This process of further appeal is never available where the Commissioners' decision is based on a question of fact. In disputes which involve large sums of money and where the correct legal interpretation of a word or phrase in the legislation is the basis for the decision, appeals will often be entered beyond the High Court into the Court of Appeal and even the House of Lords.

Scope and coverage

Until 1965 income tax had been suffered by individuals, businesses—both corporate and unincorporate, and trusts. From 1965 upon the introduction of corporation tax (see Chapter 10), only the unincorporate trading mediums of sole traders and partnerships have borne income tax on their profits while individuals and trusts have remained liable to income tax on non-trading income. Within this section aspects of personal taxation which affect the taxation of sole traders and partners will be outlined, but the treatment of income tax with particular reference to trusts is considered to be outside the terms of reference of this book.

Table 7.3 shows a format for the computation of the income tax liability of or repayment due to an individual for a tax year. This computation has been labelled (A) to (L) for convenience of the reader in following the discussion of the terminology and for cross-referencing where necessary. In general terms it should be noted that taxpayers do not suffer income tax on the full amount of their income (C) since the legislation provides for a series of deductions to arrive at the taxable income (G).

The division between earned and investment income is more of historical interest than of practical use currently; the additional relief for earned income was abolished many years ago and the penalty on investment incomes was removed more recently by the 1984 Finance Act. Nevertheless, deductions from income included at (A) and (B) are only allowed in a very strict order by the legislation, and these items will be considered after a review of the income which must be included as either earned or investment.

TABLE 7.3. *Outline personal income tax computation*

Taxpayer—Income tax computation 19xx/19xx	(£)
Earned income less allowable deductions	A
Investment income	B
	C
Less: annual payments	(D)
Total income (net statutory income)	E
Less: personal reliefs	(F)
Taxable income	G
Income tax borne on G at unified income tax rates	H
Add: tax retained on annual payments paid net of basic rate tax	I
Income tax payable	J
Less: tax suffered at source/directly assessed and paid	(K)
Income tax liability or (repayment)	L

Acknowledging that income tax is assessable on:

(i) income arising within the UK, whatever the domicile or residence status of the taxpayer; and
(ii) income arising outside the UK on any resident in the UK whatever the domicile,

the legislation lists the sources of income which are assessable using a number of schedules and subdivisions referred to as cases and specifies the basis to be used in making assessments. The legislation is extremely detailed, but Table 7.4 is a summary of the relevant detail whereby it may be ascertained that Schedule D cases I and II (self-employed persons) and Schedule E (employees) are the principal earned sources, while investment income will arise under Schedules A, B, D cases III to VI, and Schedule F. Individuals are not assessed under Schedule C directly, any assessment notice being raised on the paying agent. Nevertheless, the grossed-up equivalent of the net interest received by the taxpayer must be recorded as investment income at (B) in his computation. Similarly, building society interest received, although not allocated a schedule at all, must be treated as investment income and dealt with in the same manner as dividends from UK companies under Schedule F.

Having now established the 'gross' income at (C), the deductions allowable at (A), (D), and (F) will now be considered more fully. The legislation is, in the case of certain expenses, quite rigid as to which expenses may be set against which income, for example capital allowances relating to the carrying on of a trade must primarily be set against profits from that trade while superannuation contributions by an employee must be set against the Schedule E income from that employment. Thus, in a personal income tax computation, these items must be deducted at point (A), and it would be both technically incorrect and certainly unwise to attempt a different treatment. The legislation relating to annual payments referred to at (D) is more flexible in that these items, which include allowable interest payments, payments under deed of covenant, and other contractual annual payments are deductible from any income whether it be earned or investment. Not all interest payments are allowable, and the reader is invited to refer to the current legislation for those payments which are. Even after establishing that an item of interest is allowable for tax purposes, i.e. on a qualifying loan, a deduction may not be claimed unless the interest is paid in the year of claim. Accruals of interest are never allowed. Interest on a bank overdraft is never allowed against 'gross' income—by definition an overdraft is not a loan, but where the interest relates to a business borrowing the sums paid may be claimed as an expense in arriving at business profits which are assessable under Schedule D cases I or II.

Following the deduction of expenses and annual payments the resultant balance at (E) is referred to by the legislation as total income or net statutory income. The importance of this line being correct cannot be over emphasized in any serious study of income tax. The absolute value of total income is critical

TABLE 7.4. *The UK income tax schedules*

Schedule and case	Type of income	Basis of assessment
A	Rents from UK land and buildings	Rent due in tax year
B	Occupation of commercially managed woodlands	Fixed assessment with option to transfer to D case I
C	Income from Government stocks paid through UK paying agent	Tax deducted in tax year assessed on paying agent
D		
Case I	Profits of trade	Normally profits of accounting year ended in previous tax year
Case II	Profits of profession or vocation	
Case III	Interest and other annual amounts received	Grossed up equivalent of income received in tax year where tax suffered at source Income received in previous tax year where income received gross
Case IV	Income from foreign securities	Normally income/profits arising in previous tax year
Case V	Income from foreign possessions including overseas trades	
Case VI	Miscellaneous income/profits	Income/profit arising in tax year
E		
Cases I/II/III	Income from employment in a variety of situations	Income in tax year with special rules in some circumstances
F	Dividends and other distributions from UK companies	Grossed up equivalent of dividends etc., received in tax year

in some claims for personal tax relief, for example age allowance, and also in establishing the size of business losses which may be offset (see Chapter 8 on losses).

Finally, at (F), a taxpayer is entitled to claim reliefs which are unique to his personal circumstances and/or responsibilities and are referred to in the legislation as personal reliefs or personal allowances. Table 7.5 shows the range of personal allowances which were available for the tax years 1985/6 and 1986/7. A detailed description of the circumstances which give rise to each

TABLE 7.5. *Personal allowances claimable against total income*

	1985/6	1986/7
Single	£2,205	£2,335
Married	£3,455	£3,655
Wife's earned income relief (100%)	£2,205	£2,335
Housekeeper	£100	£100
Addition for child if:		
claimant single or claimant's wife ill	£1,250	£1,320
Dependent relative allowance:		
certain woman claimants	£145	£145
other claimants	£100	£100
Daughter's or son's services	£55	£55
Blind person	£360	£360
Widow's bereavement	£1,250	£1,320
Age allowance to replace single or married personal allowance:		
single	£2,690	£2,850
married	£4,255	£4,505
income limit	£8,800	£9,400

allowance is beyond the scope of this book. However, it should be observed that a number of these allowances increase annually, often by a figure which is higher than the annual rate of inflation. Nevertheless, for explanation purposes in the remainder of this chapter, where there is need to refer to personal allowances in a computation, the 1985/6 figures will be used. Similar remarks apply to income tax rates which were in force for 1985/6 and 1986/7. These rates are shown in Table 7.6 and are applied to the taxable income of the tax payer at (G). The income tax, which is payable, is charged at the basic rate and then at higher rates on successive bands of taxable income up to the amount shown at (G). This scale of rates introduces a measure of progressivity into the UK income tax system and is technically referred to as the unified tax system. The unified income tax system replaced the former separate income tax and surtax systems from 1973/4. Surtax on taxpayers with higher incomes was abolished and unified with the income tax system.

In certain circumstances income tax at the ruling basic rate is deductible, at source, by the payer before making an annual payment, for example interest under the MIRAS (mortgage interest relief at source) scheme. As the income tax deducted is literally put into the pocket of the payer, in order to arrive at the true income tax payable (J) the amount of the tax retained (I) must be added to the income tax borne at (H). Unless this adjustment is made income tax relief at the basic rate on the gross amount of the annual payment would be double counted.

TABLE 7.6. *Personal income tax rates for 1985/6 and 1986/7*

1985/6	
Basic rate	30%
Income tax on taxable incomes from:	
£0 to £16,200	30%
£16,201 to £19,200	40%
£19,201 to £24,400	45%
£24,401 to £32,300	50%
£32,301 to £40,200	55%
£40,201 upwards	60%
1986/7	
Basic rate	29%
Income tax on taxable incomes from:	
£0 to £17,200	29%
£17,201 to £20,200	40%
£20,201 to £25,400	45%
£25,401 to £33,300	50%
£33,301 to £41,200	55%
£41,201 upwards	60%

As previously mentioned, any income received net of basic rate income tax, such as interest on some government securities and dividends from UK companies, must be recorded in the body of the computation (B) as a gross equivalent. With the basic rate at 30 per cent the gross equivalent is the net amount received × 10/7. This adjustment is principally to ensure that where taxpayers are liable at the higher rates they are chargeable on the gross marginal £ with any relief for income tax already suffered at the basic rate being given by way of a credit. This adjustment may be made in aggregate at (K). Before examining the general example of a personal computation given in Table 7.7 it is essential to mention a further complication which is present in personal tax computations and stems directly from the basis of assessment—the previous tax year—and is relevant to most income assessed under Schedule D including business profits. The reader is invited to refer back to Table 7.4 to verify this and note also the types of income which are assessed on the basis of arising in the current tax year. Therefore it may be seen that when computing the 'gross' income (C) for say, 1985/6 there is a mixture of income from two tax years, the previous year 1984/5 and the current year 1985/6. The general example is based upon the data shown below in respect of Simon Smith, a self-employed hairdresser:

		(£)
Mr Smith	Business profits arising in 1984/5	15,655
Mrs Smith	Rents from UK property in 1985/6	8,000
Mrs Smith	Dividends from UK companies in 1985/6 (net received)	700
Mr Smith	Pays mortgage interest under a non-MIRAS scheme (gross)	4,000

Having calculated the income tax liability in Table 7.7, it merely remains to consider the methods by which the Inland Revenue will collect the tax due of £4,960. As previously explained income tax is collected either by deduction at source or by HM Inspector of Taxes raising a direct assessment. There are three main situations where income will be deducted from income by the payer before the recipient is credited with the income:

(i) Under the pay-as-you-earn (PAYE) system employers deduct income tax from earnings in accordance with instructions received from the Inland Revenue. Unlike situations (ii) and (iii) below, income tax may be deducted at both basic and higher rates dependent on the employee's level of earnings.

(ii) In the building industry payments to self-employed sub-contractors who do not hold a special exemption certificate will have tax deducted at a prescribed rate, normally the basic rate, by the main contractor from his gross payments.

TABLE 7.7. *Example of a personal income tax computation*

S. Smith—Income tax computation 1985/6		(£)
Earned income: Schedule D case II (arising in 1984/5) (A)		15,655
Investment income:		
Schedule A (arising in 1985/6) (B)	8,000	
Dividend income (arising in 1985/6) (700 × 10/7) (B)	1,000	
		9,000
Subtotal (C)		24,655
Less: annual payment paid gross (D)		(4,000)
Total income (E)		20,655
Less: married personal allowance (F)		(3,455)
Taxable income (G)		17,200
Income tax borne under unified tax system (H):		
16200 @ 30%		4,860
1000 @ 40%		400
Subtotal (J)		5,260
Less: tax suffered at source on dividend income (1000 @ 30%) (K)		(300)
Income tax liability 1985/6 (L)		£4,960

(iii) Income tax is 'deemed' to be deducted at the basic rate by a company when making a dividend payment to its shareholders (see Chapter 10). Similar treatment is extended to interest payments by building societies and banks to their depositors.

Generally, income which consists of interest from limited companies and most government securities will have had income tax removed at the basic rate by the payer or paying agent. This extremely effective collection method therefore clearly relates to income assessable under Schedules C, D case I (self-employed sub-contractors in building industry only), D case III (unless interest is received gross), E cases I and II, and F where the taxpayer is only liable at the basic rate. On any income which is assessable under the remaining schedules and cases direct assessment will be raised, and tax will be payable on certain pay-days as shown in Table 7.8.

It will be seen that for the 1985/6 year of assessment income tax at the basic rate will normally be payable either on 1 January 1986 or 1 January and 1 July 1986 with any higher rate tax being settled on or before 1 December 1986. It should also be noted that there is a small cash-flow benefit granted to businesses. In the circumstances where an assessment, which is not appealed against, is issued late then the due date of payment is 30 days after issue where this is later than the due date. If the 1985/6 Schedule A assessment on Smith were issued on 1 January 1986 the tax would not be due until 30 January 1986. The situation which arises on appeals against direct assessments has been outlined earlier. In either circumstances the taxpayer should be aware the Inland Revenue has powers to charge interest on overdue tax and does so! The number of assessments raised upon Simon Smith, the tax due, and normal

TABLE 7.8. *Normal due date of payment of income tax on direct assessments*

(i)	Schedule A	1 January in assessment year
	Schedule B	1 January in assessment year
	Schedule D	
	Cases I & II	1 January in assessment year and 1 July following assessment year by equal instalments
	Case III	1 January in assessment year
	Cases IV & V	1 January in assessment year unless relating to a foreign business when cases I & II dates apply
	Case VI	1 January in assessment year
	Schedule E	
	Case III	No set date except normally after end of assessment year
(ii)	Higher rate tax	1 December following assessment year

payment dates are shown in Table 7.9 where it will also be observed that as far as practicable the Inland Revenue will set annual payments and personal reliefs against a taxpayer's main source of income—in this case Smith's profits as a hairdresser.

TABLE 7.9 *Example of direct assessments, tax due, and pay dates*

Simon Smith	Taxable income (£)	Tax liability (£)	Pay date
(i) Schedule A 1985/6 assessment			
Income arising in 1985/6	8,000		
Income tax due @ 30%		2,400	1 Jan. 1986
(ii) Schedule D case II 1985/6 assessment			
Income arising in 1984/5	15,655		
Less: annual payment	(4,000)		
	11,655		
Less: personal allowances	(3,455)		
	8,200		(£1,230 per instalment)
Income tax @ 30%		2,460	1 Jan. 1986 1 July 1986
(iii) Higher rate 1985/6 assessment			
Schedule A	8,000		
Schedule D case II after offsetting annual payments and personal allowances	8,200		
Gross equivalent of dividend income	1,000		
Subtotal	17,200		
Less: income already charged at basic rate	(16,200)		
	1,000		
Income tax @ 40%		400	
Less: credit for basic rate tax already deducted		(300)	
		100	1 Dec. 1986

Husband and wife

In the earlier personal income tax computation for Simon Smith, see Table 7.7, it will be seen that his wife's rental and dividend income is assessed on him.

This situation is merely the consequence of tax legislation whereby the income of a married woman is regarded as that of her husband. There is aggregation of income and it follows that:

(i) There may be an increase in the income chargeable at higher rates (there is in the Smith example).
(ii) The husband is not only directly assessed in his name but he is also liable to account for the tax; although where a wife is employed and her salary taxed under PAYE or, as in the Smith example, there is dividend income taxed at source, he will only be liable for higher rate liabilities, the £100 calculated in Table 7.9.

Aggregation of income does not apply in three specific situations:

(i) In the tax year of marriage.
(ii) Where an election has been made by either party to the marriage for husband and wife to have their respective incomes separately assessed.
(iii) Both parties to the marriage elect to have the wife's earnings taxed spearately.

For the tax year of marriage husband and wife are treated as single persons for tax purposes, although, of course, they are legally married, with a further anomaly that the husband is entitled to the married personal allowance although this will be restricted where the date of marriage is subsequent to 5 May. Additionally, if the wife's income is insufficient to absorb her personal allowances any excess allowances cannot in general be set against her husband's income.

As indicated earlier, a married taxpayer's income tax return must contain details of not only his own income but that of his wife also. However, where either husband or wife so elects their incomes will be separately assessed, which in practical terms means each will complete his or her own tax return, will receive assessments in their own names and be responsible for the income tax due thereon. Although this election in no way results in a saving of tax it does introduce a measure of confidentiality between the marriage partners. In practice this election may be a prelude to a forthcoming separation, legal or otherwise, between husband and wife.

The separate taxation of wife's earnings election was introduced in the 1971 Finance Act to avoid excessive taxation in situations where each partner or at least the wife is self-employed or employed at high earnings levels. Providing both parties to the marriage inform HM Inspector of Taxes, in writing within generous time limits, of their desire to have the wife's earnings separately taxed for a tax year, there may be a substantial saving of income tax. The election will remain in force until such time as it is revoked. The general effect of this election is illustrated in Table 7.10 which is an extension of the earlier Simon Smith example, but assumes that Mrs Smith also has earned income from her own ladies hairdressing salon of £10,000, assessable in 1985/6. Apart from the tax saving of £599, the other important issues to note from this example are (i)

TABLE 7.10. *Example of separate taxation of wife's earnings election, 1971 Finance Act*

	Aggregated Income	Election	
	S. Smith (£)	S. Smith (£)	Mrs Smith (£)
Earned income:			
Schedule D case II			
self	15,655	15,655	—
wife	10,000	—	10,000
Investment income:			
Schedule A (wife)	8,000	—	—
Dividends (wife)	1,000	9,000	—
Subtotal	34,655	24,655	10,000
Less: annual payment	(4,000)	(4,000)	—
Total income	30,655	20,655	10,000
Less: married personal allowance	(3,455)	—	—
wife's earned income allowance	(2,205)	—	—
single personal allowances	—	(2,205)	(2,205)
Taxable income	£24,995	£18,450	£7,795

Income tax borne	Aggregated income tax liability	Income tax borne	S. Smith tax liability	Income tax borne	Mrs Smith tax liability
16,200 @ 30%	4,860	16,200 @ 30%	4,860	7,795 @ 30%	2,338
3,000 @ 40%	1,200	2,250 @ 40%	900	—	—
5,200 @ 45%	2,340	—	—	—	—
595 @ 50%	297	—	—	—	—
£24,995	*£8,697*	£18,450	*£5,760*	£7,795	*£2,338*
Tax liability by making election (£5,760 + £2,338)					*£8,098*
Tax saving by making election (£8,697 – £8098)					£599

Note: It is assumed that the annual payment is made by S. Smith.

that the wife's investment income is still taxable on the husband, (ii) the title of the election means what it says, and (iii) there is a loss of the differential between married and single personal allowance to the husband, which is however, more than outweighed by disaggregating the wife's earned income and applying her own unified tax system bands and rates to that income as if she were a single person. The reader may wish to check the general conclusion that at low levels of wife's earned income there is no tax saving by substituting an earnings level of £2,205 into the example.

The long awaited Green Paper on the reform of personal taxation, proposed in the 1985 Budget, was finally published on Budget Day 1986 (HMSO 1986). The document contains proposals to eliminate some of the anomalies referred to above by giving every taxpayer the same allowances with no discrimination between the sexes or for marital status and making provision for transfer of surplus allowances between spouses where there is an excess or deficiency of incomes situation. Confidentiality between marriage partners is also envisaged. Clearly, these changes will fundamentally change the taxation of husbands and wives but any implementation of new legislation is not expected until the early 1990s!

Concluding remarks

In this chapter we described how income tax has developed from a simple means of financing the Napoleonic Wars to an extremely complex and sophisticated direct form of taxation levied on the income of individuals and profits arising from the running of unincorporated businesses.

After examining how the legal machinery for imposing income tax is operated and stressing that tax law is created by statute law, the roles of the various administrators within the UK direct tax system were described.

The importance of the assessment procedures, particularly how to react where an estimated assessment is raised by HM Inspector of Taxes, was discussed in detail.

It has been shown how different classes of income are taxed under various Schedules A to F, and the significance of the actual and previous year bases of assessment applicable to these schedules has been fully emphasized in the computation of an individual taxpayer's liability for a year of assessment. Having established the level of liability under the unified tax system, we discuss the methods of collecting the income tax due and the dates upon which the tax was payable.

Finally, the special tax legislation relating to husbands and wives was discussed, and the options available for saving tax on joint earned incomes including profits from unincorporated businesses were explored.

Recommendations for further reading

A full account of the history of income tax may be found in Sabine (1965). For those who would like a more detailed account of the legal machinery for imposing taxation, including the role of the Inland Revenue in contributing to the Budget and Finance Bill, see chapter 7 HMSO (1984). An excellent insight is also given in chapters 3 and 4 HMSO (1984) of the work of the Inland

Revenue's operational offices and head office. Pritchard (1986) contains a detailed description of taxpayer's personal allowances for the reader who wishes to explore this topic in its current form. The future proposed structure of personal allowances has been revealed in a Government Green Paper HMSO (1986), while for an interesting criticism see Johnson (1986).

References

Hepker, M. Z. (1975), *A Modern Approach to Tax Law* (London: Heinemann).

HMSO (1984), *Inland Revenue 126th Report 1983*, Cmnd. 9305 (London: HMSO).

HMSO (1986), *The Reform of Personal Taxation*, Cmnd. 9756 (London: HMSO).

Johnson, C. (1986), 'Family Tax Reform', *Lloyds Bank Economic Bulletin*, no. 88 (April 1986).

Pritchard, W. E. (1986), *Income Tax* (*Current edition*), (Harlow, Essex: Longman).

Sabine, B. E. V. (1965), *A History of Income Tax* (Hertfordshire: Allen and Unwin).

8

Income Tax on Unincorporated Businesses

Introduction

In this chapter emphasis will be directed towards the taxation of the unincorporated business conducted and controlled through the medium of either a sole proprietorship or partnership within the UK. It will demonstrate how business profits are calculated and assessed to income tax, how relief is given for capital expenditure, how losses are treated, and review the special adaptions of income tax law to partnerships. The assumption throughout is that the reader is already familiar with the UK taxation system and relevant aspects of personal taxation including the calculation of income tax liabilities, discussed in Chapter 7.

Computation of profits

Persons are charged to income tax under Schedule D in respect of 'the annual profits or gains arising or accruing from any trade, profession or vocation'. 'Annual' in the context of the income tax legislation means 'of an income nature' and thus excludes capital gains.

Profits from carrying on a trade—a butcher, a baker, a candlestick maker—are charged under Schedule D case I, whereas Schedule D case II charges income tax on professions, i.e. the concept of an occupation requiring pure intellectual or controlled manual skills, and vocations which have from time to time been held to include, for example a dramatist, racing tipster, and jockey.

In most circumstances the distinction between Schedule D case I and D case II is one of fact, and the terms 'trade', 'professions', and 'vocations' will be treated as interchangeable for explanatory purposes.

Where a transaction gives rise to a profit or gain it does not automatically give rise to a charge under Schedule D cases I or II. The profit must have arisen from a trade which is being carried on, otherwise it will be assessed under Schedule D case VI, and the taxpayer will lose the advantages of it being classed as trading income for pension purposes. If a loss is involved, see later section for detail, the flexibility of a trading loss compared with a case VI loss is also lost to the taxpayer. Therefore, it seems critical to establish what constitutes a trade for tax purposes. The statutory definition of trade is 'including every trade, manufacture, adventure or concern in the nature of trade'. This is a very wide definition and may be described as hardly helpful. Every situation is one, primarily, of fact. Also resolution may be effected by reference to decided case law. However, there are a large number of decisions ranging over many years on the interpretation of the word 'trade' and the list is steadily growing longer. While it is encouraging that the veil of uncertainty is being steadily pushed back, a clear definition of trade appears to be a long way off. Nevertheless, in an attempt to clarify the situation, although admittedly many years ago, the 1954 Royal Commission listed 'six badges of trade' which ought to be considered when deciding whether a particular transaction is to be treated as an adventure in the nature of trade. These are:

(i) the subject matter of the realization,
(ii) the length of period of ownership,
(iii) the frequency or number of similar transactions by the same person,
(iv) supplementary work on or in connection with the property realized,
(v) the circumstances that were responsible for the realization,
(vi) the motive.

Obviously in most situations it is evident that a trade exists, even to the Inland Revenue; the discussion above is merely to outline an approach where there may be dispute between the taxpayer and the Inland Revenue. In considering the grey areas it may be useful to bear in mind the profit motive. Where profit motive is present in a transaction then there is a strong indication that a trade is being carried on.

Assuming it has been established a trade is being carried on, the next problem which is encountered is how to compute the profits which are assessable—the adjusted profits. Basically, profits should be computed in accordance with the principles of commercial accountancy unless there is a specific provision in the Taxes Acts which dictates a different treatment. Commercial accountancy in this context refers to the use of accepted accounting concepts and conventions which produce historic accounting profits. These historic accounting profits, with some adjustments, are then submitted to HM Inspector of Taxes and agreement is reached between the taxpayer or his advisor and the Inland Revenue as to the level of assessable profits. The effects and problems of taxing business profits on an historic cost basis is fully discussed in Chapter 5.

Clearly, the aim of the advisor and the Inland Revenue is the same—to measure profits for a period of time even though it be an arbitrary one such as a calendar year. However immediately this aim is recognized, it seems obvious that any accounting principle which contains an element of subjectivity will lead to a clash with tax law. Areas where this may exist are the valuation of stock and work in progress, the level of a bad debt provision, and the amount written off capital expenditure as depreciation over the lifetime of an asset. The taxpayer or his advisor no doubt knows of and may use any one of the many methods which will satisfactorily record the correct accounting entry for the arbitary time period. Obviously subjective accounting adjustments may have a major impact on commercial accounting profits so tax law, as far as possible, attempts to instil a measure of consistency and standardization to avoid undue manipulation of profits from one time period to the next. In the case of depreciation of a capital asset because the original sum is not chargeable against income, the periodic writing-off of part of the expenditure is debarred. However, in respect of certain capital expenditure the tax laws do allow a standardized system of depreciation to be used, referred to as capital allowances. This system will be examined in detail in a later section.

It should be stressed that except for the case of the very simple and small business unit, the commercial accounting profit is unlikely to be the same as the assessable (adjusted) profit. The main areas giving rise to the adjustments referred to earlier are illustrated in Table 8.1. Although this example is contrived it indicates important areas which give rise to conflict between commercial accounting practice and the tax laws and so necessitate different treatment.

In general terms, it may be seen that adjustments are required to exclude income from accounting profits which is not assessable under Schedule D cases I or II because it represents capital receipts or is assessable under some other schedule or case by statute laws. Additionally, expenditure falls into two categories (i) that which is correctly charged against profits for tax purposes (allowable) and (ii) that which is not (non-allowable).

TABLE 8.1. *Example of adjustments necessary to commercial accounting profits* (£)

(i) *Alec Philson profit and loss account*	
Net profit before crediting or charging the following	10,000
Add: rental income (a)	500
capital profit (b)	1,000
	11,500
Less: capital improvements expenditure (c)	(2,000)
entertaining (d)	(500)
proprietor's salary (e)	(5,000)
Net commercial profit	£4,000
(ii) *Alec Philson computation of assessable profit*	
Net commerical profit	4,000
Add: prohibited expenditure under Taxes Act (c) (d) (e)	7,500
	11,500
Less: income assessed under another schedule (a)	(500)
non-trading receipt (b)	(1,000)
Adjusted profit	£10,000

Non-allowable expenditure may be categorized as follows:

(i) Any expenditure which is not 'wholly and exclusively' incurred for the purposes of the trade.

(ii) Amounts paid which are appropriations of profit rather than expenses of earning profits (item e).

(iii) Capital expenditure as opposed to revenue expenditure. A more detailed consideration of the distinction will be made in a later section, but it is interesting to note at this point that although capital expenditure may be 'wholly and exclusively' incurred for business purposes it is nevertheless non-deductible in computing business profits (item c).

(iv) Certain other expenditure which is of a revenue nature and 'wholly and exclusively' incurred but is specifically disallowed by statute, for example business gifts and entertainment expenses (item d).

Now that we have outlined the principles which govern the allowability or otherwise of expenditure, the reader may find it useful to refer to Table 8.2 where a number of the more common allowable and non-allowable expenses are listed. It should be remembered this list is illustrative and not exhaustive.

Now is the time to consider a more detailed example of the adjustment of accountancy profits by analysing the case of Percy Osgood who has been trading as a retail greengrocer for many years. His most recent business accounts show the following trading and profit and loss account for the 12 months ended 30 June 19—:

		(£)
Sales		55,000
Cost of stock sold		(37,500)
Gross profit		17,500
Salaries	3,900	
Van and car expenses	675	
Rent and rates	2,500	
Depreciation of fixed assets	1,050	
Light and heat	250	
Sundry expenses	300	
		(8,675)
Net profit		8,825

The following additional information is available:

(i) Salaries are £50 per week to Percy and £25 per week to his wife who works about 20 hours each week in the shop.

(ii) Percy uses the van exclusively for business. The car is estimated to be used 20 per cent of the time for business purposes. The £675 van and car expenses are made up as follows:

	(£)
Van	400
Car	275

(iii) Percy and his wife occupy the flat above the shop. The floor areas of the flat and the shop are identical.

(iv) Sundry expenses are made up as follows:

	(£)
Entertaining local hotelier	30
Trade subscriptions	45
Cost of converting shed into storeroom	225

TABLE 8.2. *Examples of allowable and non-allowable expenditure for income tax purposes*

Allowable	Non-Allowable
Accountancy/audit fees	Annual payments made under duduction of tax
Approved pension fund contributions	
Bad debts written off/specific provision for bad debts	Bad debts general provision
Business travel	
	Capital expenditure including improvements
	Charitable donations
	Depreciation of capital assets
	Drawings on account of profits by proprietor
Contributions to approved local enterprise agency	Entertainment
	Fines and other penalties
	Gifts to customers
	Income tax
Cost of obtaining loan finance	Interest payments to proprietor
Interest on borrowed money	Legal expenses for acquisition of assets and other capital items
	Political party donations
Legal expenses for debt recovery, defence of trading rights, renewing a short lease (less than 50 years)	
National insurance contributions self-employed (part)	Proprietor's living expenses and private expenditure
Premium paid for business lease	
	Salary to proprietor
Repair expenditure	Taxation appeal costs
Rent of business premises	
Trade subscriptions	
VAT, if non-recoverable	
Wages to employees including employers' national insurance contributions	Travelling expenses from home to work
Wife's wages as employee	Wife's salary as partner

The suggested solution to this example is shown in Table 8.3, and the following narrative gives a detailed commentary on why each adjustment is made. It also enables the reader to appreciate the problem of duality which exists in some business expenditure.

(i) Clearly, the salary to Percy Osgood is an appropriation of profit and as such is non-allowable. This amount merely represents a division of the profits and if it had not been charged for accounting reasons then Osgood's profits would have been £2,600 higher. The salary to Mrs Osgood is allowable providing it is a reasonable payment for the services rendered and the amount of £25 per week is actually paid to her.

(ii) The car expenses, rent and rates, and light and heat expenditure all involve the common problem of mixed expenditure. With this type of expenditure it is indeed difficult to argue 'wholly and exclusively' for anyone or all of them. However, where it is possible to split such expenditure in a way so that the part which relates 'wholly' to business purposes is quantifiable then the test of exclusivity may be applied to that part only. In this case it is suggested agreement might be reached with HM Inspector of Taxes that any apportionment of rent and rates and light and heat might be on the basis of floor area occupied by the business and the Osgood family respectively. That part of expenditure which relates to the latter will be non-allowable. A similar approach is used for the apportionment of the car-running expenses. This represents a common situation in many small sole proprietor operations where the proprietor uses his own personal vehicle for business purposes in addition to any vehicle which is owned by and used exclusively in the business. Where there is a separate business vehicle the proportion of business use of the personal vehicle is in practice relatively small. The method adopted for apportionment is to establish Osgood's total car mileage in the year ended 30 June, say 20,000, and the business mileage included therein, say 4,000. This will establish 20 per cent business use and 80 per cent private use—a figure which

TABLE 8.3. *Computation of assessable profits for Percy Osgood* (£)

Profit for the 12 months ended 30 June 19—		8,825
Add: goods for own use		175
Add: non-allowable expenditure:		9,000
salary—self	2,600	
car expenses (80% × £275)	220	
rent and rates (50%)	1,250	
depreciation	1,050	
light and heat (50%)	125	
entertaining	30	
shed conversion—improvements	225	
Subtotal		5,500
Adjusted profit		£14,500

must then be negotiated with HM Inspector of Taxes. It should be noted that in this class of expenditure the allowable element is concessional and not mandatory.

(iii) Depreciation is as previously explained a non-allowable charge against income.

(iv) The entertaining expenditure although 'wholly and exclusively' in connection with the running of Osgood's trade is nevertheless specifically disallowed by statute. Generally it should be observed that business entertainment, including hospitality of any kind, is non-allowable unless it applies to staff or overseas customers or their non-ordinarily resident agents. Definitely not relevant in this case! Gifts fall within the definition of entertainment unless they do not consist of food, drink, or tobacco, carry an easily read advertisement, and cost less than a specified sum per recipient per annum. Perhaps Percy Osgood might be advised to consider gifts of calendars or diaries next year.

(v) Sums incurred on improvements are considered to be capital payments and therefore non-allowable.

Finally, one further explanation is needed to complete this example. It will be seen that a further addition to accounting profits is necessary to record the value of goods taken from stock by Osgood for himself and his family. As a retailer this addition is the retail value of stock so taken and is one commonly insisted upon by the Inland Revenue in small retailing organizations such as greengrocers, grocers, and tobacconists. However, the adjustment must not be made where the proprietor has correctly recorded in the sales figure the retail value of the goods taken.

Basis of assessment

Having explored how profits are computed for assessment under cases I or II of Schedule D we must now turn to how such profits are assessed to income tax. It should be observed at this point that throughout the remainder of this chapter the term profits refers to the adjusted profits of a business. The rules for the assessment of profits are both comprehensive and complex due to the fact that the method of assessment used is the previous year basis. We will commence the analysis by looking at what is referred to in the legislation as the normal basis of assessment—tax is charged for a year of assessment but the profits on which tax is payable are those of a basis period which is the accounting year ended in the previous year of assessment. This rather torturous phraseology contains two fundamental points which it is necessary to grasp for a full understanding of the assessment of unincorporated businesses at various stages in their life cycle. Fig. 8.1 is a diagrammatic illustration of the law and brings into focus the fundamental importance of the terms basis period and accounting year. As will be noted, despite holding the year of assessment for which tax will be charged constant at 1987/8 the basis

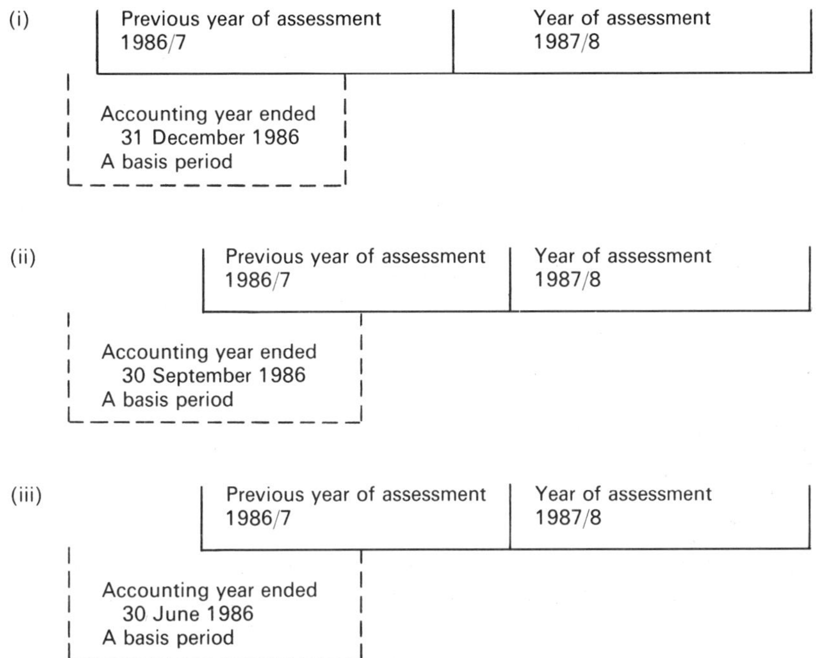

Fig. 8.1 Diagrammatic illustration of the normal basis of assessment under Schedule D cases I and II

period in the previous year of assessment 1986/7 may be any accounting year of twelve months ended between 6 April 1986 and 5 April 1987. The extreme cases are, of course, twelve-month accounting years ended on those dates both of which form the basis period for assessment in 1987/8. A further worked example of the previous year basis of assessment, basis periods, and accounting years is shown in Table 8.4 where it will be seen, in the Mercer and Cresswell situations, that despite having accounting years which end some six months apart each trader will be assessed on identical profits in the same year of assessments merely because the basis periods are common. However, contrast very carefully the Cresswell/Hogan examples where it must be observed that although the accounting years end only one day apart, because the basis periods are not common, i.e. Cresswell's profits for year ended 6 April 1986 fall within the tax year 1986/7 (admittedly only just) whereas Hogan's 1986 year-end falls within 1985/6 (completely), the years of assessment on identical profits are dissimilar. At first these points may appear trivial, but in terms of cash flows Hogan will pay tax on his £7,000 profits one year earlier than either Cresswell or Mercer. The issue of accounting dates and tax payment dates will be explored fully in Chapter 16, but the reader may wish to verify the above observation by reference to Table 7.8 in the previous chapter

TABLE 8.4. *Example of years of assessment and basis periods for different accounting years*

Mercer year ended 30 September

1986	Profits	£7,000
1987	Profits	£8,000

Year of assessment	Basis period	Assessment (£)
1987/8	falling in 1986/7 year ended 30 September 1986	7,000
1988/9	falling in 1987/8 year ended 30 September 1987	8,000

Cresswell year ended 6 April

1986	Profits	£7,000
1987	Profits	£8,000

Year of assessment	Basis period	Assessment (£)
1987/8	falling in 1986/7 year ended 6 April 1986	7,000
1988/9	falling in 1987/8 year ended 6 April 1987	8,000

Hogan year ended 5 April

1986	Profits	£7,000
1987	Profits	£8,000

Year of assessment	Basis period	Assessment (£)
1986/7	falling in 1985/6 year ended 5 April 1986	7,000
1987/8	falling in 1986/7 year ended 5 April 1987	8,000

and also investigate what cash flow advantage Cresswell has over Mercer although their profits of £7,000 are both assessable in 1987/8.

The above set of rules clearly recognizes that unincorporated businesses have complete freedom as to the date up to which they make up their accounts, but they do require that the accounts are for twelve months—no more, no less—and the accounting years are consecutive, i.e. twelve months ended 31 December 1986 is followed by the twelve months commencing 1 January 1987 and ending 31 December 1987 and so on. Although these rules will work perfectly well for a business which has been trading for a number of years there are three specific occasions when they may not apply:

(i) on the commencement of a business,
(ii) on the permanent cessation of a business, and
(iii) where the accounting date is permanently changed.

These are diagrammatically illustrated in Fig. 8.2. Obviously there would be problems if the Inland Revenue were to attempt to apply the normal rules:

(i) Where the business commenced on 1 October 1986 the accounting year ended September 1988 will form the basis period for 1989/90, but how is the September 1987 year treated? There is no earlier accounting year and therefore no continuity.

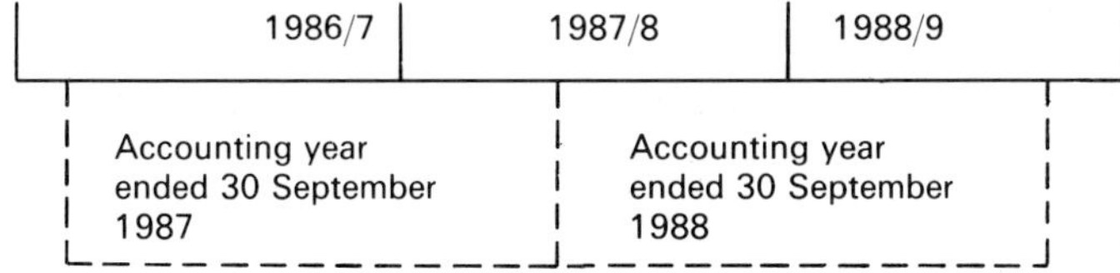

(ii) A business ceased trading on 30 September 1987 having traded for many years

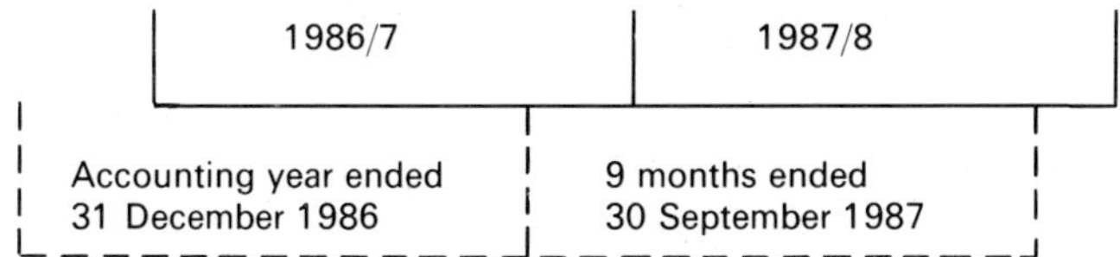

(iii) A business permanently changes its accounting date from 30 June to 31 December

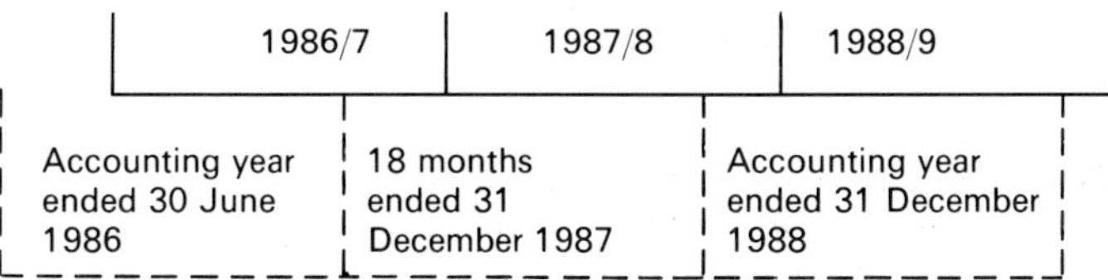

Fig. 8.2 Diagrammatic illustration of situations where normal basis of assessment cannot apply

(ii) In this situation the accounting year ended December 1986 will be the basis period for 1987/8 but what after that? Although there is continuity the final trading period is less than twelve months.

(iii) The normal previous year basis rules will establish the accounting year June 1986 as the basis period for 1987/8 and the new accounting year December 1988 as that for 1989/90, but what profits are assessed for 1988/9? One way of approaching this situation would be to merely take 12/18ths of the December 1987 profits. However, a 'gap' of six months would then exist, continuity is lost, and worst of all, from the Inland Revenue viewpoint, although of course not the taxpayer, some profits would escape assessment.

All of these special situations are dealt with in the legislation and the rules may be summarized as follows.

(i) Commencement rules

Year of assessment	*Basis Period*
Year one	Profits from date of commencement to the immediately following 5 April
Year two	Profits of the first twelve months trading
Year three	(a) Where there is an accounting year of twelve months ended in assessment year two, use that accounting year. (b) If there is no accounting year of twelve months ended in assessment year two, the profit of the first twelve months is taken again.

The operation of these rules is illustrated in Table 8.5 where a trade commenced on 1 October 1986. Profits for the years ended 30 September 1987 and 1988 are £4,000 and £8,000, respectively.

TABLE 8.5. *Example of commencement rules with opening twelve months accounting year*

Year of assessment	Basis period	Assessment (£)
1986/7 (year one)	01.10.86–05.04.87 (6/12 × £4,000)	2,000
1987/8 (year two)	01.10.86–30.09.87 first twelve months	4,000
1988/9 (year three)	01.10.86–30.09.87 accounting year twelve months ended in 1987/8	4,000
1989/90	01.10.87–30.09.88 normal previous year basis	8,000

It should be noted, from this example, that year one is invariably on an actual basis, while year three will, where the first period of trading is twelve months, almost certainly be on the normal previous year basis. The position where the first period of trading is less than twelve months is shown in Table 8.6. It is assumed the trade commenced on 1 January 1987, and it is intended to have an annual accounting date of 30 September in each year. The profits for the nine months ended 30 September 1987 and twelve months ended 30 September 1988 are £3,600 and £8,000, respectively. In this situation the particular point to note is that in year three (1988/9) it is not possible to apply the normal previous year basis, and so the basis period is established under alternative rule (b) above.

In general terms, it will have been noticed that in the early years of assessment of an unincorporated business it is necessary to apportion profits on a time basis in order to comply with the rules. This approach makes the assumption that profits accrue evenly month by month with no allowances for seasonal fluctuations. In practice the Inland Revenue will tend to allow calculations to be made to the nearest month unless the fractions of a month are material, for example profits are in £m and not £thousands. However, a more important observation to be made is that where the commencement rules are applied some profits are used more than once in establishing assessable profits—a distinct disadvantage to the taxpayer. Nevertheless, it should be pointed out that providing profits are increasing year by year there is some alleviation in that assessable profits are less than current earned profits. However, where profits after an initially good first year of trading,

TABLE 8.6. *Example of commencement rules with opening accounting year less than twelve months*

Year of assessment	Basis period		Assessment (£)
1986/7 (year one)	01.01.87–05.04.87		
	(3/9 × £3,600)		1,200
1987/8 (year two)	01.01.87–31.12.87		
	9 months to 30.09.87	3,600	
	3 months to 31.12.87		
	(i.e. 3/12 × £8,000)	2,000	5,600
1988/9 (year three)	01.01.87–31.12.87 first twelve months again as there is no twelve month accounting year ended in 1987/8		5,600
1989/90	01.10.87–30.09.88 normal previous year basis		8,000

decline drastically, severe hardship would result in that the business is faced with multiple assessments on those high profits and correspondingly large tax bills at a time when it can least afford the cash outflows. Fortunately the legislation acknowledges such a position can arise and affords the taxpayer an option whereby an election may be made to have the profits, assessable in years of assessment two and three, adjusted. This is achieved by establishing a new set of basis periods which effectively produce an actual basis of assessment. The operation of this optional basis of assessment for second and third years is shown in Table 8.7 and is calculated for a business which commenced on 1 October 1986. Profits for the three years ended 30 September 1987, 1988, and 1989 are £4,000, £500, and £8,000.

From the data in Table 8.7 it should be noted carefully that only the assessments for the years two (1987/8) and three (1988/9) are altered under the option rules. The calculations for the first year (which is always on an actual basis in any case) and fourth and fifth years are included merely to emphasize this point and also record that, even under these rules, some profits are nevertheless assessed more than once, although the effect has been minimized as far as possible. Next, the reader should observe a further fundamental point in that the election, if made, applies to both years of assessment and not just

TABLE 8.7. *Example of adjustment of second and third years of assessment to actual*

Year of assessment	Basis period		Assessment (£)
Standard commencement rules			
1986/7 (year one)	01.10.86–05.04.87		2,000
1987/8 (year two)	01.10.86–30.09.87		4,000
1988/9 (year three)	01.10.86–30.09.87		4,000
1989/90	01.10.87–30.09.88		500
1990/1	01.10.88–30.09.89		8,000
Taxpayer's option rules			
1986/7 (year one)	01.10.86–05.04.87		2,000
1987/8 (year two)	06.04.87–30.09.87		
	(6/12 × £4,000)	2,000	
	01.10.87–05.04.88		
	(6/12 × £500)	250	2,250
1988/9 (year three)	06.04.88–30.09.88		
	(6/12 × £500)	250	
	01.10.88–05.04.89		
	(6/12 × £8,000)	4,000	
			4,250
1989/90	01.10.87–30.09.88		500
1990/1	01.10.88–30.9.89		8,000

one. Thus, our taxpayer could not apply an actual basis to 1987/8 and leave 1988/9 on the previous year basis. It is, unfortunately, an all or nothing option. Both years must be compared in aggregate and where there is a net reduction overall, in this case £1,500, the election may then be made. The legislation specifies that the election must be made within seven years of the end of the second year of assessment which in this illustration is by 5 April 1995. This is not an irrevocable election, and if circumstances made it necessary to do so it could be revoked within six years of the end of the third year of assessment, i.e. 5April 1995.

(ii) Permanent cessation rules

Year of Assessment	*Basis period*
Ultimate year	Profits from 6 April immediately preceding to date of cessation
Penultimate year	Normal previous year basis
Antepenultimate year	Normal previous year basis

Table 8.8 contains an example of how these rules operate and is based upon a sole trader who has traded for many years to 31 December and chooses to permanently discontinue his trade on 30 September 1987. The profits profile for the last four years and nine months has been:

		(£)
Year ended 31 December	1983	10,000
	1984	12,000
	1985	18,000
	1986	24,000
Nine months to 30 September	1987	18,000

The most important and immediate observation which should strike the reader is that not only do the profits for the year ended 31 December 1986 no longer form the basis period for 1987/8 but also they cease to be assessed at all. Additionally, part of the profits 1 January to 5 April 1987 also escape. Recalling that in the early years of assessment some profits are assessed twice over it would not be an unreasonable conclusion to draw that perhaps after all there is some equity in tax law. However, where profits rise substantially in the closing years of a business the Inland Revenue have a similar option to that of the taxpayer in the opening years. The legislation provides effectively that the Inland Revenue is able to decide which profits escape assessment by adjusting the basis periods of the penultimate and antepenultimate years of assessment to actual. Assuming the Inland Revenue applies this optional approach the results are depicted in Table 8.8. Clearly, two issues emerge from the application of the optional rules:

(i) Some profits have still escaped assessment although the amount is now reduced to those for the year ended 31 December 1984 and the period 1 January to 5 April 1985.

TABLE 8.8. *Example of standard permanent cessation rules and Inland Revenue option*

Year of assessment	Basis period		Assessment (£)
Standard cessation rules			
1987/8 (ultimate year)	06.04.87–30.09.87 (6/9 × £18,000) actual basis		12,000
1986/7 (penultimate year)	01.01.85–31.12.85 normal previous year basis		18,000
1985/6 (antepenultimate year)	01.01.84–31.12.84 normal previous year basis		12,000
1984/5	01.01.83–31.12.83 normal previous year basis		10,000
Inland Revenue option rules			
1987/8 (ultimate year)	06.04.87–30.09.87		12,000
1986/7 (penultimate year)	01.01.87–05.04.87		
	(3/9 × £18,000)	6,000	
	06.04.86–31.12.86		
	(9/12 × £24,000)	18,000	
			24,000
1985/6 (antepenultimate year)	01.01.86–05.04.86		
	(3/12 × £24,000)	6,000	
	06.04.85–31.12.85		
	(9/12 × £18,000)	13,500	
			19,500
1984/5	01.01.83–31.12.83		10,000

(ii) It is only the penultimate and antepenultimate years of assessment which are affected.

Finally, as with the taxpayer's option in early years, the Inland Revenue must apply its right to both years involved or neither.

(iii) Permanent changes of accounting date

The detailed provisions and calculations are beyond the scope of this book but the 'gap' referred to in Fig 8.2, i.e. profits which would escape assessment in 1988/9 is minimized by a combination of legislation and Inland Revenue practice. It should be noted also that in some circumstances a change of accounting date could also result in some profits being assessed twice. Thus, the operation of law and practice is an attempt to introduce a measure of equity into the situation. This is achieved in general terms, by establishing a basis year with reference to the new permanent accounting date to be used for the 1988/9 assessment followed by the construction of a corresponding period computed by reference to a notional trading year ended 31 December 1986 to adjust the previous year's assessment 1987/8 and averaging profits as necessary. The Inland Revenue will not make adjustments unless the sums involved are significant.

Relief for capital expenditure

As outlined in the section on computation of profits, expenditure of a capital nature was not chargeable against those profits although being 'wholly and exclusively' incurred for the purposes of the business. Clearly, a definition of capital expenditure would be useful. However, the task of differentiating between revenue and capital expenditure is not easy in real life as is evidenced by the large number of cases which have appeared before the courts to settle disputes between the Inland Revenue and the taxpayer. Three important tests emerge from the morass of case law, namely the distinction between fixed and circulating capital, the enduring benefit principle, and the isolation and correct identification of assets. Therefore, for the purposes of this section capital expenditure may, as a rough yardstick, be represented by sums laid out or spent on assets which are intended to have a degree of permanency or durability within the operations of the business.

We now move on to consideration of the system whereby relief for capital expenditure is given against profits. If relief is given, and it is not given for all capital expenditure, it is by the means of a standardized form of depreciation referred to as capital allowances. As a general point it should be noted that capital allowances are given as a deduction in the assessment, not in computing the profits on which the assessment is based. This incidentally is not so in the case of corporation tax (see Chapter 10).

Over the years the Government has recognized it is important for commerce and industry to invest capital sums and from the immediate Post-World War II era to the current time a number of different incentives have been tried.

These have ranged from simple annual allowances and accelerated allowances (such as investment, initial, and first year allowances which give tax relief for each capital £ spent at the firm's marginal rate of tax) to direct grant aid such as investment grants and regional development grants. The former type of incentive, i.e. capital allowances, has been the more enduring, despite many changes in the type of allowance given and is considered so important that the detail is contained in a separate piece of legislation—the Capital Allowances Act 1968.

This act, together with modifications and additions by subsequent Finance Acts, specifies a wide range of capital expenditure which does qualify for capital allowances. The more important classifications of capital expenditure which attract allowances are:

(a) plant and machinery
(b) industrial buildings
(c) agricultural buildings
(d) hotels
(e) various buildings in enterprise zones

The rates of allowances are shown in Table 8.9.

Already we are in a position to conclude that expenditure on the acquisition of shop premises to carry on a retail trade is, even by our earlier crude definition, capital expenditure, but there is no provision for capital allowances thereon unless it happens to be situated in an enterprise zone. The point being made here is that capital expenditure which merely consists of a background or setting to the trade being carried on will not generally attract capital allowances. This point will be considered further in the section on plant and machinery below.

(a) Plant and machinery

The largest problem confronting us is that the words plant and machinery are not defined by statute. However, the generally accepted starting point as regards plant is contained in a case decided some one hundred years ago. 'There is no definition of plant in the Act; but in its ordinary sense, it includes whatever apparatus is used by a businessman for carrying on his business—not his stock in trade which he buys or makes for sale; but all goods and

TABLE 8.9. *Rates of capital allowances on various capital expenditure from 1 April 1986*

	% per annum
Plant and machinery	25 writing-down allowance
Industrial buildings	4 writing-down allowance
Agricultural buildings	4 writing-down allowance
Hotels	4 writing-down allowance
Various buildings in an enterprise zone	100 (max) initial allowance
	25 writing-down allowance

Notes:

(i) Prior to 1 April 1986 the above expenditures were entitled to accelerated capital allowances known as first year allowance in the case of plant and machinery and initial allowances for industrial, agricultural, and hotel buildings. These forms of capital allowances were phased out in stages between 14 March 1984 and 31 March 1986 by the 1984 Finance Act.

(ii) The changes in capital allowance rates were not applied to buildings within an enterprise zone.

chattels, fixed or moveable, live or dead, which he keeps for permanent employment in his business' (*Yarmouth* v. *France*, 1887). In more recent cases, apart from the fact of durability, capital assets must, it would appear, also pass a functional test of active use within the business to qualify as plant. Thus, it would be tempting to assume that buildings or parts thereof, apart from those which attract special capital allowancces or are situated in enterprise zones, do not qualify as plant and therefore for capital allowances. This is true in essence, but Table 8.10 shows in a number of situations the courts have decided otherwise. Since we now have a working definition of plant and on the presumption that the concept of a machine or machinery is understandable, it is important to consider the principles of how relief for capital allowances is given and indeed withdrawn by a balancing charge where a capital asset is disposed of.

Capital allowances known as writing-down allowances are calculated on plant and machinery at the rate of 25 per cent per annum on a reducing balance method by reference to the written-down value or qualifying expenditure brought forward from the previous period. For many years it has been possible to deal generally, there are some exceptions, with all plant and machinery acquired by a business on a collective basis known as pooling, i.e. as assets are acquired their original cost less any year of acquisition allowance is merged into a pool of qualifying expenditure and a separate monetary value lost. Prior to March 1984, when a special first year allowance of 100 per cent was given on capital expenditure incurred, the value of the plant and machinery pool from year to year was zero or negligible, but as a consequence of these capital allowances being phased out by 31 March 1986 the pool value will in the future record an upward trend in value where businesses regularly invest in capital equipment. The rate of 25 per cent will also be applied in the year of purchase to expenditure incurred on or after 1 April 1986.

As implied earlier, capital allowances are calculated for years of assessment not for accounting periods. Nevertheless, reference is made to the relevant basis period for a year of assessment when calculating the writing-down values

Table 8.10. *Some capital assets which have been classified as either actively involved in business or passively present*

Active involvement (i.e. plant)	Passive presence (i.e. non-plant)
Moveable partitions in an office building	A garage canopy over service area
A dry dock for ship repairs	A spectator stand at a football stadium
A swimming pool at a caravan site	A barge used as a floating restaurant
Lighting and decor in restaurant to create 'atmosphere'	False ceilings in a catering establishment to conceal pipes, etc.

on either additional plant and machinery or pool values brought forward. For most continuing businesses the basis period will be the accounting period on the profits of which the assessment is based. Thus, if the accounts are made up regularly to 31 December, the basis period for 1988/9 is the accounting year ended 31 December 1987. The general principles outlined above are illustrated in Table 8.11 which is based upon the following data relevant to the trading activities of Jeff Hall whose annual accounting date is and has been 31 December for many years. During the years ended 31 December 1987 and 1988 his profits were £15,000 and £20,000, respectively.

During the year 1987 he acquired plant and machinery costing £5,000 and in the subsequent year further expenditure of £10,000 was incurred on similar assets. The Schedule D case I or II assessments raised on Jeff Hall therefore become, 1988/9, profits £15,000 less capital allowances £1,375 and for 1989/90, profits £20,000 less capital allowances £3,531. It should be noted that the 25 per cent writing-down allowance is a maximum claim for the year of assessment and need not be claimed in full or at all where the trader's profits are small and wholly covered by personal allowances. This topic will be explored further in the section on losses later in this chapter.

From time to time a business will dispose of capital assets. Where the disposal relates to an item which has been 'pooled' in earlier years, the disposal value of the asset restricted to original cost, if necessary, (see Chapter 9 on

Table 8.11. *Example of capital allowances available on plant and machinery*

Jeff Hall—Capital allowances computation

Year of assessment for allowances	Basis period for allowances	Plant and machinery pool (£)
1988/9	01.01.87–31.12.87	
	value brought forward[a] (say)	500
	additions in basis period	5,000
		5,500
	writing-down allowance (25%)	(1,375)
	value carried forward	4,125
1989/90	01.01.88–31.12.88	
	additions in basis period	10,000
		14,125
	writing-down allowances (25%)	(3,531)
	value carried forward	£10,594

[a] This value may be expressed as brought forward at 6 April 1988 or 1 January 1987 and be referred to as qualifying expenditure brought forward on plant and machinery. The dating and terminology is interchangeable in practice.

capital gains tax) is deducted from the value of the pool brought forward. The effect of this adjustment is to reclaim excess allowances given in past years. It makes no difference that the contribution of the asset to the value of the pool brought forward is nil through the operation of a 100 per cent first year allowance in an earlier period. Therefore, if we continue the Jeff Hall example and assume in the year ended 31 December 1989 he sells for £2,000 an item of plant which costs £15,000 in 1983 the capital allowances claim for 1990/1 would be £2,148 computed as follows:

Pool of plant and machinery, brought forward	£10,594
Less: sale in basis period 1.1.89–31.12.89	(2,000)
	8,594
Less: writing-down allowance (25%)	(2,148)
Value, carried forward	£6,446

In certain situations a balancing charge may arise by reason of the disposal value exceeding the pool value brought forward. Supposing in this example Jeff had sold the item of plant for £20,000. Remembering to exclude the capital profit of £5,000, i.e. disposal value £20,000 less original cost £15,000, the capital allowances computation would read:

Pool of plant and machinery, brought forward	£10,594
Less: sale in basis period 1.1.89–31. 12. 89	(15,000)
Balancing charge	£4,406

The balancing charge of £4,406 will be added to the profit of the year ended 31 December 1989 as part of the 1990/1 Schedule D cases I or II assessment. Specifically the reader should note that in the latter example there will be no pool value to carry forward for the 1991/2 capital allowances computation. Generally, it is useful to observe that with the abolition of 100 per cent first year allowances the chances of a balancing charge arising in future years is less likely for most businesses.

In the special situation of a business permanently ceasing to trade either there will be a balancing charge or another form of capital allowance could arise. This special allowance is referred to in the legislation as a balancing allowance and arises where the final disposal value of capital assets in the pool is less than the value brought forward, i.e. an additional allowance for assets not fully depreciated. No writing-down allowances are calculated for the ultimate year of assessment, but any balancing allowance will be given as a deduction against profits of the basis period for that ultimate year of assessment.

The permanent cessation of an unincorporated business or indeed the commencement gives rise to a further problem in the calculation of capital allowances which stems from the special rules for the assessment of profits summarized earlier in Tables 8.5, 8.7, and 8.8. After careful study it will be observed that basis periods overlap, where the same profits are assessed more than once, in start up situations and leave gaps in permanent cessations. Therefore, it might be tempting to assume that capital expenditure at the outset of the business could be treated as incurred two to three times over and in the case of permanent cessation sales could be timed to coincide with the gap where profits escape assessment, i.e. 1 January 1986 to 5 April 1987 or in the Inland Revenue option 1 January 1984 to 5 April 1985. Nevertheless, the legislation has been too tightly drawn to allow these obvious loopholes to be exploited. The additional rules laid down which identify basis period and year of assessment for expenditure and disposal purposes may be summarized as follows:

(i) Where two basis periods overlap, the period common to both is deemed to fall in the first period only.
(ii) Where there is a gap between two basis periods, then
  (a) If the second of the basis periods is the year in which the business is assessed as discontinued, the period of the gap is added to the first of the basis periods in question.
  (b) In any other case, the period of the gap is added to the second of the basis periods.

This all looks extremely complex but is capable of translation into understandable language by reference to the data given in Table 8.12 and the following additional information.

In scenario (i) as the period 1.10.86 to 5.4.87 is common to 1986/7, 1987/8, and 1988/9 rule (i) above applies, and any expenditure incurred between those two dates is deemed to qualify for capital allowances from 1986/7 onwards. The period 6.4.87 to 30.9.87 is common to both 1987/8 and 1988/9 and again rule (i) applies. Thus, expenditure between these latter dates qualifies for capital allowances from 1987/8 forward. The reader should note that no additional expenditure can be added to the pool for calculation of 1988/9 capital allowances, but writing-down allowances are given on the value of the pool brought forward from 1987/8.

In scenario (ii) the changes in the basis periods made necessary by the election to actual for 1987/8 and 1988/9 should be closely observed. Again rule (i) is being applied. Clearly, capital expenditure incurred from 1.10.87 to 30.9.88 will qualify for capital allowances against profits somewhat earlier—either in 1987/8 or 1988/9 dependent on the precise date the expenditure is incurred. It should be pointed out that this may give rise to a major recalculation of capital allowances in the opening four or five years of assessment.

The third scenario (iii) has a gap from 1.1.86 to 5.4.87 which is added under rule (iia) to the first basis period, namely 1.1.85 to 31.12.85 as the second basis period 6.4.87 to 30.9.87 is the year in which discontinuance takes place.

Had the assessments for 1985/6 and 1986/7 been recalculated on an actual basis under the Inland Revenue option for the penultimate and antepenultim-

TABLE 8.12. *Example of special rules for basis periods and capital allowances*

Year of assessment	Basis period for profits	Basis period for capital allowances
(i) A business commencing 1 October 1986 and making up accounts to 30 September in future.		
1986/7	01.10.86–05.04.87	01.10.86–05.04.87
1987/8	01.10.86–30.09.87	06.04.87–30.09.87
1988/9	01.10.86–30.09.87	nil
1989/90	01.10.87–30.09.88	01.10.87–30.09.88
(ii) Same commencement and annual accounting dates as above, but taxpayer's election made for 1987/8 and 1988/9 assessments to be based on actual.		
1986/7	01.10.86–05.04.87	01.10.86–05.04.87
1987/8	06.04.87–05.04.88	06.04.87–05.04.88
1988/9	06.04.88–05.04.89	06.04.88–05.04.89
1989/90	01.10.87–30.09.88	nil
1990/1	01.10.88–30.09.89	06.04.89–30.09.89
(iii) A business making up accounts to 31 December is permanently discontinued on 30 September 1987.		
1987/8	06.04.87–30.09.87	06.04.87–30.09.87
1986/7	01.01.85–31.12.85	01.01.85–05.04.87
1985/6	01.01.84–31.12.84	01.01.84–31.12.84
1984/5	01.01.83–31.12.83	01.01.83–31.12.83

ate years, the gap would have been from 1.1.84 to 5.4.85 and would have been added under rule (iib) to the second basis period, namely 6.4.85 to 5.4.86. Thus, the final basis periods in this fourth scenario would be:

1987/8	6 April 1987 to 30 September 1987
1986/7	6 April 1986 to 5 April 1987
1985/6	1 January 1984 to 5 April 1986
1984/5	1 January 1983 to 31 December 1983,

which differ considerably from those in scenario three and again it could involve a major recalculation of the plant and machinery pool where there have been many acquisitions or sales of capital assets in the gap periods.

Earlier it was mentioned that there were some exceptions to plant and machinery expenditure which could be included in the pool of qualifying expenditure. These exceptions which are designed principally to cater for assets in special categories, are as follows:

(i) short life assets acquired on or after 1 April 1986,
(ii) any asset used partly for non-business purposes,

(iii) cars costing more than £8,000,
(iv) motor cars acquired on or after 1 April 1986 which prior to that date would not have qualified for first year allowance.

It might be added that by keeping a separate record of year by year capital allowances on these assets avoids the necessity, in practice, of numerous subsidiary calculations when disposal takes place.

A brief description of non-pooled assets now follows:

(i) The short life asset legislation was introduced by the 1985 Finance Act to enable a business to obtain full relief for capital expenditure over the life of the asset. A separate pool for each short life asset is established and providing an asset is disposed of within five years for less than the written-down value of its separate pool, a balancing allowance will arise which enhances the capital allowances due on the general pool expenditure for the appropriate year of assessment. As explained earlier balancing allowances will not arise on the general pool unless a permanent cessation of the business occurs. It should be noted that a balancing charge could arise where disposal value exceeds the separate pool value. Where no disposal takes place within the five-year period the written-down value on the separate pool will be transferred to the general pool. Taxpayers must make the election for each asset they require to be dealt with on this special basis within two years of the end of the accounting (basis) period in which the expenditure was incurred. Once made the election is irrevocable. Finally, this treatment cannot be applied to any asset which falls into categories (ii), (iii), and (iv).

(ii) In circumstances where an asset is used partly for non-business purposes for example a vehicle used by a sole trader or partner for private mileage, a separate pool must be established for each such asset. Thus, in a partnership of five persons each with a vehicle and some element of private use, there would need to be five additional columns of calculations to establish capital allowances due on each vehicle. Additionally, the writing-down allowance for the appropriate year of assessment must be restricted to ensure that only the proportion of allowances applicable to business use are given against trading profits. The manner by which this is achieved is shown in Table 8.13 whereby it will be seen that the full allowances are deducted in the main body but only £1,150 of writing-down allowances will be given against Brown's 1987/8 Schedule D case I assessment. Where a subsequent disposal takes place of either of these vehicles any balancing allowance or balancing charge will be similarly adjusted to the business proportion.

(iii) Cars which cost more than £8,000, whether they have private use or not, must also be kept in a separate pool—again a pool for each such vehicle. With this class of asset the writing-down allowance is restricted to £2,000 or 25 per cent of the pool value brought forward, whichever is the smaller. If we assume that the second vehicle which Brown purchased cost £10,000 in the year ended

TABLE 8.13. *Example of adjustment of capital allowances where assets are used partly for non-business purposes*

Edward Brown has traded for many years. During the year ended 31 December 1986 he acquired a second vehicle for £6,000. Business usage of vehicles as agreed with HM Inspector of Taxes is: vehicle one 80%; vehicle two 50%.
The calculation of capital allowances for 1987/8 is:

	Vehicle one (£)	*Vehicle two* (£)
Value brought forward (say)	2,000	—
Addition in basis period	—	6,000
Writing-down allowances (25%)	(500) × 80% = 400	(1,500) × 50% = 750
Value carried forward	1,500	4,500

31 December 1986 the capital allowances computation for 1987/8 and the following two years would have read:

	(£)	*Allowed* (£)
Addition in basis period	10,000	
1987/8 writing-down allowance (25%) but limited to	(2,000) × 50%	= 1,000
	8,000	
1988/9 writing-down allowance (25%)	(2,000) × 50%	= 1,000
	6,000	
1989/90 writing-down allowance (25%)	(1,500) × 50%	= 750
Value carried forward	£4,500	

When the car is sold a balancing allowance or charge will arise. It should be emphasized that any car which costs more than £8,000 must be dealt with on a separate pool per asset basis the question of non-business use being only incidental to the general illustration.

(iv) For many years prior to 1 April 1986 motor cars including estate cars were considered generally not to qualify for first year allowances and from June 1980 it was enacted that all such cars should form part of a special car pool rather than merge into the general plant and machinery pool. Although first year allowances were discontinued on 31 March 1986 it would appear that separate pooling will still apply to motor cars. However, it should be noted that this piece of legislation only applies to cars costing less than £8,000, where there is no private use by the proprietor and prior to 1 April 1986 they would not have qualified for first year allowances. Therefore, in general we are referring in this section to cars which are relatively inexpensive and provided by the employer for employees, for example a fleet of estate cars for sales representatives. The most important point to appreciate is that the special car pool is an aggregate situation similar to the general plant and machinery pool, i.e. a separate record for each car does not need to be kept as in (i), (ii), and (iii) above. Thus, acquisitions and disposals will be adjusted on the separate pool value brought forward (which might represent the unexpired expenditure on several cars) after which the normal 25 per cent writing-down allowance will be calculated. It should be noted that although it is possible for a balancing charge to arise, a balancing allowance will only be given on the permanent cessation of a trade. Now compare this position carefully with categories (i), (ii), and (iii) above and with the general plant and machinery pool as regards balancing adjustments.

(b) Industrial buildings

Unlike the case of plant and machinery, the statute law does provide a definition of an industrial building, albeit that the wording contained in the Capital Allowances Act 1968 is both long and complicated. However, an industrial building is basically one which is in use for the carrying on of a qualifying trade such as operations in a mill or factory and which tend to cover the trades of manufacturing or processing goods or materials. Manufacturers' warehouses which are used to store raw materials for processing or undelivered finished goods are included, but a wholesale warehouse is excluded. Generally, free-standing offices, showrooms, and shops are excluded (but see section on enterprise zones). However, a drawing office has been considered to be ancillary to a manufacturing process despite being a separate structure from the workshops (*CIR* v. *Lambhill Ironworks*, 1950). Conversely where an office is an integral part of the qualifying building, providing the expenditure relative to that office does not exceed 25 per cent of the cost of the whole structure, the whole building will be treated as an industrial building.

From 1 April 1986 the only capital allowance available on industrial buildings (other than within an enterprise zone) is an annual writing-down allowance, on qualifying expenditure incurred, of 4 per cent per annum. However, in contrast to plant and machinery allowances, the 4 per cent is calculated on a straight-line basis year on year and perhaps more importantly will only be given for years of assessment where the building is in use for a qualifying purpose at the end of the relevant basis period. Clearly, the intention is that the qualifying expenditure will be written off over a period of 25 years. One further point to note in connection with the writing-down allowances is that the 4 per cent rate is only available on new qualifying capital expenditure; it does not apply to costs of second-hand industrial buildings.

Mention has been made above to qualifying expenditure which for the purposes of this relief can be broadly taken to mean, where the taxpayer himself erects the structure, the costs of construction including land preparation, for example levelling and footings but excluding the cost of the land. The main principles of industrial buildings allowance on a new structure are now presented in Table 8.14 and are based on the expenditure of Walter Halford, a manufacturer who has traded for many years.

The relevant data for the computation is:

(a) Expenditure incurred in year ended 31 March

1987	Land	£90,000
1988	Construction Costs	£45,000
1989	Construction Costs	£52,500
1990	Construction Costs	£22,500

(b) The factory was completed on 30 November 1989 and in use shortly after.

(c) The construction costs included £20,000 relative to the administration office which was an integral part of the factory structure.

In the case of new buildings it may be that the first user, in our example Halford, may not want the problems associated with construction. Therefore, Halford may (a) have engaged a builder or alternatively (b) purchased from another person. In either of these other situations the qualifying expenditure, in each case excluding the cost of land, will be (a) the purchase price or (b) the lower of the purchase price or the cost of construction. In the Halford example he acquired what is referred to in the legislation as a 'relevant interest' in the building. In the main example this was because he incurred the expenditure personally, but it is also possible to acquire a relevant interest by purchase as outlined in the alternatives. Finally, Halford may have also established a relevant interest by taking a long lease on the premises from the owner. The granting of writing-down allowances on industrial buildings assumes that the first user will continue to carry on a qualifying trade for the full 25 years or

TABLE 8.14. *Example of general principles of industrial buildings allowance on a new qualifying structure*

(i) Walter Halford's qualifying expenditure totals:		
year ended 31 March 1988	45,000	
31 March 1989	52,500	
31 March 1990	22,500	
	£120,000	
(ii) The allowances due are as follows:		
writing-down allowances (4%)		£4,800

Notes:

(i) The cost of land £90,000 is not qualifying expenditure.

(ii) The cost of the administrative office £20,000 is not excluded as it does not exceed 25% of total expenditure of whole structure (25% × £120,000 = £30,000).

(iii) Writing-down allowance of £4,800 will be first available against the 1990/1 Schedule D case I assessment. This results from the factory not being used until the basis period ended 31 March 1990.

(iv) A similar sum of £4,800 will be available against the 1991/2 assessment et seq., until the whole qualifying expenditure of £120,000 has been fully relieved.

indeed the structure will continue to physically exist for at least that length of time.

However, the legislation does acknowledge this may not always be the case and provides that balancing adjustments, in the form of the familar balancing charge or allowance, are made where the relevant interest is sold, the building is destroyed, or the lease is terminated before the time span of 25 years is exceeded.

The general effect on the first purchaser, of the required adjustments, is to withdraw excess allowances—a balancing charge or make up any shortfall in allowances by way of a balancing allowance. As regards the second and subsequent purchasers the writing-down allowances are no longer a fixed percentage but are calculated by use of the following formula:

$$\frac{\text{lower of purchase price to current purchaser or original qualifying cost}}{\text{unexpired part of 25 years from the date building first used.}}$$

When computing the balancing adjustments on the vendor and claim to relief by the purchaser, care must be taken to exclude any part of the sale price (purchase price) which relates to land and, further, to treat any excess of sale price over qualifying costs of the structure as a capital gain in the vendor's hands. By using the original qualifying costs in the purchaser's computation (see formula above) any sum treated as a capital gain in the vendor's hands should be automatically excluded for industrial buildings allowance purposes.

An elementary example of these adjustments is given in Table 8.15 which illustrates the necessary computations on the assumption that Halford, from our previous example, disposes of the factory to Payne exactly four years after bringing it into qualifying use. The sale proceeds, exclusive of land, received during the year ended 31 March 1994 were £150,000.

There are three points which the reader should note about this system. Firstly, the further the sale date is from the construction date up to a maximum of 25 years, any subsequent writing-down allowances will approach 100 per cent in the next purchaser's hands. Secondly, although the computations appear complex all the system is doing is to pass the original qualifying cost on each time the relevant interest changes hands. Finally, it should be clear that if the relevant interest changes hands after the 25-year tax relief period the subsequent purchaser will have no claim, whatever price is paid—the denominator in the formula is zero! There are, of course, no corresponding balancing adjustments on the vendor.

In addition to the above general principles there are detailed rules to deal with periods of non-qualifying use and sales of these structures, but the complexity is thought to be beyond the scope of this book.

(c) Agricultural buildings

As the title suggests the relevant sections of the Capital Allowances Act 1968 relate to special reliefs for the farming and forestry industries. What qualifies as

TABLE 8.15. *Balancing adjustments and industrial buildings allowances arising on disposal within 25 years of first use*

Halford		(£)
Qualifying expenditure:		120,000
1990/1 writing-down allowances	4,800	
1991/2 writing-down allowances	4,800	
1992/3 writing-down allowances	4,800	
1993/4 writing-down allowances	4,800	(19,200)
Written-down value prior to sale		100,800
1994/5 Sale proceeds excluding capital gains £30,000		120,000
Balancing charge (sale proceeds – written-down value)		£19,200

Payne

$$\frac{\text{lower of purchase price or qualifying cost}}{\text{unexpired part of 25 years}} = \frac{120{,}000}{21}$$

$$= \text{£}5{,}714 \text{ per annum}$$

Notes:

(i) There will be a balancing charge of £19,200 on Halford in 1994/5, the basis period of disposal being year ended 31 March 1994.

(ii) Payne may claim industrial buildings allowance of £5,714 per annum (4.76%) the year of assessment being decided by the basis period for his business.

an agricultural building is defined by statute and covers new but not second-hand agricultural structures, so barns, cowsheds and the like are included plus cottages for the occupation of farm-workers. In addition, one-third of the cost of construction of a farmhouse (for the farmer's and family occupation) will also qualify. The definition also includes capital and improvement costs on agricultural and forestry works, for example fencing, drainage, and reclamation of land. The costs of plant and machinery do not fall within the definition but do qualify in the normal way as plant and machinery.

For expenditure after 1 April 1986 the capital allowances available consist of a writing-down allowance of 4 per cent per annum calculated on a straight-line basis which effectively spreads the relief over a 25-year period.

The relief itself is given to the person who incurs the expenditure which may be the owner or tenant of agricultural land or perhaps both. Sir Peter Fuller (landlord) leases farmland to Tom Smith (tenant). Sir Peter incurs expenditure of £40,000 on the provision of farm buildings, and Tom incurs expenditure of £10,000 on new fencing, drainage, and land clearance. Assuming the expenditure is after 1 April 1986 each would have a claim to agricultural buildings allowance of £1,600 and £400 per annum respectively. Their respective claims would be set primarily against agricultural income with any excess allowances set off against any other income.

To establish which year of assessment qualifies for the allowance in respect of new expenditure it is important to note that the normal basis period rules do not apply. For individuals the allowance will commence generally in the year of assessment immediately following the year ended 31 March in which the expenditure was incurred. However, the taxpayer (a farmer) may agree with HM Inspector of Taxes that the normal accounting period be used instead of year ended 31 March. To illustrate the effect of this approach let us assume that the expenditure incurred by Sir Peter and Tom was on 1 August 1986, and Tom has agreed his normal accounting year-end of 30 June be substituted. Sir Peter will be able to claim £1,600 for the first time against 1987/8 assessable income (basis period year ended 31 March 1987) while Tom's claim for £400 will be set against his 1988/9 assessment (basis period year ended 30 June 1987). If, on the other hand, Tom's year-end had been 30 September the first assessable income available for relief would be 1987/8!

Prior to April 1986 when agricultural buildings or works were sold no balancing adjustments were made on the vendor—the sale price being irrelevant. The purchaser merely took over the unexpired portion, if any, of the original cost with the allowance for the year of sale being apportioned on a time basis. Additionally, there existed an almost feudal piece of legislation which gave any unexpired expenditure of the tenant back to the landlord where a tenant farmer gave up a lease or received no payment towards such expenditure from the incoming tenant. However, from April 1986 it would appear that, at the taxpayer's option, balancing adjustments will be available when an agricultural building is sold, destroyed, or demolished.

(d) Hotels

Hotels were originally excluded from the definition of industrial buildings but by the 1978 Finance Act industrial buildings allowance with certain modifications has been extended to capital expenditure on qualifying hotels after 11 April 1978. The word hotel is not defined statutorily, but the definition contained in any English dictionary would appear to suffice. However, a qualifying hotel must satisfy all the following conditions:

(i) the accommodation must be of a permanent nature,
(ii) be open for at least four months between 1 April and 31 October each year,
(iii) have at least ten bedrooms available for public letting between the above dates,
(iv) the bedrooms in (iii) must offer sleeping accommodation, and
(v) the services provided must include breakfast and evening meal, cleaning and bedmaking.

The rates of allowance for all expenditure incurred on or after 1 April 1986 is a writing-down allowance of 4 per cent per annum calculated on a straight-line basis by reference to that expenditure. Essentially, and not surprisingly, the operation of this relief is very similar to that of industrial buildings allowance including the making of balancing adjustments on the vendor where a sale, termination of lease, or destruction of the building occurs. Additionally, a balancing adjustment may occur where there is a change of trade and the building ceases to be a qualifying hotel.

(e) Enterprise zones

Under the provisions of the 1980 Finance Act the Secretary of State was empowered to designate certain areas within the UK as enterprise zones. The general idea behind the creation of those special areas was to stimulate new development in derelict industrial hinterlands, for example Tyneside Enterprise Zone. As part of a general package of inducements for firms to move into these areas, industrial buildings allowance in these areas was substantially extended both as to type of qualifying building and rates of allowance. The package of inducements is only available on expenditure incurred in the first ten years after the zone is established. As the first generation was created from June 1981 onwards (Corby, Swansea) this point is currently of academic interest only.

In addition to industrial buildings, as already defined including the extension to qualifying hotels, all other commercial buildings sited within an enterprise zone will qualify for the industrial buildings allowance. A commercial building would include such structures as shops, showrooms, offices, and wholesale warehouses providing they are used for the purposes of a trade, profession, or vocation. A dwelling-house is specifically excluded.

The rates of allowance, which are the same for expenditure incurred either before or after 1 April 1986 are merely an accelerated version of the capital allowances already reviewed.

If the owner of the relevant interest wishes he or she may write off 100 per cent of the qualifying expenditure in one year against assessable income. However, the claimant may elect not to take the full 100 per cent initial allowance in which case the balance of qualifying expenditure will be written off by means of writing-down allowances of 25 per cent of cost per annum calculated on a straight-line basis. Providing the qualifying expenditure is incurred within the first ten years of the zone being established, it is expected that all such expenditure will have been relieved against profits within four years. Table 8.16 illustrates the operation of capital allowances within the zones in three different situations. Where the qualifying building is disposed of within 25 years, balancing adjustments will be made.

We have now reviewed the more common and important systems of relief for capital expenditure, but it should not escape the reader's attention that there are also special reliefs of minor application to businesses in respect of scientific research expenditure and also patents and know-how.

TABLE 8.16. *The operation of capital allowances within an enterprise zone* (£)

(i) 100% initial allowance claimed immediately:	
cost of new office block incurred in year ended 31 December 1987	1,000,000
1988/9 initial allowance	(1,000,000)
(ii) 75% initial allowance only in first year:	
cost of new wholesale warehouse incurred in year ended 31 December 1987	1,500,000
1988/9 initial allowance	(1,125,000)
	375,000
1989/90 writing-down allowance 25% of cost	(375,000)
(iii) 35% initial allowance only in first year:	
cost of new industrial building incurred in year ended 31 December 1987	2,000,000
1988/9 initial allowance	(700,000)
	1,300,000
1989/90 writing-down allowance 25% of cost	(500,000)
	800,000
1990/1 writing-down allowance 25% of cost	(500,000)
	300,000
1991/2 writing-down allowance 15% balance of cost	(300,000)

Losses in unincorporated businesses

Within the UK tax system losses, for which some form of tax relief may be given, fall into two main categories:

(i) Trading losses, i.e. losses arising under Schedule D cases I and II, and less frequently case V.

(ii) Non-trading losses rising under Schedule A and Schedule D case VI, and losses from investment in shares in an unquoted trading company by an individual.

As this section is concerned with business taxation it will concentrate on trading losses in category (i) above and primarily deal with such losses arising under Schedule D cases I and II. The position regarding Schedule D case V losses will be dealt with in summary form.

Relief for trading losses is contained in sections 168, 169, 171, 172, and 174 of the Income and Corporation Taxes Act 1970 and the 1978 Finance Act section 30. Before considering how the detailed provisions of each section are operated, it may be useful to establish how a trading loss is calculated. Put at its simplest, trading losses are computed in exactly the same way as profits, i.e. the commercial profit or loss shown by the annual accounts is adjusted in the normal way to arrive at the assessable (adjusted) profits. However, the effect of these tax adjustments is to produce a negative adjusted profit or, put another way, an adjusted loss. Consider the two computations below which explain, particularly in computation (ii), how a commercial accounting profit may become an adjusted loss for tax purposes.

(i) Arnold Bennett has traded for many years to 31 December. His Schedule D case I computation of assessable profit is:

Net loss for the 12 months ended 31 December 1986	£4,000
Less: Depreciation	(500)
Adjusted loss	£3,500

(ii) Gordon Bennett has traded for many years to 30 September. His Schedule D case I computation of assessable profit is:

Net Profit for the 12 months ended 30 September 1986	£1,000
Less: Income assessable under Schedule A	(1,500)
Adjusted loss	£500

The respective adjusted losses of £3,500 and £500 are the trading losses with which we are concerned—the trading losses of each trader. Throughout the remainder of this section and indeed the chapter the term loss/losses will refer to trading losses. There are two immediate consequences of the above losses arising:

(i) The D case I assessments for 1987/8 for each trader will be nil by reference to their basis (accounting) periods ended 30 September or 31 December 1986.
(ii) Each trader has established a loss, but relief will not be given for it until Arnold or Gordon make their respective claims.

The analysis of the available claims will be started by looking at section 168 and using the Arnold Bennett data for explanatory purposes. The general application of this section is that an adjusted loss (£3,500) may be used to relieve total income of the tax year of loss (1986/7), i.e. the tax year in which the basis period (12 months to 31 December 1986) ends and for the following tax year (1987/8). Therefore, if we assume further data for Arnold, as shown below, the possible claims under sections 168 are shown in Table 8.17:

		Trading profits
Year ended 31 December	1985	£1,200
	1986	£(3,500)
		Other Income
Year ended 5th April	1987	£1,500
	1988	£1,500

A point which must be noted about a section 168 claim is that it is voluntary, that is, no one including the Inland Revenue can force Arnold into the claim. However, if Arnold wishes to proceed, it is imperative that he notifies HM Inspector of Taxes within two years of the end of each year of assessment for which he wishes to offset the loss, i.e. by 5 April 1989 and 1990, respectively. Thus, the options open to Arnold are claim for neither year, claim only for 1986/7, claim only for 1987/8 or both years as shown in Table 8.17. The key feature of these claims is therefore one of complete flexibility, but this very feature has led to legislative restriction in certain circumstances to avoid abuse of setting trading losses against other income. Losses incurred in 'hobby' trades are not available for relief under section 168 and in farming or market-gardening trades, where a loss is made for the sixth consecutive year, this loss is similarly prohibited.

Care should also be taken in using this flexibility. It will be observed this is an 'all or nothing' claim in that Arnold must set £2,700 of his loss relief against total income not taxable income. If Arnold had personal allowances of say £2,200 available in 1986/7 before a claim were made his taxable income would have been £500. What he cannot do is use £500 of the loss in 1986/7 to leave total income of £2,200 to be covered by his personal allowances. Remember the golden rule in any section 168 loss relief claim is that losses can be carried forward from tax year to tax year but personal allowances cannot.

In addition to a trading loss most firms will have a claim to capital allowances for the year of assessment which has a nil Schedule D case I assessment as a consequence of that loss. Arnold has a nil 1987/8 D case I assessment, but let us say he has capital allowances amounting to £700 for that year. He has a number of alternatives (i) he may waive the writing-down allowances altogether as suggested in the previous section on capital allowances, (ii) he may carry them forward to set against future profits of the same trade, or (iii) invoke the operation of section 169. Taking these choices in order (i) unlikely, (ii) still unlikely, after all, who knows what the future may bring? (iii) assuming Arnold considers the cost of irretrievably losing personal allowances is less than the benefit of claiming loss relief at the earliest moment; go for section 169.

Section 169 allows capital allowances for the year of assessment (1987/8) for which the period of account in which the loss was incurred was the basis period

TABLE 8.17. *Example of relief for trading loss under section 168 (ICTA 1970)*

	Assessments (£)	
	1986/7	1987/8
Schedule D case I	1,200	nil
Other income	1,500	1,500
Total income	2,700	1,500
Less: S.168 relief	(2,700)	(800)
Taxable income	nil	700

(year ended 31 December 1986) to be added to a trading loss (£3,500) or used to convert a profit into a loss for section 168 purposes. The results of Arnold extending section 168 by the operation of section 169 are shown in Table 8.18.

We next consider the most straight forward of the loss relief sections—section 171, under which relief for the loss is obtained by carrying it forward against future profits from the same trade. If we return to the Arnold Bennett example and assume (i) he does not wish to claim under section 168, and (ii) for the 12 months ended 31 December 1987 he has an adjusted profit of £2,500, the loss of £3,500 would reduce the 1988/9 Schedule D case I assessment to nil, but on the assumption his other income continues at the same level as before Arnold's total income for 1988/9 would be £1,500. Three points to note regarding relief under section 171 are as follows:

(i) The claim is mandatory and against the first available profits of the same trade in full—there may be some loss of personal allowances where other income is insufficient to cover them.
(ii) The unrelieved loss of £1,000 is carried forward against the immediate next profits from the same trade with no time limit (but see below).
(iii) No part of other income can be reduced under this section.

A claim to section 171 must strictly be made within six years of the year of assessment in which the loss-making basis period ends. Thus, Arnold Bennett should notify HM Inspector of Taxes by 5 April 1993 at the latest. In practice, providing a computation is submitted to the Inland Revenue indicating the loss of £3,500 is being carried forward, Arnold need make no formal claim.

TABLE 8.18. *Example of relief for trading loss under section 168 (ICTA 1970) as extended by section 169*

Computation of section 168 loss	
Trading loss for year ended 31 December 1986	3,500
Add: capital allowances 1987/8 (basis period 12 months ended 31 December 1986)	700
	£4,200

	Assessments (£)	
	1986/7	1987/8
Schedule D case I	1,200	nil
Other income	1,500	1,500
Total income	2,700	1,500
Less: S.168 relief	(2,700)	(1,500)
Taxable income	nil	nil

If the loss-making trade permanently ceases, including a change in the nature of trade, or the business is transferred to a limited company, any unused losses 'die' with that permanent cessation.

Finally, we briefly review Schedule D case V, which applies to trades, professions, or vocations carried on and controlled wholly from abroad. The way in which these losses may be relieved is fairly limited. Any such losses may be set against certain other earned income from abroad using similar rules to those used for UK trading losses under Schedule D cases I or II. However, it is not possible to set a case V trading loss against unearned foreign income as most certainly is the case for UK trading losses. There is very little flexibility in reality!

As mentioned above, the benefit of trading losses being carried forward under section 171 will be lost if an unincorporated business is transferred to a limited company. This would be particularly unfair where the cessation is a technical one. By this we mean a situation where a sole trader has decided to conduct his trading activities through the medium of a limited company in the future. Perhaps, it might be argued that he should have chosen more carefully at the outset of his business (see Chapter 16). However, the legislation is more compassionate in that section 172 is drawn to cover this change of heart by a proprietor.

The provisions of section 172 allow any unused losses under section 171 to be relieved against income the sole trader receives from the company firstly in the form of earned income and then as investment income. Needless to say, there are some conditions contained in the statutes which insist that the same trade is carried on by the company, the sale consideration was satisfied mainly by the issue of shares, and those shares are held by the former sole trader in any tax year for which a claim is made.

All these conditions must be met before a claim can be successful. The operation of this relief is shown in Table 8.19 based on the following data relating to John Greaves who transferred his business to J.G. Limited on 1 January 1987 wholly in exchange for shares.

(i) The losses unused, after all other available reliefs have been claimed, were £10,000.
(ii) He became a director of J.G. Ltd. and received a salary of £3,000 and dividends of £710 (net) during 1986/7 and a salary of £9,000 and dividends of £1,420 (net) for 1987/8.
(iii) He still holds the original shares at 5 April 1988.
(iv) Other investment income amounted to £4,260 (net) each year.
(v) Basic rate income tax is assumed to be 29 per cent.

As indicated in (i) above the losses used in John's claim are those remaining after prior loss claims under section 168 and terminal loss relief have been made. It must also be understood that losses for section 172 purposes do not include unused capital allowances. However, this is not too much of a practical

TABLE 8.19. *Example of relief for trading loss after incorporation of a business*

John Greaves		
Total income computation 1986/7		
Earned Income: Schedule E	3,000	
Less: Section 172 relief	(3,000)	
Investment income: Dividends J. G. Ltd.		nil
(gross)	1,000	
Less: Section 172 relief	(1,000)	
	nil	
Other dividends (gross)	6,000	6,000
Total income		£6,000
Total income computation 1987/8		
Earned income: Schedule E	9,000	
Less: Section 172 relief (balance)	(6,000)	
		3,000
Investment income: Dividends (gross)		8,000
Total income		£11,000

point since they have probably been absorbed in the aforementioned prior claims.

Where a business permanently ceases to trade either technically or through natural wastage any trading loss in the last twelve months of trading may be set against assessments of the same trade for the three years prior to the cessation year. In certain circumstances capital allowances for the same twelve months may be added to the loss. This is an outline of the provisions of section 174 and as can be seen from Table 8.20 operates in a similar way to section 171 except that the loss is carried back in time rather than forward. The data from which Table 8.20 is calculated refers to Neil Farmer, who closed his business finally on 5 April 1987 after trading for many years. His results have been:

		(£)
Year ended 5 April	1987 (loss)	(4,950)
	1986 profit	100
	1985 profit	750
	1984 profit	1,650
	1983 profit	2,100

Because there is a limitation on how far back the loss may be carried the sum of £450 is lost forever. However, if Neil had total income and personal allowances greater than £4,950 in 1986/7 it would probably pay him to claim for the loss under section 168 in that year.

TABLE 8.20. *Example of terminal loss relief upon permanent cessation of trading*

Neil Farmer

(i) *Assessments on cessation*[a] (£)

1986/7 (basis period 5.4.87)	nil
1985/6 (basis period 5.4.85)	750
1984/5 (basis period 5.4.84)	1,650
1983/4 (basis period 5.4.83)	2,100

(ii) *Terminal loss relief claim*

	Schedule DI assessment	S.174 claim	Net assessment
1985/6	750	750	nil
1984/5	1,650	1,650	nil
1983/4	2,100	2,100	nil
		4,500	

Remaining loss which cannot be relieved is £450

[a] It is unlikely the Inland Revenue would wish to calculate the 1985/6 and 1984/5 assessments on an actual basis.

The 1978 Finance Act introduced special legislation whereby a sole trader who incurs a loss in his first year of assessment, or the immediately following three years of assessment, may offset that loss against total income for the three preceding years of assessment, preceding that in which the loss is suffered. The relief is given against the earlier years first. The practical operation of this relief can become extremely complex in that section 168 may or may not operate for the loss-making year dependent on whether the taxpayer has other income, and there are special rules for calculating losses for sections 168 and 171 purposes in the opening years of a business. However, abstracting from these difficulties, it is possible to show the general principles of this piece of legislation at work.

Jo Baker commences her trade on 1 October 1986 and for the year ended 30 September 1987 she incurs a loss of £20,000. Thus, her Schedule D Case I assessments for 1986/7, 1987/8, and 1988/9 will be nil. As she has no other income for these years no valid claim under section 168 is possible, and further, even if the results for the year ended 30 September 1988 show a profit, relief under section 171 could not be claimed until 1989/90. Prior to commencing her own business Jo had been a highly paid executive with an advertising agency, and her earned income in 1983/4, 1984/5 and 1985/6 had been in the region of £50,000 per annum. The provisions of section 30 of the 1978 Finance

Act are clearly needed to obtain a tax repayment to tide over the ailing business. First, we must calculate the loss in the first year of assessment (1986/7). This loss must be computed on an actual tax year basis and is, therefore, £10,000 (i.e. October 1986 to 5 April 1987 = 1/2 × £20,000). Noting 1986/7 is excluded by the three preceding years of assessment rule—the earliest year against which the £10,000 loss may be claimed is 1983/4 and the latest 1985/6. Because the section 30 relief is considerably smaller than Jo's total income for 1983/4 the part loss is fully relieved. However, the balance of the full loss, namely £10,000, falls in 1987/8 and a further claim is available against 1984/5, 1985/6, and 1986/7 subject to the 30 September 1988 results. A profit of say £5,000 to 30 September 1988 would result in section 30 relief being $\frac{1}{2}$ × £20,000 loss plus $\frac{1}{2}$ × £5,000 profit = £7,500. This would be claimed against total income for 1984/5.

Partnerships

Many unincorporated businesses are run as partnerships, particularly in the professions where the regulations of the professional association forbid the formation of a limited company to carry on the business. The principles outlined in the preceding sections of this chapter also apply, in the main, to any business carried on by two or more persons in partnership. There are a number of modifications and peculiarities, and it is to these that attention will be drawn.

In English law a partnership is not a separate legal entity as distinct from its members. However, where a trade or profession is carried on in the form of a partnership the UK tax legislation stipulates income tax must be computed and stated jointly in one sum and a joint assessment shall be made in the partnership name. The assessment, although being in one sum, always breaks down the liability between the partners. Thus, each partner should pay his share of the liability, but if he does not do so the Inland Revenue may extract payment from the other partners. In practice the cheque for the total partnership tax bill is often drawn on the firm's bank account, and the respective partners' shares are charged to their drawings accounts.

This procedure follows the general principles, outlined in Chapters 7 and 8, whereby income is computed and assessed according to the schedules, in this case Schedule D cases I or II, and then the unique circumstances (personal reliefs) of the individuals sharing in that income are deducted to arrive at the overall tax liability.

In computing the profits of a partnership care must be taken to disallow items charged in the annual accounts which, in reality, are merely appropriations of profit. Salaries paid to partners and interest on capital, two popular forms of equating work-loads or capital contribution rights between partners, are examples of typical appropriations of profits. However, two interesting points emerge from these generalities. Salaried partners are treated as employees, not partners, while interest on capital is treated as earned income except where it is paid to a sleeping partner.

The basis of assessment applied to partnership profits is, apart from new businesses and permanent cessations of trades or professions, the normal previous year rule. Garfield and Sobers have traded in partnership for many years, their annual accounting date being 30 September. The profits for the year ended 30 September 1986 are £50,000 which are assessed in 1987/8, and the claim to capital allowances totals £5,000 which gives a net Schedule D case I assessment on the partnership of £45,000 for 1987/8.

We now run into a peculiarity of partnership taxation, i.e. how the sum of £45,000 is divided between the partners. Here care is needed because having arrived at the assessment it is well to forget where the figure came from. This is because profits are apportioned between the partners in accordance with profit-sharing arrangements in the year of assessment. Where the same profit-sharing split continues from year to year no difficulty presents itself so where Garfield and Sobers are dividing profits equally, as they have always done, at 5 April 1988 then each partner will be assessed on £22,500. However, suppose that from 6 April 1987 it is agreed between the partners that Garfield will now receive two-thirds of profits and Sobers one-third. The result of this decision is that Garfield will now be assessed on £30,000 in 1987/8 but Sobers on only £15,000. It should be noted carefully that the share of profits in the basis period is unaffected. There is an anomaly whereby Garfield receives profits of £22,500 but is assessed on £30,000. Where changes in profit-sharing occurs other than on 6 April it is more likely to be an accounting anniversary, the year of assessment is time-apportioned and the respective profit-sharing ratios applied to each time span. Table 8.21 illustrates the allocation of the 1987/8 assessment where Garfield and Sobers delayed the change until 1 October 1987.

TABLE 8.21. *Example of division of partnership assessment where there is a change in profit-sharing ratios*

Garfield and Sobers—Schedule D case I assessment 1987/8 (£)

Profit in basis period ended 30 September 1986	50,000
Less: capital allowances	(5,000)
Net assessment for division	£45,000

	Total	Garfield	Sobers
Period to 30.09.87 ($\frac{1}{2}$ × £45,000)	22,500	($\frac{1}{2}$) 11,250	($\frac{1}{2}$) 11,250
Period from 1.10.87	22,500	($\frac{2}{3}$) 15,000	($\frac{1}{3}$) 7,500
	£45,000	£26,250	£18,750

Apart from a partnership ceasing to trade by natural wastage or transferring its business to a limited company, there is also a deemed cessation of trade for tax purposes occasioned by a change in the number of partners either up or down. Where a partner retires or dies or a new member is admitted into the firm the standard permanent cessation rules are applied to the 'old' firm up to the date of change and the commencement rules with some modifications (see below), to the 'new' firm from the same date. It is immaterial that the name of the partnership remains unchanged or no break in trade occurs, it is the changes in the individual parties which are important. The above rules also apply where a sole trader admits a partner or a partnership of two becomes a sole proprietorship. If we assume that instead of merely changing profit-sharing ratios on 1 October 1987 Garfield and Sobers had admitted Holder into partnership sharing profits equally, this would affect the 'old' firm's assessments by using actual profits from 6 April 1987 to 30 September 1987 to fix the 1987/8 assessment. The years 1986/7 and 1985/6 may also be adjusted at the Inland Revenue's option (see Table 8.8 earlier). Whatever the Inland Revenue does at this juncture there will, nevertheless, be some profits which escape assessment. However, from 20 March 1985 the commencement rules for partnerships, where there is at least one person in common in the 'old' and 'new' firms and an election to a continuation election could have been made but was not, are as follows:

Year of Assessment	*Basis period*
Year one	Profits from date of commencement to the immediately following 5 April
Years two, three, and four	From 6 April in one year to 5 April, i.e. an actual basis
Year five onwards	Profits of twelve-month accounting period ended in assessment year four, i.e. previous year basis.

Therefore the 'new' firm of Garfield, Sobers, and Holder will have assessments for 1987/8 to 1990/1 based on the actual profits arising between 1 October 1987 and 5 April 1991 calculated by time-apportionment of the twelve-month accounting periods ended 30 September 1988 to 1991 inclusive. The fifth year of assessment 1991/2 will have a basis period of twelve months ended 30 September 1990 having reverted to the normal previous year basis. The 'new' firm has the option of electing for an actual basis to apply to the fifth and sixth years of assessment rather than second and third under the standard commencement rules for new businesses. Such an election would be made by 5 April 1999, i.e. within six years of the end of the sixth year of assessment.

The reason for this new set of commencement rules from 20 March 1985 in the case of continuing operations linked with changes of partners but not, it should be stressed, for sole traders or newly set up partnerships stemmed from a growing tax avoidance strategy. This strategy used the then normal cessation and commencement rules to obtain a reduction in tax liability by maximizing the amount of profits escaping assessment by repeating the change process every five or six years. The new rules were codified in the 1985 Finance Act.

Mention has been made above to the so-called continuation election which effectually means the cessation and commencement rules do not apply in assessing the profits of the business. Garfield, Sobers, and Holder have this option open to them, and the effect of taking it is shown in Table 8.22. Clearly, the 1987/8 assessment is based on the normal previous year basis, i.e. profits for the twelve months ended 30 September 1986 and similarly the 1988/9 assessment will have the year ended 30 September 1987 as its basis period. It should be observed that where this election is made no profits escape assessment, and Holder is assessed upon profits which he has not received.

The decision whether to make this election or not may, even taking the new commencement rules into account, result in a clash of tax interests between the old and new partners. This is particularly so in the case of incoming partners such as Holder in our example. The situation is aggravated because, to be effective, any election for continuation must be made in writing to HM Inspector of Taxes, within two years of the change, i.e. by 1 October 1989, and must be signed by all old and new partners. Therefore, it is obligatory that Holder sign any such election along with Garfield and Sobers. On the assumption the election is made, the resultant tax payments are a matter for resolution between the three of them although the division of profits which gives rise to these payments is statutorily laid down.

From time to time, businesses carried on as partnerships will incur trading losses rather than produce assessable profits. The rules of sections 168 and 171 (TA 1970) apply in the normal way, and each partner may claim his share of the trading loss to his best tax advantage completely independent from the other partners.

When dealing with loss reliefs in partnerships, care must be taken not to produce an artifically inflated loss for one partner and assessable income for

TABLE 8.22. *Effect of an election for continuation basis of assessment on partnership profits*

Garfield, Sobers, and Holder—Schedule D case I assessment 1987/8

	Total	Garfield	Sobers	Holder
Net assessment profits 12 months to 30 September 1986	45,000			
Period to 30.9.87	22,500	11,250	11,250	—
Period from 1.10.87	22,500	7,500	7,500	7,500
	£45,000	£18,750	£18,750	£7,500

another by the charging of salaries or interest on capital. It must be remembered that it is the firm which is assessed and a partner cannot be given relief for a loss for use under sections 168 and 171 which exceeds the overall loss of the firm, and there is simply no loss relief available to any partner where the firm makes an overall profit.

There are some restrictions on loss relief arising from partnership trading losses, for example from 'hobby' trades and farming or market-gardening activities (see earlier section on losses). More importantly, the 1985 Finance Act introduced legislation to reduce the attraction of limited partnerships as tax saving vehicles. From 20 March 1985 the amount of a limited partner's share of the firm's loss that may be set against other income under section 168 is to be restricted to the amount of the limited partners capital at risk. There is no similar restriction on the amount of loss which may be carried forward under section 171!

Concluding remarks

This chapter has concentrated on four key areas of income tax principles relevant to unincorporated businesses operated and controlled from within the United Kingdom, namely computation of profits, basis of assessment of those profits, relief for capital expenditure and trading losses.

The chapter commenced with a definition of profits and trade before analysing in depth the difference between commercial accounting and assessable or adjusted profits for taxation purposes. This theme was further developed through a detailed discussion of various items of expenditure which are either allowable or non-allowable in computing trading profits under Schedule D cases I and II.

Once the principle of trading profit had been established, the methods by which the Inland Revenue assesses these profits were explored. The concepts of years of assessment and basis periods were introduced and linked with the firm's accounting year. The normal previous year basis of assessment was then explained in detail before considering difficulties which are occasioned by the use of this basis where a trade commences or permanently ceases and how the legislation provides a solution. This section then concluded by looking at the double assessment of profits in the early years of trading and the gap which exists upon the permanent cessation of operations together with the respective options open to the taxpayer and the Inland Revenue to alleviate these anomalies.

After a brief introduction as to the definition of capital expenditure considerable attention was devoted to the reliefs for such expenditure granted under the Capital Allowances Act 1968. Five classes of expenditure were discussed in detail, namely plant and machinery, industrial buildings, agricultural buildings, hotels and various buildings in enterprise zones. The reader was systematically introduced to the differing principles underlying the various claims including the use of writing-down allowances, balancing charges or allowances and pooled and non-pooled expenditure. Special problems regarding basis periods in the opening and closing years of assessment were discussed and the rules for resolution presented.

It was then considered appropriate to introduce the sections of the Income and Corporation Taxes Act 1970 and subsequent legislation whereby relief for trading losses is given. After a brief introduction as to how a trading loss is computed, the detailed provisions of sections 168 and 171 (TA 1970) were examined. The differences between the two sections were made clear including the voluntary nature of section 168 compared with the mandatory legislation contained in section 171. The reader's attention was also drawn to certain 'trading' situations where a loss would not be allowed for section 168 purposes. Losses and the relief thereof in new businesses, closing businesses, and transfers of operations to a limited company were also discussed.

Finally, there was a concluding section which described how the four key areas affected partnerships and also highlighted some necessary modifications of the general tax legislation including a new set of commencement rules in certain circumstances and restriction of trading losses of limited partners.

Recommendations for further reading

A more detailed explanation of what constitutes a trade may be found in an article by Sinclair (1985) and the six badges of trade are discussed in depth, with extensive reference to case law in Butterworth (1985), chapter 7. This reference also includes an excellent analysis of the distinction between capital and revenue expenditure. The fundamental changes in the assessment of partnerships, upon a change in membership, from March 1985 is further discussed and illustrated by Greene (1985). For the reader wishing to explore the complex effects of a change of accounting date on tax assessments, detailed examples are available in Bertram and Edwards (1986) and Pritchard (1985).

References

Bertram, D., and Edwards, S. (1986), *Comprehensive Aspects of Taxation—1986–87* (London: Holt, Rinehart and Winston).

Butterworth (1985), *Butterworths UK Tax Guide* (London: Butterworths).

Greene, C. (1985), 'Partnerships—what the new tax rules will mean', *Accountancy*, 96 (no. 101): 14–15.

Pritchard, W. E. (1985), *Income Tax 1985/86* (Harlow, Essex: Longman).

Sinclair, W. (1985), 'What is a Trade?', *The Accountant*, (6 November 1985): 18–19.

9
Capital Gains Tax

Introduction

In this chapter we will, after an historical perspective recording the development of capital gains tax, review initially the scope and coverage of the tax followed by an introduction to the general principles applicable to basic computations of gains or losses. The special rules for assets acquired prior to 1965 will be considered together with the concept of indexation of asset costs.

Following this general approach to principles the remainder of the chapter will be devoted to exemptions and reliefs which directly affect the business.

Business in the context of this tax refers not only to trades, professions, or vocations carried on by sole proprietors or partnerships, but also to limited companies. The inclusion of corporate trades gives rise to some presentational problems because of the assessment link with corporation tax. However, modifications of general principles or law will be dealt with in this chapter leaving only specialized points be be dealt with in Chapter 10 on corporation tax.

History and development

Current taxation of capital profits on disposal of capital assets has its foundations in the 1962 Finance Act which introduced, from 6 April 1962, new legislation to attack short-term gains. Generally, short-term gains or losses arose on the disposal of an asset within twelve months of acquisition although in the case of land this period was extended to three years.

However, short-term gains tax as it became known was not a true capital tax in that the statute governing it was a newly-created case 7 of Schedule D, and income tax rates were applied to the assessable amounts. It was assessed on an actual basis.

In the 1965 Finance Act, the government imposed a true capital gains tax. A completely new, complex piece of legislation was introduced which attacked long-term gains, i.e. where the period between purchase and sale of assets exceeded twelve months. This was an entirely new tax, with its own rate of tax to apply to long-term gains arising on or after 6 April 1965. As with all recent forms of newly introduced taxes in the UK it was assessable on an actual basis; the first gains were therefore assessable in 1965/6.

Until the tax year 1970/1 both short-term and long-term gains taxes operated side by side. The 1971 Finance Act abolished the short-term gains legislation from 6 April 1971, and the long-term arm was extended to cover gains arising from disposals of assets irrespective of the period of ownership.

All legislation from 1965 up to and including that introduced by the 1978 Finance Act was consolidated into the Capital Gains Tax Act 1979 and is currently operative plus major and minor amendments introduced by subsequent Finance Acts. Two significant changes in recent years have been the introduction of indexation and changes to retirement relief in the 1982 and 1985 Finance Acts, respectively.

As a form of raising cash for the government, capital gains tax has been relatively unsuccessful. In 1984/5 the amount collectable totalled some £700 m which represented something less than 1 per cent of the total UK tax revenue. In percentage terms its zenith was in 1973/4 when the tax accounted for nearly 2 per cent of the total tax revenue of that year. It is probably not coincidental that this period of time was one of rapid price inflation and more than not gave rise to the allegation that capital gains tax was 'a tax on inflation'. With the introduction of indexation to combat this allegation it is unlikely the dizzy heights of 1973/4 will be achieved again. Indeed it has been estimated that the collection of capital gains tax will drop (in 1984/5 prices) to £475 m in 1990/1 and £339 m by 1995/6. Conversely, the costs of collection by the Inland Revenue are estimated to rise from approximately 2p to nearly 10p in the £ (King 1985). Somewhat like old soldiers if capital gains tax is not abolished it will merely fade away! Nevertheless until such time as this occurs students of business taxation and others are advised to be conversant with the general operation of the tax.

Scope and coverage

As the name implies it is a tax on capital profits, and it follows these arise from the disposal of capital assets. If a business person disposes of an asset which is part of his circulating capital, for example stock, the profit will be of an income nature and assessed under Schedule D case I. However, where the same trader disposes of an enduring asset which represents fixed capital, for example property (see Chapter 8 on capital expenditure), we are referring to a capital asset, and the resultant profit, if any, may be subjected to capital gains tax.

It must, of course, be appreciated that the tax is equally applied to disposals of capital assets by non-trading persons. Generally it may be said that where a capital profits arises, whatever the circumstances, there may be a capital gains tax liability.

However, this broad brush approach is merely a starter and to obtain a better overview of the impact of this tax reference is necessary to the statutes.

The main charging section of the Capital Gains Tax Act 1979 says 'tax shall be charged in accordance with this Act in respect of capital gains, that is to say chargeable gains computed in accordance with this Act and accruing to a person on the disposal of an asset.'

A careful study of this wording will highlight two fundamental points. The legislation distinguishes between a capital gain and chargeable gain, i.e. all chargeable gains arise from capital gains, but not all capital gains will give rise to a chargeable gain. This distinction is a direct consequence of the necessity for three factors to be present before a chargeable gain can arise:

(i) a chargeable person,
(ii) a chargeable disposal, and
(iii) a chargeable asset.

(i) A chargeable person may be either a UK or foreign subject. What is more important, for a person to be chargeable, is the fact of being resident or ordinarily resident in the UK. A UK subject resident or ordinarily resident in the UK is liable to tax on gains arising world-wide, for example profits on holiday homes in the Welsh Mountains and the Algarve.

A foreign national (German), resident or ordinarily resident in the UK is liable to tax on gains arising in the UK, but gains arising in Germany will only be charged to tax if the profit is remitted to the UK.

Neither UK nor foreign subjects who are non-residents will be charged to tax on gains arising outside the UK. This seems sensible since there would appear to be no justification for the UK government to be able to levy UK capital gains tax on a Spaniard, living in Madrid, selling his business there at a profit. However, a non-resident who trades in the UK will be liable on chargeable gains arising from the disposal of business assets in the UK.

Already the number of possible chargeable persons has been substantially reduced, but what is a person for capital gain tax purposes? A person may include an individual, a company, trustees, and personal representatives of deceased persons. There are a number of statutorily exempt persons including local authorities, charities, unit and investment trusts, and superannuation funds approved by the Inland Revenue.

Husband and wife are treated as one person for this tax unless one of them makes application to be separately assessed. There is no saving of capital gains tax under this election.

(ii) Chargeable disposals are not defined by the law but they may be accorded a normally accepted meaning, i.e. a sale or gift. Additionally, the legislation adds situations which are to be treated as disposals, for example compensation for loss of assets, sums received for forfeiture or surrender of rights, and the granting of an option.

Transactions between husband and wife are not regarded as disposals nor are transfers of assets between companies within a group of companies. In these circumstances the transferee merely subsumes the original cost to the transferor for use in calculating the chargeable gain arising on a subsequent disposal to a third party. Similar treatment is applied where personal representatives of deceased persons transfer assets to legatees. Death is not a disposal for capital gains tax purposes.

(iii) All types of capital asset both tangible and non-tangible are looked upon as chargeable assets, for example buildings or goodwill, unless specifically exempted by the legislation. Table 9.1 indicates a selection of the exempt categories.

It is critical that all these factors are present when a capital gain arises otherwise there can be no chargeable gain for assessment. It is only necessary for one of the three to be absent, and it makes no difference which. Hopefully, it will also become clear in the following sections that unless a situation is immediately recognized as one which cannot, because of legislation, give rise to a chargeable gain considerable time may be spent producing unnecessary computations.

In addition to the exemption of certain classes of assets there is an annual exemption to which all individuals are entitled. This exemption is £6,300 for 1986/7 and is increased annually by index-linking to the retail prices index (RPI). There is only one annual exemption available to husband and wife. Companies are not treated as an individual for this exemption. Effect is given to this annual exemption by deduction from the aggregate chargeable gains for the year of assessment. In 1986/7 Pauline Jackson, who is single, has aggregate chargeable gains amounting to £7,300. After deduction of her annual exemption, assessable gains will be reduced to £1,000. If her aggregate gains had totalled £5,000, the assessable gains for 1986/7 would be reduced to nil. Unfortunately, the unused portion of the £6,300 exemption cannot be carried forward to 1987/8.

TABLE 9.1. *Assets exempted from a charge to capital gains tax*

[a] Motor cars including veteran and vintage vehicles
[a] Non-marketable government securities, e.g. National Savings Certificates
[a] Marketable government securities, e.g. 3½% War Loan
Foreign currency for use outside the UK, e.g. holidays
Decorations for valour except where purchased
[a] Winnings from gambling, e.g. betting and lotteries
[a] Rights under a life assurance policy except where acquired from original owner
[a] Individual's only or main residence
Additional residence for a dependent relative in certain circumstances
[b] Chattels sold for less than £3,000
[b] Wasting chattels unless used in a business
Qualifying corporate bonds
Compensation or damages for personal or professional wrong or injury

[a] Commonly held or arising and therefore of interest to most taxpayers.
[b] These categories have particular relevance to business taxation.

The rate of tax applied to assessable gains for the tax year 1986/7 is 30 per cent so Pauline would ultimately receive an assessment asking her for tax of £300, if the data in the first example above were operative. It is interesting to observe that the effective rate at which an individual taxpayer bears this tax increases as the level of chargeable gains rises, but never quite reaches the full 30 per cent because of the exemption threshold. Pauline has an effective rate of 4.1 per cent on her chargeable gains $\left(\frac{300}{7{,}300} \times 100 = 4.1\%\right)$ or approximately 4p for each £ of gain. A limited company will, on the other hand, always pay at the full 30 per cent for each capital gain £ whatever the level of chargeable gains.

The tax is a direct tax and as such is under direct control of the Commissioners of Inland Revenue with the taxpayer or his advisor having most dealings with HM Inspector of Taxes or Collector of Taxes. Although special returns exist, it is unusual for these to be issued by the Inland Revenue in practice. In most cases it will be sufficient if the appropriate section of the income tax return is completed to disclose relevant details of capital transactions. Assessment and appeal procedures are similar to those existing in income tax legislation (see Chapter 7 on administration and practice).

Payment of the tax is due on 1 December following the end of the year of assessment for which it is due or 30 days after the issue of the assessment if this later. Therefore, the liability for 1986/7 is due on 1 December 1987 providing the Inland Revenue has issued the appropriate assessment by 1 November 1987. If it were issued on 1 December 1987 the tax must be remitted to the Collector of Taxes by 31 December of that year. These rules are only applicable to assessments on individuals, whatever their capacity, i.e. non-trader, partner in trading firm, or trustee of a settlement. They do not apply to limited companies who pay tax on their chargeable gains as part of the corporation tax assessment. The appropriate date is, therefore, variable (see Chapter 10).

Basic computations

The general principles of a capital gains tax computation are straightforward and Table 9.2 illustrates the principal features which might be included where the asset, in question, is acquired after 6 April 1965 and disposed of after 6 April 1982. A commentary on the items included now follows.

It should be noted that although consideration for disposal will normally be the gross sale price, in some circumstances, for example gifts of assets or disposals to connected persons, the price if any, at which it changes hands will no doubt be less than a similar disposal of the same asset to a third party who is a stranger. In such transactions the consideration for disposal is the open market value. The term 'connected persons' encompasses, in general terms, close family members, business partners, trustees of family settlements, and companies under family control. Clearly, key areas for saving capital gains tax

TABLE 9.2. *Outline capital gains tax computation* (£)

Consideration for disposal		40,000
Less: acquisition costs	10,000	
incidental costs of acquisition	1,000	
capital expenditure on enhancement of asset	5,000	
incidental costs of sale	4,000	(20,000)
Capital gain		20,000
Less: indexation allowance (say)		(2,000)
Chargeable gain		£18,000

at the time of disposal, by nil or nominal sale prices, were it not for the open market value rule!

Acquisition costs are, we feel, self-explanatory, but the reader should be aware that the costs must be reduced by any contribution from public money including overseas contributions. Obviously the consideration for disposal £40,000 is the acquisition cost in the purchaser's hands.

Often additional expenditure will be incurred in improving the property. To be deductible this type of expenditure must have enhanced the value of the asset and be reflected in that value at the time of disposal. James Green acquires a derelict barn and two tumbledown cottages. He intends to convert each unit into a holiday cottage. He incurs architect's fees of £500 to obtain planning permission on the barn, but the permission is refused. To unlock capital tied-up in this property he sells at a profit shortly after but the £500 fees are not deductible in arriving at that profit. Conversely, the structural conversion work which he incurs on the two cottages trebles their market value so that, if or when he sells, there will be a deduction for this enhancement work.

Items of expenditure which are of repair or maintenance character, or rank as deductions for income or corporation tax purposes or might be deductible if trade were being carried on, are specifically debarred by law.

Incidental costs of buying and selling cover a wide range of professional services including surveyors, valuers, auctioneers, accountants, estate agents, and legal advisors. Costs of transfer or conveyance are also included together with stamp duties thereon. Advertising costs for a buyer or seller complete the list. Additionally, costs of establishing the market value, where required (see transactions between connected persons above) may be included as an incidental cost of sale. Costs of preparing the actual computation, submitting to, and agreeing with the Inland Revenue are on the other hand not deductible.

From the gross gain, there may be deducted an additional allowance to allow for the effects of inflation. The first positive step toward reducing the effects of inflation was introduced by the 1982 Finance Act with effect from 6 April 1982 (1 April 1982 for companies). After some ten years of debate as to whether it should be costs that were boosted or disposal values reduced, the first piece of legislation was a disappointingly imperfect model. Having come down in favour of indexation of costs, by applying the increase in the RPI as the measure of inflation, it effectively ignored there was inflation prior to April 1982. The use of the RPI as the measure of inflation for capital assets is probably debatable, but to imply there was no inflation prior to April 1982 was simply incorrect. This latter criticism was met by the Government pointing out there was a substantial increase in the annual exemption for 1982/3 compared with the amount in 1981/2 and earlier years. There were also restrictions imposed which excluded the first twelve months of ownership, where this commenced after April 1982, from inflationary increases and treated capital losses unfavourably. Subsequent improvements were incorporated into the legislation by the 1985 Finance Act, including the abolition of the restrictions referred to above. Nevertheless the model is still imperfect in that only capital assets purchased in or after April 1982 and disposed of subsequent to April 1985 are totally inflation-proofed as measured by the RPI.

For disposals on or after 6 April 1985 (1 April 1985 for companies) the indexation allowance is computed by comparing the increase in the RPI between a base month and the month in which the disposal was made. The base month is to be the later of March 1982 or the month in which the expenditure was incurred. Assuming the RPI was 396 at the date of disposal and 313 at March 1982 (the expenditure being prior to that date) the indexation allowance to be applied to costs is 0.265 (rounded to three decimal places in accordance with the legislation). The following formula was used to obtain this result:

$$\frac{Is - Ib}{Ib}$$

where Is = RPI for month of disposal, and
Ib = RPI for base month.

An example of the operation and calculation of the indexation allowance is shown in Table 9.3. The reader should carefully note the way in which the indexation allowance must be calculated for every item of expenditure where the dates are not identical, i.e. base months differ. Additionally, the base month for the original cost is pushed back to March 1982. Incidental costs of acquisition would normally also have indexation allowances, but incidental costs of sale would not attract any indexation allowance.

A further modification to the indexation rules is that where expenditure was incurred prior to 31 March 1982 and the disposal is after 6 April 1985 (1 April 1985 for companies) an election may be made to calculate the indexation allowance by reference to the value of the asset at 31 March 1982. This does not

TABLE 9.3. *Computation of chargeable gain and indexation allowance*

Alan Pye acquired an asset for £10,000 on 1 February 1981. He incurred £2,500 in August 1982 on capital improvements and sells the asset for £36,250 on 9 April 1985.

Assume RPI March 1982 = 313.4
August 1982 = 327.0
April 1985 = 361.0

Computation of capital gain 1985/6		
Sale Price		36,250
Less: original cost (February 1981)	10,000	
improvements (August 1982)	2,500	
Subtotal		(12,500)
Gross gain		23,750
Less: indexation allowance:		
original cost		
$10{,}000 \times \frac{361.0 - 313.4}{313.4}$ (0.152)	1,520	
improvements		
$2{,}500 \times \frac{361.0 - 327.0}{327.0}$ (0.104)	260	
Subtotal		(1,780)
Chargeable gain		£21,970

mean the market value in 1982 is substituted in the body of the computation, merely that the indexation allowance might be increased at the option of the taxpayer. If we assume the asset acquired by Alan Pye in February 1981 had a market value at 31 March 1982 of £15,000, the indexation allowance would become £2,280(0.152 × £15,000) and the chargeable gain would be reduced to £21,210. The gross gain remains unaltered at £23,750.

Finally, in the Alan Pye example, assume he sells (i) for £13,750 or (ii) for £10,625 but no 31 March 1982 election is available. In situation (i) a loss of £530 occurs while in (ii) the loss amounts to £3,655 (we leave it to the reader to verify these figures). What happens to the loss? Generally, the legislation recognizes that not all capital transactions will result in a profit and where a computation reveals a loss this is referred to as an allowable loss. Of course, losses on exempt asset transactions or disposals where either of the other two necessary factors is missing are not allowable losses, i.e. they are ignored in exactly the same way as a gain would be for assessment purposes. The rules for offset of allowable losses are illustrated in Table 9.4 based on the following information provided by Ian Charles, a single man:

	Chargeable gains (£)	*Allowable losses* (£)
1985/6	2,500	4,450
1986/7	12,300	5,300

Priority must always be given to the offset of allowable losses of the current year against current year chargeable gains, and the computations for both 1985/6 and 1986/7 show this procedure. The offset must be in full even where the net chargeable gains are reduced below the annual exemption threshold. This situation occurs in 1985/6 and not only restricts the amount of allowable losses which may be carried forward but also means that the annual exemption for 1985/6 is not needed and cannot be carried forward. However, in subsequent years the treatment of unused allowable losses *vis-à-vis* annual exemption is somewhat more lenient. It is only necessary to use enough of the losses brought forward (£700) to reduce the 1986/7 current year gains (£7,000) to the annual exemption limit (£6,300). The operation of this rule leaves an additional amount of losses (£1,250) available to carry forward to subsequent years for set off as soon as possible. The rules are much simpler for limited companies in that a company does not qualify for the annual exemption. Allowable losses cannot, with minor exceptions, be either carried back or set against profits of an income nature assessable to either income tax or corporation tax in the case of companies.

TABLE 9.4. *An illustration of the treatment of allowable losses for capital gains tax purposes*

Ian Charles—Computation of assessable gains		(£)
1985/6		
Chargeable gains		2,500
Allowable losses		(4,450)
Excess losses carried forward		1,950
Assessable gains		nil
1986/7		
Chargeable gains		12,300
Allowable losses		(5,300)
		7,000
Losses brought forward	1,950	
Utilized	(700)	(700)
Net chargeable gains		6,300
Annual exemption		6,300
Assessable gains		nil
Losses available to carry forward		1,250

Up until this point we have assumed both the acquisition date and therefore disposal date were after 6 April 1965 the day upon which capital gains tax became effective. However, a moment's reflection upon the position of capital asset ownership at that point of time will pinpoint the need for some necessary adjustments to the basic computation presented in Table 9.2 if the asset disposed of had been held at 6 April 1965. In the early days of capital gains tax immediately following 6 April 1965 it followed that all disposals which were caught by the new tax must have been held on 6 April 1965. Recall, that if they have been bought and sold within twelve months, any gain would have been assessed under Schedule D case VII. One of the greatest exemptions which the capital gains tax legislation granted was that gains accruing prior to 6 April 1965 were completely outside the scope of the tax. In other words it was not a retrospective piece of legislation and had to make certain that where chargeable gains were assessable on post- 6 April 1965 disposals of assets held on that date, only the gains arising since that date were caught. Of course, accrued losses are likewise excluded.

The draughtsmen of the legislation approached this problem by establishing two categories of assets and then producing rules for each. The categories of assets are:

(i) quoted securities and land with development value, and
(ii) all other types of assets including unquoted securities.

Quoted securities are those quoted on a recognized Stock Exchange in the UK or elsewhere on 6 April 1965 or within the previous six years. This definition includes units in unit trusts where there is regular publication of bid and offer prices. Land with development value is land within the UK acquired before 6 April 1965 the value of which has been enhanced by the granting of, or possibility of, the grant of planning permission for development under the Town and Country Planning Acts.

The general principle underlying this division was merely that the legislators considered it would be easy to establish the 1965 value of the category (i) assets, even where disposal took place many years after 1965: quoted securities by reference to the Stock Exchange Official List or a specialized service such as that provided by Extel; land with development value by reference to the district valuer. For category (i) assets the gain or loss arising was, in general terms, to be calculated firstly by assuming the taxpayer sold the asset on 6 April 1965, i.e. Budget Day 1965 (BD 1965) and immediately re-acquired it at its market or budget day value 1965 (BDV 1965) then secondly comparing the actual sale proceeds with the BDV 1965. There are, nevertheless, general rules which limit the chargeable gain or allowable loss by reference to the original cost. The taxpayer has no choice in this procedure; the Inland Revenue merely operates the basis which produces the smaller gain or loss or indeed in some cases what is known as a 'no gain no loss situation'. Ignoring indexation these general rules are shown in Table 9.5.

TABLE 9.5. *Computation of chargeable gain or allowable loss on quoted securities held at 6 April 1965*

Briggs sells his holdings in the following four companies in December 1986. He acquired the securities in 1959.

Computation of capital gain 1986/7

	Dee plc[a] (£)	Mirror plc[b] (£)	Fade plc[c] (£)	Green plc[c] (£)
Sale proceeds	1,305	1,087	942	580
Less: BDV 1965	1,145	1,160	1,015	362
Gain or (loss)	160	(73)	(73)	218
Sale proceeds	1,305	1,087	942	580
Less: original cost 1959	1,044	1,305	870	1,015
Gain or (loss)	261	(218)	72	(435)
Chargeable gain or (allowable loss)	160	(73)	nil	nil

[a] The Inland Revenue will accept the BDV 1965 computation where use of original cost would produce a larger gain.

[b] The BDV 1965 computed loss is applied by the Inland Revenue—it is smaller than that produced by the original cost computation.

[c] The BDV 1965 basis recording a loss of £73 and a profit of £218 is ignored because original cost computations show a profit and loss respectively. This is a no gain no loss situation.

The rules are relatively simple to operate, but in the case of quoted securities difficulties in the application of the rules exist. These difficulties stem from the very nature of the asset. Holdings in quoted securities tend to fluctuate over the years irrespective of whether the original holding was purchased prior to or subsequent to 6 April 1965, for example bonus or rights issues, part disposals of holdings, and additional purchases. Also, the introduction of indexation by the 1982 Finance Act produced complex but necessary anti-avoidance legislation for share identification although this has now been relaxed due to indexation changes in the 1985 Finance Act.

Although a detailed study of the complex capital gains tax identification rules is not considered necessary, after all it is mainly individuals or specialized businesses which deal in quoted securities, a brief summary is included here for the interested reader.

Where shares have been bought in the same company on different occasions the price will differ as well. The identification rules spell out how disposals must be matched with acquisitions, for example if 200 shares are purchased in Zena plc at £2 each and a further 400 shares at £4 each and then 100 shares are sold, what is the cost (base) price used in computing the gain? The answer will be dependent on when the shares that were sold were originally purchased as follows:

(i) with any acquisitions made on the same day,
(ii) with any acquisitions made in the previous nine days—using the first in first out principle,
(iii) with the pool, i.e. any shares in Zena plc purchased between 6 April 1982 up to nine days before the disposal (an average price will be used for the cost or base price),
(iv) with a separate pool representing any shares in Zena plc acquired between 6 April 1965 and 5 April 1982,
(v) with any acquisitions made before 6 April 1965.

We now turn to the category (ii) assets which the legislators realized would become more difficult to value on 6 April 1965 the further the disposal date was in the future. On or around BD 1965, there was a great deal of activity by taxpayers in having likely chargeable assets valued.

However, over time, pieces of paper become mislaid or are destroyed. Thus, another set of rules were devised for category (ii) assets which initially relieve, the taxpayer of any need to go to the expense of having to produce a BDV 1965, say thirty years after.

In essence the operation of the rules are extremely straightforward. The computation commences in the normal way by calculating the gain, after indexation, over the whole period of ownership which in Fig. 9.1 is 30 years. However, to arrive at the chargeable gain it is then necessary to apportion an indexed gain between the two time periods *A* and *B*, where period *A* represents the gain accruing in the five years from purchase to BD 1965 and period *B* represents that gain which has accrued from BD 1965 to date of sale. This is

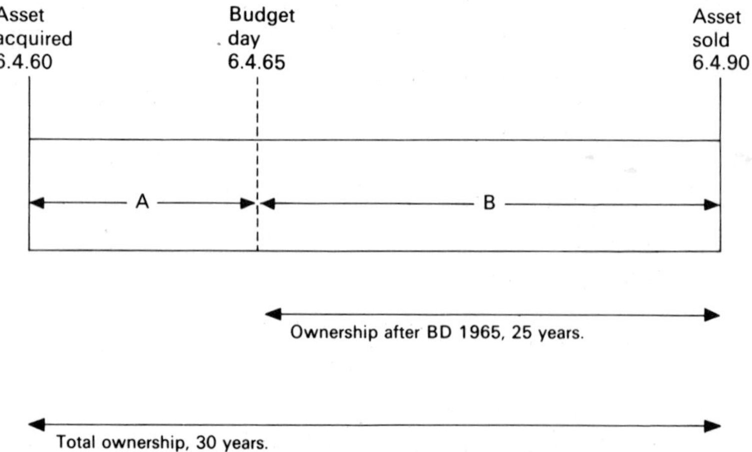

Fig. 9.1 The principle of time apportionment applied to assets held on 6 April 1965

achieved by calculating the gain arising in period *B* only (remember only gains accruing since BD 1965 are chargeable) by applying the fraction $B/(A + B)$ to the overall indexed gain where the numerator (25 years) represents the period of ownership since BD 1965 and the denominator (30 years) the total period of ownership. Any part of the gain which falls in period *B* is chargeable while the remainder, which is attributed to period *A* under these rules, is non-chargeable.

If an indexed loss had arisen overall the part apportioned to period *B* would be allowable whereas the remainder relating to period *A* is non-allowable. Table 9.6 contains a worked example of these principles. It is normal to work in months and fractions of months since clearly not all taxpayers are considerate enough to acquire or dispose of their capital assets on the 6th of a month.

Because time is the unit of apportionment in this set of rules it is referred to as the time-apportionment basis (TAB). Clearly, it applies to a wide range of asset disposals including most business capital assets, for example freehold properties, goodwill, and wasting chattels (which are exempted in a non-business situation).

Unfortunately, the TAB rules make a sweeping assumption which is that the gain or loss accrues evenly over the whole period of ownership. If in the Hanson example the relationship between time and increasing value of the asset were indeed linear, then the TAB has provided the correct solution by calculating a chargeable gain of £3,907. However, in most circumstances it is unrealistic to assume a linear relationship. If we assume the Hanson property

TABLE 9.6. *Calculation of a capital gain on asset held at 6 April 1965*

Hanson acquired an investment property on 6 October 1963 at a cost of £8,000 plus incidental costs of £200. He sold the property on 6 October 1986 for £13,200 net of selling expenses.

Computation of capital gain 1986/7	(£)
Net sale proceeds	13,200
Less: original cost plus incidentals	(8,200)
Gross gain	5,000
Less: indexation allowance (say)	(820)
Indexed gain	£4,180

Chargeable gain 1986/7 is:

$$\text{indexed gain} \times \left(\frac{\text{ownership after BD 1965}}{\text{total ownership}}\right)$$

$$£4{,}180 \times \left(\frac{258 \text{ months } (21\tfrac{1}{2} \text{ years})}{276 \text{ months } (23 \text{ years})}\right) = £3{,}907$$

recorded a value of £11,000 at BD 1965, then this indicates that most of the gain did, in fact, accrue before 6 April 1965. Therefore, the legislation allows the taxpayer to make an election, within two years after the end of the tax year in which the disposal took place (Hanson must elect by 5 April 1989), to have the gain calculated by reference to the BDV 1965. The effect of this election is similar to the mandatory treatment of category (i) assets with some restrictions on size of loss by reference to original cost and allowance for a no gain no loss situation.

The reader should note that in the case of other, i.e. category (ii), assets the taxpayer must take positive action to operate this alternative method of calculating the post-BD 1965 gain—it is not automatically applied as with category (i) assets. Table 9.7 shows the re-calculated chargeable gain arising for 1986/7 if Hanson takes his option.

On the assumption that Hanson's annual exemption and losses, if any, have been fully used in 1986/7 the case for making the election would appear to be overwhelming since, by informing his local HM Inspector of Taxes, there is a tax saving of approximately £840 (£3,907 – £1,100) × 30 per cent. However, Hanson should be warned of the following difficulties surrounding this election:

(i) The Inland Revenue requires, in addition to the written election, a copy of the TAB computation and some evidence for the valuation of £11,000.

(ii) Upon receipt of this information HM Inspector of Taxes will invite his colleague the district valuer to recommend a figure to represent the BDV 1965.

(iii) Normally the taxpayer's and district valuer's figures do not correspond, and unfortunately it is the district valuer's valuation which will hold

TABLE 9.7. *The alternative method of computing a chargeable gain on asset held at 6 April 1965*

Assume the same initial data as shown in Table 9.6, but the BDV 1965 of Hanson's investment property is £11,000

Computation of capital gain 1986/7 (£)	
Net sale proceeds	13,200
Less: BDV 1965 substituted for original cost	(11,000)
Gross gain	2,200
Less: indexation allowance (based on BDV 1965)	(1,100)
Chargeable gain	1,100

Notes:

(i) Providing Hanson makes the election by 5 April 1989 he may apply the alternative basis as there appears to be a tax saving.

(ii) In addition to substituting BDV 1965 for original cost the indexation allowance is also recalculated on BDV 1965.

precedence. This could produce an amended chargeable gain under the alternative basis which was higher than that calculated by TAB.

If this situation did develop what rights has Hanson under the legislation? Unfortunately for Hanson the answer is none. The election, once made, is irrevocable and could result in more, rather than less, tax being paid. The moral of this episode is that where the BDV 1965 substitution option is being considered by a taxpayer, it is the validity of the taxpayer's BDV 1965 valuation which needs thorough checking before the election is made.

Exemptions and reliefs

We commence this section by reference to chattels, i.e. assets which are 'tangible movable property'. Movable in this sense means either under their own power or by human exertion. Thus, a wide range of personal belongings, for example furniture, works of art, racehorses, and some business assets such as plant and machinery, and commercial vehicles, fall within this definition. Clearly, business assets such as buildings and goodwill cannot be chattels by definition.

For the purposes of capital gains tax a subdivision of chattels is made between non-wasting (durable) and wasting chattels. Wasting chattels are those which at the time of disposal have an estimated useful life of less than 50 years. By reference back to Table 9.1 it will be seen that this subdivision is important when it comes to the question of which business assets, if any, are exempted from tax.

Durable chattels whether they be personal or business assets are exempted from tax where the consideration for sale is £3,000 or less. This exemption has a practical application in that only disposals of valuable personal belongings, for example antique furniture or jewellery; will give rise to a chargeable gain or an allowable loss. Where the disposal price is only. marginally in excess of £3,000 the computed chargeable gain cannot exceed 5/3 of the excess proceeds over £3,000. It is difficult to visualize a durable business asset which would be chargeable or exempted under this rule.

Wasting chattels receive a different treatment under the legislation, and based on the proposition that many business assets are wasting chattels, by definition this differential is significant in a study of business taxation. Broadly, the legislation provides that wasting assets are exempted from the capital gains tax whatever the amount of the disposal value. However, there is an exception to this general exemption where the sale price exceeds £3,000 and the wasting asset has been used for the purposes of a trade, profession, or vocation, and capital allowances have been or could have been claimed thereon. In these latter circumstances a chargeable gain may arise although there can never be an allowable loss (see below). Thus, where a private yacht which cost £40,000 is sold for £50,000, the gain of £10,000 is exempted.

However, if the yacht had been part of a yacht chartering business then it would have qualified as plant and machinery, and the gain of £10,000 is chargeable. It should be noted that it is irrelevant whether capital allowances have been actually claimed on the yacht. The fact that the expenditure is eligible is sufficient for capital gains tax legislation. It must not be overlooked that the £40,000 would be deducted from the 'pool' value to establish any balancing charge or reduced value of the 'pool' upon which future writing-down allowances are claimed (see Chapter 8 on plant and machinery).

In the business situation if the yacht had cost £50,000 and it was sold for only £40,000, the loss of £10,000 would be given within the capital allowances system and allowed against the Schedule D case I profits. Therefore, to avoid a double tax allowance the capital loss is not eligible for relief for capital gains tax purposes.

We will now review a relief which is extremely important in business capital taxation and commonly referred to as the roll-over principle. It should be stressed at the outset that this relief is not a true exemption because the tax man catches up later rather than sooner. However, it is a useful principle which may well confer significant liquidity advantages on an expanding business, interest free! The operation of the principle will be outlined in two distinct but commonly met business situations, namely the replacement of business assets and the transfer of an unincorporated business to a limited company.

The general principles of roll-over relief may be best explored within the framework of the replacement of asset situation. The relief applies to both unincorporated businesses and limited companies where a chargeable gain arises on the disposal of a business asset and the proceeds of the sale are reinvested in further business assets. James purchases a building to carry on his business for £100,000 in 1985. After three successful trading years he feels the need to acquire new premises to cope with the growth of his operations. He sells the first building for £140,000 and immediately reinvests the proceeds in a second building which costs £185,000. Ignoring indexation and the annual exemption band, the chargeable gain arising in 1988 is £40,000, and the capital gains tax payable would be £12,000. Without the operation of roll-over relief James, in addition to raising finance of £45,000 to purchase his second building, would also have to pay the Inland Revenue a further £12,000 at a critical period in his firm's development. However, James may elect to postpone the liability of £12,000 by deducting the chargeable gain of £40,000 from the actual cost of the replacement asset and arriving at a 'deemed' cost for future computational work, for example the subsequent disposal of the second building. Table 9.8 shows the detailed computations relating to the first disposal, claim to roll-over relief, and final disposal by James when he ceased trading in 1990. Some general points which should be appreciated about this relief are that capital gains tax may be postponed for a very long time, without any interest charge arising and on a whole series of replacement asset

TABLE 9.8. *The general principles of roll-over relief*

James	
Capital gains computation 1988/9 (£)	
Sale price of building 1 (May 1988)	140,000
Less: cost May 1985	(100,000)
Chargeable gain	40,000
Chargeable gain rolled-over against cost of building 2	(40,000)
Assessable gain	nil
Actual cost of replacement building	185,000
Less: gain on building 1 rolled-over	(40,000)
'Deemed' cost for subsequent transactions	145,000
Capital gains computation 1990/1 (£)	
Sale price of building 2 (May 1990)	200,000
Less: 'deemed' cost May 1988	(145,000)
Chargeable gain	55,000

Note: The assessable gain in 1990/1 represents the sum of the true gain on building 2 (£15,000) and the rolled-over gain of £40,000 from 1988/9.

transactions—not merely the one as used in this example. Additionally, it is interesting to note that if the second building were sold for merely £145,000 there would be no chargeable gain in 1990/1 which effectively means the rolled-over gain of £40,000 escapes assessment, and it follows the Inland Revenue cannot collect the deferred tax of £12,000.

As with most tax legislation there are certain conditions which are laid down with regard to the roll-over principle and replacement of business assets. There is a restriction on the class of asset to which the relief applies. These special classes are land and buildings, ships, aircraft, goodwill, hovercraft, and fixed plant and machinery. Apart from this apparently rather narrow grouping of business assets which qualify for the relief it is, nevertheless, important to note that the old and new asset need not be within the same class. Thus, the chargeable gain arising on the sale of a retail shop may be rolled-over against the cost of an executive aircraft. A further interesting extension of this flexibility is that, apart from the general rule that both the old and new asset must be used in a business, the legislation currently allows the taxpayer to elect for the relief not only within the same trade but also between trades. It follows that the chargeable gain on say, the disposal of goodwill in a bookmaker's business may be rolled-over against the cost of a building to carry on a ladies' hairdressing salon providing, of course, the two businesses are carried on by the same person. Person for this purpose includes a limited company, and groups of companies are treated as one, so that where one group member sells to a third party and another group member buys the replacement external to the group, relief is available. The time limited for making the claim on the replacement asset is within the range twelve months before to three years after the disposal of the old asset.

There are two further important restrictions on roll-over a relief where either (i) only part of the sale proceeds are reinvested, or (ii) the replacement asset is a depreciating asset.

The first restriction is introduced to counter abuse of the relief in that the law makes certain that where cash is or should be available, the tax bill must be settled on the due date. If we assume, for instance, that James in the earlier example had replaced his first building with a second building that cost merely £130,000 then only that part of the gain which is reinvested (£30,000) may be rolled-over leaving the balance of £10,000 to be assessed in 1988/9. There is a net cash increment to the business of £7,000 after the tax bill has been settled. Where no part of the gain is reinvested there is no question of a claim, the vendor being treated as if he were making a final disposal without replacement.

The second restriction, is where a replacement asset is established to be depreciating, i.e. at the time of purchase it has an estimated useful life of not more than fifty years, or will so within ten years of purchase, for example a 55-year lease. When this is the case the taxpayer cannot elect for roll-over relief in its pure form but is nevertheless entitled to defer the gain being assessed until the earliest of the following events:

(i) the replacement asset is disposed of,
(ii) it ceases to be used in the taxpayer's business, or
(iii) the tenth anniversary of its acquisition.

Although tax is postponed in a similar manner to that allowed under the roll-over relief claim, the taxpayer nevertheless has a finite time horizon by which the tax bill must be paid, and it cannot be extinguished by a loss arising on the disposal of the replacement asset.

Having reviewed the roll-over principle it is now possible to apply it to the situation where a sole trader or partnership may want to transfer their business to a limited company. At the outset it is important to note that this is a strictly one-way process, and there is no possibility of any relief where a corporate business becomes unincorporated or indeed where one company transfers its business to another corporate entity. The actual transfer of the business to a company produces a chargeable disposal for capital gains tax purposes which, in turn, may produce a chargeable gain on the assets being transferred. The principal assets giving rise to a gain are land, buildings, and goodwill. However, subject to certain conditions the chargeable gain on the business assets may be rolled-over and offset against the value of the shares issued by the company in exchange for those assets. The conditions specify that it is essential the business be transferred as a going concern and that all business assets must be assigned other than for cash. In addition, the consideration for the transfer must be wholly or partly for shares issued by the acquiring company to the transferor of the business.

In circumstances where the consideration is wholly for shares the computational aspects are relatively straightforward. Suzanne Green has decided to transfer her business, which has a net worth of £60,000 to a new limited company S.G. Limited. It has been agreed the new company will issue her with 60,000 £1 ordinary shares in exchange. The first step is to compute any chargeable gains arising on Suzanne in the normal way comparing agreed values for assets against original costs. The only chargeable gain arising (£40,000) is that on goodwill, all other assets being exempt. The next step is for Suzanne to elect for this gain to be rolled-over against the cost of her shares in S.G. Limited. If this is done the 'deemed' cost of the S.G. Limited shares is reduced to £20,000 for subsequent computational purposes, for example a sale of the shares by Suzanne. However, if there is a mixed consideration for the business, i.e. part shares and part other assets (usually cash), then the proportion of the chargeable gain arising on the transferor relative to the non-share consideration cannot be deferred. This complication is illustrated in Table 9.9 and is based upon the previous example, but now Suzane receives £50,000 in S.G. Limited shares and £10,000 in cash. It will be seen that the effect of the restriction in roll-over relief gives rise to some immediate tax liability on part of the disposal of goodwill (£6,667) whereas tax on the balance is effectively deferred until such time as Suzanne disposes of her shares in S.G. Limited. The

TABLE 9.9. *Transfer of a business to a company for a mixed consideration*

Chargeable gain arising on transfer to S. G. Ltd.		£40,000
Consideration issued by S. G. Ltd.:		
50,000 £1 ordinary shares	50,000	
cash	10,000	
	£60,000	
Computation of final chargeable gain and roll-over relief (£)		
Chargeable gain		40,000
Less: relief, $\frac{A}{B} \times \text{gain} = \frac{50{,}000}{60{,}000} \times 40{,}000$		(33,333)
Non-deferred chargeable gain		6,667
where A = value of shares given in exchange by S. G. Ltd.		
B = total value of whole consideration received from S. G. Ltd.		
'Deemed' cost of S. G. Ltd. shares for future disposals by Suzanne (£)		
Actual cost of shares		50,000
Less: gain rolled-over		(33,333)
'deemed' cost for subsequent transactions		16,667

reader is left to check this is so by verifying the chargeable gain arising on Suzanne is £83,333 if, at some future date, she sells all her shares in S.G. Limited for £100,000.

This section will be concluded by a review of the retirement relief legislation which, unlike the roll-over principle, is a true exemption from tax upon an individual retiring from business. This piece of legislation does not apply to limited companies although it does apply in certain situations to shares in a family trading company (see below).

Generally, the transfer or sale of an unincorporated business or the disposal of shares in a family company, upon retirement, is a chargeable disposal for capital gains tax purposes. Clearly, substantial tax liabilities might arise on a taxpayer at a time in his life when any reduction in his available capital might be critical to his being able to live in the manner to which he has become accustomed. Thus, this exemption was introduced whereby all or part of the gains arising on the business assets, up to the maximum of £100,000, become non-chargeable. Originally the exemption was only granted to individuals aged over 60, but the 1985 Finance Act introduced additional legislation which extends the relief to persons under the age of 60 who have to retire on the grounds of ill-health. In the latter circumstances the retiring taxpayer must make formal election to the Inland Revenue for the relief to apply and also produce medical evidence showing he or she is incapable of carrying on the business. Where the Inland Revenue decides the grounds are insufficient, the decision is final, and there is no appeal procedure. For the over 60 taxpayer the application of the relief is automatic, and it is interesting to note that it is not even necessary for the taxpayer to go into retirement, merely that he makes a material disposal of business assets. Apart from these distinctions between the two age categories the remainder of the legislation is applied evenly, for example the concept of a material disposal.

A material disposal is defined as the disposal of a business, or part of it, providing the business has been owned by an individual for a minimum of one year prior to the date the business ceased. The business may be either a sole proprietorship or a partnership. A material disposal may also be extended to a disposal by an individual of shares in a company owning the business, providing that company is a family trading company and the individual is a full-time working director of that company. A family company is any company where the individual owns at least 25 per cent of the voting rights or his own share is at least 5 per cent of such rights and together with close relatives (e.g. his wife) owns more than 50 per cent. To attract the relief the individual must, in general terms, have satisfied the voting rights and full-time working director requirements for the minimum period of one year prior to the disposal of the shares.

Business assets which qualify for the relief are also defined, although this is by exclusion rather than inclusion. Specific exclusions are shares or other assets held as investments and any assets on which no chargeable gain would arise on a disposal because of exemptions, for example durable or wasting chattels sold for less than £3,000, stock , debtors, and cash. Clearly, the list of chargeable business assets becomes somewhat truncated by these exclusions and for most practical purposes will only include goodwill and premises. However, it is important for the reader realize, although shares or assets held as investments are not chargeable business assets they, nevertheless, are chargeable assets for capital gains tax purposes.

The maximum relief available against chargeable business assets is £100,000 but will be reduced proportionately where the business has not been owned for a full ten years or, in the case of shares in a family company, the director has not been a full-time working director for a similar period of time prior to the disposal. Therefore, a qualifying time span of 10 years attracts 100 per cent relief, 5 years 50 per cent relief, and 1 year 10 per cent with appropriate adjustments for parts of a year. Clearly, there is a minimum relief of £10,000 since any period of ownership under a year would debar a claim to relief. The computation of the relief upon a material disposal by two sole traders is illustrated in Table 9.10. The reader should note particularly the dual restriction of the relief available to Desmond Quick, and in the case of Ian Jones the period of ownership in excess of 10 years is ignored. Desmond will have a chargeable gain of £5,000 arising from the sale of the commercial vehicle.

Where the material disposal is of shares in a family company there is an added complication in that the consideration received by the vendor for those shares is arrived at by reference to the assets of the company. Thus, only part of the consideration will normally relate to chargeable business assets while the remainder is related to chargeable assets. It follows that any resultant gain will be similarly allocated, and so as to maintain equity between the different circumstances of taxpayers, the legislation provides that the part of the gain which attracts retirement relief be calculated as follows:

$$\text{Gain on shares} \times \frac{\text{Chargeable business assets}}{\text{Chargeable business assets plus chargeable assets}}$$

A worked example of this necessary variation is given in Table 9.11. The chargeable gain after relief is £15,000. What is most important for the reader to realize in this situation is, that the value of the company's assets is only relevant for apportionment of the gain arising on the disposal of the shares. It does not enter directly into the calculation of the gain. The gain referred to is calculated by reference to the sale consideration received by Patch, less his cost of acquisition.

Concluding remarks

After a brief introduction recording the history and development of capital gains tax, the remainder of this chapter has concentrated on a systematic

TABLE 9.10. *Computation of retirement relief for a sole trader*

(a) Desmond Quick disposes of his business which he has owned throughout the previous $7\frac{1}{2}$ years. His age at retirement is 62. The gains arising on the disposal are:

	(£)
business properties	50,000
business goodwill	20,000
commercial vehicle	5,000

The maximum relief available is 75% × £100,000 = £75,000.
The actual relief available is limited to £70,000 (i.e. the gains arising on chargeable business assets—properties and goodwill).

(b) Ian Jones, aged 48, has owned his business for 15 years. Unfortunately he has suffered a physical disability which has forced him into an early retirement. He has negotiated a sale of the business and the gains arising on the disposal are:

	(£)
business properties	70,000
business goodwill	40,000

The maximum and actual relief available is 100% × £100,000 = £100,000.

TABLE 9.11. *Computation of retirement relief upon the disposal of shares in a family trading company*

Patch who is 64 years old sells his shares in a family trading company realizing a gain of £45,000. He had been a full-time working director of the company for the previous 5 years. On his retirement the company's assets were valued:

	(£)
property	30,000
goodwill	30,000
trade investment	30,000
	90,000

The maximum relief available is 50% × £100,000 = £50,000.
The actual relief available is limited to:

$$45{,}000 \times \frac{60{,}000}{90{,}000} = £30{,}000$$

(i.e. the proportion of the gain relative to chargeable business assets).

development of the reader's knowledge and appreciation of an important UK tax on capital assets.

The first part of the chapter concentrated upon introducing, with the aid of basic computations, the underlying concept of the legislation including important terminology such as consideration for disposal, allowable capital costs, gross and chargeable gains. The necessity for the introduction of indexation and how the allowance is computed were outlined followed by a short explanation of how allowable losses are relieved under the legislation.

The chapter then continued by introducing the reader to the special rules which have had to be devised to deal with disposal of assets acquired prior to 6 April 1965. The rules are complex, and a rigorous examination of the principles of time-apportionment and substitution of market value 1965 was undertaken.

In the final section of the chapter a number of exemptions and reliefs were introduced which modify the basic computations. A discussion of the problem of wasting chattels in a business context was undertaken and the inter-relationship with income tax and the capital allowance system was outlined. The important principle of roll-over relief was analysed in detail and its application to an important business decision—the transfer of an unincorporated business to a limited company—illustrated.

Finally, the provisions of retirement relief legislation including the extension of the law to encompass ill-health retirements were reviewed, and a comparison was made between the computations necessary for sole traders and vendors of shares in family trading companies.

Recommendations for further reading

For those readers requiring a more advanced approach to general computations, including indexation and losses, reference may be made to Bertram and Edwards (1986) and Pritchard (1985). An explanation, cross-referenced to the statutes, of the relationship between capital gains tax and capital allowances, the transfer of an unincorporated business to a limited company, and retirement relief may be found in chapter 20, Butterworth (1985). An in depth explanation of the operation of the roll-over relief and indexation is given in a two-part article by Sandy (1985).

References

Bertram, D., and Edwards, S. (1986), *Comprehensive Aspects of Taxation—1986–87* (London: Holt, Rinehart and Winston).

Butterworth (1985), *Butterworths UK Tax Guide* (London: Butterworths).

King, J. (1985), 'What future for Capital Gains Tax?', *Fiscal Studies*, 6, no. 2 (May 1985): 71–7.

Pritchard, W. E. (1985), *Income Tax 1985/86* (Harlow, Essex: Longman).

Sandy, C. (1985), 'Rollover Relief', *The Accountant*, (16 May 1985): 20–1 and (23 May 1985): 23–4.

10
Corporation Tax

Introduction

Corporation tax was introduced as a separate tax on corporate profits in 1965, and within this chapter we will present a review of its development to the current time.

After this brief review an explanation of the general operational principles will be given and comparisons will be drawn, where relevant, to the taxation of unincorporated businesses (Chapter 8). As the explanation develops the reader will observe that the legislation relating to corporation tax is in some respects an extension, with modifications, of that applied to non-corporate organizations.

The remainder of the chapter will concentrate upon specific parts of the law which are unique to corporate taxation and cover such areas as the quarterly accounting system, family, associated, and groups of companies.

History and development

Prior to 1965, companies were subject to direct assessment of income tax on their profits with some modifications to recognize that although they were separate legal entities, they were not individuals for tax purposes, i.e. they were not entitled to the range of personal allowances. During the period 1915 to 1965 it was the threat of, or the outbreak of war and the consequent need by the nation for additional finance which led to the first separate tax on company incomes.

However, these discriminating taxes came and went, and it was through the 1965 Finance Act that corporation tax was finally introduced. Overnight, companies found a completely new piece of legislation specifically drawn to tax corporate profits.

From the outset the tax had its detractors. The objections ranged from the impossibility of changing from a previous year basis of assessment of income tax to that of an actual basis for the new tax (see following section on scope and coverage) to more fundamental issues such as the dual taxation of distributed profits.

The first type of objection rapidly evaporated as professional advisors discovered the benefits stemming from an actual-based tax. However, the

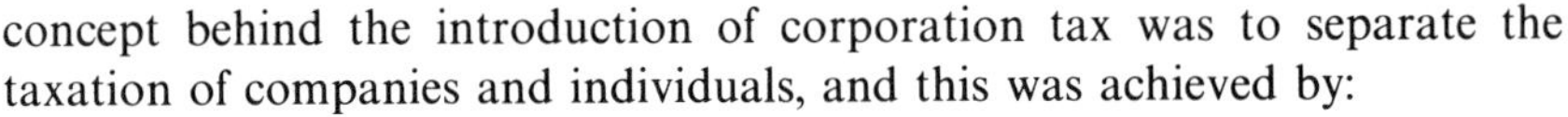

concept behind the introduction of corporation tax was to separate the taxation of companies and individuals, and this was achieved by:

(i) imposing a flat or uniform rate on all company profits whether they were retained or distributed in the form of dividends—the classical system,
(ii) creating a new Schedule F whereby companies were liable to deduct income tax at the basic rate from distributions and account for these deductions to the Inland Revenue on behalf of the recipients.

Clearly, there was dual taxation of distributed profits, and it took a considerable time for the objectors to obtain a necessary change in law albeit that it was not through the abolition of corporation tax.

The 1972 Finance Act introduced the necessary changes which came into effect on 1 April 1973. This new piece of legislation introduced the imputation system, which is still currently operative, the essential elements of which are:

(i) A company is chargeable to corporation tax on its profits whether retained or distributed.

(ii) A company distributing profits will, in addition, be required to make an advance payment of corporation tax (ACT) to the Inland Revenue (see later section on quarterly accounting system).

(iii) The ACT payment is considered to belong to the individual recipient (i.e. it is ascribed to or imputed to him), and it is from this process the title imputation system is derived. The tax payment entitles the shareholder to a tax credit of a corresponding amount which is set off against his liability to income tax at the basic rate on the 'gross' dividend (i.e. dividend received plus the tax credit, see Chapter 7).

(iv) When the company pays its corporation tax bill, the ACT paid will be deducted from the gross liability calculated on all profits.

Thus, dual taxation on distributed profits is now avoided, and yet the concept of a separate corporation tax for companies is retained while income tax is still applicable to individuals.

Scope and coverage

Although it should be reasonably clear to the reader that limited liability companies are chargeable to corporation tax, the legislation casts a rather wider net. Companies, for the purposes of this tax, are those resident in the UK incorporated under the various Companies Acts plus any other body corporate, for example a public corporation created by an Act of Parliament and unincorporated associations. Although the wording, unincorporated associations, does not include partnerships it does include a wide range of organizations such as sports clubs, and the Inland Revenue has sought, successfully, to establish a nunnery to be within this definition. However, they did fail in the Court of Appeal, to prove the Conservative and Unionist Central Office was an unincorporated association!

The main exempted bodies, other than partnerships, are local authorities, local authority associations, and charities.

In certain circumstances non-resident companies may fall within the scope of UK corporation tax, but this overseas aspect will be dealt with in Chapter 17.

We must now consider, in general terms, how a company's corporation tax liability is assessed and upon what profits. It should be noted that for the remainder of this chapter 'company' is to include the wider definition outlined above. For corporation tax the word profit has a precise meaning and represents the company's income plus chargeable capital gains. A company's income is computed using the income tax schedules and cases and the various computational rules which apply to each schedule (see Chapter 7). The chargeable gain element of profit is computed using the principles outlined in Chapter 9. There is also an extended meaning of profit which we will discuss in detail under the section on small companies rate of corporation tax. Turning now to the question of assessment, as a matter of statutory convenience a company will only receive one piece of paper, i.e. an assessment notice, covering all sources of income and chargeable gains forming part of the profit. The reader is invited to compare this to an individual taxpayer with sources of income under Schedules A, D cases I and III, and a chargeable gain. In the latter situation the individual may receive as many as four direct assessment notices and certainly a minimum of two. However, returning to the point of one assessment notice on companies; although this may have statutory convenience it does pose a problem in arriving at the correct tax payable upon any chargeable gains realized by a company. This problem will be demonstrated, together with its solution, in the section on computation of profits. The most important feature of assessment of corporation tax must now be stressed. Although income is computed in accordance with income tax rules a company is always assessed on an actual basis. If Clarke Limited has been trading for many years to 30 September and its Schedule D case I income is £40,000 for the year 1987, then it will receive a corporation tax assessment on those profits for a chargeable accounting period ended 30 September 1987. However, if Clarke had conducted his trading activities as a sole trader, Schedule D case I income would be assessed for the tax year 1988/9. Recognizing that a chargeable accounting period corresponds to a year of assessment for taxing purposes it will be seen that for Clarke Limited the basis period and chargeable accounting period coincide (actual basis) whereas for Clarke the basis period and year of assessment fall in two different tax years (previous year basis). So we may sum up by saying that tax is charged on an actual basis for a chargeable accounting period which is normally a company's accounting year or period of account. Once we have examined the features of a chargeable accounting period the simplicity of assessment of corporate trades compared with unincorporated trades (which is given by escaping the shackles of the previous year basis) is astounding.

A chargeable accounting period is a period of time for which corporation tax is charged on a company. This time period may not exceed 12 months, i.e. it may be less but never more. This causes a minor problem where a company prepares its accounts for a period of account longer than 12 months, for example Flag Limited makes up its accounts for the 19 months ended 30 September 1987. To arrive at the chargeable accounting period for assessment purposes, the twelve-month rule is applied by splitting the period of account on a time basis. Thus, for Flag Limited two chargeable accounting periods are established, namely from 1 March 1986 to 28 February 1987 (12 months) and 1 March 1987 to 30 September 1987 (7 months). It is important to observe that the period of twelve months must come first, followed by the balance, never the other way round. Clearly, subject to the general legislation outlined above, chargeable accounting periods may be for any length of time—normally consecutive—which may commence or cease on the occurrence of the following:

(i) a company's trading year commencing or ceasing,
(ii) the commencement or cessation of a trade,
(iii) a company becoming or ceasing to be resident in the UK, or
(iv) the passing of a resolution to wind-up.

A general example is included in Table 10.1. However, it is purely illustrative due to the restrictions imposed by company law on changes of accounting dates. Unashamedly a contrived example, it nevertheless illustrates the comparative ease of calculating taxing periods for corporate trades particularly avoiding the complex commencement and permanent cessation rules

TABLE 10.1. *Establishing a chargeable accounting period*

Crypt Ltd. commenced trading on 1 October 1986 and had the following profile of trading periods until it went into liquidation:

12 months ended 30.09.87
12 months ended 30.09.88
15 months ended 31.12.89
9 months ended 30.09.90

A resolution to wind-up the company was passed on 30 November 1990.

The chargeable accounting periods are:

12 months ended 30.09.87 (commencement of trade to end of trading year)
12 months ended 30.09.88 (commencement/end of trading year)
12 months ended 30.09.89 (commencement of trading period for maximum 12 months)
3 months ended 31.12.89 (balance of trading period)
9 months ended 30.09.90 (commencement/end of trading period)
2 months ended 30.11.90 (commencement of trading period to start of winding-up)

required for unincorporated traders (see Chapter 8). Clearly, there is no double taxing of profits in early years although conversely, upon permanent cessation, no profits drop out of assessment as they would under income tax law. The reader should also have detected that the complex basis period legislation for capital allowances becomes similarly redundant—capital allowances being generally computed for the relevant chargeable accounting period. Although profits are assessed by reference to chargeable accounting periods, the rate of corporation tax to be applied to those profits is fixed for financial years. Within the corporation tax legislation a financial year has a precise meaning and must not be confused with a company's trading year. Its equivalent in income tax law is the year of assessment. However, more sensible dates are used, and a financial year is deemed to run from 1 April in one calendar year to 31 March in the next and is identified by the calendar year in which it commences, for example the financial year 1986 spans the period 1 April 1986 to 31 March 1987. As for income tax, the rate is announced in the Chancellor's Budget Speech and becomes law in the subsequent Finance Act. For many years, unlike income tax, the rate was fixed in arrears but the 1984 Finance Act fixed the rate not only for the financial year 1983 (i.e. 1 April 1983 to 31 March 1984) but also for the future years 1984, 1985, and 1986. The 1986 Finance Act made a further fine tuning adjustment to the small companies rate for 1986, interestingly once again in advance. So at the time of writing we know both the full and small companies rates up to and including 31 March 1987. The appropriate rates, including the ACT fraction, are given in Table 10.2 and will be used for later computational work in this chapter. Strictly speaking, the ACT rate is set for the income tax year i.e. 6 April to following 5 April, and is always set in advance because of its direct relationship with the basic rate of income tax as part of the imputation system described earlier. While the basic rate of income tax remained at 30 per cent, the corresponding ACT rate was 3/7 but subsequently when the basic rate became 29 per cent in the 1986 Finance Act a change in the ACT rate for 1986/7 became necessary.

We now consider the question of when the tax is payable. The answer is dependent upon whether the liability is settled as ACT on distributed profits or by direct assessment on all profits (with or without an appropriate deduction for ACT) often referred to as mainstream corporation tax (MCT). Where ACT is payable, then generally, the due date may not exceed $3\frac{1}{2}$ months from the date of the associated distribution of profits under the quarterly

TABLE 10.2. *Corporation tax rates for recent years*

Financial year	1983	1984	1985	1986
Full rate	50%	45%	40%	35%
Small company rate	30%	30%	30%	29%
ACT rate	3/7	3/7	3/7	29/71

accounting system. A liability to MCT is due for payment 9 months after the end of the chargeable accounting period or 30 days after the issue date of the assessment notice, whichever is the later. This rule applies to all companies commencing to trade after 1 April 1965. For a company with a chargeable accounting period ended 30 June 1987 this means the MCT is due on 31 March 1988 unless the Inland Revenue issues the assessment after 1 March 1988. However, for companies trading prior to 1 April 1965 we should recall that companies paid income tax on their profits under the previous year basis of assessment. Therefore, we must consider the effect on company cash flows upon the change over to corporation tax. Under the old system a company with a 30 June 1964 year-end would have received a 1965/6 tax assessment showing tax due on 1 January 1966 (there was no equal instalment provision for companies). Upon the introduction of corporation tax the MCT due on profits for a year ended 30 June 1965 would be payable on 31 March 1966. The resultant one-off double tax bill within one trading year would almost certainly put a strain on the cash resources of the best regulated company. To avoid this unnecessary hardship the legislation allowed companies trading pre-1965 to retain the original tax lag from the end of their trading period. Thus, the pay date would become 1 January 1967 i.e. 18 months from the end of the chargeable accounting period 30 June 1965. The 18-month interval is effective in all future years, and the company in our example would continue to pay MCT on 1 January each year, unless it were to change its accounting year-end. A change in accounting date, forward by 3 months, to 30 September merely gives a chargeable accounting period ended on that date. The new date for payment of tax will also move forward by the same number of months, i.e. to 1 April. This illustrates the general rule that the due date for payment of MCT will remain the same time interval after the chargeable accounting period as existed before the change.

Corporation tax is another direct tax so is administered by the Commissioners of Inland Revenue. The procedures for raising assessments, lodging appeals, making applications for postponement of disputed tax, interest provisions, and the collection are therefore generally the same as for income tax (see Chapter 7 on administration and practice).

Computation of profits

For an appreciation of the fundamental principles which are involved in the computation of profits Table 10.3 shows, in outline, the format of a typical company tax computation. Naturally, in practice, it would be unusual if every line had a value. For the purist it should be explained that profits chargeable to corporation tax (PC) should technically be arrived at by taking income from all sources (d) plus chargeable gains (NCG) to give total profits less charges on income (e). However, we consider the layout adopted makes for an easier presentation of certain key issues; the more technically correct format is

TABLE 10.3. *Outline corporation tax computation*

Denton Ltd.—Corporation tax computation for the chargeable accounting period ended ..... 19xx (£)	
Corporation tax income:	
Schedules A, B, D case I, D cases III–VI	a
Unfranked investment income (UFII) (gross)	b
Building society interest (gross)	c
	d
Less: charges on income (gross)	(e)
Net taxable income	NTI
Add: chargeable gains (proportion)	NCG
Profits chargeable to corporation tax	PC
Add: franked investment income (FII) (gross)	f
Profits for small companies rate	PS

reverted to later after the reader has completely mastered the basic principles of computation.

Before analysing in detail the various items which could appear in a corporation tax computation it must be emphasized that the terms net taxable income (NTI), profits chargeable to corporation tax (PC) and profits for small companies rate (PS) do initially cause the tiro of the tax some confusion. However, for any serious student of corporation tax it is vital that the differences between these three terms becomes absolutely clear.

We will commence the analysis by considering net taxable income (NTI) which consists of all income of the company less charges on income during the chargeable accounting period. For sources of income computed in accordance with the income tax schedules (a) it should be noted that income tax Schedules C, D case II, and E do not appear. Unless the company is a UK paying agent of income from government stocks it cannot receive an assessment under Schedule C, and in this respect individual companies are in exactly the same position as an individual under income tax legislation. Companies are deemed to carry on a trade and therefore income from their main activities are assessed under Schedule D case I and never D case II. Schedule E does not apply to companies as they cannot hold offices of employment in the same way that individuals can.

It is normal to commence the computation with the Schedule D case I adjusted profit, and the same underlying principles of allowable and non-allowable expenditure, as discussed in Chapter 8 in relation to unincorporated businesses, prevail. There are, nevertheless, some important differences. A number of the more common allowable and non-allowable expenses for Schedule D case I purposes, as applied to companies, are given in Table 10.4. Those items which have a fundamentally different treatment under corporation tax legislation are marked with an asterisk and are decribed below:

(i) Approved pension fund contributions relate to the company's portion of the premiums paid on behalf of all employees including directors.

(ii) Capital allowances are treated as a trading expense in the main body of the computation and not, as for income tax, a deduction against the assessment. Balancing charges are deemed to be a trading receipt.

(iii) The cost of obtaining loan finance, for example debentures, is deductible but for ordinary share capital is not.

TABLE 10.4. *Examples of allowable and non-allowable expenditure under Schedule D case I for corporation tax*

Allowable	Non-allowable
Accountancy/audit fees	* Annual payments made under deduction of income tax
* Approved pension fund contributions	Bad debts general provision
Bad debts written off/specific provision	
* Capital allowances	Capital expenditure including improvements
Contributions to approved local enterprise agency	Charitable donations
	Corporation tax
	Depreciation of capital assets
* Cost of obtaining loan finance	* Dividends to shareholders
	Entertainment
* Directors' emoluments	Fines and other penalties
Interest on borrowed money	Gifts to customers
Legal expenses for debt recovery, defence of trading rights, renewing a short lease (less than 50 years)	Legal expenses for acquisition of assets and other capital items
	Political party donations
Premium paid for business lease	* Preliminary expenses on company formation
	Taxation appeal costs
Repair expenditure	
Rent of business premises	
Trade subscriptions	
VAT, if non-recoverable	
Wages to employees including employers' national insurance contributions	

(iv) Directors' emoluments include payments of fees, salaries, commission, and benefits in kind, for example use of company car and provision of living accommodation. It should be noted that a director is for tax purposes an employee of a company, thus in general all such payments are deductible in full. Put another way they are not regarded as appropriations of profit. This does not mean that an individual who chooses to run his business activity as a limited company, rather than as a sole trader, achieves a tax advantage particularly in respect to benefits. As with all income from employment the director is assessable under Schedule E to income tax including the private element of expenses and the use of capital assets provided by the company. This approach means that it is unnecessary to record separately, for capital allowance purposes, assets where there is an element of non-business use. Also expenses incurred in respect of such assets are chargeable in full against profits. Cinque Limited has five directors all of whom use a company vehicle. Their business mileages exceed 2,500 miles per annum but all have some private mileage in addition to that incurred on company business. The total running costs of the vehicles is £7,500. Providing none of the vehicles originally cost more that £8,000 the company's capital allowance computation would not show any of these vehicles separately, i.e. the written-down values would be incorporated in the special car pool. Additionally, there is no restriction, by reference to the private use, of the capital allowances which may be claimed by the company for the chargeable accounting period. If one of the vehicles had cost more than £8,000 originally then this vehicle would be shown separately as an expensive car—mainly to ensure the writing-down allowance does not exceed £2,000 per annum. Again the computed writing-down allowance is in no way restricted by reference to any private use. The running costs of £7,500 will be allowed in full in computing Cinque's Schedule D case I profit. Ultimately, each director will receive a Schedule E assessment valuing the benefit of the private use of his car which is calculated in accordance with a pre-determined scale of charges. Thus, the Inland Revenue obtains their 'pound of flesh' albeit from the individual rather than his company.

(v) Annual payments made under deduction of income tax cover payments of interest excluding bank interest, deeds of covenant (including those to a charity) and patent royalties. These payments are collectively referred to as charges on income and although non-allowable in the computation of trading profits are nevertheless deductible from a wider range of company income (see item (e) in outline computation). However, to be deductible the charges must have been paid in the chargeable accounting period.

(vi) Dividend payments to shareholders are, unlike charges on income, totally non-allowable for corporation tax purposes. Thus, they are always paid out of post-tax profits, and this discrimination between the two types of payments and its effects on financing and investment decisions are more fully explored in Chapter 13 and 14. In the context of this chapter dividends are regarded by the legislation as appropriations of profit and as such are not deductible.

(vii) Preliminary expenses arising upon the formation of a company i.e. bringing it into legal existence, are non-allowable. Clearly this expenditure cannot be deductible under the 'wholly and exclusively' principle. However, care must be taken not to confuse preliminary expenses, which create the company, with pre-trading expenditure of a revenue nature. The latter class of expenditure may in certain circumstances be deductible from trading profits.

Having established the Schedule D case I profit, we believe the remaining income arising under section (a) needs little further explanation. Similar to an unincorporated business, a company may receive rents from UK land and buildings (Schedule A) and occupy commercially managed woodlands (Schedule B), although more likely an election to have this assessed under Schedule D case I will have been made. A company may receive interest (Schedule D case III) and also overseas income (Schedules D cases IV and V). It is important to remember that any income received by a company under these schedules is assessed to corporation tax on an actual basis and not the previous year basis applied to similar income under income tax legislation. Finally, any miscellaneous income or profits of the company will be dealt with under the rules of Schedule D case VI.

Income to be included under unfranked investment income (UFII) at point (b) includes all income received under deduction of income tax. The main sources of income included under this heading are: debenture and loan interest from other UK companies, certain government securities, and patent royalties. Because the changes in the 1984 Finance Act relating to the application of the composite rate system to bank deposit account interest does not apply to deposits by corporate investors such interest is received gross by companies and cannot by definition be classed as UFII. It is Schedule D case III income. As described earlier, companies are no longer liable to income tax on their income or profits, and it is therefore necessary to gross up any UFII received by the appropriate rate. Corporation tax is then charged on the gross marginal £ at the correct corporation tax rate and credit given for the income tax suffered. This procedure is similar to that applied to individual taxpayers where income is received under deduction of tax at source (see Chapter 7). There are, however, some important differences, and these are dealt with under the later section on the quarterly accounting system. Perhaps the reader might at this stage consider the proposition that charges on income and UFII are merely two sides of the same coin where debenture interest is paid by one UK resident company to another.

Where a company, normally an unincorporated association, receives building society interest (c) the amount received is deemed to have suffered income tax at source. Thus, it is essential the gross equivalent be included as corporation tax income with credit being given for the income tax deemed to have been suffered, against the MCT liability. Where the tax credit exceeds the MCT, a repayment of the excess will be made to the company. This repayment procedure is totally different to that for individuals under income tax legislation where any excess building society interest tax credit is never refundable.

To establish the level of profits chargeable to corporation tax (PC) it is also necessary to include any chargeable gains (NCG) assessable on the company in respect to the disposal of capital assets during the chargeable accounting period. However, only a proportion of the full chargeable gain is chargeable. Applying capital gains tax principles Extra Limited computes it has a chargeable gain of £4,000 in its chargeable accounting period ended 31 March 1986. On the assumption that the company is liable to corporation tax at the full rate of 40 per cent for the financial year 1985 the total tax payable would appear to be £1,600 (i.e. 40% × £4,000). Now consider the same gain chargeable on an individual for 1985/6. Ignoring the annual exemption limit the capital gains tax payable would be £1,200 (i.e. 30% × £4,000). Clearly, unless some adjustment is made to a company's chargeable gain, an unintentional distortion is built into the corporation tax legislation because of the statutory convenience, referred to earlier, regarding the method of raising assessments to corporation tax. Although this situation vexes many students of corporation tax at the outset it must, nevertheless, be accepted and the method of eliminating the distortion understood.

As a first step the law stipulates the amount of the gain be reduced by a specified fraction which, for the financial year 1985, has been fixed at 1/4. The object of the fractional reduction is to tax a company at an effective rate of 30 per cent on its chargeable gains. This is achieved by charging the balance of the gain (3/4 for the financial year 1985) at the full rate of corporation tax. Therefore, Extra Limited would include as part of its chargeable profits £4,000 × 3/4 = £3,000 and pay corporation tax of £1,200 thereon (i.e. £3,000 × 40%). Justice is seen to be done but the reader might recall that the annual exemption granted to individuals under the capital gains legislation does not extend to companies!

The full corporation tax rates, specified fraction to reduce chargeable gains, and capital gains tax rates are shown in Table 10.5. Technically, the gains for any financial year should be reduced by using the appropriate specified fraction. Nevertheless, it is normal to arrive at the chargeable gain by taking the full gain and multiplying by the complementary fraction as in the Extra Limited example.

TABLE 10.5. *Corporation and capital gains tax rates and specified fractional reductions for recent years*

Financial Year	1983	1984	1985	1986
Full corporation tax rate	50%	45%	40%	35%
Capital gains tax rate	30%	30%	30%	30%
Chargeable gains fractional reduction	2/5	1/3	1/4	1/7

If Extra Limited has also an allowable capital loss in its chargeable accounting period ended 31 March 1986 of say, £2,000, then this must be set off against any gains arising in the same period. The resultant net gain is then reduced by the appropriate fraction leaving £1,500 to include as part of the chargeable profits. Because allowable capital losses can only be set against capital gains any net losses, after aggregation, in a chargeable accounting period may only be carried forward and offset against future capital gains. Such setoffs must occur before the fractional reduction is operated. If this order of computation were not followed, relief for capital losses in terms of tax would be greater than the effective rate of 30 per cent applied to capital gains.

The following general points regarding capital gains and companies should be observed:

(i) The pay-day for tax thereon is variable by reference to the company's chargeable accounting period and not fixed as it is for individuals.
(ii) Roll-over relief will apply to the disposal and replacement of certain capital assets.
(iii) Retirement relief is never applicable to companies.
(iv) Special treatment is afforded to groups of companies where capital assets are transferred within the group (see later section).

To establish whether a company is liable to pay corporation tax at the full rate or the small companies rate it is necessary to take account of any franked investment income (FII) received. Where such income exists then it must be shown in the computation at point (f). FII is defined in the legislation as being qualifying distributions, normally dividends, received from other UK companies plus an associated tax credit. If it is recalled that earlier we said that dividend payments by a company are not deductible for corporation tax purposes and any such distribution requires the payment of ACT, two points should be evident:

(i) The dividend received is made from the post-tax profits of the paying company, and the underlying tax on those profits is passed on to the recipient through the imputation system.
(ii) As with any income received net of tax the grossing up procedure is necessary.

As a consequence of (i) above, the amount of FII is included in the computation merely to establish at which rate of tax the recipient company is liable, but it is not chargeable to corporation tax. If FII were chargeable then clearly double taxation would occur on every £ of distributed profits—once in the paying company's hands and once via the recipient company.

With regard to point (ii) above two observations are necessary, the first of which is that unless the amount received is grossed up the value inserted in the computation is not FII by definition. Secondly, the tax credit used in the grossing up operation cannot be set against the corporation tax liability of the recipient company otherwise no tax charge would arise on the distributed £ of profits—after all, the FII is not chargeable to corporation tax. However, if the recipient company passes on the dividend received in the form of dividends to its own shareholders, the tax credit is also passed to them. The means by which this is achieved is illustrated fully in the section on the quarterly accounting system.

Finally , it is important to note that the following are not FII:

(i) Debenture and loan interest received from other UK companies. This will be UFII and must be shown at point (b).

(ii) Dividends received from overseas companies. This income is assessable under Schedule D case V and would be shown at point (a).

A number of the general principles previously introduced are now illustrated in Tables 10.6 and 10.7 and are based upon the following data supplied by Cresta Limited for the year ended 31 March 1986:

		(£)
Profit		52,109
After charging:	(£)	
Depreciation	5,000	
Directors' fees	12,000	
Debenture interest paid	1,093 (gross)	
And crediting:		
Bank deposit interest	252	
Building society interest	488	
Loan interest from UK company	1,219 (net)	
Income from letting property	287	
Dividends from UK company	175 (net)	
Capital allowances claimed		£6,250
Dividend paid during year, for year ended 31 March 1985		£7,000
Gain on sale of investments		£11,250
Capital losses brought forward		£3,125

We feel that a detailed commentary on the various items which appear in the suggested solutions in unnecessary, but a limited number of general observations are given below:

(i) The format adopted in Table 10.7 is that introduced earlier with important sub-totals clearly notated. It is agreed that the line PC £57,509 should more strictly be computed as under:

	(£)
Corporation tax income	52,508
Add: net chargeable gain (NCG)	6,094
Total profits	58,602
Less: charges on income	(1,093)
	57,509

TABLE 10.6. *Computation of Schedule D case I income for Cresta Ltd.* (£)

Profit for the 12 months ended 31 March 1986		52,109
Add: non-allowable expenditure:		
depreciation	5,000	
debenture interest paid	1,093	
Subtotal		6,093
		58,202
Less: non-trading income:		
bank deposit interest	252	
building society interest	488	
loan interest received	1,219	
rental income	287	
dividends from UK company	175	
Subtotal		(2,421)
		55,781
Less: capital allowances		(6,250)
Adjusted profit for schedule D case I		£49,531

TABLE 10.7. *Corporation tax computation for the chargeable accounting period ended 31 March 1986*

Cresta Ltd.		(£)
Corporation tax income:		
Schedule D case I		49,531
Schedule A		287
Schedule D case III		252
UFII (£1,219 × 10/7)		1,741
Building society interest (£488 × 10/7)		697
		52,508
Less: charges on income, paid		(1,093)
Net taxable income (NTI)		51,415
Add: net chargeable gains (NCG):		
Gain on sale	11,250	
Less: losses brought forward	(3,125)	
	8,125	
Less: fractional reduction ($\frac{1}{4}$)	(2,031)	
		6,094
Profits chargeable to corporation tax (PC)		57,509
Add: FII (£175 × 10/7)		250
Profits for small companies rate (PS)		£57,759

but we consider our initial presentation emphasizes that charges on income are primarily given against income of the chargeable accounting period and only excess charges are set off against capital profits, if any.

(ii) In the computation of Schedule D case I income, Table 10.6, it should be noted carefully that the values for adjusting profits are those shown in the company's accounts, for example dividends received are shown as £175 net. It is only in the main computation, Table 10.7, that the grossing up addition is effected.

(iii) Capital allowances are computed for chargeable accounting periods on an actual basis. Thus, assets acquired in the year ended 31 March 1986 qualify for the full writing-down allowance and are relieved against trading profits for that year. If the expenditure were in an enterprise zone, so attracting accelerated capital allowances by way of a 100 per cent initial allowance, then full relief for the expenditure could be given against trading profits for the chargeable accounting period ended 31 March 1986.

(iv) The treatment of the capital losses of £3,125, which have been brought forward from an earlier accounting period, clearly illustrates that capital losses may only be utilized against future capital gains.

(v) Net chargeable gains are computed by deducting the fractional reduction for the chargeable accounting period from the aggregate gains. The value of £6,094 could also have been calculated by using the complementary fraction approach referred to earlier, i.e. £8,125 × 3/4. What is truly important is that the two methods are not confused!

(vi) Although not part of the profits chargeable to corporation tax it is essential to include FII, whatever its value, in the computation as its inclusion or indeed incorrect exclusion may affect the rate at which corporation tax is paid (see following section on small companies rate).

(vii) The dividend paid is an appropriation of profits and not deductible for computational purposes.

Small companies rate

The small companies rate of corporation tax, which for the financial year 1986 has been fixed at 29 per cent, is in some ways a misnomer. It in no way refers to the size of the company, i.e, in terms of annual turnover, number of employees, or asset base, but to the level of profits for the chargeable accounting period. It is worthwhile remembering that 'blue chip' companies such as ICI would qualify for the small companies rate if their profits were small.

The definition of profits for the small companies rate is NTI + NCG = PC + FII = PS. In addition to the legislation fixing the small companies rate of tax it also gives thresholds of profits below which the small companies rate applies and above which the full rate is always operative. Table 10.8 shows the profit levels for recent financial years and repeats for easy reference the small and full rates of corporation tax. By reference to the Cresta Limited

TABLE 10.8. *Corporation tax upper and lower levels of profit for recent years*

Financial year	1983	1984	1985	1986
Small company rate	30%	30%	30%	29%
Level of profit under	£100,000	£100,000	£100,000	£100,000
Full rate	50%	45%	40%	35%
Level of profit over	£500,000	£500,000	£500,000	£500,000
Marginal fraction	1/20	3/80	1/40	3/200

computation it can be seen that for the chargeable accounting period ended 31 March 1986 that PS is well below the threshold of £100,000, and the company qualifies for the small companies rate of 30 per cent.

However, having established this fact extreme care must now be taken in deciding which elements comprising PS are taxable at the small companies rate. Certainly, for the reasons outlined earlier, FII is not chargeable to any rate of corporation tax in the recipient company's hands. Then we must consider NCG of £6,094. If we recall that the purpose of the fractional reduction is to produce an effective tax rate of 30 per cent on the full gain (£8,125 × 30% = £3,437) then clearly £6,094 × 30% will produce an effective rate less than 30 per cent. The rule is quite specific in these circumstances; the full rate of corporation tax is always applied to NCG. By a process of elimination we are therefore left with NTI (£51,415), and it is to this subtotal only that the small companies rate of 30 per cent applies.

The true significance of the inclusion of FII now begins to emerge. If we assume that Cresta Limited received, in its accounting year, dividends from other UK companies of a substantial value, for example £310,000, PS would total £500,366 and the company would be chargeable at the full rate of 40 per cent on its profits. Despite the FII not being chargeable to tax in Cresta's hands it nevertheless means that an additional £5,141 corporation tax bill would be levied on the company.

We must now consider what happens in the circumstances where PS falls between the upper and lower level thresholds. In this situation the legislation produces a rather horrendous solution to the problem in the form of marginal relief. As a first step NTI is taxed at the full rate of corporation tax, and the resultant tax calculation is then reduced by the marginal relief computed by the following formula:

$$(UL - PS) \times \frac{NTI}{PS} \times MF$$

where UL = upper level of profits for financial year
PS = profits as defined for small companies rate purposes
NTI = net taxable income
MF = marginal fraction for financial year.

These extremely important rules are summarized in Table 10.9, using the notation already introduced throughout the chapter, of which practical examples are provided in the next section.

Irregular periods of account

Up until this point we have, for ease of exposition, mainly used examples where a company has a 12-month period of account ended 31 March with a consequent chargeable accounting period which fits neatly into a financial year for taxation purposes. Unfortunately, the real world is not so straightforward. In this section we will briefly examine the modifications required to cater for:

(i) chargeable accounting periods which are less than 12 months in length,
(ii) chargeable accounting periods which do not coincide with a financial year,
(iii) periods of account which cover a period of more than 12 months.

Where a company has a period of account less that 12 months it will have a correspondingly short chargeable accounting period. Short Limited has traded for many years to 30 September but has now decided to change its trading year-end to 31 March. For the 6 months to 31 March 1987 it shows a trading profit of £60,000. It has no other profits for this period. The only problem in this situation is that the lower and upper limits for rates of tax are annual sums and require scaling down pro rata where a chargeable accounting period is less than 12 months. If this were not so Short Limited would be liable on NTI at 29 per cent. However, having recognized we are dealing with the

TABLE 10.9. *A summary of the rules fixing the rate of corporation tax applicable to profits*

For the financial year 1986
(i) if PS $\geq$ £500,000
tax NTI @ 35% (full rate)
NCG @ 35% (full rate)
(ii) if PS $\leq$ £100,000
tax NTI @ 29% (small company rate)
NCG @ 35% (full rate)
(iii) if £100,000 < PS < £500,000
tax NTI @ 35% (full rate initially)
Less: marginal relief (see below)
tax NCG @ 35% (full rate)

Marginal relief formula for financial year 1986 is:

$$(500{,}000 - \text{PS}) \times \frac{\text{NTI}}{\text{PS}} \times \frac{3}{200}$$

financial year 1986 (i.e. 1 October 1986–31 March 1987) it is apparent the lower and upper limits become £50,000 and £250,000, respectively. As NTI = PS (£60,000) for this company we are faced with a marginal relief calculation which is shown in Table 10.10. The operation of the marginal relief gives Short Limited an effective rate of 30.25 per cent on each £ of profit.

We now move on to consider Credit Limited which has a chargeable accounting period for the 12 months ended 31 December 1986. It has a trading profit of £200,000 but no other income or profits during the period. The difficulty here is that, the chargeable accounting period spans two financial years, i.e. 1985, the period from 1 January to 31 March 1986, and 1986, the period 1 April 1986 to 31 December 1986. Because two financial years are involved it is first necessary to apportion the profit on a time basis. This gives, for the financial years 1985 (1/4) and 1986 (3/4), £50,000 and £150,000, respectively.

TABLE 10.10. *Examples of corporation tax computations based on irregular periods of account*

(i) *Short Ltd.—6 months accounting period ended 31 March 1987*

Profits (NTI)=(PC)=(PS)	£60,000
Initial tax due at full rate (35%)	21,000
Less: marginal relief:	
$(250{,}000-60{,}000)\times\frac{60{,}000}{60{,}000}\times\frac{3}{200}$	(2,850)
Gross corporation tax liability	£18,150

$$\text{Effective rate}=\frac{18{,}150}{60{,}000}\times 100=30.25\%$$

(ii) *Credit Ltd.—12 months accounting period ended 31 December 1986*

	FY 1985 (£)	FY 1986 (£)
Profits (NTI)=(PC)=(PS)	50,000	150,000
Initial tax due at full rate	20,000 (40%)	52,500 (35%)
Less: marginal relief:		
FY 1985 $(125{,}000-50{,}000)\times 1\times\frac{1}{40}$	(1,875)	—
FY 1986 $(375{,}000-150{,}000)\times 1\times\frac{3}{200}$	—	(3,375)
Gross corporation tax liability	18,125	49,125
Effective rates	36.25%	32.75%

Next, it is vital to calculate the scaled down lower and upper limits for the appropriate parts of each financial year in order to fix the correct rates of tax applicable to the levels of profits. These are shown under:

Financial year 1985: lower limit £100,000 × 1/4 = £25,000
upper limit £500,000 × 1/4 = £125,000,
Financial year 1986: lower limit £100,000 × 3/4 = £75,000
upper limit £500,000 × 3/4 = £375,000.

It is now immediately obvious that Credit Limited is liable to tax at a rate in excess of the small companies rate, and because the boundaries of two financial years are crossed, at a different effective rate per £ of profit in each. It is most important in this type of calculation that the correct rates and marginal fractions are applied. The suggested solution incorporating marginal relief is shown in Table 10.10. In this example we have ignored, for explanation purposes, other sources of income and profits. However, their inclusion causes no particular problem other than subtotals at NTI, NCG, PC, and PS are each time apportioned to the appropriate financial year.

However, where a company has a period of account exceeding 12 months the simple time apportionment method of computing assessable profits (and indeed profits for small companies rate) is abandoned. The procedure to be followed is briefly outlined here. If we assume Long Limited has a period of account lasting 15 months to 31 March 1987 we must first compute the adjusted profit for Schedule D case I purposes as described earlier (see Table 10.6) with one very important exception. Although the normal adjustments for non-allowable expenditure and non-trading income are made, the computation stops, prior to deduction of capital allowances. This is because capital allowances are given for chargeable accounting periods. Thus, the next step is to apportion the D case I profit before capital allowances, by the familiar time basis using the fractions (12/15) and (3/15). Having established the two chargeable accounting periods and trading income arising therein the capital allowances for each separate time period are calculated and deducted from the respective income to establish the taxable Schedule D case I income. It is now possible to build up for each chargeable accounting period the subtotals NTI, NCG, PC, and PS. This is achieved by allocating other sources of income to the period in which they are received. Charges on income are deducted in the period of payment. Chargeable gains are allocated by reference to the date of disposal and franked investment income in accordance with the date of receipt.

Quarterly accounting system

In the earlier sections of this chapter reference has been made to a company having suffered ACT on dividends it receives from other UK companies and having to account in advance for some of the gross corporation tax liability of its accounting period where a dividend is paid during that accounting period. Therefore, a company may, during its accounting period, end up in a situation where it has ACT payable to the Inland Revenue but perhaps ACT reclaimable where it is merely passing on a dividend to its own shareholders out of dividends received.

Before examining the system whereby the company accounts for payments of ACT, we must briefly see what the legislation says as regards payments upon which an ACT liability arises. Broadly, the law refers to qualifying and non-qualifying distributions with the former category being assets which have passed or about to pass out of a company, for example a dividend whether from income or capital providing it is a capital dividend and not a repayment of capital. Non-qualifying distributions are those which relate to assets which will pass from the company at some future date, such as a bonus issue of redeemable share capital. Qualifying distributions produce an almost immediate liability to ACT; non-qualifying distributions do not. Where a company makes a qualifying distribution the ACT is calculated on the amount paid, at the appropriate fraction, by reference to the financial year in which it is paid. Thus, Distribution Limited makes an interim dividend payment to its shareholders of £14,000 on 30 June 1985 relating to its accounting period ended 31 December 1985. As the dividend date falls within the financial year 1985 the ACT is at the rate of 3/7 giving a liability to ACT of £6,000. The net distribution plus the ACT payable is referred to as a franked payment (FP).

The sum of £6,000 reduces the company's gross corporation tax liability for the accounting period ended 31 December 1985 on its net taxable income (NTI). Additionally, it is also passed on to the individual shareholders of Distribution Limited in the form of tax credits and is used to satisfy any one shareholder's liability to income tax at the basic rate—the imputation system at work! Where the shareholder is not liable to tax a refund will be made by the Inland Revenue. Naturally, the Inland Revenue is only willing to repay because they have already collected the tax via the quarterly accounting system. The mechanics of how this is achieved now follow.

The legislation provides that a company must make quarterly returns (CT61) for ACT purposes made up to the end of March, June, September, and December. Therefore, Distribution Limited is expected to produce four returns during its chargeable accounting period ended 31 December 1985. Where, as is likely, a company makes up its accounts to a date which does not end on one of the above dates for example 30 November each year, there will be five return periods. The first will run from 1 December to 31 December (one month) followed by three quarterly returns and a fifth for the remaining two months 1 October to 30 November. Whatever the length of the return period a return must be made within 14 days of its end, and any ACT due on qualifying distributions, within the return period, made at the same time. So Distribution Limited must complete the return for the three months to 30 June 1985 and send this to HM Inspector of Taxes together with a cheque for £6,000 no later than 14 July 1985. A point to note here is that if the dividend had been paid on the 1 July 1985 the ACT liability of £6,000 would not have been payable until 14 October 1985.

Where a company is in receipt of FII (i.e. UK dividends received plus a related tax credit) then with certain restrictions it is possible to reduce the ACT payable on the FP by reference to the tax credits attached to FII. If during the quarter ended 30 June 1985 Distribution Limited had received FII of £20,000 (net dividend £14,000 plus tax credit £6,000), then because the distribution to its shareholders merely represents the passing on of another company's income no additional ACT is collectable from Distribution Limited. After all if it were, clearly the Inland Revenue would then hold 60p of tax credits for each £ distributed. It can, therefore, be concluded that ACT will only be payable by a company where FP > FII and then only on the excess of FP − FII. Conversely, it is not correct to conclude there will be a repayment of tax credits to a company in all circumstances where FII > FP. The general operation of the rules for quarterly accounting for ACT are illustrated in Table 10.11 which

TABLE 10.11. *Quarterly accounting for ACT*

Mega Ltd.—Chargeable accounting period ended 31 March 1986

(i) *Return period 3 months ended 30 June 1985*
No return is required. Although FII (£375) > FP (£nil) during return period no repayment of tax credit suffered can be obtained, as the overriding rule that a repayment will only arise where ACT has been paid in a previous return period during the overall accounting period (i.e. 1 April 1985 to 31 March 1986) is applicable.

(ii) *Return period 3 months ended 30 September 1985*
No return is required.

(iii) *Return period 3 months ended 31 December 1985*

	(£)
FP 10 December 1985	11,812
FII 14 May 1985	(375)
	11,437

ACT payable by 14 January 1986 £11,437 @ 30% = £3,431

(iv) *Return period 3 months ended 31 March 1986*

FP	nil
FII 21 February 1986	562

A repayment is available on £562 FII because ACT in excess of the amount repayable £562 @ 30% = £169 has been paid in a previous return period during the overall accounting period.

is based upon the following data for Mega Limited. During the year ended 31 March 1986, the company received and paid:

		(£)
14 May 1985	FII	375
10 December 1985	FP	11,812
21 February 1986	FII	562

Based upon the computations in Table 10.11 it will be seen that Mega Limited has net ACT of £3,262 to set against the gross corporation tax liability for the chargeable accounting period ended 31 March 1986. This amount for ACT represents FP (£11,812) – FII (£937) = £10,875 @ 30%.

In certain circumstances, at the end of the accounting period, an excess of FII over FP exists. Such an excess is described as surplus FII, and it may be either carried forward and treated as FII received on the first day of the next accounting period of the company or used to obtain a repayment where the company makes a trading loss. In the first alternative an offset of tax credits will occur when FII $\leqslant$ FP in some future return period. The second alternative will be investigated further in the later section on losses.

A slight complication arises where there is a change in the ACT rate, such as in the 1986 Finance Act, and the company's accounting period straddles the date of change. For ACT purposes the accounting period is split into two. One period is deemed to end on 5 April 1986 and the other starting on 6 April 1986. The effect of this ruling is that FII received after 5 April 1986 cannot be set against a FP made on or before that date and will be carried forward to the subsequent accounting period as surplus FII as indicated in the previous paragraph.

In addition to the quarterly system for ACT there also exists, within the legislation, similar rules to handle the income tax which companies must deduct from their charges on income and remit to the Inland Revenue and basic rate income tax provisionally suffered on UFII and ultimately repayable by the tax authorities. The use of the quarterly accounting system for income tax may speed up the refund of income tax suffered by companies on their UFII.

The operation of the system for income tax requires the completion of returns, four or five dependent on the company's accounting date. These returns are in fact a different part of the form CT61. The time scale for completion is identical. Within each return period the rules for set off of income tax due to the Inland Revenue against provisional income tax suffered are the same as those for the ACT system. If we now return to Mega Limited we find that during the year ended 31 March 1986 the company also received and paid:

	(£)
10 August 1985 loan interest received	862 (gross)
9 October 1985 loan interest paid	1,625 (gross).

The suggested completion of the required quarterly return is illustrated in Table 10.12 where it may be seen that the company has effectively obtained repayment of the income tax suffered on UFII by 14 January 1986 rather than by offset against the corporation tax liability on 1 January 1987. It should also be observed that unlike the ACT calculations it is quite in order to work in amounts of tax. This point is only significant where there is a change in the basic rate of income tax. At such a change point, as in the 1986 Finance Act, there is no need for a deemed split of a company's accounting period for income tax accounting where it straddles the 5 April.

However, a fundamental difference exists at the end of a company's chargeable accounting period where the income tax suffered on UFII has not been fully recovered. This situation would arise where there have been no charges on income or UFII exceeds such charges during the accounting period. Unlike the ACT system there is no equivalent to surplus FII carried forward with the result that any excess provisional income tax suffered is set off against the corporation tax payable or a repayment is made where the corporation tax liability is nil or lower than the income tax excess.

Finally, it should be stressed that the two systems must never be intermuddled. Thus, it is totally incorrect to set ACT suffered on FII against income tax deducted from a charge on income and due to the Inland Revenue. Of course the design of the form CT61 makes this likely to be a theoretical rather than a practical problem.

TABLE 10.12. *Quarterly accounting for income tax*

Mega Ltd.—Chargeable accounting period ended 31 March 1986

(i) *Return period 3 months ended 30 June 1985*
No return is required.

(ii) *Return period 3 months ended 30 September 1985*
No return is required. Although income tax provisionally suffered on UFII (£862 @ 30% = £259) > tax witheld on charges (£nil) no repayment can be obtained, as the overriding rule that a repayment will only arise where income tax has been paid in a previous return period during the overall accounting period (i.e. 1 April 1985 to 31 March 1986) is applicable.

(iii) *Return period 3 months ended 31 December 1985*

	(£)
Income tax witheld on loan interest paid 9 October 1985	487
Income tax suffered on loan interest received 10 August 1985	(259)
Income tax payable by 14 January 1986	£228

(iv) *Return period 3 months ended 31 March 1986*
No return required.

Surplus ACT

As already indicated ACT paid during an accounting period and excess income tax suffered at the end of that accounting period may be offset against the gross corporation tax liability of a company. There is a general rule that ACT is deductible before excess income tax. The reason for this stems from a further piece of legislation which restricts the amount of ACT which may be set off to an amount equal to basic rate income tax on net taxable income, i.e. corporation tax income less charges on income but excluding chargeable gains, if any. This latter situation is illustrated in Table 10.13 where it is assumed Mega Limited has an adjusted Schedule D case I profit of £9,000 and a chargeable gain of £2,000 after the fractional reduction. In this example there is no further deduction relative to excess income tax suffered, this already having been refunded on 14 January 1986 (see Table 10.12). The surplus ACT of £791 in this case may be carried back and set against the corporation tax payable for the six previous chargeable accounting periods or carried forward without time limit. Where the carry back option is chosen the surplus is offset against latest years first, for example 31 March 1985 to 31 March 1980 and will normally result in a repayment of corporation tax.

TABLE 10.13. *Offset of ACT and surplus ACT*

Mega Ltd.—Chargeable accounting period ended 31 March 1986 (£)		
Corporation tax income:		
Schedule D case I		9,000
UFII		862
		9,862
Less: charges on income, paid		(1,625)
Net taxable income (NTI)		8,237
Add: chargeable gains (NCG)		2,000
Profits chargeable to corporation tax (PC)		10,237
Add: FII		937
Profits for small companies rate (PS)		£11,174
Corporation tax payable:		
NTI 8,237 @ 30%		2,471
NCG, 2,000 @ 40%		800
		3,271
Less: net ACT during accounting period	3,262	
maximum set-off 30% × 8,237 (NTI)	2,471	(2,471)
Mainstream corporation tax payable		£800

Note: There is a surplus of ACT of (£3,262 − £2,471) = £791.

Loss reliefs

As for unincorporated businesses (see Chapter 8), the UK tax system recognizes that companies are also likely to incur losses in their operations. Similarly, these losses will fall into two main categories:

(i) trading losses arising under Schedule D case I,
(ii) Non-trading losses arising from capital transactions and also possibly under Schedule A and Schedule D case VI.

Before considering how relief for trading losses is given we will briefly refer to the treatment of non-trading losses. As regards losses on capital assets it should be recalled these may only be set against capital profits—the detailed rules being contained in the earlier section on computation of profits. Losses under Schedule A and D case VI can only be set against similar income arising in the same accounting period or carried forward against future profits of the same class. We can see that there is very little flexibility in the way relief is given under the statutes.

Relief for trading losses is far more flexible, and provision is made for different classes of claim in sections 177, 178, and 254 of the Income and Corporation Taxes Act 1970. The alternatives which are open to a company for relief of a trading loss in a chargeable accounting period are:

(i) set off against total profits of the same accounting period,
(ii) carried back against total profits of an earlier accounting period,
(iii) carried forward against future trading profits,
(iv) carried back against earlier trading profits where the loss occurs upon the cessation of a trade,
(v) set off against surplus FII.

However, before dealing with each of these loss claims it is considered useful to establish how a trading loss may arise for an accounting period. Generally, this should present no difficulty since a trading loss under Schedule D case I is computed in precisely the same way as a trading profit, i.e. the normal add-backs and deductions are made. In order that the reader feels confident on this point we suggest that he or she rework the earlier Cresta Limited example (Table 10.6), assuming the profit after charging and crediting the specified items reads (a) £1,000 and (b) loss £52,109. The adjusted Schedule D case I loss calculated should be (a) £1,578 and (b) £54,687 remembering that in this latter case capital allowances which are treated as trading expenses for corporation tax purposes should be added to the adjusted loss.

Even more important to a complete understanding of the various loss reliefs available is the need to realize the type of profits which enter into the claims (i) to (iv) above. In alternatives (i) and (ii) reference is made to totals profits while in (iii) and (iv) profits are trading profits. When dealing with loss claims for companies the term total profits has its generally accepted meaning within the corporation tax legislation, i.e. corporation tax income plus net chargeable gains. Thus, in the outline corporation tax computation in Table 10.3 the lines NCG and (e) are exchanged and in summary form would appear as under:

	(£)
Corporation tax income	d
Add: chargeable gains (proportion)	NCG
Total profits	TP
Less: charges on income (gross)	(e)
Profits chargeable to corporation tax	PC
Add: FII (gross)	f
Profits for small companies rate	PS

The term trading profits relates solely to Schedule D case I adjusted income and nothing else.

Because trading losses are set against total profits before charges on income are deductible, situations may develop where after loss relief, there are insufficient total profits to cover the charges. The interaction of loss claims and charges is an extremely complex subject and considered to be beyond the scope of this book. However, in general terms, unrelieved trading charges, for example debenture interest, may be carried forward as a trading loss and used against a future Schedule D case I trading profit. An unrelieved non-trading charge, such as a charitable deed of convenant, cannot be carried forward in this way. It must be utilized against the total profits of the chargeable accounting period in which it is paid or not at all.

We are now in a position to commence our discussion.

(i) Under section 177 a trading loss arising in any chargeable accounting period may be set against total profits of the same period. The way in which Cresta Limited may claim relief for its trading loss of £1,578 incurred in the chargeable accounting period ended 31 March 1986 is shown in Table 10.14. Clearly, the company will still have a tax liability for this accounting period at the small companies rate of 30 per cent. However, care must be exercised in calculating the gross corporation tax due because the offset of a trading loss is firstly against income and then chargeable gains, while charges are primarily set against income. Thus, Cresta Limited has chargeable profits of £6,400 of which £306 is charged at 30 per cent and £6,094 is liable at the full rate of 40 per cent. Overall it should be realized that this claim may be made i.e. it is voluntary and not mandatory, and the full loss of £1,578 could have been carried forward (see (iii) following). Where the company wishes to exercise the claim then, it must do so within two years of the end of the loss-making period, i.e. by 31 March 1988.

(ii) Section 177 also provides that where a trading loss has been set against total profits of the same period, but not fully relieved, the balance remaining

TABLE 10.14. *Use of a trading loss against total profits of the same chargeable accounting period*

Cresta Ltd.—Corporation tax computation for chargeable accounting period ended 31 March 1986 (£)

Corporation tax income:	
Schedule D case I	nil
Schedule A	287
Schedule D case III	252
UFII	1,741
Building society interest	697
	2,977
Add: chargeable gains	6,094
Total profits	9,071
Less: trading loss of current accounting period	(1,578)
	7,493
Less: charges on income	(1,093)
Profits chargeable to corporation tax	6,400
Add: FII	250
Profits for small companies rate	£6,650

Note: The figures used above are those calculated in detail in Table 10.7.

may be carried back against total profits of an earlier accounting period. It is then mandatory to effect the current period claim first.

There is an important restriction within the carry-back rules which dictates that the carry-back period must be equal to the loss-making period. Briefly, the effect of this rule is that where a company has consistent 12-month accounting periods then the loss will be available against the immediately preceding accounting period's total profits. However, if the immediately preceding accounting period was of eight months duration, assuming the loss-making period was twelve months, part of the loss might be carried back into the next previous accounting period. Profits of these earlier accounting periods are apportioned on a time basis to obtain the maximum total profits which can be offset by the trading loss.

The general operation of this carry-back claim will be illustrated by assuming Cresta Limited had a bad trading year to 31 March 1986 which resulted in the trading loss of £54,687 computed earlier. We will also assume the total profits for the year ended 31 March 1985 have been agreed with the Inland Revenue at £45,000. Because the current year claim must be made first the loss available to carry back is reduced to £45,616, i.e. trading loss £54,687 minus total profits for accounting period to 31 March 1986. This calculation may be checked by reference back to Table 10.14 and also it might be noted that the trading charges of £1,093 are no longer utilized. They can, of course, be carried forward and utilized as explained earlier. As both the loss-making period and the immediately preceding accounting period are equal in length the total profits of £45,000 may be fully extinguished by the carried back losses. The remaining balance of the loss (£616) cannot be carried back further and may only be carried forward as explained in (iii) following. The time limit for making this further claim must be lodged with the Inland Revenue by 31 March 1988. The claim is not mandatory although, if effected, it does signify the current year claim becomes so and under both claims the company cannot choose to use part only of its total profits. They are all or nothing claims!

(iii) Irrespective as to whether a company makes claims under (i) and (ii) above the general provisions of section 177 allow it to carry forward unutilized trading losses against the first available trading profits (i.e. Schedule D case I income) from the same trade. With regard to the trading loss of £1,578 made by Cresta Limited, if a current year claim was not made, then the loss is carried forward indefinitely until a Schedule D case I profit arises. As soon as a trading profit is made the loss must be offset as this part of the legislation is mandatory. In the scenario where Cresta had an appalling trading year, assuming both current year and carry-back claims were made, the unrelieved balance of £616 must be dealt with as described under the carry-forward rules. Although the loss may be carried forward for an indefinite period of time a company must agree on the amount of the loss with the Inland Revenue within six years after the end of the loss-making period i.e. by 31 March 1992.

(iv) Where a company ceases trading and a trading loss, computed under the rules of Schedule D case I, occurs for the last twelve months of trading it may claim to carry back that loss against earlier trading profits. Section 178 governs the operation of this claim which is known as terminal loss relief. In some ways this relief is similar to the carry-forward rules in that it may only be set against trading profits. However, there is one distinguishing factor whereby the legislation stipulates only trading profits arising in the three years preceding the final twelve months may be extinguished by the terminal loss on a last in first out basis. Additionally, any current year or carry-back loss claims under section 177 against total profits become mandatory; in other words terminal loss relief is one of last resort. If the final period of trading is less than twelve months an appropriate proportion of the profits from the previous accounting period is taken to complete the twelve-month period. An example, abstracting from the complications of charges on income, is given in Table 10.15 to show how the general principles operate. It is computed from the data relating to Disaster Limited which ceased trading on 31 July 1987:

		(£)
4 months to 31 July 1987	(loss)	10,000
year ended 31 March 1987	(loss)	1,000
year ended 31 March 1986	(profit)	2,000
year ended 31 March 1985	(profit)	2,000
year ended 31 March 1984	(profit)	3,000

In presenting the solution in Table 10.15 it is also assumed that the above profits and losses are all relative to trading operations. The various stages in the calculation are shown at (a), (b), and (c) with (c) showing how time apportionment is applied to chargeable accounting periods falling wholly or partly within the three-year time span. Unfortunately, as a result of the three-year rule only £5,000 of the terminal loss is relieved and the balance of £5,000 is lost forever. Providing the company makes a claim within six years of ceasing to trade, i.e. by 31 July 1993, a repayment of corporation tax paid for the accounting periods ended 31 March 1984, 1985, and 1986 will be obtained.

(v) Under section 254 the legislation provides a temporary relief to companies where a surplus of FII arises with no immediate prospect of being able to set this against a future franked payment, for example a dividend payment. This situation is often the result of a company hitting a bad trading patch and as a consequence accumulating losses which cannot be relieved against profits. The essence of this piece of legislation is that a temporary 'loan' may be obtained from the Inland Revenue by allowing a company to set a trading loss against a surplus of FII. However, the temporary relief for the losses used in this way is calculated at the basic rate of tax for each £ of loss surrendered and not at the corporation tax rate.

TABLE 10.15. *Example of terminal loss relief upon a permanent cessation of trading* (£)

Disaster Ltd.	
(a) Prior loss claim for chargeable accounting period to 31.3.86	
Profit for year to 31.3.86	2,000
Loss brought back from 1987 under section 177	(1,000)
Chargeable profits	1,000
(b) Calculation of terminal loss relief for last twelve months	
Loss, four months to 31.7.87	10,000
Loss, eight months of year to 31.3.87	
8/12 × 1,000 (but already used)	nil
	10,000
(c) Terminal loss relief claim for three years ended 31.7.86	
four months, 1.4.86–31.7.86	nil
twelve months, 1.4.85–31.3.86	1,000
Less: terminal loss relief (part)	(1,000)
twelve months, 1.4.84–31.3.85	2,000
Less: terminal loss relief (part)	(2,000)
eight months, 1.8.83–31.3.84	
8/12 × £3,000	2,000
Less: terminal loss relief (part)	(2,000)

Ultimately, where a company achieves an excess of franked payments at some future date, a compensatory adjustment arises. The consequence of the compensatory adjustment is to reinstate the loss relief and for the Inland Revenue to obtain a repayment of the 'loan' from the company. Thus, over a period of time, providing there is no change in the rates of corporation tax, the total tax bill is identical whether the section 254 claim is made or not. However, in terms of cash-flow timing and in an era when corporation tax rates are changing annually the value of this piece of legislation might easily be overlooked (Spratley 1985).

Close companies

Many companies resident in the UK are controlled and operated by a small family unit, for example father, wife, and two children. Often such companies are run by one individual merely to attract the advantages of limited liability to his or her trading operation. These companies may be used as vehicles to minimize tax liabilities in ways which are not open to large companies with a wide share ownership, for example where the top marginal rate of personal tax on shareholders is 60 per cent it would be cheaper in terms of tax to retain profits within the company rather than pay a dividend.

Because a trading company which is also a close company does not have to concern itself any longer with an enforced distribution of trading income, one of the major problems of being a close company has been removed. Thus, in this section we concentrate on the legislation which (a) identifies what constitutes a close company, and (b) takes steps to prevent abuse of this status. For this reason our discussion will be necessarily brief but nevertheless the reader will be made aware of the major issues involved.

Generally, a close company is one which is controlled by five or fewer participators or by its directors however many there are. A participator is defined as any shareholder, loan creditor, or option holder. Attempts to dilute a person's shareholding by spreading it, for example to close family members, are rendered inoperative as the statutes regard shareholdings of associates as being those of the participator. Associates for the purpose of close company legislation broadly include immediate relatives, business partners, and trustees of family settlements. There are some exemptions which apply despite close company status being established under the detailed rules. Examples of exemptions include any non-resident company, any registered industrial, provident or building society, and any company controlled by a non-close company.

Control is established principally by owning more than 50 per cent of the voting power. Thus, although the definition of a close company is involved and complex, in most everyday situations it is fairly simple to identify a close company. In the illustrations at the start of this section if the father, wife, and each child hold 25 per cent of the voting capital, a close company status exists—there are only four participators who control 100 per cent of the voting power. If they are also directors, as is most likely the case, then double jeopardy exists. Even more common is the one person business where the husband or wife owns 99 per cent of the voting capital with the remaining 1 per cent held by the spouse to satisfy company law requirements. Additionally, both are directors. Clearly, a close company exists for corporation tax purposes.

Obviously a close company is potentially subject to all the corporation tax principles discussed in the earlier sections, but there are extensions of the legislation to counter tax avoidance by such a company. The main areas of potential abuse are excessive retention of profits, already referred to, and where distributions are made, an attempt may be made to disguise them in some way. The main theme behind these ploys is to save higher rate tax on distributions to the shareholders.

Close companies tend to approach the distribution problem in two ways—by providing benefits in kind or making non-repayable loans to participators who are not directors or employees. Strategies in the first category are caught as qualifying distributions by an extension of the definition by the legislation. The effect of this extended meaning is threefold: such payments are non-allowable for computing Schedule D case I profits of the company; ACT is payable at the appropriate rate on the value of the benefit; and higher rate personal tax rates may be payable by the recipient.

Where a loan of any amount is made is to a participator, and directors or employees in excess of £15,000, the amount of the loan is treated as if it were a distribution. It is important to note that the loan is not a distribution. Therefore, although the Inland Revenue will raise an assessment showing tax due by the company at the appropriate ACT rate the tax is not ACT and cannot be set against the gross corporation tax liability of the company. Further, since the loan is not regarded as a distribution it is not treated as income of the recipient for higher rate tax purposes. If at some future date the loan is repaid by the participator a repayment will be made to the company by the Inland Revenue.

One further piece of legislation must be acknowledged for those who feel they have detected a loophole in the loan situation. Why not, after a reasonable time, write off the loan?. If this does occur the legislation provides that the amount is then regarded as a qualifying distribution and becomes income of the recipient with the normal personal tax consequences.

As regards non-distribution of profits by a close company the Inland Revenue have powers under the tax statutes to raise assessments to collect higher rates of income tax from participators in a company. The assessments are based upon the excess of the 'relevant income' of the company over the actual distributions made by it in respect of a chargeable accounting period. Such excess is apportioned among the participators, and a notional tax credit is deemed to be attached. This means the recipient will only be liable to higher rate tax on his share of the apportioned income, and no ACT is actually paid by the company. For these reasons the notional tax credit is not available for repayment in a non-liable participator's hands.

The computational and procedural rules are long and complex, but a brief outline is now given. At the present time 'relevant income' does not include the trading income of a trading company and only part of any estate income (for example Schedule A or Schedule B income) or investment income. Where the distribution of estate or investment income would prejudice the business of the company, e.g. a cash crisis or future expansion plans, the 'relevant income' figure may be further reduced by negotiation with the Inland Revenue. The rules for non-trading companies are more stringent, particularly as regards one with investment income only. The legislation defines a trading company as one which exists wholly or mainly for the purposes of carrying on a trade or any company where the investment income is not the main source of income. Therefore, it would appear that at the current time a close company which is also a trading company with relatively small amounts of estate or investment income has little to fear from the apportionment legislation.

Associated and group companies

Until this point we have purposely illustrated the principles of corporation tax by reference to the sole company. However, in practice, the problem of common control exists with its attendant advantages and disadvantages.

The concept of common control is shown in Fig. 10.1 where it is assumed Jason and all the companies are UK resident. Control for this purpose is

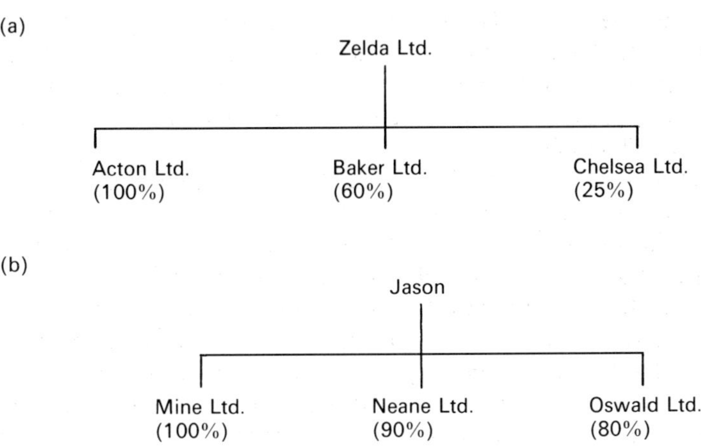

Fig. 10.1 Examples of common control

defined by section 302 Income and Corporation Taxes Act 1970 as beneficial ownership by a person or persons of over 50 per cent of the voting capital or able to receive over 50 per cent of the company's income or net assets in a winding-up. Persons may be individuals or companies. Therefore, in situation (a) Acton and Baker are under the control of Zelda Limited (a company). Clearly, Chelsea Limited is not under common control. In (b) all three companies are under the control of Jason (an individual). Despite common control existing in both situations there is an important distinction between (a) corporate control and (b) individual control.

Tax legislation specifies that companies are associated when they are under the control of the same person or persons. It follows, therefore, that Zelda, Acton, and Baker Limited are associated companies and Mine, Neane, and Oswald Limited are also although the companies in (a) and (b) are not. However, if Jason were to acquire a majority holding in Zelda Limited all six companies would become associated.

The principle disadvantage of associated companies is that a piece of anti-avoidance legislation exists to counter an otherwise too obvious a strategy by taxpayers. Assuming Jason carried on his trading activities through a single company and chargeable profits were £300,000 then that company will pay tax at an effective rate between 29 and 35 per cent for the financial year 1986. Marginal relief will be in operation. Now we assume Jason carried on the same activities through the three associated companies with each company having chargeable profits of £100,000. In this latter strategy each company would only be liable at the small companies rate of 29 per cent for the financial year 1986, or would they? The answer is no as a result of the tax rules which specify that where there are associated companies the upper (£500,000) and lower (£100,000) limits must be reduced by the number of associated companies involved; in this case three. Therefore, in the computation of each company's gross corporation tax liability for the financial year 1986 the upper and lower limits become £166,667 and £33,333 respectively. Because the chargeable profits of any one company now fall within the reduced range, tax will be calculated initially on £100,000 at the full rate reduced by marginal relief. As a result of the upper limit being reduced there is a consequent adjustment to the marginal relief formula for each company.
It will read:

$$(166{,}667 - PS) \times \frac{\text{NTI}}{PS} \times \frac{3}{200}$$

Similar remarks apply to the Zelda, Acton, and Baker structure where we will assume the chargeable profits are £200,000, £150,000, and £30,000, respectively. In computing the liabilities of each company it should be noted carefully that Zelda Limited will be liable at the full rate, Baker Limited at the small companies rate, and only Acton Limited will apply marginal relief to its calculations.

We now consider common corporate control which exists in the Zelda case but not that of Jason. Here we have what is loosely described as a 'group' of companies for tax purposes as well as associated companies. Although the tax laws do not formally treat corporate groups as a single tax structure they do nevertheless bestow certain benefits, dependant upon certain criteria. It must be stressed that what is described below cannot apply to the Jason structure and by definition excludes Chelsea Limited from the Zelda group.

Where a group structure consists of a holding company and there are 75 per cent subsidiaries, for example Zelda and Acton form a 75 per cent group, then trading losses and certain other expenses may be passed between group members. The technical term for this transfer is surrender. If Acton Limited makes a trading loss for its accounting period ended 31 March 1986, it may surrender this loss to Zelda Limited (the claimant company) for a corresponding accounting period. Zelda Limited may set the loss against its own total profits. This whole process is referred to as group relief. Within a 75 per cent group there are also provisions to enable capital assets to be transferred between group companies without a chargeable gain arising. The transferee company, say Acton Limited will assume the original cost and purchase date of Zelda Limited if and when the asset is finally disposed of external to the 75 per cent group. Additionally, roll-over relief (see Chapter 9) operates in such a way that a chargeable gain by Acton Limited may be held over where the replacement asset is acquired by Zelda Limited.

If a group structure is a holding company and 51 per cent subsidiaries, for example Zelda, Acton, and Baker form a 51 per cent group, there are further relaxations of corporation tax regulations which principally avoid the necessity to comply with the quarterly accounting system. Thus, it is possible, following the appropriate elections being made, for both Acton and Baker to pay dividends to Zelda Limited without accounting for ACT. Indeed it would be possible for Acton to pay Baker a dividend in this way or vice versa. However, this is unlikely. The payments are referred to as group income instead of franked payments and franked investment income. Similar arrangements exist for the payment of charges on income from any group company to another. ACT, normally surplus ACT, paid by the holding company may be surrendered to 51 per cent subsidiaries. It cannot be surrendered the other way but presumably if surplus ACT is likely to arise in the subsidiary, a group income election should be made. Although the subsidiary, say Baker Limited, may use the surrendered ACT against its current or future corporation tax liabilities it cannot be carried back.

Concluding remarks

This chapter has concentrated upon the introduction of the basic principles which are laid down in the corporation tax legislation. It has shown there are many similarities between the taxation of corporate and unincorporated businesses. Nevertheless, the separate corporation tax legislation contains many technical terms which have been rigorously explained. Without a full understanding of this terminology, study of even simple computations and calculations becomes difficult and more advanced work impossible.

In the concluding section more complex ideas were introduced regarding associated and groups of companies. Clearly, within the group structure the interaction of corporation tax principles is extremely complex. However, this brief introduction was intended to show some of the exciting challenges open to those who have grasped the basic principles.

Recommendations for further reading

More advanced computations of profits may be found in Pritchard (1984) while those readers who wish to pursue their understanding of irregular periods of account and carry back of trading losses will find excellent examples in the relevant chapters of Bertram and Edwards (1986). The detailed rules of setting a trading loss against franked investment income are in an article by Spratley (1985).

References

Bertram, D., and Edwards, S. (1986), *Comprehensive Aspects of Taxation—1986–87* (London: Holt, Rinehart and Winston).

Pritchard, W. E. (1984), *Corporation Tax* (Stockport: Polytech).

Spratley, D. (1985), 'Section 254 TA 1970—a time for review and action', *Accountancy*, 96 (no. 1097): 105–6 and 96 (no. 1099): 165–6.

11
Value Added Tax

Introduction

Value added tax (VAT) was introduced by the 1972 Finance Act to be operative from 1 April 1973 and to replace two separate taxes, purchase tax and selective employment tax. Although now somewhat buried in history its introduction was as a direct consequence of the UK's wish firstly to co-operate with European tax harmonization and secondly to be prepared for the forthcoming membership in the EEC.

Although VAT was put on the statutes by the 1972 Finance Act it was approximately twelve months before the tax became effective. The reason for this long lead time was merely one of practicability in that all businesses affected by the new tax should be given adequate time to assimilate its requirements, register with Customs and Excise (C & E), and ensure the detailed accounting procedures, which were necessary, were understood and acted upon. This period of twelve months also enabled C & E to train or retrain a large number of officers to monitor the new tax.

Of the four major taxes which we discuss in Part Two VAT is the only indirect tax and as for all similar taxes its administration is the responsibility of C & E.

That VAT has become an established source of revenue for the Government since its inception is illustrated in Table 11.1. Here it can be observed that in the decade from 1973/4 the contribution has risen from £1.5bn. to an estimated £18.0bn. in 1984/5. During this time the sums collectable have risen from under 25 per cent to over 50 per cent of all C & E tax collections and less than 9 per cent to 20 per cent of the total tax revenue of the UK.

Concept of value added revisited

VAT is a common method of indirect taxation in the EEC. An indirect tax may be identified by reference to the split in the administrative process between those persons upon whom assessments are raised and tax collected and the persons who are statutorily deemed to bear that tax. In the case of VAT, although C & E raises assessments and collects the tax due from firms adding value, it is the man or woman in the street, the ultimate consumer, who bears the VAT bills. Thus, it may be seen that VAT uses consumption (expenditure)

TABLE 11.1. *VAT as a source of revenue for Government 1973/4–1984/5*

	Tax collectable by Customs & Excise £(bn)	VAT contribution £(bn)	VAT as % Customs & Excise	VAT as % total tax revenue
1973/4	6.3	1.5	23.8	8.6
1974/5	7.4	2.5	33.8	8.9
1975/6	9.2	3.4	36.9	12.1
1976/7	10.9	3.8	34.9	11.7
1977/8	12.3	4.2	34.1	11.5
1978/9	13.8	4.8	34.8	11.8
1979/80	18.3	8.2	44.8	16.2
1980/1	21.9	10.9	49.7	18.3
1981/2	25.2	11.8	46.8	16.7
1982/3	27.9	13.8	49.5	18.1
1983/4	31.4	15.2	48.4	18.8
1984/5	35.0	18.0	51.4	20.3

Sources: Adapted from 74th and 75th Reports of Customs and Excise and 126th Report of Inland Revenue.

as a tax base, and again it is a general feature of indirect taxes that the tax base is one of consumption as opposed to income or capital.

We now reconsider the concept of value added, which we introduced in Chapter 2, and the general operation of a tax thereon in the example shown in Table 11.2. What we must assume for this illustration is a product which is manufactured from a raw material and is then distributed through a typical wholesaler/retailer chain to the general public.

The first firm in the chain is A which represents an extractor of the raw materials, for example a mine or quarry and as is often assumed in such examples the cost of extraction to this firm is nil—a gift of nature. Obviously this is quite unrealistic, but this assumption in no way invalidates the general nature of the exposition which follows. Clearly the amount of VAT A suffers on costs must be nil but in respect of sales to B of £100 an addition of £15, i.e. VAT at 15 per cent will be added giving a tax inclusive price of £115. This latter sum is the amount paid by B to A and therefore, of course, received by A as part of its cash flows. The tiro might at this stage be forgiven for thinking the profit made by A is £115, namely the tax inclusive selling price £115 less tax inclusive cost price nil.

However, it is part of the VAT system that firms selling at a tax inclusive price—this necessarily implies a positive tax rate—must account to C & E within a specified time period for the tax on value added. Thus in the example firm A will forward a payment of £15 representing tax at 15 per cent on value added of £100.

TABLE 11.2. *An example to illustrate the general operation of VAT and the concept of value added*

		Prices exclusive + of VAT (£)	VAT % rate =	Prices inclusive of VAT (£)	VAT (suffered) or added (£)
A supplier of raw materials	Cost	—	15	—	—
	Sales to B	100	15	115	15
	Value added	100	at 15% due to C & E		15
B manufacturer	Cost from A	100	15	115	(15)
	Sales to C	200	15	230	30
	Value added	100	at 15% due to C & E		15
C wholesaler	Cost from B	200	15	230	(30)
	Sales to D	300	15	345	45
	Value added	100	at 15% due to C & E		15
D retailer	Cost from C	300	15	345	(45)
	Sales to E	400	15	460	60
	Value added	100	at 15% due to C & E		15
E consumer	Cost from D	400	15	460	—

Next we shall consider the position of firm B within the VAT system where it will be observed there is one fundamental difference to that of firm A; firm B has paid (suffered) £15 tax on its costs. Despite B having to make an addition of £30, i.e. VAT at 15 per cent on £200 sales to C, in order to keep within the concept of tax on value added B is entitled to deduct the £15 tax suffered on its purchases from A and need only forward C & E a payment for the net sum of £15, i.e. tax on value added by B only.

Finally, an examination of the VAT situation of E, the ultimate consumer of the product, shows that he or she pays D £400 for it plus VAT at 15 per cent giving a tax inclusive price of £460. E, as the consumer, adds no further value but does, of course, bear the tax of £60 on the expenditure as the ultimate consumer. No direct payment is necessary to C & E as this has already been accounted for by the firms in the manufacturing and distribution chain; A(£15) + B(£15) + C(£15) + D(£15) = £60 or put another way the tax on the total value added by the four firms is £400 at 15% = £60.

It should be apparent that all firms in the chain act as tax collectors for the Government albeit unpaid, an undoubted plus from the Government's viewpoint, and by enforcing the payment of tax at each point of value added the Government's cash flows are significantly improved.

Registration

Having outlined in the previous two sections the introduction, importance, operation, and concept of VAT we are now in a position to consider a more detailed examination of the tax. As in the study of any tax it is vital for a complete understanding to come to grips with a number of key words—the terminology—which are specific to that tax. VAT is no exception, so in outlining the vital importance of registration we will also introduce a range of terminology, complementary topics, and issues.

As described earlier VAT was introduced in the 1972 Finance Act which, with various amendments in subsequent Finance Acts, has now been consolidated in the Value Added Tax Act 1983. This latter act plus numerous statutory instruments govern the operation of VAT at the current time.

The main charging section of the legislation indicates VAT is chargeable on the supply of goods and services in the UK and on the importation of goods and certain services into the UK. The tax will apply to all such goods and services where they are taxable supplies made in the course or furtherance of any business by a taxable person. The detailed consideration of what constitutes taxable supplies will be dealt with in the next section, entitled goods and services, but generally means all supplies not specifically exempted by law. A taxable person may be any one of the normal trading mediums i.e. sole trader, partnership, or limited company, or be an unincorporated body, public corporation, nationalized industry, or local authority. However the feature which all taxable persons have in common is a level of taxable supplies or turnover which exceeds or is likely to exceed an amount prescribed by law.

In 1973 this threshold was £5,000 per annum and currently is £19,500 per annum. It is important to note that the period of one year does not necessarily coincide with the organizations trading year. A has a normal trading year from 1 June to 31 May, and the provision of taxable supplies totals £19,000—A is not a taxable person. On 1 July, A makes a general increase in prices of 10 per cent which will give him an expected total taxable turnover of £20,900 per annum. A has become a taxable person and must immediately notify C & E. In the case of a new business commencing, if the proprietors have reasonable grounds in believing the level of taxable supplies will exceed the currently prescribed threshold in the coming year, C & E must be notified. Liability to notify C & E will also arise where certain quarterly thresholds are exceeded.

Notification to C & E is the first stage in the registration process by a taxable person. A form VAT 1 is obtained from any local VAT office and after completion is returned. Registration is then effected by C & E who issue the certificate of registration indicating the effective date and most importantly the taxable person's unique VAT number.

Once registration is complete the taxable person assumes certain obligations and entitlements which do not apply to non-registered persons. These are summarized in Table 11.3 where it would seem the obligations outweigh

TABLE 11.3. *Certain obligations and entitlements of taxable person registered for VAT*

(i)	Obligation to charge output tax to customers and issue tax invoices
(ii)	Entitled to reclaim input tax charged by suppliers
(iii)	Must keep certain records of transactions
(iv)	Required to complete a VAT Return (VAT 100) for a specified VAT period

the entitlements. However, a more detailed examination of each specific requirement may partially dispel this impression. Where a taxable person supplies goods and services to his customers these are referred to as outputs, and the VAT charged on them is output tax. However, if such supplies are zero-rated (see following section on goods and services) no VAT is chargeable. Where taxable supplies are chargeable at a positive VAT rate, i.e. a rate in excess of zero rate to another taxable person, it is obligatory to issue a special invoice commonly referred to as a tax invoice. This document, in addition to including the normal detail shown on a sales invoice, must also include the tax point, which is the relevant date for calculating the tax, supplier's VAT registration number, rate of VAT charged, amount of VAT charged, and tax exclusive total of supplies. However, where either the supplies are zero-rated to a customer who is a taxable person or positive rated to a non-taxable person, the issue of a tax invoice is optional although in practice it would be unusual in the first circumstance for a tax invoice not to be issued.

Thus, if we momentarily return to Table 11.2 and look at the transaction between B and C, both taxable persons, it follows that B would send C a tax invoice recording the sale of £200 + (VAT at 15%) £30 = £230. C as a taxable person will be charged with VAT by all his suppliers, including B, for goods supplied to him and this tax invoice in C's hands is evidence of the VAT suffered. Since these goods are for C's business they are described as inputs, and the tax on them is his input tax. In addition to goods acquired for resale, expenses such as telephone, stationery and accountant's services will be incurred. Providing the suppliers of these services are registered taxable persons then C has additional inputs and input tax. One further important feature of the VAT system is that no distinction is made between once-off capital expenditure and regular day to day revenue expenditure. Therefore if C acquires a major item of fixed plant from a taxable person, C will receive a tax invoice in the normal way. For VAT purposes all these different classes of expenditure are merely referred to as inputs, and C would be entitled to set off the related input tax against output tax he has charged his customers and must hand over the balance to the C & E.

In certain circumstances input tax may exceed output tax, for example where a taxable person's outputs are primarily zero-rated or large sums have been expended on capital items. A refund of the excess may be obtained which is a useful entitlement and may partially or totally, in the view of the taxable person, compensate for the cost of complying with the obligations already described and the expense of maintaining records and completing VAT returns.

With regard to the records which C & E require taxable persons to keep and preserve, although there are a number of formal general and special requirements as to content, the records do not have to be kept in any special manner providing the format will enable C & E officers to check the completeness and accuracy thereof. Table 11.4 illustrates the general content of the records to be maintained. Generally it may be observed that a record must be kept of all taxable (including zero-rated) goods and services that are received or supplied in the course of the business and exempt supplies if applicable. It is also obligatory to record ány taxable self-supplies and goods applied to non-business or personal use. In addition all records must be kept up to date and be sufficiently detailed to complete the VAT return. Supporting documentation, principally tax invoices issued and received, must be available for inspection and preserved for a prescribed period of time. Records may be preserved on microfilm or held on computer storage media provided that in both cases legible copies may be produced for inspection by C & E if so required.

The taxable person is required to complete regularly VAT returns (VAT 100). These returns are prepared for the tax periods which are normally every

TABLE 11.4. *General content of records to be maintained by a taxable person for VAT purposes*

Outputs	(£)	Inputs	(£)
Total sales: (item by item) excluding VAT	x	Taxable inputs: (item by item) excluding VAT	—
Analysis of sales: (item by item)		VAT suffered: (item by item)	—
zero-rated sales	—		
taxable sales (excluding tax)	—		
exempt supplies	—		
Sub-total	y		
VAT charged	—		
	—		—

Note: The sub-total at y must equal the sum at x.

three months, apart from the first return and situations where a repayment position is consistently arising because taxable supplies are wholly or mainly zero-rated. In this latter case a taxable person has the option to submit monthly returns, thus obtaining earlier repayment of input tax, although this advantage must be weighed against the disadvantage of having to produce twelve returns instead of the usual four in any one year. The VAT return in its simplest form is merely a comparison of output and input tax for the tax period culminating in the VAT payable to or refundable from C & E. In addition the return includes certain statistical information. The return is issued by the VAT Central Unit located at Southend-on-Sea and after completion is returned, not later than one month after the end of the tax period, together with a remittance for the amount due to C & E. If a refund is due this will be made by C & E by giro credit into a bank account as directed by the taxable person.

Goods and services

Under the VAT legislation all goods and services are divided into two broad categories, i.e. taxable supplies and non-taxable supplies. Taxable supplies are currently further subdivided into those supplies taxed at a positive rate 15 per cent, referred to as the standard rate, and those which are legally taxable but the rate of tax is nil. This latter type of taxable supplies are known as zero-rated goods and services.

It can, therefore, be seen that at the present time the UK operates a two-tier VAT system. This has not always been the case. Between November 1974 and June 1978 a three-tier system was operated whereby certain goods and services were taxed at a higher positive rate, initially at 25 per cent subsequently reduced to $12\frac{1}{2}$ per cent. On 1 July 1978 the higher rate of $12\frac{1}{2}$ per cent and the then standard rate of 8 per cent were merged into one standard rate of 15 per cent.

In order to simplify as far as possible supplies of goods and services which are taxable and those which are not, the legislation specifically lists the exempt cagetories and those items which are zero-rated. If a business by scrutiny of these lists cannot trace its supply of goods and services as being either exempt or zero-rated, then by a process of deduction they fall within the standard rate category. Table 11.5 shows the main classes of exempt and zero-rated supplies, but the reader should be aware of the necessity of checking the small print in the wording of the legislation since there are many exceptions to the general listed categories. As an example of this although food and drink are generally zero-rated, goods or services which relate to food and drink supplied in the course of catering, alcoholic or soft drinks, and pet food are excepted from the zero-rating classification and are therefore standard rate items.

We must now look at the perplexing but fundamental difference between persons making exempt non-taxable supplies and those making zero-rated

TABLE 11.5. *Main goods and services specified as exempt or zero-rated*

Exempt	Zero-rated
Land	Food and drink (with exceptions)
Insurance	Sewerage services and water
Postal services	Fuel and power (excepting road fuel)
Betting, gaming, and lotteries	Construction of buildings (with exceptions)
Finance	Transport
Education	Young children's clothing and footwear
Health	
Burial and cremation	

Note: Supplies of any goods are also zero-rated if those goods are exported or shipped as stores on a voyage or flight to a destination outside the UK.

taxable supplies. Although neither person is liable to charge their customers tax on those supplies, exempt suppliers suffer from the dual problem of not being able to register and therefore not be in a position to reclaim any tax on related inputs. This as we have already seen is not true in the case of zero-rated suppliers who may reclaim any related input tax from C & E providing they are registered as a taxable person. Table 11.6 indicates the relative positions of four traders under the UK VAT system. What should be immediately observed is that an element of hidden tax may enter into the price of exempt supplies, i.e. the supplier of exempt outputs would have to pass on the non-reclaimable input tax of £15 to his customers in order to produce the same profit level of £100. There is no remedy. The same problem also exists for very small firms where their supplies, although taxable at either standard or zero-rate, are below the prescribed annual limit. However, in this latter situation the small firm may remedy the problem by applying to C & E for voluntary registration. The small trader, if his application is accepted, assumes the same obligations and entitlements as described in the previous section. The costs of compliance must, of course, be carefully weighed against the amount of tax reclaimable and therefore the benefit of being more price competitive. Quite clearly if all the small firm's inputs were zero-rated there would be no advantage in a voluntary registration.

Special situations

This section is particularly concerned with providing additional information about the VAT system. Each topic will be dealt with in general terms only, but nevertheless it does provide an insight into a number of varied practical points which surround the basic VAT legislation as outlined in the two previous sections.

TABLE 11.6. *Relative position of four traders under UK VAT system*

	(£)	(VAT 100) (£)
(i) Registered taxable person making standard rated outputs		
Outputs	230	30
Less: inputs	(115)	(15)
	115	15
Less: net tax due to C & E	(15)	
Profit	100	
(ii) Registered taxable person making zero-rated outputs		
Outputs	200	nil
Less: inputs	(115)	(15)
	85	(15)
Add: tax refund from C & E	15	
Profit	100	
(iii) Non-registered person making 100% exempt outputs		
Outputs	200	—
Less: inputs	(115)	—
Profit	85	—
(iv) Non-registered person making taxable outputs < annual threshold		
Outputs	200	—
Less: inputs	(115)	—
Profit	85	—

Although it has been generally indicated that registered taxable persons are entitled to deduct input tax it should be noted that certain items give rise to non-deductible input tax in their hands. Thus any input tax relative to business expenditure on private cars (as opposed to commercial vehicles) must be excluded from the entries included on the VAT 100.

As previously indicated the VAT system requires that a taxable person must record an item by item account of each transaction as well as the issue of tax invoices. Retailers, in particular, would find compliance with these general obligations extremely tedious with regard to volume and small amount of each supply. Fortunately the legislation has been modified in two ways to assist this class of taxable person. Firstly, a taxable supply of goods or services to the general public need not be accompanied by a tax invoice unless specifically requested and even where the customer does require such a document, unless the tax inclusive price is £50 or more, a short form tax invoice may be offered. Secondly, to cope with the volume of transactions, a number of special retailer schemes exist which enable the calculation of output tax to be simplified. There are currently nine such schemes designated A to J (I is omitted). The input tax of retailers is not considered to require any special arrangements as to the manner in which they are recorded.

Generally speaking within the VAT legislation no difference is made between supply of new or second-hand goods. However certain traders consistently acquire their goods for resale from members of the public who almost certainly are non-registered for VAT purposes. The goods involved are invariably second-hand, for example second-hand car, boat, or caravan dealers. The problem for the trader is that if he is required to charge output tax on his selling price—there can be no input tax to deduct because his supplier is non-registered—the tax due to C & E would be consistently greater than that on the amount of value added by him. Again special schemes have been devised which, not surprisingly, are referred to as the second-hand goods schemes. Briefly the aim of these schemes is to redress the balance between dealers in second-hand as compared with dealers in identical new goods by allowing the trader to calculate his VAT on the margin, i.e. the difference between his buying and selling price both of which are regarded as tax-inclusive.

It should be noted that C & E issue guidance booklets on the detailed operation of both retailers and second-hand goods schemes, both sets having statutory authority as to the special rules which must be complied with. Non-compliance in any respect will invalidate its operation, and the cost of ignorance will fall on the taxable person.

In the previous section on goods and services we discussed the problem of a business with 100 per cent exempt supplies. Often a business will have a mixed range of goods and services which poses a problem in view of our earlier exposition. However the legislation contains a number of detailed and complex rules to deal with this situation and it is probably sufficient to say the problem of partial exemption is quite adequately, if not always equitably, solved by that legislation.

Groups of companies or companies carrying on their business through a number of separate divisions have certain entitlements as to how they may organize their structure for VAT purposes. Providing they are under common control a group of companies may elect for group registration. This election has the effect of creating a super VAT entity whereby all sales by the individual companies in the group covered by the election are treated as being made by one of the companies, and output tax is calculated accordingly. A claim for input tax is also made on a joint basis. One benefit of such an election is that only external outputs and inputs are recorded in the VAT records; the necessity for charging VAT on inter-company items is dispensed with. Conversely a single company with divisions may register each division as if it were a separate company.

VAT is payable on goods imported into the UK, and this obligation applies whether the importer is a taxable person or not. Prior to November 1984 the importer could defer paying the VAT at the time of importation and account for the tax on the next VAT return with a corresponding deduction for input tax.

Therefore in normal circumstances an importer who was also a taxable person need never finance personally this tax. However from 1 November 1984 VAT must be paid upon importation or removal of goods from a bonded warehouse or under special arrangements one month after importation or removal. The effect of this change has meant importers will have to finance this tax for anything up to three months before it may be recouped. Output tax will be chargeable in the normal way by the importer to his customer when the goods are sold.

Where the whole or part of a business is sold as a going concern, providing both the vendor and purchaser are taxable persons, it is not necessary to account for VAT on the sale consideration, and the purchaser, therefore, has no input tax to reclaim. This seems an eminently sensible arrangement. However, this exception does not apply to the disposal of the sale of assets piecemeal.

Finally, the question of de-registration should be briefly explained. Registration as outlined earlier is an important feature of the VAT system, but the act of registration is not irrevocable. A taxable person may cease to make taxable supplies in which case upon C & E receiving notification of this fact the registration will be cancelled. However cancellation of registration may be applied for if a taxable person's turnover in the next twelve months and previous two years does not exceed specified thresholds. The purpose of the two-year rule is to deter reckless voluntary registrations which, having achieved their purpose, i.e. a substantial refund, would be revoked immediately. Other events which give rise to a de-registration are cessation of the business, a sole trader taking in a partner or a partnership becoming a sole proprietorship, and change of business medium from sole trader to limited company or vice versa. In any of these events C & E should be notified within ten days.

Concluding remarks

We have in this chapter considered the introduction of VAT in 1973 and traced its rise to the position of being the main source of indirect taxation revenue for the Government in the following decade.

The concept of value added was examined within a detailed example to show the operation of the VAT system in the UK and the features of an indirect tax. The tax base of VAT was found to be that of consumption, a feature common to indirect taxes. It was also noted that firms in the VAT chain act as unpaid tax collectors.

In the section entitled registration, not only was the vital importance of registration by taxable persons explored, but also a range of complementary topics and issues were introduced. It was explained that registration will mean a taxable person assumes a number of obligations and entitlements under VAT legislation. The special nature of the tax invoice and its role within the VAT system was outlined. The terms output tax and input tax were introduced, and explained, and a brief description was given of the necessary accounting procedures with C & E including the VAT return (VAT 100).

Goods and services were identified as being of two types—either taxable or non-taxable supplies. The terms standard, zero-rated, and exempt supplies were explained and the fundamental difference between zero-rated and exempt supplies was examined in detail. The significance of voluntary registration with particular reference to small firms was outlined.

Finally, the chapter concluded by reviewing a number of fairly common special situations which arise within and because of the VAT legislation. Prominence was given to the retailer and second-hand goods schemes plus an explanation of what is meant by partial exemption—a common phenomenon in VAT practice—and the changed cash flow situation of UK importers was discussed.

Recommendations for further reading

A more detailed explanation of VAT rules and procedures is provided by HM Customs and Excise (1984). Detailed guidance on features of VAT which arise less frequently or only affect certain types of business are covered by separate VAT notices and leaflets which are freely available from any local VAT office. A general index to these is produced by HM Customs and Excise (1986).

References

HM Customs and Excise (1984), *The VAT guide No. 700* (Printed in the UK for HMSO).

HM Customs and Excise (1986) *VAT Publication No. 700/13/86* (Printed in the UK for HMSO).

12
Other Taxes

Introduction

This chapter will take a brief look at a number of revenue raisers for central and local Government, namely national insurance contributions, customs and excise duties other than VAT, local authority rates, and North Sea oil taxation. It may be arguable whether the four selected areas are taxes in the accepted sense. However, all the payments which are dissussed are compulsory and levied by public bodies, although clearly in the case of national insurance contributions and local authority rates the payer does receive some direct benefits. Nevertheless, the estimated value of the revenue raised in 1985/6 from these sources, some £60 billion, suggests their impact on the business community cannot be insignificant and merits some further discussion.

National insurance contributions (NIC)

Although the total cost of the UK social security system is not fully met by NIC, the estimated sum to be collected in 1985/6 through NIC was £24 billion. This amount represents sums extracted from the pockets of employees, employers, the self-employed, and non-employed persons. All but the last category are in the form of compulsory contributions. Dependent upon the circumstances of the contributor the rate of contributions varies, as does the entitlement to benefits. The method by which the contributions are collected also varies—again by reference to the contributor's status—but for the reasons outlined much of the contributions are collected by the Inland Revenue on behalf of the Department of Health and Social Security (DHSS).

Under the current legislation there are four classes of contributions:

(i) class 1—relating to employees and employers,
(ii) class 2 and 4—for self-employed persons,
(iii) class 3—voluntary contributions for the non-employed.

For convenience it is useful to outline the legislative provisions which are contained in the Social Security Act 1986 under two headings, employed and self-employed persons. Contributions under class 3 are of no relevance to businesses and are, therefore, omitted from the discussion.

(i) Class 1 contributions are payable by the employee and employer based upon the gross pay of the employee. Thus, national insurance contributions are earnings related, and Table 12.1 shows the rates in force from 6 April 1986. It will be noticed that there is a level of graduation built into the system. This has existed since October 1985. Where the pay of the employee does not exceed £38 per week there is no liability to NIC by either the employee or the employer. However, if this threshold of £38 is crossed, for example, the employee's pay is £39 in a week, the full £39 is liable to NIC at 5 per cent. A small increase in pay of £1 from £37.99 leaves the employee some 95p a week less in his pay packet after the £1 has been taken into account.

The same effect will be experienced at the other thresholds of £60 and £95 when the employee will automatically have to account for 7 per cent and 9 per cent on each £ of pay. However, where the employee's pay exceeds £285 per week the maximum weekly NIC is £25.65. It will be further observed that in the range £38 to £140 the employer is committed to paying the identical sum of NIC for each employee but an additional 1.45 per cent on each £ of employee's pay between £140 and £285. Once an employee earns more that £285 per week the employer is considerably worse off since there is no maximum weekly NIC as there is for employees. Thus, an employee with pay at £500 per week will have class 1 NIC of £25.65 whereas the employer will make contributions of £52.25.

This relatively new level of graduated NIC rates has received mixed reaction from the business community. Sectors which traditionally have a high number of low-paid workers, such as retailing, should show a decrease in NIC costs, but high pay service industries, including banking, expect a large increase. Also, there may be discrimination between similar firms who trade in London and the south-east—traditional high pay areas—and those whose activity is based in the south-west. Before leaving this point it is interesting to note that employers are entitled to deduct for Schedule D case I purposes the cost of NIC. This means for an unincorporated business, where the proprietor pays tax on his profits at the basic rate for 1986/7, the cost of contributions for the £500 per week employee is reduced to £37 while at the top marginal rate (60%) the cost is reduced to £21. A corporate employer paying at the full rate (35%) for the financial year 1986 would incur an after-tax NIC cost of £34 for the

TABLE 12.1. *Class I national insurance contributions from 6 April 1986*

Not contracted out rates on weekly earnings (£)	Employee %	Employer %
38.00–59.99	5	5
60.00–94.99	7	7
95.00–139.99	9	9
140.00–284.99	9	10.45
285 and over	—	10.45

same employee. It is perhaps worth noting, by contrast, that the employee receives, for income tax purposes, no deduction from his total income for class 1 NIC.

In addition to the general NIC system outlined above there are a number of situations where the employee or employer, may bc exempted from class 1 contributions entirely or pay at a reduced rate. The principal exempt categories of employees are persons aged under sixteen, or employed outside the UK, or members of visiting Armed Forces. By implication the employer is also exempted. An employee who is aged over 65 (man), 60 (woman) may apply for exemption, although in these circumstances the employer still remains liable at the non-contracted-out rates where the aged employee's pay exceeds the lower threshold.

Next, we consider the position of contracted-out employees who along with their employers pay class 1 contributions at reduced rates. If the employer runs an approved occupational pension scheme, then the employer may partially contract-out of the Government retirement pension scheme. The effect of this election for 1986/7 is that employees pay 2.15 percentage points less in contributions across the whole range of thresholds apart from the first £38 which remains at the non-contracted-out rate. Thus, a contracted-out employee with pay of £145 per week would contribute £38 × 9% + £107 × 6.85% = £10.75. The employer receives a reduction of 4.10 percentage points on the non-contracted-out rates except for the first £38. This special rate, however, only applies up to the maximum figure of £285, so that the employer's contributions at that level would be £38 × 10.45% + £247 × 6.35% = £19.65. Where the employee's pay exceeds £285 the employer receives no further concessionary rate and must contribute at the normal rate of 10.45 per cent for every £ in excess of £285. A comparison of class 1 contributions for a £500 per week employee are:

	Non-contracted-out	*Contracted-out*
Employee (maximum)	25.65	20.34
Employer (no maximum)	52.25	42.12
	£77.90	£62.46

However, when deciding to contract out, it must be remembered that the employee's share of NIC is recovered from him, by deduction from his pay, leaving a saving of £10 on costs to the employer. If we assume a business has ten employees earning £26,000 per annum, the saving to the business is £5,200. This is intended to offset the costs of setting up and running the occupational pension scheme.

The decision is further complicated in that where an employee is contracted out of the Government scheme he will, upon retirement, only receive the basic state pension, the entitlement to the earnings-related portion being relinquished by contracting-out. Of course, this missing income is replaced by a pension under the employer's scheme since an employer cannot contract out unless his occupational pension scheme offers benefits, at the worst, equal to the benefits forgone under the Government scheme. It is thus interesting to note that directors of a company are treated as employees of that company. This is true even where an individual has merely sought the protection of limited liability for his trading activities. In these circumstances, which also includes family companies, it is not uncommon for the company, as the employer, to retain a non-contracted-out stance. This would enable the employees including the owners, as directors, to have their cake and eat it too! Presumably the additional current costs are deemed to be outweighed by future benefits.

Conversely, owners of unincorporated businesses cannot be regarded as employees for pension purposes and contracting out may be more likely.

Although employers may have choices, as indicated above, the operation of the NIC system is mandatory, and it is obligatory to maintain a record showing the class 1 contributions in respect to each employee. The DHSS issue weekly and monthly tables for use by the employer to calculate the NIC. Clearly, these tables are for use where employees have regular pay intervals. Where irregular pay intervals exist for employees and in the case of all directors, there are special regulations. It is the obligation of the employer to remit class 1 NIC to the Inland Revenue on a monthly basis as part of the PAYE income tax system.

(ii) Any self-employed person, which includes any proprietor of his own business be it on his own or in partnership, must pay both class 2 and class 4 NIC. However, the DHSS has its own criteria for deciding whether a person is self-employed or in fact an 'employed earner'. Clearly, it is important for a person to know which category he is in because an 'employed earner' is liable to class 1 NIC. The interested reader is referred to the current DHSS leaflet entitled 'National Insurance and Contract of Service' for precise details.

The method for collecting classes 2 and 4 NIC is fundamentally different to that for class 1. Because the class 2 and class 4 contributions are also collected in different ways we shall outline the two systems separately.

As regards class 2 NIC any self-employed persons, aged 16 and over or under pension age, i.e. men 65, women 60, are liable. However, where a person's self-employment is subsidiary to a main employment, the DHSS may rule that the person is not liable for class 2 contributions. Similarly, a self-employed person with small earnings (1986/7 below £2,075) may apply for exemption also. Additionally, persons working outside the UK, or incapable or work, or in receipt of certain state benefits in any week, will not be liable for class 2 NIC in those particular weeks.

For the year 1986/7 class 2 contributions are payable at a flat rate of £3.75 per week, and these payments entitle that person to a range of state benefits. Important benefits for which the self-employed person does not qualify are unemployment and the earnings-related supplement on the state retirement pension. The payments may be made either by purchase of a special stamp from a post office or by direct debit to the DHSS. This one contribution covers all self-employments conducted by a person.

In addition to the weekly flat rate contribution under class 2 a self-employed person may also be liable to class 4 NIC at a fixed percentage. The fixed percentage for the year 1986/7 is 6.3 per cent and is applied to profits between £4,450 and £14,820. Where profits are less than £4,450 there is no liability, and the maximum payable is £653. Apart from the exemption for profits below £4,450, any self-employed person between the age of 16 and under pension age, i.e. men 65, women 60, is liable where profits exceed that figure. However, where these higher profits exist, exemption from contribution is nevertheless granted to non-resident UK individuals, sleeping partners, and certain divers and supervisors engaged in exploration activities around the coastline of the UK.

The word 'profits', for the purposes of class 4 NIC calculation, broadly covers those arising and assessable under Schedule D cases I and II (see Chapter 8). The collection of the contributions is the responsibility of the Inland Revenue and will form part of the Schedule D cases I or II assessment and be payable at the same time as the income tax (see Chapter 7). This class of contribution carries no right to state benefits, but from 1985/6 onwards 50 per cent of any such contributions are deductible from an individual's total income in computing his tax liability. Thus, a self-employed taxpayer taxable at the highest marginal rate will contribute £326 + £327 × 40% = £457 to the costs of the UK social security system.

Customs and excise duties

Excluding VAT, which was dealt with as a separate customs and excise duty or tax in Chapter 11, the estimated amount collectable in 1985/6 is £18 billion. An analysis of the main duties involved is given in Table 12.2. Statistics for VAT

TABLE 12.2. *Analysis of tax collectable by Customs and Excise 1985/6*

Tax	£bn	% Customs and Excise duties
Hydrocarbon oil	6.5	17.9
Tobacco	4.3	11.8
Alcoholic drink	4.2	11.5
Customs duties	1.4	3.8
Miscellaneous	1.6	4.4
	18.0	49.4
Value added tax	18.3	50.6

Source: 76th Report of Customs and Excise based on Budget estimates.

are also included for comparison purposes to indicate it is clearly the most important tax collected by Customs and Excise (C & E). However, the other heads of duty contribute substantial sums to the Government's pocket; they are and have been valuable revenue raisers for decades. All these various other duties are indirect taxes, and therefore the responsibility for collection falls upon the C & E. Part of these responsibilities are now to the European Economic Community (EEC), rather than the UK Government, in respect to customs duties.

The tax base for C& E duties is either specific or *ad valorem*; the former bases the duty upon weight, size, or quantity while the latter applies a duty to values. The duty on hydrocarbon oils and alcoholic drinks is specific while customs duties are *ad valorem* relative to the value of imports. The duty on tobacco is a mixture of both systems, i.e. specific as regards most tobaccos but specific and *ad valorem* on cigarettes.

Before analysing the effects of C & E duties on the business community we set out below a brief outline of the methods of charge under the main heads of duty:

(i) Hydrocarbon oil, petrol substitutes, and gas oil used as road fuel are charged excise duty at various basic rates per litre dependent on the category. The main sub headings are light oil and heavy oil. Heavy oil is further subdivided into that which is used as road fuel, such as derv, and carries no rebate from the basic rate for users, and non-road use which carries a substantial rebate. There are also reliefs from duty for certain users, for example fishing boats and lifeboats and heavy oil used in ships in home waters. There are also reliefs for agricultural users.

(ii) Tobacco products include cigarettes, cigars, hand-rolling tobaccos, and other smoking and chewing tobacco. Cigarettes are charged at a percentage rate of the retail price for a packet of 20 king-size plus an amount per 1,000 cigarettes. The remaining categories are charged at a rate per kilogram of the finished product. No rebates or reliefs are granted.

(iii) Alcoholic drinks are chargeable to basic duty under various categories. The subheadings are spirits, beer, wine from fresh grapes, made-wine from concentrated grape-juice, cider, and perry. Across all subheadings there is a complex range of duties applied to a hectolitre of alcohol. Spirits are an exception in that the basic duty is per litre of alcohol. There is an exemption from cider duty where the production level does not exceed 70 hectolitres per annum.

(iv) Customs duties relate to goods imported into the UK or goods manufactured therefrom. Upon entry by the UK to the EEC, protective duties against imports from other member states were phased out along with preference for imports from the commonwealth. The duties now applied to imports are part of the EEC Common Customs Tariff. The general purpose is to protect industries of member states but allow some preferential treatment to trade with certain non-member states. Developing countries are given preference for a wide range of goods under a scheme referred to as the Generalized System of Preference. As described earlier, these duties are collected for the benefit of the EEC, but 10 per cent of the amount collected is returned to the UK to cover costs.

(v) Miscellaneous heads of duty include betting and gaming tax, duty on matches and mechanical lighters, and car tax.

From the above outline it would seem that most of the excise duties are collected from a very narrow range of manufacturers. Brewers, distillers, oil, and tobacco companies would tend to head the list. Clearly, all businesses which acquire imported goods as part of their trading operations will have to pay customs duties. The car industry, principally main-dealers, bookmakers, and weekly football pool operators will collect and account to C & E for well over £1 billion in car tax and betting duties during 1985/6.

As with most indirect taxes including VAT, excise duties are a tax upon expenditure. Unlike VAT, however, they are in general terms hidden taxes. There is no statutory requirement for the duty levied to be shown separately for goods and services. No equivalent of the tax invoice in VAT legislation (Chapter 11) exists. Thus, unlike VAT where it is clear, at least theoretically, that the incidence of tax falls upon the ultimate consumer, excise duties are not typical indirect taxes, i.e. the taxes are levied on the producer but only borne to some extent by the consumer. The extent of the 'shifting' of these duties is undisclosed in the chain from the producer or importer to the final consumer. Of course, there are instances where the consumer acts in a manner which signifies awareness of who bears the incidence. This is particularly prevalent around the time of the Budget where increases in excise duties on drink, petrol, and tobacco are announced. The man or woman in the street will often acquire more than the normal amount of these products merely to delay the effects of the price increases. Similarly, persons placing bets will normally pay betting tax on their stake money rather than on their winnings, if any, to minimize the effects. Conversely, if a foreign-made transistor radio is purchased the customer is unaware of any customs duty being included and certainly has no idea of the amount included in the price paid. What is the most important factor is the price paid and if this is cheaper than an identical radio in the shop next door it may be purchased. The difference in price quoted by the two retailers may signify more efficient control, but it may also be attributed to the retailer bearing part of the customs duty and reducing his net profit margins thereby. Other examples of C & E duties being borne by the business community, rather than the consumer, are petrol stations (regular price wars), cut-price wine and spirit merchants, and the 1p or 2p price cut on popular brands of cigarettes offered by large retail tobacconist chains.

From this necessarily general analysis of the effects of C & E duties it is nevertheless possible to draw some conclusions:

(i) C & E duties are attractive revenue raisers for the Government which acts as if it believes the incidence is borne by the consumer, for example reliefs are given against the basic excise duties on hydrocarbon oils in a limited range of business occupations.

(ii) C & E duties are regressive in nature not only to the non-domestic consumer but also to businesses who bear part of the incidence themselves. This situation arises because these forms of taxes are allowable deductions in computing Schedule D cases I or II profits assessable to income tax or corporation tax. Thus, dependent upon the top marginal rate at which a business is liable to direct taxes, £1 of C & E duty will cost between £1 (for the loss-making business) and 40p (for the highly profitable sole trader). Clearly, because of the presumption of the Government in (i) above, regarding incidence, this is an unintended subsidy of the indirect tax system by the direct, but nevertheless it may occur. The less well-off firm in terms of profit levels is at a disadvantage, and there is also discrimination between the unincorporated and corporate business venture with the same profit levels above, say, £50,000 at current rates of income and corporation tax.

Local authority rates

At the present time the topic of local authority rates is a political 'hot potato'; not, it might be added, for the first time in the past ten years. Leaving aside all political issues a succession of government papers—4 Green, 1 Blue, and 1 White—have left in their wake a confused picture of what the future of rates is going to be.

Clearly, this situation has presented us with difficulty in explaining this important tax on businesses. We, therefore, intend to discuss briefly the present system of rates as regards businesses and then introduce the latest proposals for the future.

Rates are a levy by local authorities to partially offset the costs of the services provided including education, housing, libraries, recreation, and leisure facilities, while a large proportion of the balance is met by central government grants. The estimated amount to be collected in 1985/6 from domestic and non-domestic ratepayers is approximately £14 billion. Of this sum 2/5 (£5.6 billion) arose from the domestic ratepayer and 3/5 (£8.4 billion) from the non-domestic, i.e. the business ratepayer.

Each local authority will fix its levy of *X*p and apply it to the rateable values of rateable property within its boundaries for the year from 1 April to the following 31 March. A business with premises and plant with a rateable value of £4,000 in a local authority area, which imposes a rate of 200p per £ of rateable value, will receive a rates bill of £8,000, i.e. 4,000 × 200 p. The business may be the owner of the property or occupying it as a tenant under a lease where the tenant is liable for the rates. A domestic ratepayer with a dwelling having a rateable value of £300 will have a rates demand for £600. The rateable value of domestic premises is based upon accommodation space and not the number of occupants. In aggregate terms the rateable values of all properties within its boundaries × the levy for a particular year will provide the local authority with its rates income.

The method of raising cash through the rates system is probably the least complex form of taxation we have discussed. However, its very simplicity is open to criticism and we shall discuss this below:

(i) Local authorities appear to have little accountability; those who elect may not pay and those who pay may receive little or no benefit from the services provided. This is particularly true of business ratepayers who receive no vote in local elections and receive very little, if any, benefits. Things were slightly improved under the Rates Act 1984 whereby provision was made for discussion between local authorities and their industrial and commercial ratepayers on the rate-fixing process.

(ii) Perhaps what is more evident from the earlier examples is that no account is taken of the ability to pay. Rates are levied without reference to business profits or incomes of domestic ratepayers. Thus, rates are a regressive form of taxation for either category. In the business sector the incidence of rates is highest upon those firms paying no tax because of trading losses or having very low profit levels. At high profit levels a £1 of rates will be reduced to 40p after taking the top marginal rate of income tax into account.

(iii) There is considerable variability in business rates from one geographical area to another. Holding the rate in the £ constant nation-wide, the rate bills faced by firms trading in the south-east, particularly London, tend to be higher than those for the rest of the country. This reflects the high rateable values applicable in the London area. Next, we must acknowledge that each local authority fixes its rate relative to its own requirements, i.e. the rate in the £ is not constant nation-wide. It follows that in our earlier example if the property and plant were moved to a neighbouring local authority who have imposed a rate of 150p in the £ the business would receive a rate demand for £6,000.

These problems with the current local authority rates system present economic distortions between (i) the domestic and business ratepayer, (ii) business competitors in different local authority areas or wider geographical areas, (iii) low and high profit level firms, and (iv) unincorporated and corporate businesses in post-tax terms. The latest Government Green Paper (HMSO 1986) has published a number of proposals for the future of rates. The general conclusions suggest that domestic rates should be abolished and replaced by a comumunity charge while business rates would be recast with a uniform business rate. The essence of the uniform business rate system is that after a transitional period a uniform rate nation-wide emerges. Clearly, these proposals would eliminate distortions (i) and part of (ii) above. However, if rateable values are the base for calculating the amount due from businesses those located in the North would have a rates advantage over firms operating from central London. The issue of ability to pay appears to have been completely ignored and thus leaves (iii) and (iv) above as unresolved problems.

Whatever legislation, if any, finally emerges from this Green Paper we feel the commencement of its operation is not imminent, and firms should be prepared to accept the current, albeit imperfect, rates system in the short to medium term.

North Sea oil taxation

The taxation of the exploitation of energy resources in the North Sea is in one way unique when compared with all other taxes we have discussed in Part Two. It is known it will end at some future point in time although that point is not yet established. This is because the energy reserves, which are being exploited, will be exhausted. Current oil production forecasts for 1990 show a 30 per cent reduction from the expected out-turn for 1986. Thus, this taxation system may be viewed as essentially short-term as a major source of revenue for the UK Government and may already be in decline. The other important factors which may affect future tax revenue are the price of oil and the US $ against the £ exchange rate. Significant changes in these clearly affect the revenue upon which the tax is based, for example between December 1985 and March 1986 the price of crude oil fell from US $30 to US $10. This massive reduction in price caused a downward forecast for North Sea oil tax revenues from £11.5 billion in 1985/6 to £6 billion for 1986/7. For these reasons we will keep our discussion of this topic brief.

The taxation system may be divided into two distinct phases; the period 1975–83 and 1983 onwards. In the 1975–83 period the system included four distinct methods of taxation—licence royalties (LR), petroleum revenue tax (PRT), supplementary petroleum duty which was replaced by advance petroleum revenue tax, and corporation tax (CT). The first three of the taxes were applied on a field basis while CT was levied upon companies involved in the operation of the fields. Following pressure from the oil companies, significant changes were introduced in the 1983 Finance Act; LR for new fields was abolished and advance petroleum revenue tax was to be phased out before its intended departure date of 1985. Therefore, the operative taxes with which we shall concern ourselves are licence royalties on older fields, petroleum revenue tax, and corporation tax.

Royalties, which are levied at $12\frac{1}{2}$ per cent on the gross revenue of a field licensed before April 1982, have their roots in the Petroleum (Production) Act 1934 for onshore fields and the Continental Shelf Act 1964 which extended coverage to offshore fields. Where fields are licensed after April 1982 they are exempted from LR in legislation introduced by the Petroleum Royalties (Relief) Act 1983. Because royalties use gross revenue as a base, rather than profits (see Chapter 2), this exemption will substantially assist future high-cost marginal fields.

Next, we will consider PRT which was a completely new tax and is principally governed by the Oil Taxation Act 1975 with amendments contained in subsequent Finance Acts. Although the word 'revenue' appears in its title PRT is not a tax on revenue but is levied on the profits of fields. In its simplest form PRT is charged at 75 per cent on the excess of net revenue over exploration and operating costs and capital expenditure. The term 'net revenue' in this context signifies that, where applicable, for example a pre-1982 field, royalties are also deductible for the purposes of PRT. There is provision for the carrying forward of losses.

A number of concessions were introduced in the original 1975 legislation. The first of these, to reduce the burden of PRT on marginal fields, was in the form of an oil allowance. This allowance exempts one-half million tonnes of oil per chargeable period with an upper cumulative ceiling of ten million tonnes per field.

Second, in general terms, capital expenditure on exploration and development was allowed at more that 100 per cent of cost by the use of an adjustment referred to as uplifit. This additional relief for capital expenditure is now only granted until payback is realized, i.e. a profit after all expenses, capital or revenue, and royalties where applicable but before charging PRT. This limitation was imposed in 1981.

Third, we have the complicated provision of safeguard which limits the PRT liability in any chargeable period by reference to the excess of net income over cumulative capital expenditure. Net income for this purpose would be net revenue (see above) less operating costs. There are also limits on how long safeguard may be claimed.

A chargeable period for PRT purposes is one of six months. During each period of six months the tax is paid on a monthly basis being a fixed percentage of the previous chargeable period's final liability. Any adjustment resulting from changes between six monthly assessments is accountable for two months after the end of the current period. Therefore, assuming PRT due for the six months ended 31 December 1986 was £90,000 and for the six months ended 30 June 1987 it was £100,000, the payment would be £90,000 × 75% ÷ 6 per month, i.e. £11,250. Each month from January to June 1987, £11,250 is payable with a final payment of £32,500 due on 30 August 1987.

Finally, we must review the operation of corporation tax. This tax which had been operating since 1965 (see Chapter 10) was levied upon companies participating in the North Sea fields on the same basis as for onshore companies. However, in order to prevent the offset of onshore losses against offshore profits, a line was drawn on the map designating where onshore activities ceased and offshore activities commenced. In addition to this special piece of legislation both LR and PRT are deductible in computing profits for corporation tax purposes. Here there arises a slight problem in that the former taxes are levied on a field basis, and many of the fields have several participant companies, while corporation tax is levied on a company basis. Fortunately, a simple but effective solution is adopted whereby the liability to LR and PRT is apportioned to the participants by reference to their respective shares in the field.

Capital allowances are claimable by companies in respect of all relevant categories of capital expenditure in the normal way (see Chapters 8 and 10). Allowances of a particular interest to companies are scientific research expenditure, and mines and oil wells allowances. Scientific research covers activities in the fields of natural or applied science. It is of either a capital or revenue nature. Capital expenditure qualifies for a 100 per cent write-off in the chargeable accounting period in which it is incurred. This 100 per cent allowance has been unaffected by the 1984 and 1985 Finance Acts which withdrew first year and initial allowances on most classes of capital expenditure.

For expenditure which qualifies for mines and oil wells allowances there have been fundamental changes in respect of expenditure incurred on or after 1 April 1986. The previous system which provided for initial and writing-down allowances involving the use of formulae relative to output and royalty values has been abolished. Relief for qualifying expenditure incurred after 1 April 1986 or residue of expenditure from prior to that date is similar to the general capital allowances system, i.e. the rate of allowance will be 25 per cent on a reducing balance basis.

Concluding remarks

In this chapter we discussed a number of important taxes, in terms of revenue raised, which affect a wide range of different persons. It was shown that national insurance contributions applied to employees, employers, and self-employed persons. Illustrations were included of the effects of a graduated scale of contributions, and the consequences of contracting-out where the employer maintains an approved occupational pension scheme were presented.

The general operation of customs and excise duties was examined, and it was found that excise duties are extracted, initially, from a small number of producers. The shifting of excise duties to the ultimate consumer was analysed in general terms, and it was demonstrated that where partial shifting occurs the duties are regressive.

Local authority rates were discussed against a background of proposed radical changes. The conclusion being that, currently rates are regressive to firms and will remain so as long as they use a base for calculations which is other than profits.

The system for the taxation of North Sea oil revenues was introduced together with a brief discussion of its likely decline over the next decade. It was found to be a system composed of three separate taxes, each with a different base for calculation. A general examination of the interaction between corporation tax, royalties, and petroleum revenue tax was made. Finally, we concluded by outlining the systems of capital allowances which would be of particular interest to oil companies.

Recommendations for further reading

For the reader wishing to acquire a detailed knowledge of particular NIC topics, it is suggested reference be made to a wide range of booklets and pamphlets which may be obtained from local DHSS offices. More detailed comment about the main heads of customs and excise duties may be found in the latest report of HM Customs and Excise (HMSO 1985, Chapter 3). A wide selection of statistical information and rates of basic duty are also included in that chapter. The full proposals for change in local rates are published in a Green Paper (HMSO 1986) while an interesting criticism of the community tax and comment on the confusion of objectives contained therein is presented by Johnson (1986). Johnson (1986) also puts forward alternatives to the suggested uniform business rate proposals which address the problem of ability to pay. An excellent paper giving an analysis of North Sea oil taxation past, present, and future has been prepared by Devereaux and Morris (1983) as part of the IFS project on Taxation of North Sea Oil. We have deliberately excluded any reference to inheritance tax but, for the reader requiring an introduction to this tax, Homer & Burrows (1986) might be a useful starting point.

References

Devereaux, M. P., and Morris, C. N. (1983), *North Sea Oil Taxation: The Development of the North Sea Tax System* (London: Institute for Fiscal studies).

HMSO (1985), *HM Customs and Excise 75th Report 1983*, Cmnd. 9391 (London: HMSO).

HMSO (1986), *Paying for Local Government*, Cmnd. 9714 (London: HMSO).

Homer, A., and Burrows, R. (1986), *Tolley's Tax Guide 1986/87* (Croydon, Surrey: Tolley).

Johnson, C. (1986), 'Local rate scrapping', *Lloyds Bank Economic Bulletin*, no. 90 (June 1986).

PART THREE

Tax Implications of Selected Business Decisions

In Part One we provided a fairly rigorous analysis of alternative tax systems and, in particular, explained under what conditions tax provisions may not interfere with the efficient selection of capital projects and financing methods. Then in Part Two we described the broad principles of the main taxes in the UK relevant to businesses. Our task is now to apply the concepts learned from our knowledge of tax theory to the particular circumstances of selected business decisions. Chapter 13 concentrates on corporate financial policy and is followed by an analysis of the impact of tax upon capital investment decisions and leasing in Chapters 14 and 15, respectively. The choice of business medium, whether a sole proprietorship, partnership, or a limited company, is evaluated in Chapter 16. Finally in Chapter 17 we examine the fiscal implications of overseas operations.

13
Corporate Financial Policy

Introduction

We analysed the implications for dividend policy under a partial imputation system in Chapter 4. Our intention now is to expand our analysis so that we may take account of some of the detailed UK personal and corporate tax rules discussed in Part Two. We begin with an examination of dividend policy, then turn our attention to debt finance, the overall cost of capital, and capital structure.

The cost of dividends

When a company pays a dividend there are at least three sets of cash flows associated with the transaction. First, net dividends are paid to the shareholders. Second, there is normally a payment of advance corporation tax (ACT). Third, there is a reduction in net mainstream corporation tax for this or another accounting period.

If there is no franked investment income, the ACT is paid 14 days after the end of the quarter in which the dividends are paid. Alternatively, if the company has some franked investment income, then the incremental ACT occurs further into the future. For example, assume initially that there is franked investment income of £10,000 in the first quarter and a planned franked payment of £10,000 in the third quarter. In this instance, there is no ACT due. However, if the company then decides to make an additional franked payment of £10,000 in the first quarter, then there is no ACT in the first quarter because the franked investment income cancels the franked payment. However, ACT arises on the franked payment made in the third quarter because there is no longer any offsetting franked investment income. Thus, because of the existence of franked investment income, the extra dividend in the first quarter gives rise to an additional ACT payment due 14 days after the end of the third quarter. The time lag could even be longer than this if there were no other franked payments yet due. Furthermore, if the franked payments exceed franked investment income, there may be more than one incremental ACT payment. For example, assume initially that the franked investment income in the first quarter is £5,000 and that there is a planned franked payment of £10,000 in the third quarter. The result of this is an ACT liability of (£10,000 − £5,000) × 29% = £1,450 for the third quarter assuming an

ACT rate of 29/71. An additional £10,000 franked payment in the first quarter results in an ACT liability of (£10,000 − £5,000) × 29% = £1,450 for the first quarter and a liability of £10,000 × 29% = £2,900 for the third quarter. Thus, the additional ACT liabilities are £1,450 for the first quarter and £2,900 − £1,450 = £1,450 for the third quarter.

The advance corporation tax setoff against the gross corporation tax liability reduces the cost to the company of paying a dividend. When the setoff is restricted, because the advance corporation tax payments exceed the maximum setoff limit, then the cost of the dividend is increased when account is taken of the time value of money. To illustrate more fully how to evaluate the cost, to the company, of paying a dividend let us consider the following example. Under plan A in Table 13.1, net dividends of £3.55 m are paid on 1 January of year one. Franked investment income of £10 m is received in the first quarter, and so there is no ACT payable. The firm earns net taxable

TABLE 13.1. *Taxation implications of dividend policy: a complex example* (£m)

	Plan A	Plan B	Incremental cash flow
Year 1			
Franked investment income in first quarter of year 1	10.00	10.00	
Dividends paid on 1 January of year 1	3.55	14.20	(10.65)
Franked payments in first quarter	5.00	20.00	
ACT payable on 14 April of year 1	—	2.90	(2.90)
Net taxable income for year 1	8.00	8.00	
Tax at 35%	2.80	2.80	
ACT setoff (restricted)	—	2.32	
ACT carried forward	—	0.58	
Mainstream corporation tax, payable on 1 January of year 3	2.80	0.48	2.32
Year 2			
Surplus franked investment income b/fd	5.00	—	
Franked payment in first quarter	5.00	5.00	
ACT payable on 14 April of year 2	—	1.45	(1.45)
Net taxable income for year 2	10.00	10.00	
Tax at 35%	3.50	3.50	
ACT setoff	—	2.03	
Mainstream corporation tax, payable on 1 January of year 4	3.50	1.47	2.03

income of £8 m for the first year, and thus the mainstream corporation tax payable is £2.8 m, on the basis of a 35 per cent corporate tax rate. Because franked payments during year one are only £3.55 m × 100/71 = £5 m, assuming an ACT rate of 29/71, which is £5 m less than the franked investment income, then the surplus franked investment income of £5 m is offset against franked payments in the next year. We assume that franked payments of £5 m in year two occur during the first quarter, and so there is no ACT payable at that stage. Since net taxable income for year two is £10 m, there is a mainstream corporation tax liability of £3.5 m.

The tax implications of additional dividends of £10.65m on 1 January of year one are quite fascinating. This is shown under plan B in Table 13.1. During the first quarter of year one, franked payments are now £20m, and so there is an ACT payment of £(20m – 10m) × 29% = £2.9m. However, ACT setoff is restricted because the ACT exceeds 29 per cent of net taxable income. The setoff is equal to 29% × £8m = £2.32m, with the result that the remaining ACT is carried backwards or forwards. We assume that the ACT setoff cannot be carried backwards because of restrictions in previous years, and so the ACT carried forward is equal to £2.9m – £2.32m = £0.58m. The mainstream corporation tax liability under plan B is thus:

$$£8\text{m} \times 35\% - £2.32\text{m} = £2.8\text{m} - £2.32\text{m} = £0.48\text{m}.$$

In year two, under plan B, the franked payment gives rise to an ACT liability of 29% × £5m = £1.45m. This ACT, together with the ACT brought forward from the previous year, represents the ACT setoff for year two of:

$$£1.45\text{m} + £0.58\text{m} = £2.03\text{m},$$

and so the mainstream corporation tax for year two, under plan B, is:

$$£3.5\text{m} - £2.03\text{m} = £1.47\text{m}.$$

In Table 13.1 we also see the incremental cash flows arising from the payment of the extra dividends of £10.65m. There is additional ACT of £2.9m due 14 weeks into year one, and £1.45m due 66 weeks from the beginning of year one, totalling £4.35m. This represents 29/71 of the net dividend:

$$29/71 \times £10.65\text{m} = £4.35\text{m}.$$

Also, there is an incremental mainstream corporation tax saving of £2.32m, which arises two years after the dividend in year one, on the assumption of a tax time lag of one year and one day from the end of the accounting year, ended 31 December, and a £2.03m saving due three years after the dividend. These total £4.35m and are equal to the ACT saving. However, if account is taken of the time value of money then, given a discount rate of, say, 8 per cent per annum, the after-tax cost of the £10.65m dividend is equal to (£m):

$$10.65 + 2.90/(1.08)^{14/52} - 2.32/(1.08)^2 + 1.45/(1.08)^{66/52} - 2.03/(1.08)^3$$
$$= 11.205084.$$

Thus, the cost of the dividend is increased by £11,205,084 – £10,650,000 = £555,084, when compared with its pre-tax cost, and represents over 5 per cent of the net dividend.

The cost of debt and the weighted average cost of capital

The explicit cost to the company of paying interest on debt is given by (i) the net interest, plus (ii) the payment of income tax at source, less (iii) the reduction in the mainstream corporation tax liability arising from the gross interest being deducted in the derivation of taxable profits.

Given a basic rate of income tax of 29 per cent, on gross debenture interest of £15m, the company pays only the net interest of 71% × £15m = £10.65m to debenture holders, and 29% × £15m = £4.35m is normally deducted at source and paid to the Inland Revenue on behalf of the debenture holders. Through interest deductibility, the firm's mainstream tax liability is reduced by 35% × £15m, or £5.25m, assuming a 35 per cent marginal tax rate. The after-tax cost, which comprises the three components, is thus:

$$\text{£}10.65\text{m} + \text{£}4.35\text{m} - \text{£}5.25\text{m} = \text{£}9.75\text{m}.$$

But the fundamental relationship is that the cost of the interest is reduced to the product of the gross interest and one minus the corporate tax rate:

$$\text{£}15\text{m}\ (1 - 0.35) = \text{£}9.75\text{m}.$$

However, this approach obscures the underlying cash flows which are important when account is taken of the time value of money.

The weighted average cost of capital is found by calculating the component costs of each source of finance and weighting each cost according to the proportionate value of each source. For example, let us assume that shareholders require the company to pay gross dividends of 24 per cent or to retain funds to be reinvested at 24 per cent and that debenture holders require a yield of 15 per cent. Retentions form 20 per cent of finance, new issues represent 50 per cent, and 30 per cent is raised through borrowing. We assume a corporation tax rate of 35 per cent, a basic rate of income tax of 29 per cent, and an ACT rate of 29/71.

We have already discussed the role of ACT setoff for the cost of dividends. If the company regularly pays full dividends and raises equity finance from new issues, then such a policy needs to reflect ACT payments as well as issue costs. Let us assume that issue costs are 5 per cent, that ACT is paid three months after the respective dividend, and that the setoff is made against a tax liability due one year after the dividend payment. A 24 per cent gross dividend return would imply an equity cost of capital of 18.8 per cent. This is found by solving for k in the following evaluation equation:

$$100{,}000 - 5{,}000 = \frac{24{,}000}{k}\left(0.71 + \frac{0.29}{(1+k)^{0.25}} - \frac{0.29}{(1+k)}\right) \qquad (13.1)$$

$$\text{or } k = \frac{0.24}{0.95}\left(0.71 + \frac{0.29}{(1+k)^{0.25}} - \frac{0.29}{(1+k)}\right) \tag{13.2}$$

By trial and error we find that, to satisfy equation (13.2), k is 0.188. The right-hand side of equation (13.1) represents the net amount of finance raised after issue costs for each £100,000 gross. The left-hand side shows the capitalized value of the costs to the company. For each £100,000 of finance, the company pays a gross dividend of £24,000. The term in the brackets of equation (13.1) converts the gross dividend into the present value of three cash flows: first, the dividend which is assumed to be 71 per cent of its gross equivalent; second, 29 per cent of the gross dividend, which represents the ACT payment discounted for one-quarter of a year; and third, a deduction for ACT setoff discounted for one year. By dividing by k, we capitalize those dividends and hence produce a discounted value of all the dividends and ACT payments less ACT setoffs.

The after-tax cost of debt is derived by a similar process. Let us assume that the company pays £15,000 gross interest on every £100,000 debt. We assume that there are issue costs of 5 per cent, which are tax-deductible, unlike issue costs for equity. The reduced corporation tax liability, through the deduction for issue costs for tax purposes, is assumed to occur one year later. For every £15,000 gross interest, there are three cash flows: first, a net payment of interest which represents 71 per cent of the gross equivalent; second, an income tax liability, three months later, equal to 29 per cent of the gross value; and finally, a reduced mainstream corporation tax liability through interest deductibility, discounted for the one year delay, between the payment of the net interest and the payment of a reduced corporation tax liability. If we assume that the debt is irredeemable and that the corporation tax rate is 35 per cent, then we can capitalize the interest payments at i, which denotes the after-tax cost of debt. The evaluation equation now reads:

$$100{,}000 - 5{,}000 + \frac{5{,}000(0.35)}{1+i} = \frac{15{,}000}{i}\left(0.71 + \frac{0.29}{(1+i)^{0.25}} - \frac{0.35}{(1+i)}\right) \tag{13.3}$$

The first three terms in this equation represent the discounted value of each £100,000 raised less issue costs, after tax relief on issue costs. The remainder shows the capitalized value of interest payments after income tax deductions at source and corporation tax savings. By trial and error we find that to satisfy the equation, an approximate value for i is 10.5 per cent.

Hence, if we apply the costs of retentions, new issues, and debt to the respective proportions of finance raised by these three methods, we can calculate the weighted average cost of capital:

$$0.20 \times 24\% \text{ (retentions)} + 0.50 \times 18.8\% \text{ (new equity)}$$
$$+ 0.30 \times 10.5\% \text{ (debt)} = 17.35\% \text{ (overall).}$$

A firm which earns 17.35 per cent and is financed according to the stated proportions can produce sufficient income to match the rates of return required by each category of investor.

Personal taxation and corporate financial policy

In the preceding example we may note that the cost to the company of a retention is more expensive than paying dividends and raising new equity. Given this result, is it wise for the company to retain profits? In order to answer this it is important to examine the personal tax position of the representative shareholder. For every 24p of gross dividends, the discounted cost to the company was found to be 18.8p. Hence, if the company retains the profits, instead of paying dividends, the 18.8p should represent a capital gain to the shareholder. If the gain is realized, the capital gain would be worth:

$$18.8\text{p} \times (1 - 30\%) = 13.16\text{p},$$

on the basis of an assumed capital gains tax rate of 30 per cent. If the shareholder has a high marginal rate of income tax, the capital gain should be preferred to a dividend. However, at the margin, investors should be indifferent to a retention-induced capital gain if the after-tax value of the retention is worth the same as the after-tax value of the dividend. The equilibrium marginal rate of income tax on gross dividend income, which we denote by m^*, is thus found when:

$$24\% \ (1 - m^*) = 13.16\% \text{ or, } m^* = 45\% \text{ (approx.).}$$

Hence, the dividend policy of the firm is rational provided shareholders suffer income tax at 45 per cent and capital gains tax at 30 per cent.

Let us now turn our attention to the debt finance. The rate of interest on debt we assume to be lower than that on equity, since it is less risky for the investor. We know that under the UK tax system, interest is tax-deductible at the corporate level. But, through the setoff of ACT, dividends also reduce mainstream taxes. However, provided the corporate tax rate exceeds the basic rate of income tax, from which the ACT rate is assumed to be determined, a company can save more tax through higher levels of gearing. Thus, should a firm increasingly use debt finance at the margin? Furthermore, does this imply that as more firms seek debt finance, interest rates will be pushed upwards? If this is correct, does the increase in interest rates offset the initial tax advantage? Hence, with higher interest rates, should degrees of gearing make any difference to the value of the firm? The general equilibirum theory of capital structure supports the view that demand interest rates on debt must rise in order to attract investors in higher income tax brackets, who could otherwise largely avoid taxes by seeking out other investments which generate capital gains rather than income. But rational firms should be willing to supply debt at a rate of interest in excess of that which would be determined in the absence of tax deductibility of interest. After appropriate adjustments have been made for risk, the marginal investor should be indifferent between (i) low-taxed capital gains from shares and (ii) high-taxed income from debt, which has been inflated due to the tax inducement through interest deductibility at the corporate level. In general market equilibrium the rise in interest rates would wipe out the tax benefits.

In order to illustrate the main issues at work, let us assume that there are three groups of potential lenders A, B, and C, who have marginal income tax rates of 29, 35, and 40 per cent, respectively. There is no capital gains tax, and investors can earn in the market 15 per cent on risk-free growth stocks. For simplicity we shall ignore tax time lags. Now, a firm is considering how to fund several risk-free projects which, if financed by retentions, would earn 15 per cent per annum after corporation tax at 35 per cent. For shareholders, it would be an acceptable proposition on the basis of a 15 per cent opportunity cost for risk-free growth stocks. However, the firm could, instead, finance the projects by debt on which interest could be paid at a rate of 21.13 per cent per annum. The reason for this is that the after-tax cost to the company, allowing for interest deductibility, is only:

$$21.13\%\ (1-35\%) = 13.73\%\ \text{(ignoring tax lags for simplicity)},$$

which is cheaper than finance by retentions. It is financially worthwhile to borrow on this basis, since the cost is less than the internal rate of return on the projects. Group A investors should be willing to lend since they could earn a rate of return after personal tax of:

$$21.13\%\ (1-29\%) = 15\%,$$

which is comparable with the 15 per cent opportunity cost relating to growth stocks. However group B investors should be unwilling to lend unless interest rates increased to 23.08 per cent. Since they pay personal tax at 35 per cent, they could earn an after-tax return of:

$$23.08\%(1-35\%\ \text{(personal tax)}) = 15\%,$$

which is equivalent to the return on growth stocks. At this rate of interest the after-tax cost to the company, which pays corporation tax at 35 per cent, is:

$$23.08\%\ (1-35\%\ \text{(corporation tax)}) = 15\%,$$

which is equivalent to the internal rate of return on the projects and should therefore be acceptable to the company. However, if interest rates exceeded 23.08 per cent, the cost to the company would exceed the cost of retentions and could therefore be unattractive. Furthermore, group C investors would not wish to lend at only 23.08 per cent, since their return after personal taxes, of 40 per cent, would be:

$$23.08\%\ (1-40\%) = 13.85\%,$$

which is inadequate compared with an opportunity cost of 15 per cent. Hence, in equilibrium, rates of interest would be forced upwards until the rate of personal tax of the marginal investor (from group B) is equal to the rate of corporation tax. In this way, the tax saving at the corporate level is wiped out by the income tax at the personal level. Those who gain are the lenders (from group A), whose personal tax rate is less than that of the marginal investor (from group B).

In Chapter 4 we derived the relationships between marginal tax rates at which the firm should be indifferent between retentions and debt, which we expressed as:

$$(1-t)=(1-T)(1-g), \tag{13.4}$$

where $t=$ the marginal rate of income tax on gross interest received,
$T=$ the corporate tax rate, and
$g=$ the rate of capital gains tax.

In our present example the capital gains tax rate is zero, and so from equation (13.4) we find that $t = T$, i.e. the personal tax rate on interest received should be equal to the corporate tax rate.

The general equilibrium theory suggests that the debt-equity ratio should not affect the cost of capital and hence should make no difference to the value of the firm. However, where different firms have different tax profiles, the choice of finance can be significant. For example, suppose that investors in groups A, B, and C can also invest in a second firm, which can earn the 15 per cent after-tax return on risk-free projects. If the second firm has a different marginal tax rate from the first firm, perhaps at only 29 per cent, then it can only afford to pay interest at a rate of up to 21.13 per cent. At this rate the after-tax cost of debt is:

$$21.13\% \ (1-29\%)=15\%,$$

which we assume to be equal to the cost of retentions. However, investors will be unwilling to lend to the second firm, since they can earn a higher return in the first firm. If the second firm paid a market determined rate of interest of 23.08 per cent, then its value would be reduced, for the after-tax cost of debt would be:

$$23.08\% \ (1-29\%)=16.39\%,$$

which exceeds the 15 per cent rate of return earned on projects and is therefore too costly. Thus, taxation can be a significant factor in the determination of gearing levels. Furthermore, an important practical constraint is that if a firm invests in risky assets, there are potential receivership or liquidation costs if the firm defaults on debt.

Conclusion

When a company pays a dividend, there are normally at least three associated cash flows: the net dividend, the ACT payment, and the mainstream corporation tax saving through ACT setoff. However, where a company also has franked investment income, there can be more than one incremental ACT payment. A further complication is that through ACT setoff restrictions, the discounted after-tax cost of paying dividends can be substantially increased.

Similarly, there are at least three sets of cash flows relating to debenture interest payments: the net interest, the income tax payment, and the saving in mainstream corporation tax through interest deductibility. In present value terms, such complexities can significantly alter the cost of dividends and debt, and the weighted average cost of capital.

We also reviewed the implications of interest deductibility for interest rates. Because of the tax savings from debt finance, firms can offer debt at attractive rates of interest, with the result that market rates of interest may tend to increase. In our illustration, this occurred until the point at which the personal tax rate on interest received by the marginal investor equals the corporate tax rate. Hence, under the general equilibrium theory of capital structure the tax advantage at the corporate level is eliminated through personal taxation. This suggests that the debt-equity ratio should not affect the value of the firm. However, where firms have different tax profiles, the role of taxation can be an important issue in corporate financial policy.

Recommendations for further reading

The general equilibrium theory of capital structure, attributable to Miller (1977), is still a contentious issue. An important paper by Mayer (1984) considers corporate tax progressivity through tax losses and re-establishes the relevance of gearing at the corporate level. Dissenting views also include those by Patterson (1985), on empirical evidence, and Ross (1985), who argues on theoretical grounds that in the presence of uncertainty each firm has a unique debt-equity ratio. For further reading on capital structure the reader is referred to standard texts such as those by Davis and Pointon (1984) and Franks, Broyles, and Carleton (1985). Finally, empirical studies of the effects of UK taxation of dividend valuation and dividend policy have been made by Poterba and Summers (1984) and Edwards, Mayer, Pasherdes, and Poterba (1985).

References

Davis, E. W., and Pointon, J. (1984), *Finance and the Firm* (Oxford: Oxford University Press).

Edwards, J., Mayer, C., Pasherdes, P., and Poterba, J. (1985), 'The Effects of Taxation on Corporate Dividend Distributions', IFS Working Paper No. 78 (June).

Franks, J. R., Broyles, J. E., and Carleton, W. T. (1985), *Corporate Finance* (Boston: Kent).

Mayer, C. (1984), 'Corporation Tax, Finance and the Cost of Capital', IFS Working Paper No. 81, Second Revision (October).

Miller, M. H. (1977), 'Debt and Taxes', *Journal of Finance*, 32, no. 2 (May): 261–75.
Patterson, C. S. (1985), 'Debt and Taxes: Empirical Evidence', *Journal of Business Finance and Accounting*, 12, no. 2 (Summer): 187–206.
Poterba, J., and Summers, L. H. (1984), 'New Evidence that Taxes Affect the Valuation of Dividends', *Journal of Finance*, (December): 1387–415.
Ross, S. A. (1985), 'Debt and Taxes and Uncertainty', *Journal of Finance*, 60, no. 3 (July): 637–57.

14
Capital Investment Decisions

Introduction

In Part One we provided a fairly rigorous analysis of alternative tax systems and explained under what conditions tax provisions may not interfere with the efficient selection of capital projects. Later, in Chapter 10, we described particular features of the UK corporate tax system. Our task is now to apply the concepts, learnt from our knowledge of tax theory, to particular circumstances operative in the UK. Although the prime focus will dwell upon the tax provisions needed for tax neutrality, we shall also highlight features which may give rise to potential incentives or disincentives to invest. For the sake of brevity, our illustrations will draw upon just three types of rules for capital allowances: 100 per cent allowances for buildings in enterprise zones, zero allowances for commercial buildings not in enterprise zones, and 25 per cent writing-down allowances on plant and machinery. As to the tax effects on financing, which we introduced in Chapter 13, we shall make clear distinctions between retentions, new equity, and debt finance. Finally, we shall focus our attention on the need, induced by the complexities of the tax provisions, to assess projects in combination, and to evaluate investment and financing decisions simultaneously. For simplicity we shall ignore risk.

Investment incentives in enterprise zones

Throughout the course of the book, we have made a number of references to the specific features of tax design which would imply a neutral effect on the capital investment decision. The question which now presents itself is whether such features are displayed within the present UK tax system, which we described in Part Two.

In Chapter 3 we developed three models of a cash-flow tax system. Under Model I tax is raised on cash receipts less payments, ignoring transactions relating to long-term finance. Thus, are there any circumstances under which the present tax system can be represented by Model I? If so, then there should be a neutral effect on the investment decision. We know from Chapter 4 that when finance is from retentions rather than debt, for instance, there is no tax deduction at the corporate level. This represents one requirement of Model I. Now let us consider the differences between profit and operating cash flow, which we discussed in Chapter 5. We recall that where there is no periodic investment in net working capital, profit before depreciation is equal to net operating cash flow. Thus, the remaining point at issue is whether there are circumstances under which tax depreciation is equal to the cash outflow for capital expenditure. An example of capital allowances at 100 per cent is that relating to industrial or commercial buildings in enterprise zones. Hence, we are now moving towards a scenario under which the UK tax system should have a neutral effect on the investment decision.

Consider an investment of £1m on industrial buildings in an enterprise zone, which would earn an internal rate of return of 20 per cent per annum through the generation of profits before depreciation of £200,000 per annum for the foreseeable future. The firm pays taxes at 35 per cent. The tax time lag is one year; there is no periodic investment in net working capital, and all projects are financed by retentions. Under these rigid circumstances, the UK tax system can be represented by Model I, and hence the internal rate of return before tax is the same as the internal rate of return after tax. Discounting at the rate r, we derive the internal rate of return, at which rate the net present value is zero:

$$-1\text{m}\left(1-\frac{0.35}{(1+r)}\right)+\frac{0.2\text{m}}{r}\left(1-\frac{0.35}{(1+r)}\right)=0.$$

which gives $1\text{m}=0.2\text{m}/r$, and $r=20$ per cent. The expression, $1-0.35/(1+r)$, when applied to the outlay converts the pre-tax cost of the outlay into the discounted cost after immediate tax relief on the full expenditure, for which the benefit is received one year later. Hence, tax rate is discounted for one year. Similarly, the same expression when applied to the discounted value of the inflows, of $(0.2\text{m}/r)$, converts the pre-tax discounted value of the inflows into a post-tax valuation. The final result shows that the internal rate of return before tax is equal to the internal rate of return after tax.

Although the circumstances described are quite rigid, we can relax some of the assumptions and discover whether there are potential incentives or disincentives to invest. For example, if the same project were debt-financed and if there were no perceived increase in risk, then because of the interest deductibility, there would be additional tax savings. Thus, the internal rate of return after tax would increase.

Alternatively, the project may be financed by retentions, but there may be a substantial initial investment in working capital. Since we know, from Chapter 5, that net operating profit is equal to profit before depreciation less the periodic investment in net working capital, then a tax on profit is effectively a tax on working capital investment as well as a tax on cash flow. Although working capital will be released in future years, because of the time value of money the discounted value of the future tax benefits, when taxable profit is less than cash flow, is less than the discounted value of the initial tax penalty when taxable profit exceeds cash flow. Under these circumstances, the internal rate of return on the same project is now reduced.

Another variation might be that all projects are financed by new equity. Ignoring issue costs, which we have already discussed in Chapter 13, then where the returns to shareholders are in the form of dividends, there is a tax saving at the corporate level through ACT setoff. Because of these additional tax savings, when compared with finance from retentions, the internal rate of return after tax will increase.

We have demonstrated that for a retention-financed project, with no working capital investment, an investment in an enterprise zone with 100 per cent capital allowances should have a neutral effect on the investment decision. Hence, if capital allowances are less generous, then the project earns a lower internal rate of return. Thus, if the project requires investment in plant and machinery, on which the capital allowances are at the rate of 25 per cent per annum on a reducing-balance basis, then the discounted value of the capital allowances is reduced, because the allowances are spread further into the future. Consequently, the internal rate of return is reduced.

Debt-financed projects

In Chapter 3 we described another variant of the cash-flow tax system which we labelled Model II. Under this model there are taxable inflows and tax-deductible outflows, additional to those under Model I, which take account of cash transactions between the firm and suppliers of borrowed funds. Interest costs and debt capital repayments are tax-deductible, whereas debt capital receipts are taxable. Although such a system does not presently operate in the UK, the model does provide a useful insight into the analysis of debt-financed projects on which there are no capital allowances. We shall assume, for the sake of convenience, that the projects are risk-free. Now, under Model II debt capital receipts are taxable, whereas 100 per cent capital allowances are given immediately. But, for debt-financed projects, the tax on the cash inflow from holders of debt is exactly cancelled by the tax saving on the capital expenditure, because borrowed funds match the expenditure. Hence, this is equivalent to no relief for capital expenditure and no taxes on borrowed funds. If the debt is irredeemable, then taxes are paid on net operating cash flows, interest on debt is tax-deductible, and effectively there are no further tax payments or savings.

Provided the projects involve no working capital investment, then risk-free projects in the UK, which are financed by irredeemable debt and which require capital expenditure only on commerical buildings not in enterprise zones, can be represented by Model II. Although there is no tax relief for capital expenditure on commerical buildings not in enterprise zones, the interest on debt used to finance the projects is tax-deductible. The result is that there is no tax distortion in that the internal rate of return before tax is equal to the internal rate of return after tax. For example, let us assume that the firm borrows £1m of irredeemable debt for 100 per cent financing, to acquire a commercial building, on which interest is payable at 15 per cent per annum. The project earns operating profits of £200,000 per annum before tax, there is no working capital investment, and the tax rate is 35 per cent, paid one year in arrears. The after-tax cost of debt is 10.23756 per cent per annum.[1] Hence, the net present value after tax is:

$$-\text{£}1\text{m}+\frac{\text{£}0.20\text{m}}{0.1023756}\left(1-\frac{0.35}{1.1023756}\right)=\text{£}333{,}333.$$

The annual inflows are divided by the discount rate in order to capitalize them into a present value equivalent. One plus the discount rate is divided into the tax rate to allow for the one year lag in paying taxes on inflows. But, the net present value before tax is given by:

$$-\text{£}1\text{m}+\text{£}0.20\text{m}/0.15=\text{£}333{,}333,$$

which is the same as the net present value after tax. Thus, with interest deductibility but no capital allowances, the decision to invest in debt-financed projects, that are risk-free and require no working capital investment, should be unaffected by the presence of UK corporate taxes.

It is clear from the above analysis that if such projects had attracted some capital allowances, then the net present value after tax would increase. But since, in the absence of capital allowances, the net present value before tax is equal to the net present value after tax then, given the assumptions discussed, the internal rate of return after tax is the same as the internal rate of return before tax. Such a scenario is one of economic efficiency.

One critical assumption relates to the absence of any periodic investment in net working capital. We have already stated that a tax on profits is effectively a tax on cash flow plus a tax on the periodic investment in net working capital, and thus, if the above-mentioned debt-financed project required an initial investment in net working capital, then the after-tax net present value of the project would be reduced. To wipe out the net present value completely, the initial investment in working capital would have to be very substantial although, in the case of a project which has a relatively small net present value before tax, the working capital implications could be critical.

[1] Assuming a one year tax time lag, the after-tax interest rate, denoted a, is given by:

$$a=b(1-T/(1+a)),$$

where b is the before-tax cost and T is the corporate tax rate. Multiplying by $(1+a)$ and collecting terms, we have:

$$a^2+(1-b)a-b(1-T)=0.$$

From the square root formula for quadratic equations and ignoring negative roots:

$$a=0.5\{(1-b)^2+4b(1-T)\}^{0.5}-0.5(1-b).$$

Thus, for $b=0.15$ and $T=0.35$:

$$a=0.5\{0.85\times0.85+4\times0.15\times0.65\}^{0.5}-0.5(0.85)$$
$$=0.1023756.$$

A knowledge of the impact of tax on debt-financed projects with no working capital investment, and no capital allowances, also provides an insight into projects financed by equity. Given that the former scenario has a neutral effect on the investment decision, then when the financing source offers tax relief which is less attractive than that offered by debt finance, then the internal rate of return after tax of a project which cannot attract any capital allowances and is undertaken by an all-equity financed firm, will be less than the internal rate of return before tax. If the project is marginal before tax, then it would be unattractive after tax. Furthermore, since firms are not 100 per cent debt-financed, the overall tax relief of financing costs is likely to be less than that obtained for our hypothetical firm which we assumed to be 100 per cent debt-financed. Consequently, for projects which are marginal before tax, there is a disincentive to invest after tax if there are no capital allowances, on the assumption that profits are taxed at a constant rate.

An exception to the rule, however, is for firms who pay taxes at the small companies rate. For the sake of convenience, we shall assume that profits, as defined for small companies rate, are the same as net taxable income. Thus, where the small companies rate is at 29 per cent, for example, then the mainstream corporation tax saving on £1 gross debenture interest is 29p, whilst the mainstream corporation tax saving, through ACT setoff on a £1 gross dividend, is also 29p, assuming an ACT rate of 29/71, on the net dividend. Thus, where the returns to shareholders are solely in the form of dividends, and not through retention-induced capital gains, then the after-tax internal rate of return on a project with no capital allowances is normally the same as the before-tax internal rate of return, whether the firm is financed mainly by debt or equity. For example, let us assume that the pre-tax cost of finance is 15 per cent per annum for an all-equity financed firm. The tax time lag for the ACT setoff is one year, and the ACT rate is 29/71 on the net dividend. The small delay between dividends paid and the associated ACT payment will be ignored for convenience. A project which costs £1m is expected to earn £0.2m per annum before tax. There are no capital allowances and there is no working capital investment. The after-tax cost of finance, denoted k, which allows for the mainstream corporation tax saving one year in arrears, is:

$$k = 0.15(1 - 0.29/(1 + k)).$$

and so k is 11.08404 per cent:

$$0.15(1 - 0.29/1.1108404) = 0.1108404.$$

Hence, the after-tax net present value of the project is:

$$-\text{£}1\text{m} + \text{£}0.20\text{m}(1 - 0.29/1.1108404)/0.1108404 = \text{£}333{,}334.$$

Note that the 29 per cent tax rate is discounted for one year and that the after-tax inflows are capitalized through division by the after-tax discount rate.

Hence, apart from the £1 rounding error, the after-tax net present value is the same as the before-tax net present value, which is:

$$-£1m + £0.2m/0.15 = £333,333.$$

Thus, when small companies rate applies, even with no capital allowances, the financial attraction of a project is unaffected by the implications of corporation tax. We do, of course, assume a constant tax rate and no working capital investment.

Writing-down allowances

Our analysis so far has primarily focused upon two extremes: investments attracting either zero or 100 per cent instantaneous capital allowances. For many types of investment we know that capital allowances are frequently spread over a number of years, and so the present value of tax savings from capital allowances is normally less than that resulting from 100 per cent instantaneous relief.

As an illustration, let us consider an asset which costs £1m and attracts writing-down allowances at the rate of 25 per cent per annum on a reducing balance basis. Before tax, the project earns a constant perpetual cash stream at 20 per cent per annum, and there is no working capital investment. The firm is financed solely by equity capital, although there are no retentions. Issue costs are ignored. The corporate tax rate is fixed at 35 per cent, the ACT rate is 29/71 on the net dividend, and there is a one year tax time lag. The before-tax cost of capital is 15 per cent per annum.
The after-tax cost of capital is given by:

$$k = 0.15(1 - 0.29/(1 + k)) = 0.1108404, \text{ as previously.}$$

The present value of tax savings from capital allowances is found by formula[1] to be:

$$\frac{AJT}{A+k} = \frac{0.25 \times £1m \times 0.35}{0.25 + 0.1108404} = £242,489.$$

[1] Let $A = 0.25$, $J =$ asset cost, and $T =$ corporate tax rate. If capital allowances are claimed on a reducing balance basis, then the first tax saving in one year's time is AJT, the next in two years' time is $A(1-A)JT$, and the next is $A(1-A)^2JT$ and so on. Thus, discounting at k, the present value of tax savings from capital allowances is:

$$AJT/(1+k) + A(1-A)JT/(1+k)^2 + A(1-A)^2JT/(1+k)^3 + \ldots .$$

This geometric progression has a common ratio of $(1-A)/(1+k)$, and thus reduces to:

$$\frac{AJT}{(1+k)\{1-(1-A)/(1+k)\}} = \frac{AJT}{1+k-(1-A)} = \frac{AJT}{A+k}.$$

The after-tax net present value of the project, ignoring capital allowances, is:

$$-£1\text{m}+\frac{£0.20\text{m}}{0.1108404}\left(1-\frac{0.35}{1.1108404}\right)=£235{,}873,$$

and so the value of the project is £235,873 + £242,489 = £478,362.

But the striking feature is that the before-tax net present value is only:

$$-£1\text{m}+£0.20\text{m}/0.15=£333{,}333.$$

Hence, the tax provisions actually increase the present value of the project.

For firms that can reduce the after-tax cost of capital by the introduction of debt finance into the capital structure, the tax benefits will be even greater. However, if such projects also require very substantial working capital investments, which attract no tax relief, the incentive to invest may be eliminated.

Other tax complexities

We need to remind ourselves that any general conclusions on the effects of taxation on capital investment are reached strictly in accordance to the rigid assumptions made on a whole range of questions. Is the marginal tax rate constant? Does the firm have sufficient profits against which to offset capital allowances? Is there any periodic investment in net working capital? Are there any restrictions in ACT setoff? Are issue costs of new debt or equity igrnored in the calculation of the after-tax cost of capital? Are several tax time lags assumed to be zero, such as those relating to the quarterly accounting for ACT or income tax? Has personal taxation been ignored? How does the analysis change when risk is introduced?

A particularly important aspect is whether the firm may temporarily experience periods in which no taxes are paid, on account of the existence of tax losses. During this period, capital allowances may be carried forward, which will reduce their present value equivalent, unless the marginal tax rate increases dramatically. On the other hand, the after-tax cost of debt may be substantially increased, since the present value of the tax savings which arise through interest deductibility may be reduced, as the interest is carried forward. When the firm does move into a taxpaying position, initially the marginal tax rate may be at the lower small companies rate, and then as taxable profits increase over time, the marginal tax rate may increase as relevant profits lie within the marginal relief limits and then fall slightly to the full companies rate. The existence of tax losses can also have ramifications for ACT setoff, as net taxable income may be reduced to nil, with the result that no ACT may presently be offset. Unless the ACT can be carried back and offset against previous mainstream corporation tax liabilities, such a tax position increases the cost to the company of paying dividends, through the time value of money.

One interesting tax feature is that of project interdependencies. The tax implications of one project is potentially affected by the acceptance or rejection of other projects. It is the tax position of the firm as a whole, or the group or consortium of companies, which determines the marginal tax rate, the ACT setoff provisions, and the sufficiency of profits against which to offset capital allowances. Yet, when several divisions of a firm are appraising projects independently, some may be unaware of some of these assumptions, in particular the sufficiency of taxable profits. Hence, combinations of projects need to be considered jointly.

But the reduction in net taxable income, as a result of heavy capital allowances, may distort too the marginal tax rate at which relief is obtained on debenture interest; and where capital allowances fully wipe out taxable profits, any reductions in mainstream corporation tax liabilities through charges on income may be delayed for many years. In present value terms, the after-tax cost of the interest may be increased substantially. Thus, not only do projects need to be appraised simultaneously, but also the firm's total investment programme and financing decision policies need to be analysed together.

Conclusion

Under certain specified conditions, the after-tax internal rate of return of a project is the same as the before-tax internal rate of return. One example of this is an investment in a commerical building in an enterprise zone, on which 100 per cent capital allowances are given. We assume that there is no periodic investment in net working capital and that all projects are financed by retentions. Other requirements are that the marginal tax rate is fixed through the duration of the project and that the tax time lag is constant. An alternative example is that of a risk-free debt-financed project on which no capital allowances are given. Once again, there is assumed to be no periodic investment in net working capital, and tax rates as well as tax time lags are treated as constant throughout the project's life.

On account of the time value of money, capital allowances at the rate of 25 per cent per annum are less attractive than 100 per cent immediate relief, given a constant marginal tax rate. However, under the UK corporation tax system, when account is taken of tax relief for financing costs, the net result is that there are potential incentives to invest in projects, which attract a 25 per cent writing-down allowance, unless the firm is financed solely by retentions.

Apart from instances when small companies rate applies, the benefits to the firm of the tax deductibility of interest payments are generally greater than those from ACT setoff, arising from dividend distributions. Depending upon the level of interest rates, the after-tax cost of capital may be affected by the firm's capital structure, an issue which we introduced in Chapter 13. Thus, the choice of the firm's financing methods is important in project appraisal because of the tax implications.

We also noted other tax complexities which make it difficult to reach broad conclusions on the effects of taxation on project appraisal. These included changes in marginal tax rates, tax losses, ACT setoff restrictions, and working capital investment which is not tax-deductible. Finally, we explained that, on account of the tax provisions, investment and financing decisions are interrelated, and projects arising within divisionalized firms, groups of companies, or consortia need to be appraised in combination.

Recommendations for further reading

Examples of project interdependencies are provided by Grundy and Burns (1979), whilst Berry and Dyson (1979) and Pointon (1982) explain how to develop mathematical programming models to encapsulate taxation-induced interdependencies within an optimization framework. The impact of the UK tax system since 1984 is discussed by Devereux and Mayer (1984) and Pointon (1987).

References

Berry, R. H., and Dyson, R. G. (1979), 'A mathematical programming approach to taxation-induced interdependencies in investment appraisal', *Journal of Business Finance and Accounting*, 6, no. 4 (Winter): 425–41.

Devereux, M. P., and Mayer, C. P. (1984), *Corporation Tax: The Impact of the 1984 Budget*, IFS Report Series No. 11 (June).

Grundy, G., and Burns, P. (1979), 'Taxation-induced interdependencies in project appraisal', *Accounting and Business Research*, 10, no. 37 (Winter): 47–53.

Pointon, J. (1982), 'Taxation and mathematical programming', *Journal of Business Finance and Accounting*, 9, no. 1 (Spring): 43–50.

Pointon, J. (1987), 'Taxation and Capital Project Appraisal', *Management Research News*, 9, no. 2: 19–21.

15
Leasing

Introduction

This chapter is concerned with the effect of taxation on the evaluation of a decision to lease or buy equipment. We begin with an explanation of the nature of a finance lease and proceed to show why, in theory, leasing or purchasing should be financially equivalent, given symmetric tax positions of lessor and lessee and perfect capital markets. We proceed to illustrate how the existence of different tax rates for lessor and lessee may give rise to different evaluations for leasing or purchasing. Finally, we demonstrate how to adjust the discount rate when the lessee is temporarily in a position of having a negative taxable capacity.

The nature of a finance lease

There are basically two types of lease: an operating lease and a finance lease. Under an operating lease an asset is hired for a short period, during which time the lessee, which is the firm that makes use of the asset, may cancel the commitment and return the asset to the lessor, which is the owner firm. Typically the lessor of an operating lease, which is normally responsible for maintenance and other services, rehires the same asset to many customers.

By contrast, under a finance lease, there is an agreement to lease for the expected useful life of the asset. Unlike that of an operating lease, the commitment cannot be cancelled. Essentially, the lessee reaps the rewards of ownership and bears the risks, without obtaining the legal title of ownership. A stream of leasing rentals are paid to the lessor for the benefits of using the asset. However, the discounted cash flows, associated with the productive use of an asset which is bought, are not necessarily financially equivalent to those associated with the usage of a leased asset. The principal reason for any discrepancy may very well be due to the tax implications of the decision to lease or buy.

Symmetric tax positions

The tax implications of leasing are essentially that for the lessor, or leasing company, the inflows from periodic rentals are treated as taxable income, whereas the capital expenditure on equipment is likely to be eligible for capital allowances. By contrast, for the lessee who uses the equipment, there are no capital allowances, but all the rental payments are tax-deductible.

Given perfect competition in the leasing industry, lessors can expect to earn the required rate of return. Hence, for the lessor, the discounted value of the inflows from rentals after tax, should be equal to the cost of the asset, less the present value of the tax relief on capital allowances. If the user leases rather than purchases the asset, then the lessee incurs tax-deductible payments, but loses the benefits from capital allowances, although the lessee does not incur the outlay for the asset's purchase cost. Therefore, the net present value of the net benefit from leasing, as opposed to purchasing, is given by the cost of the asset less the present value of capital allowances, less the discounted value of the rental payments after tax relief. But if both lessee and lessor have the same discount rate and pay taxes at the same marginal rate, then the cost of the asset less the present value of capital allowances for the potential user should be the same as the cost of the asset less the present value of capital allowances for the lessor. Likewise, the discounted cost to the lessee of outflows for rental payments, after tax relief, should be equal to the discounted value to the lessor of inflows for rental income after tax. Hence, the net present value of the net benefits from leasing, as opposed to purchasing, should be zero. Given a symmetry of taxable capacity for lessees and lessors there should not normally be any financial advantage to leasing in a competitive market.

In order to demonstrate this let us consider the case of a lessor who can buy a piece of equipment for £100,000 at the end of year zero and obtain capital allowances at 25 per cent per annum on a reducing balance basis for five years, at the end of which the equipment is sold for £23,731, its tax written-down value. The present value of the capital allowances tax shield is set out in Table 15.1 and shown to be £19,377. We assume a discount rate of 10 per cent per annum on the basis of a before-tax cost of debt of 14.7 per cent per annum and a one year tax time lag. The after-tax cost of debt is equal to its before-tax cost less the tax saving through interest deductibility discounted for one year at the after-tax cost:

$$i = 0.147\ (1 - 0.35/(1 + i)),$$

and so i is just over 10 per cent:

$$0.1002 = 0.147\ (1 - 0.35/1.1002).$$

We have chosen the after-tax cost of debt as an approximation to a relatively risk-free rate of interest since we are discounting a set of cash flows which are reasonably certain.

The disposal proceeds are assumed to be more risky and discounted at 20 per cent to give a present value of: $£23{,}731/(1.20)^5 = £9{,}537$. We have ignored any tax complications arising on disposal, which would arise if the asset were sold for an amount other than its tax written-down value.

TABLE 15.1. *Present value of the capital allowances tax shield* (£)

		Tax shield	Discount factor	Present value of tax shield
Cost	100,000			
Capital allowances (25%) yr. 1	(25,000) × 0.35	= 8,750	× $1/(1.10)^2$	= 7,231
Written-down value (end of yr. 1)	75,000			
Capital allowances (25%) yr. 2	(18,750) × 0.35	= 6,562	× $1/(1.10)^3$	= 4,930
Written-down value (end of yr. 2)	56,250			
Capital allowances (25%) yr. 3	(14,062) × 0.35	= 4,922	× $1/(1.10)^4$	= 3,362
Written-down value (end of yr. 3)	42,188			
Capital allowances (25%) yr. 4	(10,547) × 0.35	= 3,691	× $1/(1.10)^5$	= 2,292
Written-down value (end of yr. 4)	31,641			
Capital allowances (25%) yr. 5	(7,910) × 0.35	= 2,768	× $1/(1.10)^6$	= 1,562
Written-down value (end of yr. 5)	23,731			
Present value of the capital allowances tax shield (35% tax rate)				19,377

If the rental income from leasing the asset is £25,003 per annum for five years, payable annually in advance, then the after-tax present value of the rental income is £71,086 as shown in Table 15.2, and the after-tax net present value to the lessor is zero:

> – 100,000 (cost) + 19,377 (capital allowances tax shield) + 9,537 (present value of disposal proceeds = $23{,}731/(1.20)^5$) + 71,086 (present value of rental income after tax) = 0 (£).

TABLE 15.2. *Present value of lessor's rental income after tax at 35 per cent* (£)

End of year	Rental income	Tax on rental income (at 35%)	Discount factor	Present value
0	25,003		× 1	= 25,003
1		(8,751)	× $1/(1.10)$	= (7,955)
1	25,003		× $1/(1.10)$	= 22,730
2		(8,751)	× $1/(1.10)^2$	= (7,232)
2	25,003		× $1/(1.10)^2$	= 20,664
3		(8,751)	× $1/(1.10)^3$	= (6,575)
3	25,003		× $1/(1.10)^3$	= 18,785
4		(8,751)	× $1/(1.10)^4$	= (5,977)
4	25,003		× $1/(1.10)^4$	= 17,077
5		(8,751)	× $1/(1.10)^5$	= (5,434)
Present value of lessor's rental income after tax				71,086

If the rental income were quoted at a rate higher than the £25,003 base rental, other leasing firms could in theory provide the same service at the base rental and earn the required return, whereas if the actual rental were less than the base rental, leasing would be uneconomic to the lessor, since the net present value would be negative.

Let us now evaluate the leasing or purchase decision for the lessee. We assume that the equipment will be used to generate pre-tax net operating cash flows of £33,000 per annum, arising mid-year for five years. The marginal tax rate for the lessee is assumed to be 35 per cent, with taxes payable one year after the year-end date. Leasing rentals are payable at the beginning of each year. From Table 15.3 we see that the present value of the lessee's net operating cash flows after tax, discounting at the rate of 20 per cent per annum for risky cash flows, is £79,325. The present value of the capital allowances tax shield has already been shown to be £19,377 from Table 15.1. Hence, the net present value of the purchase alternative is:

> −100,000 (cost) +19,377 (capital allowances tax shield) +79,325 (present value of operating cash flows after tax) +9,537 (present value of disposal proceeds) = £8,239.

However, if the firm decides to lease the equipment, the discounted cost to the lessee, of the leasing rentals after tax relief, amounts to £71,086 as derived in Table 15.4. Hence the net present value of the leasing alternative is given by:

> −71,086 (discounted cost of leasing after tax relief) +79,325 (present value of operating cash flows after tax) = £8,239.

TABLE 15.3. *Present value of lessee's net operating cash flows after tax at 35 per cent* (£)

Year	Net operating cash flow before tax	Tax on cash flow	Discount factor	Present value
0.5	33,000		$1/(1.20)^{0.5}$	30,125
2.0		(11,550)	$1/(1.20)^{2}$	(8,021)
1.5	33,000		$1/(1.20)^{1.5}$	25,104
3.0		(11,550)	$1/(1.20)^{3}$	(6,684)
2.5	33,000		$1/(1.20)^{2.5}$	20,920
4.0		(11,550)	$1/(1.20)^{4}$	(5,570)
3.5	33,000		$1/(1.20)^{3.5}$	17,433
5.0		(11,550)	$1/(1.20)^{5}$	(4,642)
4.5	33,000		$1/(1.20)^{4.5}$	14,528
6.0		(11,550)	$1/(1.20)^{6}$	(3,868)
Present value of net operating cash flows after tax (£)				79,325

TABLE 15.4. *Present value of lessee's leasing rentals after tax relief at 35 per cent* (£)

End of year	Rental payment	Tax relief on rental payment (at 35%)	Discount factor	Present value
0	(25,003)		1	(25,003)
1		8,751	1/(1.10)	7,955
1	(25,003)		1/(1.10)	(22,730)
2		8,751	$1/(1.10)^2$	7,232
2	(25,003)		$1/(1.10)^2$	(20,664)
3		8,751	$1/(1.10)^3$	6,575
3	(25,003)		$1/(1.10)^3$	(18,785)
4		8,751	$1/(1.10)^4$	5,977
4	(25,003)		$1/(1.10)^4$	(17,077)
5		8,751	$1/(1.10)^5$	5,434
Present value (cost) of leasing rentals after tax relief (£)				(71,086)

But this is identical to the net present value of the purchase alternative. The reason for this result is twofold: first, the lessor charges a competitive rate for leasing and does not earn excess returns; and second, the tax position of the lessor is identical to that of the lessee. Effectively, the tax position of the lessee is symmetric to that of the lessor. The discounted cost to the lessee of leasing, after tax relief, is £71,086, whereas the present value of rental income to the lessor, after tax, is also £71,086. Similarly, the present value of the capital allowances tax shield, to the user firm, of £19,377 is equal to the present value of the capital allowances tax shield to the lessor, which is also £19,377.

Differential tax positions

The theoretical indifference between leasing and buying does not necessarily hold when the lessor and potential lessee pay taxes at different rates. To illustrate this, let us assume that all lessors suffer taxes at 35 per cent and that the market-determined leasing rental is £25,003 per annum, as before. However, the potential lessee pays tax at only 30 per cent. The present value of the lessee's net operating cash flows after tax is £83,438, as shown in Table 15.5. In order to determine the after-tax net present value of the purchase alternative, we need to deduct the outlay of £100,000, to include the present value of the disposal proceeds and to add back the present value of the capital allowances tax shield. But because the tax rate is lower than previously, the after-tax cost of debt is now increased to:

$$i = 0.147\ (1 - 0.30/(1 + i)),$$

TABLE 15.5. *Present value of lessee's net operating cash flows after tax at 30 per cent* (£)

Year	Net operating cash flow	Tax on cash flow	Discount factor	Present value
0.5	33,000		$1/(1.20)^{0.5}$	30,125
2.0		(9,900)	$1/(1.20)^{2}$	(6,875)
1.5	33,000		$1/(1.20)^{1.5}$	25,104
3.0		(9,900)	$1/(1.20)^{3}$	(5,729)
2.5	33,000		$1/(1.20)^{2.5}$	20,920
4.0		(9,900)	$1/(1.20)^{4}$	(4,774)
3.5	33,000		$1/(1.20)^{3.5}$	17,433
5.0		(9,900)	$1/(1.20)^{5}$	(3,979)
4.5	33,000		$1/(1.20)^{4.5}$	14,528
6.0		(9,900)	$1/(1.20)^{6}$	(3,315)
Present value of net operating cash flows after tax (£)				83,438

and so i is 10.72 per cent:

$$0.1072 = 0.147\,(1 - 0.30/1.1072).$$

In Table 15.6 we show that the net present value of the purchase alternative is £9,234, which may be compared with a net present value of £8,318 associated with a decision to lease, which is evaluated in Table 15.7. Thus, it is preferable to buy rather than to lease the equipment.

A more complex case to analyse, however, is when the potential lessee is temporarily in a position of having a negative taxable capacity for a few years, after which it can expect to resume paying taxes, after relief for tax losses brought forward. The net operating cash flows which arise during the useful life of the project will reduce the tax losses carried forward. The capital allowances of the purchase alternative will serve to increase the tax loss carried forward and so too will the leasing rentals increase the loss, if the firm decides to lease. However, the main analytical problem is that the after-tax cost of debt becomes more difficult to calculate because the time lag, between when the interest is incurred and when the tax benefit is reaped from interest deductibility will vary from year to year, because the interest is carried forward for tax purposes on account of the tax losses.

In the next example we build upon the previous illustration, but now assume that the potential lessee does not have any taxable capacity before year four, but from year four onwards, the firm is liable to tax at 35 per cent. Any interest for year four will attract tax relief in year five, assuming a one year tax time lag. For year four onwards, the after-tax cost of debt is given by the before-tax cost of 14.7 per cent times the term, one minus the discounted tax rate, as shown in Table 15.8. However, the tax savings on interest in years one, two, and three

TABLE 15.6. *Net present value, after tax at 30 per cent, of the purchasing alternative* (£)

	Year	Cash flow	Discount factor	Present value
Cost	0	(100,000)	1	(100,000)
Net operating cash flows after tax (see Table 15.5)	—	—	—	83,438
Disposal proceeds	5	23,731	$1/(1.20)^5$	9,537
Capital allowance tax shield	2	$25{,}000 \times 0.30$	$1/(1.1072)^2$	6,118
Capital allowance tax shield	3	$18{,}750 \times 0.30$	$1/(1.1072)^3$	4,144
Capital allowance tax shield	4	$14{,}062 \times 0.30$	$1/(1.1072)^4$	2,807
Capital allowance tax shield	5	$10{,}547 \times 0.30$	$1/(1.1072)^5$	1,902
Capital allowance tax shield	6	$7{,}910 \times 0.30$	$1/(1.1072)^6$	1,288
Net present value of the purchasing alternative				9,234

TABLE 15.7. *Net present value, after tax at 30 per cent, of the leasing alternative* (£)

	Year	Cash flow	Discount factor	Present value
Net operating cash flows after tax (see Table 15.5)	—	—	—	83,438
Leasing rental	0	(25,003)	1	(25,003)
Tax relief on rental	1	7,501	$1/(1.1072)$	6,775
Leasing rental	1	(25,003)	$1/(1.1072)$	(22,582)
Tax relief on rental	2	7,501	$1/(1.1072)^2$	6,119
Leasing rental	2	(25,003)	$1/(1.1072)^2$	(20,396)
Tax relief on rental	3	7,501	$1/(1.1072)^3$	5,526
Leasing rental	3	(25,003)	$1/(1.1072)^3$	(18,421)
Tax relief on rental	4	7,501	$1/(1.1072)^4$	4,991
Leasing rental	4	(25,003)	$1/(1.1072)^4$	(16,637)
Tax relief on rental	5	7,501	$1/(1.1072)^5$	4,508
Net present value (lease)				8,318

will also occur in year five, since they will be deductible against taxable income in year four, but will be subject to the one year tax lag. In the derivation of the after-tax discount rate for year three, the tax saving is discounted for two years, to reflect the delay between years three and five. We see from Table 15.8 the

TABLE 15.8. *After tax cost of debt for period t (k_t)*

k_t = before tax cost × (1 − discounted tax rate) = after tax cost	
$k_6 = 0.147\ (1-0.35/[1+k_7])$	$=0.1002$
$k_5 = 0.147\ (1-0.35/[1+k_6])$	$=0.1002$
$k_4 = 0.147\ (1-0.35/[1+k_5])$	$=0.1002$
$k_3 = 0.147\ (1-0.35/[(1+k_4)(1+k_5)])$	
$= 0.147\ (1-0.35/[1.1002\times 1.1002])$	$=0.1045$
$k_2 = 0.147\ (1-0.35/[(1+k_3)(1+k_4)(1+k_5)])$	
$= 0.147\ (1-0.35/[1.1045\times 1.1002\times 1.1002])$	$=0.1085$
$k_1 = 0.147\ (1-0.35/[(1+k_2)(1+k_3)(1+k_4)(1+k_5)])$	
$= 0.147\ (1-0.35/[1.1085\times 1.1045\times 1.1002\times 1.1002])$	$=0.1123$

application of two discount rates, denoted k_4 and k_5. Similarly, in order to calculate the discount rate for the second year, we need to know the discount rates for years three, four, and five, so that the tax saving, which occurs at the end of year five can be evaluated. Finally, the after-tax discount rate for year one takes account of the after-tax interest rates for years two to five, which are used to discount the tax savings, in year five, on interest carried forward from year one.

Having derived the after-tax cost of debt, we can evaluate the lease or buy decision. In Table 15.9 we set out the present value of the purchasing alternative. The disposal proceeds, net operating cash flows, and taxes on net

TABLE 15.9. *Present value of the purchasing alternative* (£)

	Year	Workings	Present value
Purchase cost	0	—	(100,000)
Disposal proceeds	5	$23{,}731/(1.20)^5$	= 9,537
Capital allowances tax shield (see Tables 15.1 and 15.8)	5	$(8{,}750+6{,}562+4{,}922+3{,}691)/(1.1123\times 1.1085\times 1.1045\times 1.1002\times 1.1002)$	= 14,514
Capital allowances tax shield (see Tables 15.1 and 15.8)	6	$2{,}768/(1.1123\times 1.1085\times 1.1045\times 1.1002\times 1.1002\times 1.1002)$	= 1,526
Net operating cash flows before tax (see Table 15.3)	—	$30{,}125+25{,}104+20{,}920+17{,}433+14{,}528$	= 108,110
Tax on net operating cash flows	5	$(11{,}550+11{,}550+11{,}550+11{,}550)/(1.20)^5$	= (18,567)
Tax on net operating cash flows	6	$11{,}550/(1.20)^6$	= (3,868)
Present value of the purchasing alternative			11,252

operating cash flows are all discounted at the 20 per cent per annum risky rate, and the capital allowances are discounted at the after-tax cost of debt. However, because of the negative taxable income for years one to three, the capital allowances for the first four years are all setoff against income in year four, which results in a tax saving in year five. The discount factor for five years is determined by the annual after-tax cost of debt for years one to five, respectively. The present value of the tax shield on the first four years' capital allowances is £14,514 as shown in Table 15.9. The capital allowances for the fifth year produce a tax saving at the end of year six and are thus discounted for six years. We see from Table 15.9 that the discount factor is based upon the individual after-tax costs of debt for each of the six years. We also set out the present value of the net operating cash flows and the incremental tax payments in years five and six on (i) the sum of the first four cash flows, and (ii) the fifth cash flow, respectively, once again taking account of the one year tax lag from the end of the year in which taxable income is positive.

In Table 15.10 we evaluate the leasing alternative. The tax savings on the rentals, which occur at the end of the fifth year, and the before-tax leasing payments are discounted at the after-tax cost of debt. The separate discount rates for the after-tax cost of debt have already been derived in Table 15.8. As previously, the net operating cash flows and the taxes on the cash flows are discounted at the 20 per cent risky rate. From Tables 15.9 and 15.10, we see that the present value of the purchasing alternative is higher at £11,252 compared with £9,411, if the firm decides to lease.

TABLE 15.10. *Present value of the leasing alternative* (£)

	Year	Workings	Present value
Rental	0	—	(25,003)
Rental	1	25,003/(1.1123)	(22,479)
Rental	2	25,003/(1.1123 × 1.1085)	(20,278)
Rental	3	25,003/(1.1123 × 1.1085 × 1.1045)	(18,360)
Rental	4	25,003/(1.1123 × 1.1085 × 1.1045 × 1.1002)	(16,688)
Tax savings on rentals	5	(25,003 × 5 × 0.35)/(1.1123 × 1.1085 × 1.1045 × 1.1002 × 1.1002)	26,544
Net operating cash flows before tax	—	(see Table 15.9)	108,110
Tax on net operating cash flows	—	(see Table 15.9) 18,567 + 3,868	(22,435)
Present value of the leasing alternative			9,411

Conclusion

Under a finance lease, the lessee reaps the rewards of ownership for the expected life of the asset, without obtaining the legal title of ownership. For the lessor, the inflows from rentals are treated as taxable income, whereas capital expenditure on equipment is likely to be eligible for capital allowances. The rental payments are tax-deductible for the lessee firm, which cannot also claim capital allowances. Given perfect competition in the leasing industry, and identical tax rates and tax lags for lessor and lessee, there should not normally be any financial advantage to leasing. However, we demonstrated that when the lessor and lessee are in different tax positions the lease or buy decision is not necessarily one of indifference.

In the evaluation procedure we discounted the capital allowances tax shield from purchasing, and the rentals and tax savings from the leasing alternative at the after-tax cost of debt. However, the proceeds from asset disposal, the net operating cash flows, and taxes on these cash flows were discounted at a risky rate of interest.

Finally, when the lessee expects to have a negative taxable capacity for a number of years, then the after-tax cost of debt needs to reflect the time lag between interest payments and tax savings from interest deductibility. Thus, the after-tax cost of debt may vary from year to year.

Recommendations for further reading

Miller and Upton (1976) provide an analysis of the financial equivalence of leasing and buying in a perfect capital market, given symmetric tax positions of both lessor and lessee. For further reading on lease evaluation models, the interested reader is referred to articles by Myers, Dill, and Bautista (1976), Franks and Hodges (1978), and Chapter 23 of a book by Franks, Broyles, and Carleton (1985). Finally, a review of theory and practice is presented by Hull and Hubbard (1980) and Fawthrop (1986).

References

Fawthrop, R. (1986), 'Equipment Leasing', in *Issues in Finance*, edited by Firth, M., and Keane, S. M. (Oxford: Philip Allan).

Franks, J. R., Broyles, J. E., and Carleton, W. T. (1985), *Corporate Finance: Concepts and Applications* (Boston: Kent).

Franks, J. R., and Hodges, S. D. (1978), 'Valuation of Financial Lease Contracts: A Note', *Journal of Finance*, 33, no. 2 (May): 657–69.

Hull, J. C., and Hubbard, G. L. (1980), 'Lease Evaluation in the UK: Current Theory and Practice', *Journal of Business Finance and Accounting*, 7, no. 4 (Winter): 619 37.

Miller, M. H., and Upton, C. W. (1976), 'Leasing, Buying and the Cost of Capital Services', *Journal of Finance*, 31, no. 3 (June): 761–86.

Myers, S. C., Dill, D. A., and Bautista, A. J. (1976), 'Valuation of Financial Lease Contracts', *Journal of Finance*, 31, no. 3 (June): 799–819.

16
The Business Medium

Introduction

To the budding entrepreneur on the verge of commencing a new business venture there are a number of problems confronting him. One of which is that he requires to know whether to trade as an unincorporated business or through the medium of a limited company so as to minimize the effects of taxation. In these days of Government support for the small firm it is a problem requiring a solution every day somewhere in the UK.

Thus, the aim of this chapter is to provide a general approach which will provide the business person with sufficient data for decision-making purposes. This approach will draw heavily upon the relevant tax principles introduced throughout Part Two. These principles will be applied to a simulated start-up situation which abstracts from the more common case by reason of the level of profits used. Nevertheless, it does enable us not only to develop the general approach to all such situations but also to highlight the tax differentials facing the entrepreneur.

Case data

The time is January 1987. Albert Campbell has decided to start a business in the UK as a wholesale distributor of tiles. The calendar year 1986 saw an upturn in demand, partly, as a result of an increase in new house building. Albert expects this trend to continue, so it is a good time to start his business. On the assumption of a 1 May 1987 start his business plan shows estimated profit levels of:

Year ended 30 April	(£)
1988	50,000
1989	75,000
1990 onwards	95,000

These projected profit figures are before charging the following:

(i) He will incur expenses of £2,000 in respect of rent and rates for a warehouse on 1 March 1987.

(ii) There is further expenditure of £30,000 of an allowable nature which may be incurred in either the year ended 30 April 1988 or the year ended 30 April 1989.

(iii) Albert intends to draw a salary of £12,000 each year on the last day of trading.

Albert is married and neither he nor his wife have any other taxable income. From this data Albert Campbell would like to know which business medium, i.e. sole trader or limited company, he should adopt to minimize the effects of taxation.

General considerations

At the outset we wish to stress that although emphasis is put upon the tax consequences for the entrepreneur it would be foolish if he were to choose his form of trading organization purely on tax considerations alone. Clearly, taxation is only one of a number of variables which enter into the best solution equation. By attempting to quantify the taxation implications it merely means our entrepreneur has more data for a balanced decision.

Apart from this extremely important overriding consideration, before commencing any computational work, a number of other issues should be resolved:

(i) Pre-trading expenses, i.e. those incurred before day one of actual trading, are frequently incurred. The general rule regarding expenditure is that it is deductible when incurred and hence cannot be allowable if incurred before trading commenced. However, if such expenditure were incurred after the business commenced trading and were of a nature that would be deductible against Schedule D cases I or II profits, i.e. it satisfies the 'wholly and exclusively' rule and is not capital expenditure, the general rule is modified. The modification provided for in the legislation is that pre-trading expenditure of a revenue nature incurred after 31 March 1980 and within three years before trading commenced is deductible. Clearly, the £2,000 payment for rent qualifies as a deductible expense. However, the way in which relief is given varies, dependent upon the trading medium adopted (see following section on computations).

(ii) The problem of when to incur allowable revenue expenditure in the early days of a business may be particularly significant where the business medium adopted is that of a sole trader. This is a consequence of having to apply the new business assessment rules in establishing the first three years of assessment to income tax. The result of having to apply these rules to the profits for the year ended 30 April 1988 is shown in Table 16.1. In calculating the assessable profits, it has been assumed, the £30,000 expenditure has been incurred in the first year's trading and all other expenses deducted in arriving at the profit of £50,000 are allowable. What should be immediately obvious is that relief for the expenses is given approximately 2.92 times $(2+\frac{11}{12})$. Admittedly the 1990/1 assessment is £75,000, whereas it would only be £45,000 were the expenses incurred in the year ended 30 April 1989. However, if this

TABLE 16.1. *Opening income tax assessments on Albert Campbell*

Year of assessment	Basis period	Assessment (£)	
1987/8	1.5.87–5.4.88		
	(11/12 × £20,000)	18,333	
1988/9	1.5.87–30.4.88	20,000	
1989/90	1.5.87–30.4.88	20,000	
1990/1	1.5.88–30.4.89	75,000	
1991/2	1.5.89–30.4.90	95,000	
Income tax computation (£)			
Profit for the 12 months ended 30 April 1988			50,000
Less: additional expenditure			(30,000)
Adjusted profit			20,000

latter approach is adopted, relief for the £30,000 is available once only, and there are additional profits of £57,500 assessable in the first four years. In this particular case no advantage may be obtained from a claim to have the second and third years of assessment being calculated on an actual basis whichever year the £30,000 expenditure is incurred in. It should, of course, be recognized that every case must be judged on its merits, so, given a different profile of profits, especially where this could be influenced at the taxpayer's option, do not overlook an actual claim.

If Albert Campbell were to choose the limited company medium there is no tax advantage whichever year bears the expenses. This is because assessments to corporation tax are computed on an actual basis. There may nevertheless be cash flow advantages (see later section) and changes in tax rates in later years may also be relevant.

(iii) Certainly in any computational work, apart from having to work with estimated profit projections, the other area of uncertainty is the future rates of tax and values for personal reliefs.

In the case under review we cannot, in January 1987, have knowledge of the income tax rates and allowances applicable for 1987/8, and we do not know the corporation tax rates beyond 31 March 1987. On the assumption that Albert must commence his trade on 1 May 1987 and therefore make decisions now, a reasonable method is to use the last known set of values in all calculations. The reasoning behind this approach is that although taxes may fall or rise in the next two or three years unless there is a fundamental change in principles the effect on the tax liabilities calculated may only be marginal.

(iv) The question of national insurance contributions should be considered. Using 1986/7 rates (see Chapter 12), as a sole trader Albert would be liable to pay class 2 contributions of £195 plus maximum class 4 contributions of £653 giving a liability of £848 per annum.

As a director, and therefore an employee of his own company, the equivalent annual class 1 contributions on the salary of £12,000 would be £12,000 × 9% = £1,080. In addition the company as the employer would need to pay £12,000 × 10.45% = £1,254, although this may be reduced if an occupational pension scheme were set up.

For Albert Campbell the sums calculated will prove to be of marginal significance in the decision process. However, it is essential that he is made aware of the rights and entitlements which he will forgo under the self-employed category.

In cases where the tax liabilities are significantly smaller, national insurance contributions and benefits gained or lost from the social security system may play an important role in the final decision.

(v) Capital expenditure which qualifies for relief under the capital allowances system may be an important factor in estimating the future taxation liabilities of a taxpayer. Where substantial amounts are to be incurred and there is flexibility as to the date of acquisition, careful planning may enable capital allowances to be set against profits in the most tax efficient way. The profits of basis periods which appear to be giving rise to assessments that are likely to be taxed at the highest rates, relative to the business medium, may be reduced by prudent use of capital allowances. Care must, however, be taken in the opening years of an unincorporated business both as regards overlap of basis periods and the changes in basis periods occasioned by an election to an actual basis of assessment. These general comments are particularly relevant to a manufacturing business which may qualify for capital allowances on industrial buildings in addition to plant and machinery.

The business which Albert Campbell intends to operate will incur capital expenditure which is insignificant relative to profit size. This assumption allows us to abstract from the unnecessary complications introduced by capital allowances and may not be unrealistic relative to the nature of his trade.

(vi) The timing of payments whether this be in respect of revenue or capital expenditure plays an important part in computing taxation liabilities. Similarly, in order to reach a valid conclusion as to the most beneficial business medium not only the size of the tax payments should be considered but also the time scale involved. It is, therefore, suggested that a discounted cash flow approach be used in all but the most obvious cases to assist the comparison.

Computations

The computations of the tax liabilities are central to the solution of the problem, and Table 16.2 shows the estimated income tax payable for all years from 1987/8 to 1991/2 inclusive. These liabilities are based upon the

TABLE 16.2. *Income tax liabilities of Albert Campbell* (£)

	1987/8	1988/9	1989/90
Earned income: Schedule D case I	18,333	20,000	20,000
Less: pre-trading expenses	(2,000)	—	—
	16,333	20,000	20,000
Less: married personal allowance	(3,655)	(3,655)	(3,655)
Taxable income	12,678	16,345	16,345
Income tax payable @ 29%	3,677	4,740	4,740

		1990/1	1991/2
Earned income: Schedule D case I		75,000	95,000
Less: married personal allowance		(3,655)	(3,655)
Taxable income		71,345	91,345
Income tax payable:			
first	17,200 @ 29%	4,988	
next	3,000 @ 40%	1,200	
next	5,200 @ 45%	2,340	16,823
next	7,900 @ 50%	3,950	
next	7,900 @ 55%	4,345	
remainder	30,145 @ 60%	18,087	—
	50,145 @ 60%	—	30,087
		34,910	46,910

assessments previously calculated and using 1986/7 tax rates and allowances. Clearly, for the first three years of assessment Albert will only be liable at the basic rate of tax, while in the later two years he is well into the top marginal rate.

It is at this point we may briefly reconsider the issue, raised earlier, regarding the timing of revenue expenditure. If the expenditure of £30,000 were deferred until the year ended 30 April 1989 there would be a tax saving on £30,000 at Albert's top marginal rate, i.e. £18,000 in the year 1990/1. However, the additional tax payable on the increased profits of the first year, which are assessed 2.92 times, would outweigh this, since Albert is liable at the higher rates in each assessment year including some liability at the top marginal rate of 60 per cent in 1988/9 to 1990/1 inclusive.

The way in which relief for the pre-trading expenditure is given for an unincorporated business is also important. Broadly, these items of expenditure are treated as a separate loss of the business and are allowable against the first tax year of assessment. The wording of the legislation does however mean that relief for this type of expenditure cannot be given more than once in the opening years of assessment. Relief is granted in a similar way to trading losses (see Chapter 8) and is available against total income of the taxpayer. Thus, Albert is entitled to deduct the £2,000 rent payment from his 1987/8 total income which in this case is entirely trading profits from his business.

As a final point it should be observed that the salary to be drawn by Albert has been ignored in computing assessable profits. This is because, in unincorporated businesses, salaries paid to proprietors are regarded as appropriations of profits. Thus effectively, any sums withdrawn by Albert from the business are from post-tax profits.

We now turn to the taxation liabilities which will arise where a limited company is formed. The computations of assessable profits are shown in Table 16.3. As explained earlier, the year in which the optional £30,000 expenditure is incurred gives no tax advantage, although cash outflows for tax payments may have a more even profile. However, to illustrate this point fully the initial computations have been prepared on the basis of (i) expenditure in year one and (ii) expenditure in the second year.

Where pre-trading expenditure is incurred by a company the legislation provides that it may be treated as an expense of the first accounting period. The actual basis of assessment precludes the need for a more complex approach, and the operational effect is to be able to claim the £2,000 against trading profits.

The final point which emerges is that the salary drawn by Albert Campbell from his company is an allowable deduction against trading profits. This

TABLE 16.3. *Opening corporation tax assessments on A. Campbell Ltd.* (£)

Chargeable accounting period ended 30 April	(i)	(ii)
1988		
Profits	50,000	50,000
Less: additional revenue expenses	(30,000)	—
pre-trading expenses	(2,000)	(2,000)
director's salary	(12,000)	(12,000)
Schedule D case I income	6,000	36,000
1989		
Profits	75,000	75,000
Less: additional revenue expenses	—	(30,000)
director's salary	(12,000)	(12,000)
Schedule D case I income	63,000	33,000
1990		
Profits	95,000	95,000
Less: director's salary	(12,000)	(12,000)
Schedule D case I income	£83,000	£83,000

amount of transferred profits will be assessed to income tax, under Schedule E, upon Albert Campbell.

Technically, only 11/12 of Albert's salary would be assessable in 1987/8, but for ease of presentation it will be assumed the full £12,000 is assessed within that tax year. This assumption has very minor effects on the overall tax liabilities. The income tax payable for each year is:

	(£)
Director's salary	12,000
Less: married personal allowance	(3,655)
Taxable income	8,345
Income tax payable at 29%	2,420

It is now possible to compute the corporation tax liabilities which will arise, and Table 16.4 presents this data again distinguishing between the optional treatment of the £30,000 revenue expenditure. It will be seen that all

TABLE 16.4. *Corporation tax liabilities of A. Campbell Ltd.* (£)

Chargeable accounting periods ended 30 April	Tax due at 29%	Financial Year			
		1987	1988	1989	1990
(i) *1988*					
£6,000 × 11/12	1,595	5,500			
£6,000 × 1/12	145		500		
	1,740				
1989					
£63,000 × 11/12	16,747		57,750		
£63,000 × 1/12	1,523			5,250	
	18,270				
1990					
£83,000 × 11/12	22,064			76,083	
£83,000 × 1/12	2,006				6,917
	24,070				
(ii) *1988*					
£36,000 × 11/12	9,570	33,000			
£36,000 × 1/12	870		3,000		
	10,440				
1989					
£33,000 × 11/12	8,773		30,250		
£33,000 × 1/12	797			2,750	
	9,570				
1990 as for (i)	*24,070*			76,083	6,917

corporation tax due has been based upon the rates and limits applicable to the financial year 1986. The company's profits are all well below the lower limit for small companies rate and 29 per cent has been applied to the profit levels. Although not necessary because the rate of corporation tax is assumed to be constant throughout, the allocation of chargeable profits to the relevant financial years has been shown for illustrative purposes. Where chargeable accounting periods are not coincident with financial years this approach is recommended and is vital if different tax rates apply to the financial years concerned.

Because it is almost certain the company will be a close company, when computing any tax liabilities the problem of enforced distributions should be considered. However, it is clear the company would qualify as a trading company with no estate or trading income (see Chapter 10) and for the purposes of our example this problem may be ignored.

National insurance contributions under class 1 have been ignored in the calculations for the reasons previously advanced.

Tax cash flows

We must now consider the total estimated tax outflows which will arise dependent upon whether Albert conducts his business as a sole trader or through the medium of a company. The results are summarized in Table 16.5 with two sets of data included for the company to represent the different treatment of the optional revenue expenditure. We initially present the data for tax cash flows on the first three years' trading only.

In preparing this summary we have allocated tax payments to the trading years of the organizations as this will be useful for future cash flow projections. The normal due dates of payment have been adopted with the consequence that the higher rate tax due on profits as a sole trader are thrown several years into the future. It has been assumed the income tax due on the director's salary will be paid over on the same date as the salary is drawn. Although this may not be totally realistic this assumption is not considered to affect the overall decision to be made.

The total estimated saving of tax, if Albert were to form a company, is approximately £43,500. In general terms, this situation will always develop above a certain level of profits because of the differentials between the basis of assessment and the marginal rates of tax applicable to individuals and companies. However, this advantage to companies is perhaps offset by the considerable cash flow advantages which accrue to unincorporated businesses as a result of the timing of tax payments. With a 30 April year-end, once the normal previous year basis of assessment is fully operational, an unincorporated business will have a twenty-month gap between the profits being earned and having to account for the first instalment of basic rate tax thereon. There are greater lags for the second instalment and higher rate tax

TABLE 16.5. *Summary tax cash flows for Albert Campbell based on first three years' profits* (£)

Payments due in year ended 30 April	Sole trader	Limited company	
		(i)	(ii)
1988			
D case I income tax 1.1.88	1,838	—	
Income tax on salary 30.4.88	—	2,420	2,420
	1,838	*2,420*	*2,420*
1989			
D case I income tax 1.7.88	1,839	—	—
D case I income tax 1.1.89	2,370	—	—
Corporation tax 31.1.89	—	1,740	10,440
Income tax on salary 30.4.89	—	2,420	2,420
	4,209	*4,160*	*12,860*
1990			
D case I income tax 1.7.89	2,370	—	—
D case I income tax 1.1.90	2,370	—	—
Corporation tax 31.1.90	—	18,270	9,570
Income tax on salary 30.4.90	—	2,420	2,420
	4,740	*20,690*	*11,990*
1991			
D case I income tax 1.7.90	2,370	—	—
D case I income tax 1.1.91	2,494	—	—
Corporation tax 31.1.91	—	24,070	24,070
	4,864	*24,070*	*24,070*
1992			
D case I income tax 1.7.91	2,494	—	—
D case I income tax 1.1.92	2,494	—	—
Higher rate assessment 1.12.91	29,922	—	—
	34,910	—	—
1993			
D case I income tax 1.7.92	2,494	—	—
Higher rate assessment 1.12.92	41,922	—	—
	44,416	—	—
Total payments	*£94,977*	*£51,340*	*£51,340*

assessments. Conversely, the newly-formed company has merely nine months to meet its tax bill on profits. So that a comparison of the tax payments may be made, taking into account the different timings of payment, we will discount the cash flows to calculate a present value for each alternative. Before doing this it is necessary to modify the data shown in Table 16.5 to show the tax cash flows for all years. Table 16.6 shows these changes.

Two problems are present in adopting this approach. The first arises because the actual due dates of payment vary considerably, but we shall assume for illustrative purposes that all payments are made on the last day of trading. The other problem is to establish a discount rate to be applied to the cash flows. In practice, this might be relative to an investment opportunity lost because of finance being diverted to tax payments. For the purposes of this example a 10 per cent opportunity rate will be used, and the discounted tax cash flows are provided in Table 16.7 for the first 25 years!

Decision

The conclusion to be reached, therefore, is that taking both the size of all tax payments into account and the timing thereof Albert should seriously consider forming a company as this will minimize the effects of taxation in the longer term. As a rider to this proposition if the discounted value of the £30,000 revenue expenditure is also acknowledged there is a marginal advantage in deferring it until year ended 30 April 1989, the discounted value of the payment being smaller.

Alternatives

As with all business decisions there are alternatives to be considered by Albert. The reason for the above decision is a direct result of the level of profits and tax rate differentials.

Clearly, some tax savings could be achieved by letting his wife become an employee of the unincorporated business particularly as she has no other income. In terms of tax a salary of £2,335 would save tax at the basic rate for the first three years of assessment and the top marginal rate of 60 per cent in the next two. This amount would be covered by the wife's earned income allowance, and the tax saved would be £4,833. To offset this saving there would be a small cost for class 1 national insurance contributions. Higher salary levels for Mrs Campbell would achieve greater tax savings in 1990/1 and 1991/2, but unless the Inland Revenue were satisfied the payments were wholly and exclusively for the purposes of the trade this strategy may be ineffective for tax purposes. Simply put, the excess salary would not be an allowable expense against profits.

However, a more attractive alternative is for Mrs Campbell to become a partner. Providing his wife takes some active part in the business operations the Inland Revenue cannot challenge the level of profits which is deemed to be hers. This suggestion should be presented to Albert together with an indication of the tax savings over a sole trader made possible when linked with an election for separate taxation of wife's earnings (see Chapter 7). Assuming

TABLE 16.6. *Summary tax cash flows for Albert Campbell based on profits for all years* (£)

Payments due in year ended 30 April	Sole trader	Limited company	
		(i)	(ii)
1988			
D case I income tax 1.1.88	1,838	—	—
Income tax on salary 30.4.88	—	2,420	2,420
	1,838	*2,420*	*2,420*
1989			
D case I income tax 1.7.88	1,839	—	—
D case I income tax 1.1.89	2,370	—	—
Corporation tax 31.1.89	—	1,740	10,440
Income tax on salary 30.4.89	—	2,420	2,420
	4,209	*4,160*	*12,860*
1990			
D case I income tax 1.7.89	2,370	—	—
D case I income tax 1.1.90	2,370	—	—
Corporation tax 31.1.90	—	18,270	9,570
Income tax on salary 30.4.90	—	2,420	2,420
	4,740	*20,690*	*11,990*
1991			
D case I income tax 1.7.90	2,370	—	—
D case I income tax 1.1.91	2,494	—	—
Corporation tax 31.1.91	—	24,070	24,070
Income tax on salary 30.4.91	—	2,420	2,420
	4,864	*26,490*	*26,490*
1992			
D case I income tax 1.7.91	2,494	—	—
D case I income tax 1.1.92	2,494	—	—
Higher rate assessment 1.12.91	29,922	—	—
Corporation tax 31.1.92	—	24,070	24,070
Income tax on salary 30.4.92	—	2,420	2,420
	34,910	*26,490*	*26,490*
1993 onwards			
D case I income tax 1 July	2,494	—	—
D case I income tax 1 Jan.	2,494	—	—
Higher rate assessment 1 Dec.	41,922	—	—
Corporation tax 31 Jan.	—	24,070	24,070
Income tax on salary	—	2,420	2,420
	46,910	*26,490*	*26,490*

TABLE 16.7. *Discounted tax cash flows* (25 years)

Year	Sole trader (£)	Limited company (£)	
		(i)	(ii)
1988	1,838/(1.10)	2,420/(1.10)	2,420/(1.10)
1989	$4{,}209/(1.10)^2$	$4{,}160/(1.10)^2$	$12{,}860/(1.10)^2$
1990	$4{,}740/(1.10)^3$	$20{,}690/(1.10)^3$	$11{,}990/(1.10)^3$
1991	$4{,}864/(1.10)^4$	$26{,}490/(1.10)^4$	$26{,}490/(1.10)^4$
1992	$34{,}910/(1.10)^5$	$26{,}490/(1.10)^5$	$26{,}490/(1.10)^5$
1993 onwards[a]	46,910/0.18917	26,490/0.18917	26,490/0.18917
Total	281,690	195,760	196,410

[a] For the sole trader for 1993 onwards, the total discounted tax cash flows are:

$$46{,}910\,(1/(1.10)^6 + 1/(1.10)^7 + \ldots + 1/(1.10)^{25})$$

$$= \frac{46{,}910 \times (1 - 1/(1.10)^{20})}{(1.10)^6 \times (1 - 1/1.10)} = \frac{46{,}910}{(1.10)^6} \times 9.3649201$$

$$= 46{,}910/0.18917.$$

an equal division of profits the amended tax liabilities for 1990/1 and 1991/2 are shown in Table 16.8. Under this alternative only relatively small tax savings would occur in the first three years of assessment due to the wife's earned income allowance. However, a separate taxation of wife's earnings election is not beneficial in these years.

The tax saved by entering into partnership would be approximately £7,900 for 1990/1 and £8,500 for 1991/2 onwards. Although this is a substantial saving, trading through the medium of a company would still produce a tax benefit over the partnership medium in discounted terms.

In conclusion, it is probably true to say that the tax differentials are probably still too wide for Albert to consider a partnership as a viable alternative to a company. Nevertheless, it should be stressed that, as a general point, a business partnership with a spouse may be the ideal medium for a new venture. This is particularly true where the profit levels are somewhat lower than in the example used. At 1986/7 income tax rates and allowances a profit of approximately £39,500 may be divided equally between husband and wife in business partnership, without incurring liabilities at higher rates providing the earnings election is made for the wife's share of profits. Thus, there would be considerable cash flow advantages and the opportunity to transfer the business to a company at a later date when profit levels rise substantially. There is an additional bonus in this strategy as a consequence of some profits escaping assessment because of the permanent cessation rules for unincorporated businesses (see Chapter 8).

TABLE 16.8. *Income tax liabilities of Mr & Mrs Campbell incorporating a separate taxation of wife's earnings claim* (£)

	Mr Campbell	Mrs Campbell
1990/1		
Earned income: Schedule D case I	37,500	37,500
Less: single personal allowance	(2,335)	(2,335)
Taxable income	35,165	35,165
Income tax payable:		
first 17,200 @ 29%	4,988	4,988
next 3,000 @ 40%	1,200	1,200
next 5,200 @ 45%	2,340	2,340
next 7,900 @ 50%	3,950	3,950
remainder 1865 @ 55%	1,026	1,026
	13,504	13,504
1991/2		
Earned income: Schedule D case I	47,500	47,500
Less: single personal allowance	(2,335)	(2,335)
Taxable income	45,165	45,165
Income tax payable:		
at all rates 29%–55% £41,200	16,823	16,823
remainder 3,965 @ 60%	2,379	2,379
	19,202	19,202

Concluding remarks

This chapter has discussed the taxation issues to be considered when deciding the medium to adopt for a new business venture. It has been established the critical issues are those of profit levels, different tax scales for income and corporation tax, the time lag between earning profits and settling the liabilities in the case of unincorporated businesses, and the personal circumstances of the taxpayer, for example a spouse who may become a business partner.

Where relatively large profits are immediately being earned it has been shown a company will have longer term tax advantages over a sole proprietorship or partnership.

Recommendations for further reading

An introduction to more advanced topics in the choice of the business medium including pensions for the sole trader and company director, tranfer of a business to a limited company, the potential capital gains penalty on retention of profits within a company, and loss reliefs may be found in Homer & Burrows (1986).

Reference

Homer, A., and Burrows, R. (1986), *Tolley's Tax Guide 1986/87* (Croydon, Surrey: Tolley).

17
International Aspects

Introduction

In Part Two we concentrated our discussion of business taxation upon the UK resident taxpayer (sole trader, partner, or limited company) carrying on a business which was both operated and controlled from within the UK. The aim of this chapter is to acknowledge there is an international dimension to taxation and examine, in general terms, some of the important issues faced by the UK resident when business operations are extended beyond the boundaries of the UK for whatever motive.

General considerations

There are two aspects to international trading which are linked by the UK tax system: those UK residents (including companies) with overseas trading profits and capital gains, and non-resident taxpayers (including non-resident companies) with sources of income and capital assets in the UK. The first category of taxpayers may find themselves taxable under the relevant schedules and cases stipulated by the ICTA 1970 excluding those which specifically relate to UK sources, for example Schedule A and B. Similarly, realized capital gains on overseas assets are within the net of the UK capital gains tax legislation. Non-resident taxpayers will be charged to UK income, corporation, or capital gains tax under the normal legislation with modifications, i.e. Schedule D cases IV and V clearly cannot apply to non-residents.

The situation outlined above relates, in general terms, to all UK resident or non-resident taxpayers. However, in this chapter we are principally concerned with how the legislation may affect the corporate or unincorporated business which falls within these categories. Thus, attention will be focused upon a fairly narrow band of the UK tax legislation within the international context.

International trading

We will commence our discussion by considering how the profits of an unincorporated business would be assessed to UK tax. Trading profits will be assessable to income tax under either Schedule D case I/II or Schedule D case V, while any capital profits, which are also chargeable gains (see Chapter 9), will be charged to capital gains tax. The extent to which these UK taxes may apply depends upon not only the residential qualifications of the proprietors but also the country in which the business trades and from which it is controlled.

The distinction between Schedule D cases I and II is merely one of fact dependent upon whether it is a trade, profession, or vocation which is being carried on. For explanatory purposes we will treat these two cases as interchangeable. Whether trading profits are assessed under Schedule D case I (profits from UK trade) or Schedule D case V (profit from overseas trades) is decided by the place of control, and not necessarily where the profits are earned. The place of control is therefore, of paramount importance and over the years has been the subject of dispute between the Inland Revenue and UK resident traders. However, a fair conclusion to be drawn is that it is extremely difficult for a UK resident sole trader to establish that a business carried on abroad is controlled from there. Therefore, the trade will be treated as a UK trade and assessed accordingly under Schedule D case I. An example of this ruling now follows.

Ray, who is a UK resident, has carried on his trade within the UK for many years. Recently, he has carried out part of the activities in Zenna with a consequent growth in profits. All of the profits are assessable under Schedule D case I. Subsequently Ray decides to move all his trading activities of Zenna, after all it is a growth area for profits, but he remains resident in the UK. Even though his control may be minimal it is nevertheless in the UK, and the profits are assessable under Schedule D case I.

The situation will be different where a UK resident is in partnership with non-UK residents. If we assume that when Ray moved his trading activities abroad he entered into partnership with three Zennans, the Inland Revenue would probably accept the business was controlled from Zenna, and Ray's share of the overseas profits as a UK resident would be assessable under Schedule D case V.

In terms of tax efficiency, since the removal of the 25 per cent relief available to UK residents on foreign earnings, it is probably more beneficial to have profits assessed under Schedule D case I rather than Schedule D case V. In loss situations there would be increased flexibility (see Chapter 8). Clearly, neither of the above strategies will exempt Ray from UK taxation and almost certainly result in his having to pay foreign tax in addition.

To escape UK taxation on his overseas profits Ray would, necessarily, have to cease to be a UK resident. If, therefore, he and his family moved to Zenna at the same time as he moved his business activities, he is in the category of a non-resident carrying on a trade controlled and carried on wholly abroad. This is true whether he becomes a sole trader or enters into partnership. Of course, Ray may still be subject to Zennan taxation and if this is at a higher rate than he suffered in the UK his only gain may be a more favourable climate! The moral of this episode is that potential UK tax exiles must choose their new country of residence, activities, and control with extreme care and seek expert advice. It is not an area for the DIY operation.

In general terms, it should be noted that where a foreign-controlled partnership carried on some trading activities within the UK, any UK resident partner will be assessed under Schedule D case I on his share of the UK profits, while his share of the profits from the overseas activities will be assessable under Schedule D case V.

The position regarding the sale of business assets and UK capital gains tax is somewhat more simple. UK residents trading partly or wholly abroad will be liable on any capital gains arising, providing chargeable assets are involved. The issue of control is irrelevant. Therefore, in our previous example where Ray is a UK resident, even his share of the profit on chargeable assets of the partnership with the three Zennan non-residents will be assessable to UK capital gains tax. Non-residents are not liable to UK capital gains tax on business assets outside the UK sold at a profit. This is merely the operation of the normal capital gains tax legislation and leaves the three Zennan non-residents with no liability to UK capital gains tax. Additionally, providing he maintains his non-resident status, if Ray eventually sells his Zennan business realizing capital profits he escapes a charge to UK capital gains tax.

However, a non-UK resident may become liable to capital gains tax where there is a trade established in the UK and business assets therein are sold at a profit.

Next, we will consider the tax position of corporate traders. As with individuals, a company may be either UK resident or non-resident. The issue of corporate residence is normally dictated by where the central management and control are situated. In this respect great importance will be placed upon where the meetings of the Board of Directors takes place. However, some timely words of warning may be needed here. If a company had three directors all of whom were UK residents the fact that all board meetings were held in a far off exotic place would not, in itself, make the company non-resident. Almost certainly the Inland Revenue would consider these meetings were mere formality to approve decisions and actions already taken by the directors in the UK. The company would be classed as UK resident particularly where the company's activities were carried on in the UK. If the company's trade were carried on abroad the classification is unlikely to be altered for such an obvious tax strategy although the profits will be assessed under Schedule D case I rather than Schedule D case V.

The most obvious example of a company which will be classed as non-resident is one where the management and control at strategic level is exercised by non-UK resident directors.

There are clearly some obvious parallels between the business carried on by a sole trader or through the medium of a single company as follows:

(i) A UK resident company, where it carries on its trade either wholly or partly in the UK or wholly abroad through a branch or agency, will be liable to UK corporation tax on all profits whatever the country of origin. Because corporation tax is payable on total profits the chargeable fraction of any capital gains on business assets, UK or abroad, is automatically included. There may also be foreign tax payable on overseas profits and gains.

(ii) A non-resident company with no part of its trading activities within the UK is not liable to corporation tax. However, where part of its trade is conducted in the UK through a branch or agency, a liability to corporation tax will arise on the world-wide trading profits of the branch. Capital gains tax will also be assessable on the non-resident company in respect of disposals of UK situated capital assets of the UK branch or agency.

From our discussion so far emerges the conclusion that for the relatively small UK business operation there is little chance of escape from the effects of the UK tax legislation. The only effective option is to impose a physical exile of both the taxpayer and the subject matter of the trade.

We will now consider the larger operation and commence by stressing that the word 'control' in the context of the previous paragraphs has a fundamentally different meaning than 'to control' signifying the ownership of shares in a company. Once this idea of the divorce of ownership and management in corporate entities is accepted then the UK resident may be able to act accordingly. Prior to 6 April 1984, the following tax strategy may have been considered.

Fast Limited, a UK resident company, sets up a wholly-owned subsidiary in Nobilia, an overseas country, to carry on a trade there. It becomes a question of fact as to whether the subsidiary is carrying on its own trade. The answer to the question depends on who has management and control of the subsidiary and not who owns the shares. Where the management and control of the subsidiary is in the hands of non-UK residents it will be probably be treated as carrying on its own trade and be classed as a non-resident company. The significance of this treatment is that only profits remitted by the subsidiary in the form of dividends or interest to Fast Limited will be subjected to UK corporation tax. Clearly, where very large profits are made in Nobilia, suffering very low tax rates and very small remittances are made to the UK, for example by dividend, a considerable tax saving is available to Fast Limited. Any dividends received by Fast Limited would be assessable under Schedule D case V—they cannot be franked investment income. Relief for any Nobilian tax suffered may be recovered under double taxation relief claims (see later section).

Since 1984 this type of operation has been attacked by the UK Government under legislation for controlled foreign companies (see later). Nevertheless, the opportunities for large, multinational companies, trading world-wide, to capitalize upon the tax laws and differentials in tax rates between countries with whom and within which they trade are immense.

Inland Revenue

The role of the UK Inland Revenue is at two levels in relation to international taxation.

It is involved in administering the domestic tax code as it relates to UK residents and non-residents. The work of checking computations, raising assessments, etc. is undertaken by the same officials whose functions were outlined in Chapter 7. These officials tend to be concentrated in tax offices sited in London and other major cities.

However, it is through two specialist units—Policy Division 5 and Technical Division 2B—that the fullest involvement with international taxation arises. The work of these units is threefold and covers necessary changes in the domestic tax legislation, the negotiation of double taxation agreements, and the protection of the UK Government against international tax avoidance and evasion.

Advice will be given to the Treasury regarding defects in the international aspects of the UK tax legislation, for example, the amendments necessary in respect of non-resident subsidiaries set up by UK resident companies in so-called tax havens. An illustration of this type of international operation was given earlier (Fast Limited). The appropriate counter-avoidance legislation was produced in the 1984 Finance Act.

It is interesting to note that when negotiating double taxation agreements the Inland Revenue may be protecting the UK resident taxpayer during the process. There is obviously some good in all of us!

Double taxation in this context means the taxation by two countries of the same income (which includes trading profits) and chargeable gains. The way in which the UK taxes its residents and non-residents is not unique, and many other countries tax their residents on a world-wide basis (including income arising abroad, for exampe the UK) and also on income arising within its boundaries to its own residents and non-residents, for example a UK resident. In general terms, therefore, overseas income may be subjected to tax twice, once in the country of residence and secondly in the country in which it arises. Specifically, in the Ray example earlier, where he remains a UK resident but trades wholly from Zenna, he is liable to UK income tax on trading profits and Zennan taxation.

To prevent double taxation of this nature it is normal for the country of residence to give credit against its own tax for the overseas tax suffered. Where no double taxation agreement exists between two countries, for example the UK and Zenna, Ray is entitled to unilateral relief at the lower of the UK tax and the overseas (Zennan) tax. If this is so, why do we have double taxation agreements? The main reasons advanced (HMSO 1985) are:

(i) Agreements give taxpayers protection against unfair and arbitrary taxation. However, the imposition of unitary tax by certain individual states in the USA is contrary to the double taxation agreement with the USA. The problem is that the agreement relates to federal and not state taxes. Nevertheless, Inland Revenue officials have supported efforts by the UK Government and business to obtain amendments which would remove its arbitrary incidence and excessive compliance costs. Presumably the already existing agreement makes such objections more possible.

(ii) The reduction of tax rates in the source country on income passing to a UK resident company from a subsidiary resident in that source country so equating tax levels between the source country and the UK. Agreement on this point will assist company cash flows and avoid the problem of unrelieved foreign tax in the UK. This does not mean the UK Government fixes the tax rates of the source country other than to prevent discrimination against non-residents of the source country.

(iii) The elimination of arbitrary adjustments for non-arm's length transactions between companies resident in the source country and UK resident companies. This tackles the problem of artificial transfer pricing by multinational groups.

(iv) To encourage investment in less developed countries by incorporating a 'matching credit' provision in the agreement. The effect is to allow tax foregone, as an encouragement to investment in the source country, as a deduction against UK tax on the income from the source country. Clearly, without this clause it would not be possible to deduct foreign tax which had not been actually paid.

(v) The exchange of information between tax authorities and, in particular, co-operation in the prevention of tax avoidance.

This is the sting in the tail, but is justifiable when consideration is given to the complex cross-international frontier transactions in which multinational groups engage.

Double taxation relief

In the previous section we outlined the concept behind double taxation agreements. Now, we consider the basic operational principles of double taxation agreements or unilateral relief, i.e. where no such agreement exists between the UK and the source country. The process of offsetting foreign tax suffered against UK taxation is referred to as double taxation relief (DTR). From discussion in the earlier sections it is clear that the large trading organization, i.e. multinational group is likely to be the chief beneficiary of DTR, and we shall, therefore, limit our consideration of principles to UK resident companies who are group members.

Where DTR is claimed as an offset or credit it is allowed by giving relief for the foreign tax suffered on income against the UK corporation tax on the same income. Where the foreign tax exceeds the UK corporation tax on the same income no relief for the excess can be given. There is similar relief for chargeable gains. A general example of the principle is given below.

Grey Limited, a UK resident company, carries on its trade in Mya. The profits arising from the trade are £50,000 and is the only income of the company. If, we assume, the UK corporation tax rate is 30 per cent and the Myan corporate tax rate is 40 per cent the DTR claim to be made by Grey Limited would be restricted to £50,000 × 30% = £15,000. The Schedule DI assessment on Grey Limited would be £15,000 less DTR £15,000, i.e. nil. Although no UK corporation tax is paid the excess Myan tax suffered of £5,000 is unrelieved. Unfortunately, this excess is 'dead money' as regards Grey Limited; it cannot be repaid nor is it possible to set it against the income of another accounting period either backward or forward. Therefore, it must be recognized that Grey Limited has a marginal tax rate of 40% for decision-making purposes.

Before taking up this point we will look at a further example of DTR. Blue Limited, a UK resident company, carries on part of its trade in Abia, a neighbouring country to Mya. Abia has a tax rate on trading profits of 20 per cent and one of 40 per cent on non-trading income. The results of Blue Limited for its accounting period are:

	(£)
UK trading income	30,000
Abian trading income before tax	30,000
Abian non-trading income before tax	2,000

The DTR claim by Blue Limited is shown in Table 17.1 assuming a UK

TABLE 17.1. *Example of DTR claim by Blue Ltd.* (£)

(i) Tax paid in Abia:

trading profits £30,000 @ 20%	6,000
non-trading profits of £2,000 @ 40%	800

(ii) DTR claim by Blue Ltd.

	Chargeable profits	UK tax chargeable	DTR	UK tax payable
Schedule D case I:				
UK trading income	30,000	9,000	—	9,000
foreign trading income	30,000	9,000	6,000	3,000
Schedule D case V:				
foreign non-trading income	2,000	600	600	—
	62,000	18,600	6,600	12,000

Note: Foreign tax paid on non-trading profits is partially unrelieved in the sum of £200 (i.e. £800 paid in Abia less £600 maximum used in DTR claim).

corporation tax rate of 30 per cent. The 'same income' rule is demonstrated in this example, i.e. DTR for tax paid on non-trading income in Abia may only be set against UK corporation tax on that income. The excess of £200 cannot be set against corporation tax due on the Abian trading profits. The other important feature is that all foreign income is included in a corporation tax computation gross. This rule is in fact no different to the treatment of UK income received by a company under deduction of UK tax. For decision-making purposes Blue Limited will have a marginal tax rate of 30 per cent although if a non-trading project were being considered the higher marginal rate of 40 per cent should be acknowledged.

On the assumption that Grey Limited and Blue Limited carry on identical trades with the same risk profiles and expected pre-tax returns then Grey is at a disadvantage to Blue in terms of post-tax returns. The options open to Grey Limited, which is a member of a UK resident group of companies, are:

(i) transfer the trade to a company which is classed as being resident in Mya, or

(ii) transfer the trade to the neighbouring country of Abia.

As regards the first option, points which would have to be considered by the UK group are:

(i) Unless Treasury consent is obtained under section 482 ICTA 1970 this transaction would be illegal.

(ii) The rate of 40 per cent imposed in Mya is applied to non-resident companies of Mya. The rate which is applicable to resident companies is 20 per cent. Therefore, providing Treasury consent is obtained the non-resident company approach seems attractive.

(iii) However, enquiries should be made regarding the possibility of a double taxation agreement between the UK and Mya in the near future under which this discrimination against non-residents who are UK resident is removed. This would be a more favourable proposition since the costs of obtaning Treasury consent and setting up the new company are avoided.

(iv) Assuming the enquiries at (iii) are negative, the UK group must then consider the tax consequences of removing Grey Limited from the group structure (see Chapter 10). In general terms if Grey Limited were to become non-resident it would still be included in the number of companies for 'associated companies' legislation but not as a member of a '51% or 75% group'.

Clearly, these decision processes are unlikely in the real world, for the sum involved, but the example is illustrative of the tax 'thinking' in the international trading arena. The most likely practical solution is that the trade will be transferred to the neighbouring country of Abia.

Two related topics which affect UK trading groups with DTR claims are those of underlying tax and advance corporation tax (ACT).

Where a UK resident company receives income in the form of a dividend from a non-resident subsidiary, the foreign tax suffered on the dividend will take the form of a withholding tax at a fixed percentage. In an earlier example Fast Limited carried on its trade in Nobilia through a non-resident 100 per cent subsidiary. Fast Limited received a dividend of £8,500 after suffering a withholding tax of 15 per cent. In its corporation tax computation Fast Limited will show Schedule D case V income of £10,000, i.e. gross of Nobilian tax. UK corporation tax of £10,000 at 30% = £3,000 less DTR £1,500 will be payable. However, where a UK company holds more than 10 per cent of the voting power in a non-resident subsidiary, relief may also be obtained for the underlying foreign taxes attributable to the profits from which the dividend is paid. The calculation of the underlying tax is complex and beyond the scope of this book. However, assuming the underlying tax has been calculated an example of how it may be used in a DTR claim is now given.

If, we assume, in the previous example that in addition to the Nobilian 15 per cent withholding tax, the underlying tax relative to the profits of the Nobilian subsidiary is 5 per cent, an additional claim under DTR may be made by Fast Limited. The computation of the UK corporation tax liability is:

		(£)
Schedule D case V income:		
£8,500 grossed at 15%	= £10,000	
£10,000 regrossed at 5%		10,526
UK corporation tax at 30%		3,158
Less: DTR		(2,026)
		£1,132

Certainly it would be advisable for Fast Limited to make this claim as its overall UK corporation tax liability is reduced from £1,500 to £1,132, a saving of £368. This is despite the necessity of having to include a grossing addition for the underlying tax suffered.

If a UK resident company makes a distribution then a liability to ACT arises (see Chapter 10). For a company with substantial overseas income a problem emerges where DTR is also claimed. The extent of the problem is shown in Table 17.2 where the results are shown on a pre-1984 and post-1984 basis. Prior to 31 March 1984 the order of setoff was ACT first then DTR. From 1 April 1984 the reverse order was provided for in the 1984 Finance Act. The earlier data for Grey Limited is used, and it is assumed Grey pays a dividend of £7,000 with basic rate tax at 30 per cent. The advantage of the change in legislation is that part of the foreign tax effectively becomes surplus ACT which can be carried back or forward by Grey Limited or surrendered to a UK subsidiary, of which Grey Limited is at least a 51 per cent holding company, for current or future use. Alternatively, where the payment of the dividend is to its own parent company with a 51 per cent minimum stake, an election for the dividend to be paid as group income could be made.

TABLE 17.2. *The relationship between ACT and DTR*

Grey Limited	(£)
Pre 1984	
Schedule D case I on overseas profits	50,000
Corporation tax @ 30%	15,000
Less: ACT	(3,000)
	12,000
Less: DTR (restricted)	(12,000)
Mainstream liability	nil
Unrelieved foreign tax	8,000
Post 1984	
Schedule D case I on overseas profits	50,000
Corporation tax @ 30%	15,000
Less: DTR	(15,000)
Mainstream liability	nil
Unrelieved foreign tax	5,000
Surplus ACT	3,000

Low tax areas

From the previous sections it will have become apparent that where a UK resident, either an individual or company, wishes to escape liability to UK taxation movement outside the boundaries of the UK is required. In the case of an individual trader, to satisfy the conditions of overseas control, it involves personal movement. For a company this may be achieved by setting up a foreign-controlled, i.e. non-UK resident subsidiary. However, these moves must be well thought through since a move to another area where the tax rates are comparable, or even higher than in the UK, would achieve nothing.

It would, therefore, seem likely that individuals and companies will seek to place themselves or trade through a number of non-UK resident subsidiaries in countries where tax rates are low or non existent. There are, of course, countries which offer this benefit quite blatantly; the so-called tax havens. Favourites include the Bahamas and Liechtenstein while nearer at hand are the Channel Islands. Other countries merely have low tax rates which may be exploited by multinational groups, for example the Republic of Ireland where there have been substantial benefits for foreign manufacturers. It is also to be borne in mind that although the UK tax system may seem oppressive to UK residents it may nevertheless be attractive to traders from relatively higher taxed countries.

An illustration of the use of low tax areas by a multinational group is shown in Fig. 17.1. The subsidiary resident in the high tax area forms a new subsidiary

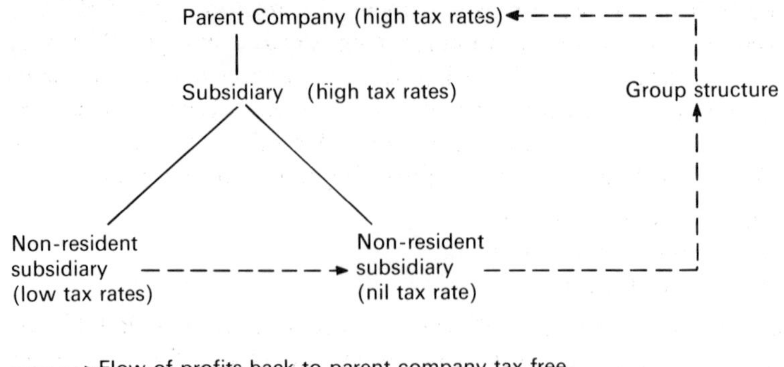

Fig. 17.1 Exploitation of low tax areas

which is resident in a low tax host area to exploit the manufacture of a new product. Apart from the low tax rates of the host country it also has the attractions of low manufacturing costs. Thus, higher profits are likely to arise in addition to tax advantages. The manufactured goods are then transferred to a sales subsidiary which has been formed in a tax haven with a nil rate of tax. The transfer of goods to this company in the second host country is barely above manufacturing cost. This will leave very small profits to be taxed in host country one. The sales subsidiary in host country two will then distribute the products onto the world markets at a substantial mark-up on cost. This effectively leaves the profit tax-free in the country in which it has been made to arise. Clearly, a way must be found to pass these profits back to the ultimate parent company in a way which renders them tax-free and this is achieved through the overall group structure. It must be stressed that this example is purely illustrative of the principles employed and in the real world would probably fail either because of double taxation agreements between the countries concerned, for example on the issue of transfer pricing, or the domestic legislation of the parent company and its subsidiary. With regard to this latter point we consider in the next section an important piece of legislation introduced by the 1984 Finance Act which applies to UK resident companies and their overseas-controlled subsidiaries.

Controlled foreign companies

In general terms it has been shown that where a UK resident company establishes a non-UK resident subsidiary there would only be a liability to UK corporation tax on profits remitted to the UK in the form of dividends. Where the bulk of the profits remain in the host country and suffer very low tax rates thereon there is clearly a tax advantage. However, from 6 April 1984 a new class of company was identified by the 1984 Finance Act. Such a company is referred to in the legislation as a 'controlled foreign company' (CFC). This relatively new set of rules is specifically designed to charge UK tax on the unremitted profits of a CFC which is situated in a low tax area or tax haven. The legislation is extremely complex and is involving very high-level meetings between multinational companies and the Inland Revenue on its application. Therefore, we will concentrate on providing a general overview of:

(i) which companies qualify,
(ii) exemptions from liability, and
(iii) assessment of profits.

A company will qualify as a CFC where in any accounting period it is resident outside the UK and is controlled by UK residents and suffers a lower level of taxation in the host country. In general terms the residence of a CFC will be decided by the test of central management and control. Providing 51 per cent of the voting capital is held by UK residents, be they individuals or companies, who may or may not be connected persons there is deemed to be control by UK residents. Broadly, where the tax paid on profits in the host country is less than 50 per cent of the corresponding UK corporation tax on those profits there is said to be a lower level of taxation. Profits for this purpose would exclude those arising from a capital transaction. If one of these factors is missing the non-UK resident company cannot be a CFC.

Where it is established a company is a CFC, the special legislation will not be invoked, where any one of the following conditions is satisfied:

(i) The activities of the CFC are exempt which broadly covers genuine commercial operations within the host country or the purposes of these operations is not with the object of reducing UK tax.
(ii) The profits of the CFC, for an accounting period, do not exceed £20,000. Where the accounting period is for less than 12 months there is a proportionate reduction.
(iii) More than 35 per cent of the voting capital of the CFC is held by the public and actively traded on a recognized Stock Exchange in the host country.
(iv) An acceptable level of distribution of profits is made by the CFC to UK residents within the accounting period or 18 months thereafter. Acceptable in this context is 50 per cent for trading companies and 90 per cent for non-trading activities.
(v) The business of the CFC is being carried on in a country which appears on a list of excluded countries prepared by the Inland Revenue. It is perhaps interesting to note that the vast majority of countries on the list have double taxation agreements with the UK.

If a CFC satisfies none of the above conditions then it is probable the Inland Revenue will apply the charging sections of the legislation. In general terms, this means any UK resident company will have a proportion, equivalent to its interest in that CFC, of the CFC's chargeable profits apportioned to it. Any apportionments to non-UK residents or UK residents who are individuals, or amount to less than 10 per cent of chargeable profits to UK resident companies, are ignored. UK resident companies with more than a 10 per cent share of the chargeable profits are assessable to corporation tax at the 'appropriate rate', which term incidentally, the Inland Revenue does not consider includes the small companies rate. To arrive at the final amount of UK corporation tax payable credit will be given for the UK resident company's share of the creditable tax applicable to the CFC's chargeable profits.

It is supposed the tax planning strategies of many international trading groups will have been affected by this recent piece of legislation and it is an interesting point with which to conclude this chapter.

Concluding remarks

This chapter has concentrated upon introducing the basic tax problems facing the international trader and the role the tax authorities play in keeping legislation in step with tax planning strategies.

We commenced our discussion with a number of general considerations indicating how the UK domestic tax system interacts with the international trader. A distinction was made between unincorporated and corporate traders, and it was shown that large multinational groups have considerable advantages over the small trader in their tax planning activities. The question of residence was established as critical to these activities.

The role which the UK Inland Revenue assume in the international tax arena was outlined with particular reference to double taxation agreements. Relief for double taxation of profits and gains was discussed, and attention was drawn to the dual problems of unrelieved foreign tax and surplus ACT where DTR claims are made. The particular problem of unrelieved foreign tax was identified as being that of high marginal tax rates for decision-making purposes.

In the section on tax havens the exploitation thereof by international trading groups was introduced. However, the scope for tax efficient trading appears to be shrinking and an important piece of major UK legislation on non-resident companies was outlined to illustrate this.

Recommendations for further reading

An in-depth coverage of residence for both individuals and companies is given in chapter 32, Butterworth (1985). For those readers wishing to acquire a fuller understanding of the Inland Revenue's role in international taxation a summary is included in chapter 7 HMSO (1985) together with additional information on double taxation agreements and a full list of agreements at 1 May 1985. The topic of underlying tax on dividends is explained by Bertram and Edwards (1986) in chapter 18 of their book. Andrews (1984) provides an excellent example of the way in which transfer pricing may be used to maximize the tax efficiency of international trading. The detailed and complex legislation relating to controlled foreign companies is unravelled by Ross (1986).

References

Andrews, J. (1984), 'The Amazing Irish Tax Dodge', *Investors Chronicle*, 69/879 (September 1984): 9–10.

Bertram, D., and Edwards, S. (1986), *Comprehensive Aspects of Taxation—1986–87* (London: Holt, Rinehart and Winston).

Butterworth (1985), *Butterworths UK Tax Guide* (London: Butterworths).

HMSO (1985) *Inland Revenue 127th Report 1984*, Cmnd. 9576 (London: HMSO).

Ross, D. (1986), *Controlled Foreign Companies* (London: The Institute of Chartered Accountants in England and Wales).

18
Conclusion

We began our exposition with a discussion of alternative bases of taxation, with particular references to the commercial activities of businesses. Particular emphasis has been placed upon the impact of taxation on decision-making. As a yardstick we have frequently used either a tax system based upon true economic income, after deduction for depreciation and interest, or a consumption-based tax system, with a uniform tax rate, of which both systems should normally have a neutral effect on the investment decision. We saw that as far as income and corporation taxes are concerned, the system of capital allowances can be much different from that of true economic depreciation. Furthermore, there is no tax relief for the periodic investment in net working capital. Additionally, especially for unincorporated businesses there is not a uniform tax rate, indeed the system is progressive and may create potential inefficiencies with regard to work effort and entrepreneurship.

As to companies, the case for a separate corporation tax is weak on theoretical grounds, although in practice it is a convenient device for the collection of revenue. The case for a cash-flow tax system, with particular reference to companies, was examined. Provided it is carefully designed, tax distortions in both investment and financing decisions can be eliminated, although there is a fundamental problem in the revenue-raising ability of such a system. The rationale for a cash-flow tax system was partly explained in terms of the theoretical superiority of a consumption-based over an income-based tax system, for economic efficiency.

A particular type of consumption-based tax system which we examined in some detail was the system of value added tax. Although the present system is an improvement on general sales taxes, especially with respect to the economic effects of multi-stage production, there are potential problems of tax-shifting on account of distinctions between standard, zero-rated, and exempt items and the role of small firms that can trade without charging VAT on sales.

For the small firm, we examined the problem of starting a new business venture and the choice of whether to trade as an unincorporated business or as a limited company, so as to minimize the effects of taxation. The critical issues were shown to be those of profit levels, different tax scales for income and corporation taxes, the tax lag between earning profits and settling tax liabilities, especially in the case of the unincorporated business, and the personal circumstances of the taxpayer, for example, a spouse who may become a business partner. Normally, where relatively large profits are immediately being earned, a company will have a long-term tax advantage over a sole proprietorship or a partnership.

For the more enterprising firm, business operations may be extended beyond the boundaries of the UK, for whatever motive. There are basic tax problems facing the international trader, particularly where the tax authorities change legislation to counteract tax planning strategies of firms. We saw that large multinational groups have considerable tax advantages over the small trader in their tax planning activities. However, the exploitation of tax havens by international trading groups for tax-efficient trading appears to be shrinking. Some attention was drawn to the problem of unrelieved foreign tax and surplus ACT, despite attempts to eliminate the double taxation of profits and gains. An insight into the variants of classical or imputation systems was provided, some of which effectively allow for full credit in personal tax computations for the underlying corporation tax. The title 'classical' or 'imputation' can indeed be misleading, for example in the case of a dual rate classical system, which applies different tax rates to distributed and undistributed profits and which can be equivalent to an imputation system under certain circumstances. In particular the UK corporate tax system can have distortionary effects in financing methods. Although the general equilibrium theory of capital structure suggests that tax advantages at the corporate level can be eliminated through personal taxation, we have stressed the importance of the role of taxation when firms have different tax profiles. Indeed such differences can account for significant fiscal benefits in another area, the lease or buy decision.

One problem we isolated was that of the impact of inflation. Distortions under the present systems of income and corporation taxes, which are very similar in design to an historic profits tax system, are more pronounced under inflation, especially with regard to the time pattern of capital allowances and the working capital cycle. Potential disincentives to invest are exaggerated when the time value of money is taken into account. Alternative inflation-adjusted tax systems were introduced including a current purchasing power tax system and a current cost tax system. Potential distortions depend upon the general rate of inflation (under a CPP system), and specific rates of inflation (under a CCA system). As far as working capital is concerned, neither system is designed to address itself to the question of volume increases. Potential distortionary effects under the methods of stock relief in the UK from 1973 to 1984 were also highlighted.

But even in the absence of inflation there are tax distortions in numerous choices facing the business enterprise. In exceptional circumstances the after-tax internal rate of return on a project can be the same as the before-tax internal rate of return. Normally, however, distortions will be particularly dependent upon: the choice of location (including overseas and UK enterprise zones), the asset category, the method of finance, any working capital investment, marginal tax rates, the business medium (sole trader, partnership, or limited company), tax positions of any associated companies, other projects under consideration, asset replacement plans (roll-over relief), existing tax losses, the commencement and cessation of a trade, the existence of occupational pension schemes, and numerous other issues. We leave it to the reader to extend the list and hope that we have stimulated his or her appetite for discovering further insights into the potential tax distortions of business activity under the UK tax system and theoretical alternatives.

Index